Critical Security Studies in the Global South

Series Editors
Pinar Bilgin, Department of International Relations, Bilkent University, Ankara, Turkey
Monica Herz, Institute of International Relations, PUC-Rio, Rio de Janeiro, Brazil

Critical approaches to security have made significant inroads into the study of world politics in the past 30 years. Drawing from a broad range of critical approaches to world politics (including Frankfurt School Critical Theory, Poststructuralism, Gramscian approaches and Postcolonial Studies), critical approaches to security have inspired students of international relations to think broadly and deeply about the security dynamic in world politics, multiple aspects of insecurities and how insecurities are produced as we seek to address them. This series, given its focus on the study of security in and of the Global South, will bring to the debate new spheres of empirical research both in terms of themes and social locations, as well as develop new interconnection between security and other related subfields.

More information about this series at
https://link.springer.com/bookseries/15576

Manuela Trindade Viana

Post-conflict Colombia and the Global Circulation of Military Expertise

palgrave
macmillan

Manuela Trindade Viana
Institute of International Relations
Pontifical Catholic University of Rio de Janeiro
Rio de Janeiro, Brazil

Critical Security Studies in the Global South
ISBN 978-3-030-96102-2   ISBN 978-3-030-96103-9 (eBook)
https://doi.org/10.1007/978-3-030-96103-9

© The Editor(s) (if applicable) and The Author(s), under exclusive license to Springer Nature Switzerland AG 2022
This work is subject to copyright. All rights are solely and exclusively licensed by the Publisher, whether the whole or part of the material is concerned, specifically the rights of translation, reprinting, reuse of illustrations, recitation, broadcasting, reproduction on microfilms or in any other physical way, and transmission or information storage and retrieval, electronic adaptation, computer software, or by similar or dissimilar methodology now known or hereafter developed.
The use of general descriptive names, registered names, trademarks, service marks, etc. in this publication does not imply, even in the absence of a specific statement, that such names are exempt from the relevant protective laws and regulations and therefore free for general use.
The publisher, the authors and the editors are safe to assume that the advice and information in this book are believed to be true and accurate at the date of publication. Neither the publisher nor the authors or the editors give a warranty, expressed or implied, with respect to the material contained herein or for any errors or omissions that may have been made. The publisher remains neutral with regard to jurisdictional claims in published maps and institutional affiliations.

Cover illustration: © Lia Lopes

This Palgrave Macmillan imprint is published by the registered company Springer Nature Switzerland AG
The registered company address is: Gewerbestrasse 11, 6330 Cham, Switzerland

À dúvida
– e às poucas certezas dessa vida,
nas figuras de Vilma, Alfredo, Diego, Paulinho.

Preface

This book is not about Colombia. It takes this country as an entry point to grasp the criteria through which Colombia now circulates internationally as a "success story". The appeal of such a story lies in its promises: putting an end to the longest armed conflict in Latin America, the regeneration of a country returning from the brink of the abyss, the hopeful future of a new Colombia. It is further compounded by the magnitude of the task: "succeeding" in a country that carried for decades the stigma of being one of the most violent in Latin America means passing "the hard test".

The idea of such metamorphosis—from a problematic country to a "success story"—has been widely contested, both by those interested in questioning the durability of the post-conflict in Colombia and by those invested in revealing the human costs behind what is claimed as a success. Even a superficial look at those debates makes it almost impossible to take a "success" for granted. And yet, Colombia continues to circulate internationally precisely in those terms. Irrespective of the contested character of that "success", this story has had concrete effects in the world, and it has been increasingly sought as a source of lessons, formulae and expertise for other problematic sites seeking to experiment that same "success". Such is the puzzle that grounds this book. To work through it, instead of adding one more set of line to the debate questioning the truthfulness or accuracy of the Colombian "success story", I am interested in exploring its conditions of possibility—not at all because I applaud it, but as a necessary step to understand that from which it derives its political strength.

This does not mean, of course, that Colombia does not matter to this book. Indeed, it matters greatly—but only insofar as "Colombia" is never simply about Colombia, never exactly where we expect it to be, and never really given as an object of thought and intervention. Thus, in the next pages, I excavate the terms within which the Colombian story has been written, disputed and valorized in order to raise questions that allow us to challenge taken-for-granted political conceptions of internal and external, civil and military, and peace and war. In doing so, I take inspiration from an interview given to Paul Rabinow in 1984, in which Michel Foucault provokes us to explore the reverse process of politics: instead of offering solutions to problems, to dig into the terms through which a set of solutions emerged to a particular understanding of a problem.

Because I am looking at Colombia in search for the politics of credentials of which it is a current expression, the possible crumbling of this "success story" would not affect the pertinence of this book. Such eventual failure might all too easily be translated into not-so-innovative claims about its reasons, leading to a renewed engagement of expert careers around a new puzzle of the policy world, all the while relocating the credentials of a model to be replicated to another promising successful case. In prying open such politics of success cases, this book hopes not only to ease their hold into our imagination, but also to contribute to the task of asking questions where they disturb the most: past the search for the best readymade solution, towards the more insidious effects of readymade problems.

Now, the project from which this book results has its own conditions of possibility. First, I am profoundly indebted to the editors of Palgrave's "Critical Security Studies in the Global South" series, Pinar Bilgin and Monica Herz, for their encouragement and patience. Most importantly, their belief that something could be learned, but also unlearned, from the reading of this book kept me going throughout the whole process. The research from which this book emerged equally benefited from scholarships granted by the Coordenação de Aperfeiçoamento de Pessoal de Nível Superior-Brasil (CAPES), Finance Code 001, and by the Conselho Nacional de Desenvolvimento Científico e Tecnológico (CNPq). The support of these Brazilian governmental agencies made my dedication to this project and my fieldwork possible—a valuable opportunity that the current dismantlement of public funding to research in Brazil has been so adamantly turning into an even scarcer privilege. Finally, previous drafts of this book were improved thanks to the attentive reading and critique of researchers and friends for whom my admiration and gratitude are immense: Monica Herz, advisor of the Ph.D. dissertation from which this book stemmed; and Rob Walker, Philippe Bonditti, Paulo Esteves, Alejo Vargas Velásquez, Rafael Duarte Villa, Didier Bigo, Vera Malaguti, Nick Onuf and Victor Coutinho Lage. Their provocations have inspired my thinking about the problems behind the solutions, and their critical spirit taught my eyes to search for many ways through which the past still pulses in the present—a disposition that I can now hope to nurture as also my own. A special gratitude I must express towards the one who, in addition to bearing the provocations and critical spirit I mentioned earlier, makes it on a daily basis: Paulinho Chamon, thank you for believing in this project sometimes more than myself, and for being my most loyal and generous reader.

This book was finished amid a pandemic full of anxiety, exhaustion, fear and, only sometimes, hope. I simply could not have done it without the soulful and sincere love of my mother, Vilma, my father, Alfredo, my brother, Diego, my love, Paulinho, and my dog, Lola. To you, I can never thank enough; to you, all of my days. There are, of course—and thankfully—many other presences that reminded me not to forget about the most important things in this world, surprising me with a love that more than often broke the walls of my isolation. My dear family and friends who made my journey possible, I am confident that your heart will be able to read your names in between these lines.

Rio de Janeiro, Brazil
July 2021

Manuela Trindade Viana

Contents

1 Introduction 1
   1.1 *Analytical Tools and Plan of the Book* 6
   References 14

Part I The Colombian "Success Story" (or, What Is Allowed to Have Happened)

2 The Problem as a Condition for Success: The Construction of Colombia as a "Problematic Country" 27
   2.1 *The Problematization of Violence in Colombia* 31
   2.2 *Fighting a Distant War: The U.S. And the Externalization of the "Drug Problem"* 42
   2.3 *Conclusion* 51
   References 52

3 The Success and Its Monsters: Disputing the Metrics, Dodging Criticism 57
   3.1 *Measuring Success: Assessing Colombia's Counternarcotic Performance* 59
   3.2 *The Silencing That Makes the Success Audible* 72
   3.3 *Conclusion* 85
   References 86

Part II The Transnational Making of the Military Professional in Latin America

4 "Technical, not Political": The Military Professional as the Citizen-Soldier — 99
  4.1 Organizing Violence: The Regulative Ideal of Modernization and the Civil-Military Divide — 101
  4.2 The Circuit of Military Savoirs and the Modernization of Post-independence Armies (or, Europe is Where Latin America is Supposed to be) — 124
  4.3 The Frictions and Fictions of the Civil-Military Boundary in the Colombian Army — 141
  4.4 Conclusion — 159
  References — 160

5 "All They Understand Is Force": The Military Professional as the Expert-Soldier — 165
  5.1 The Re-articulation of the Circuit Around Counterinsurgency, an Old New Military Savoir — 166
  5.2 (The Imperative of) Winning Hearts, Minds, and Populations in the Never-Ending Colombian War — 187
  5.3 Successful Nonetheless: The Expert-Soldier and the Re-positioning of Colombia in the Global Circuit of Military Savoirs — 207
  5.4 Conclusion — 228
  References — 230

6 Conclusion — 237
  References — 243

Bibliography — 245

Index — 265

Abbreviations

ACI	Andean Counterdrug Initiative
AFEUR	Urban Anti-Terrorism Special Forces Group
AMERIPOL	Police Community of the Americas
BACN	Counternarcotic Brigades
BINCI	Intelligence and Counterintelligence Battalion
BRIM	Mobile Brigades
CCEEU	Coordination Colombia-Europe-United States
CENAE	National Training Center
CIA	Central Intelligence Agency
CINEP	Research and Popular Education Center
COPES	Anti-Extortion and Anti-Kidnapping Special Corps
COSAS	Department of Control of Substances that Produce Physical and Psychic Addiction
CUT	Central Workers' Union
DANE	National Administrative Department of Statistics
DAS	Administrative Department of Security
DEA	Drug Enforcement Administration
DIJIN	Judicial Police and Intelligence Central Division
DIRAN	Antinarcotic Division
ELN	National Liberation Army
ESPRO	School of Professional Soldiers
FARC	Revolutionary Armed Forces of Colombia
FBI	Federal Bureau of Investigation
FIP	Ideas for Peace Foundation
FS&D	Security & Democracy Foundation
FUDRA	Rapid Deployment Force

FY	Fiscal Year
GAO	U.S. General Accounting Office
GAULA	Unified Action Groups for Personal Freedom
GOES	Special Operations Group
HRW	Human Rights Watch
IACHR	Inter-American Commission on Human Rights
IDB	Inter-American Development Bank
IEPRI	Institute of Studies on Politics and International Relations
IRA	Irish Republican Army
ISIS	Islamic State in Iraq and Syria
MOVICE	Movement of State Crime Victims
NATO	North Atlantic Treaty Organization
NGO	Non-Governmental Organization
NSDD	National Security Decision Directive
ONDCP	Office of National Drug Control Policy
SIC	Colombian Intelligence Service
SoA	School of the Americas
UNHCHR	United Nations High Commissioner for Human Rights
WEF	World Economic Forum
WOLA	Washington Office on Latin America

CHAPTER 1

Introduction

The puzzle I deal with in this book was found while I was searching for another. In 2013, I was investigating the disputes between the police and the military in Colombia deriving from their mobilization in counternarcotic operations with very similar scopes. At that time, my focus was to explore how their discursive regime was rearticulated so as to differentiate the expertise of the police from that of the military, and vice-versa, justifying, based on such terms, their respective privileged position in the security architecture in Colombia. Starting my investigations in the official journals of the Colombian National Police and the Colombian Army, the recurrence with which Mexico and Central America appeared in analyses published since the late 2000s (Montenegro and Durán 2008; Casallas 2015; Pinzón 2015) caught my attention. In those and many other articles, I found a discourse reinforcing a "Colombian success", which could serve as a reference for other "problematic countries". Are there similarities between the conditions fueling war in Afghanistan and the ones observed in the past in Colombia (Felbab-Brown 2009a)? How can Nigeria learn from the Colombian experience in dealing with terrorism and drugs (Afeikhena 2015)? What lessons can be extracted from Colombia in order to tackle the "violent drug market

© The Author(s), under exclusive license to Springer Nature Switzerland AG 2022
M. T. Viana, *Post-conflict Colombia and the Global Circulation of Military Expertise*, Critical Security Studies in the Global South, https://doi.org/10.1007/978-3-030-96103-9_1

1

in Mexico" (Felbab-Brown 2009b)? What are the risks of "Colombianizing" Mexico (Cárdenas and Casas-Zamora 2010)?—questioned some of these articles.

The exemplary position of Colombia in those approaches was quite puzzling, considering that one of the most remarkable claims about Colombia until the early 2000s was its problematic character. Indeed, the country came to be historically associated with an amalgam of variables incorporated to an equation of violence comprising guerrillas, paramilitary groups, drug trafficking, terrorism, massacres, internal displacement, and corruption, among others. A "narco-democracy" (Almario 1992; Sweeney 1995), the "most problematic country in South America" (Albright 1999), a "problematic country" (García-Peña 2006), a "protracted conflict" (Chernick 2008), a country "on the brink of state disintegration" (DeShazo et al. 2007: 50)—all expressions mobilized in order to describe the nature and the outreach of Colombia's "pathologies". As most of these expressions reveal, speaking about Colombia has generally come to mean speaking about a country whose problems irradiate beyond its boundaries, constituting a source of instability to the region and to the world (Albright 1999; Ramírez 2004; García-Peña 2006; Rojas 2006).

But how was it possible that a country historically stigmatized as problematic came to be taken as a reference for solutions regarding police and military operations? And, furthermore, how could such sliding into a "success story" be vocalized even before a peace agreement was signed with one of the main guerrillas in the country—the Revolutionary Armed Forces of Colombia (FARC, in Spanish)? Indeed, by the late 2000s, there was already a series of policy and research projects, conferences, and books on the agenda, challenges, roles and costs of the "post-conflict" in Colombia. As such, the "success" was considered "exportable" before the Peace Agreement negotiated in La Habana had been announced by the Parties, in 2016. While this could be read as evidence that the peace process with the FARC was decoupled from the "success story", I suggest that it more provocatively gestures towards the much broader web of criteria in which that story is inscribed. This book is concerned with such criteria—what I refer to as the condition of possibility of the "success story"—, with the rather specific stories they construct about problems of, and viable solutions to, violence, and with the concrete effect these have had for Colombia, for the region, and for the world.

Of course, the discourse on the Colombian "success" is far from consensual—if such a thing indeed exists. The profusion of analyses dedicated to reinforcing the "successful" performance of Colombia in solving its problems has been challenged by a myriad of angles—from the challenge in making the military achievements durable in time (Villamizar 2003; Rangel 2005) to the contestation of the "facts" constituting the "success story" (Tickner 2014; Isacson 2010), or to the systematic human rights violations failing possibilities of "success" (Coordinación Colombia-Europa-Estados Unidos 2017).

However, the contested character of the "success story" should not detract us from the historical conditions and web of credentials sustaining it, nor from their very concrete effects. For instance, from 2009 to 2013, the Colombian National Police and Army trained 10,310 professionals from Mexico; 3,026 from Panama; 2,609 from Honduras; 1,732 from Guatemala; 1,132 from Ecuador; 510 from Peru; 465 from El Salvador; and 377 from Costa Rica (Tickner 2014: 3). Furthermore, in April 2013, the Escuela de Lanceros (Lancers' School), one of the nine training schools in Fuerte Tolemaida (Tolemaida Fortress), concluded its 367th course, having resulted in the capacity building of Colombian military personnel and also of 582 "international students", from 19 different countries (among which Brazil, Canada, Ecuador, El Salvador, France, Peru and the U.S.).[1]

These numbers show that, by the late 2000s, other countries saw in the Colombian police and military an expertise to look up to. For Juan Carlos Pinzón, former Minister of Defense (2011–2015), three factors made Colombian Armed Forces[2] qualified to assist other nations: the fact that they revealed a sustained progress since the early 2000s in fighting security threats in the country; the excellence of their facilities to train its counterparts; and the fact that many countries in Latin America and other regions in the world face similar threats to those successfully combatted in Colombia (Pinzón 2015: 8). After all, their experience in fighting insurgents, drug trafficking organizations, and other transnational criminal groups is at the very source of the expertise the Armed Forces of Colombia now offer to other public forces in the world. For Pinzón

---

[1] See: http://www.cenae.mil.co/?idcategoria=344179. Accessed on 10 June 2021.

[2] The Colombian Armed Forces are formed by the Military Forces—Army, Air Force, and Navy (*Armada*)—and by the National Police.

(2015: 8), this experience is what "makes it uniquely capable and qualified to assist other nations that today, or one day, may face similar threats".

Hence, the privileged position of the Colombian Armed Forces' expertise among its regional partners was not a mere side effect of the "success story": it was bred from within it. If violence was at the core of the stigmatization of Colombia as a problematic country, the protagonism of the Armed Forces in the pacification of violence therein came to be portrayed as a fundamental condition for the emergence of a successful "new Colombia". In this sense, the conditions under which the Colombian Armed Forces capitalized their experience into expertise are part and parcel of the conditions that allowed for the discourse that the war in Colombia was won.

Here, Plan Colombia becomes key, for it is unequivocally presented as a turning point in narratives about the performance of the Colombian Armed Forces in the war against "narcoterrorism" (Felbab-Brown 2009a, b; DeShazo et al. 2007; Davis et al. 2016; Pinzón 2015). That the adherence of the "success story" is located around the late 2000s is not a coincidence: this period was marked by the ignition of the second phase of Plan Colombia, intended to consolidate the work undertaken from 1999 to 2005 (Rojas 2007). In addition to the promotion of an intensive "modernization" of the Colombian Armed Forces through training, equipment and weapons (Villamizar 2003; Rojas 2006; Rangel 2005), the Plan aimed at turning facilities such as Fuerte Tolemaida into centers of excellence in military and police training[3] (Villamizar 2003). The protagonism of the Armed Forces in the "success story" was, therefore, given impulse by Plan Colombia, through a combination of material resources and expertise from the U.S.

Interestingly, the same strength of the Colombian Armed Forces that was seen as a solution to the problem of violence came to be framed as a problem in the "post-conflict" context. Indeed, the profusion of studies and policy recommendations celebrating the economic prosperity of the country that was inaugurated by the stabilization of violence indicators (Mills 2016) was followed by concerns regarding the Armed Forces in times of "peace" (Vargas 2003; Ciro and Correa 2014; Velásquez 2015). More specifically, if violence is expected to be controlled within a context of peace, the historical involvement of the military in internal operations

---

[3] See: https://www.cenae.mil.co/?idcategoria=362512. Accessed on 26 June 2021.

(Atehortúa and Vélez 1994; Pizarro L. 1987a, b, 1988; Vargas 2012) is incorporated to the "post-conflict" debates as a problem. What function could be attributed to the military in a "peaceful" Colombia (Vargas 2003; Ciro and Correa 2014; Ruiz 2014; Velásquez 2015)? Such discussions were simultaneously focused on the need to build a "more human" police force in the "post-conflict", since the Colombian National Police was expected to take up a privileged position in ordering practices in times of "peace" (Castro 2004; Carvajal 2004; Manrique 2013; Velásquez 2015).

In other words, war times required a violence that is claimed as no longer necessary in the "post-conflict". More than this: it is unwanted as a mechanism for social order in peaceful contexts. Underlying those concerns are two important assumptions. First, that the violence deemed appropriate for war times does not belong to times of peace. Second, that war is undertaken by the military, while social order in pacified spaces is the work under the authority of the police. Through these lines, the boundary drawn between war and peace in the "post-conflict" discourse operates with a logic of presence/absence of violence.

With this in mind, instead of discussing the "success story" as one allegedly inaugurating peace in Colombia, this book proposes that we think of the war-peace relation as one traversed by processes of reorganization of violence. To make sense of such reorganization, it takes seriously the conditions under which the problem of violence and the success over violence were articulated in the making of a "post-conflict" in Colombia. Given the central position of war in the portrayal of Colombia as a "problematic country", what are the conditions that allowed for the protagonist role of the military in the making of the Colombian "success story"? And, relatedly, how is violence then organized in the context of peace?

To do so, I offer a sociological account of the biographical footprints of the production of the military professional in Colombia and, more specifically, an epistemological analysis of the specialized *saviors*— i.e. the authority derived from a technical knowledge extracted from the combination of theoretical formulations and practical experience—that came to be valorized in the pacification of the country. By analyzing the professionalization programs implemented in military schools and training centers in Colombia, I reflect on the historical transformation of the *savoirs* through which state violence is taught and trained in the preparation for war, as well as explore how they are rearticulated across times of "war" and "peace".

Nonetheless, and perhaps counterintuitively, this is not a book about Colombia. As I argue in the chapters to follow, both the discursive construction of Colombia as a "problematic country" and the production of the military professional I investigate emerged from criteria that circulate and are validated transnationally. In this sense, this book discloses the transnational adherence of the credentials with which Colombia circulates either as a problem or as a solution, rather than remaining confined to national conceptions of one or the other. Thus, Colombia is better seen as an analytical point of entry for us to grasp the transnational circulation of renderings of violence and the military *savoirs* invested against them. With that in mind, the next pages present the two main axes structuring this book, each of them worked out through an analytical tool: problematization and transnational circuit of *savoirs*.

1.1 Analytical Tools and Plan of the Book

The structure of this book emerged from three main discomforts, each stemming from a different form of discursive confinement. The first is the confinement of the "problem of violence" into the national container we came to know as "Colombia". Here, I am not referring to the dispute about Colombia's problematic character or not, but to a discursive frame that is repeatedly evoked when tackling the problem of violence: that is, as a national anomaly. It is under these terms that we often encounter renderings of problems in international politics: the failed *state* problem, the problematic *country*, or the "narco-*democracy*", encapsulating the national political regime as a problem.

We could go further and note that the ontology reproduced by such discursive articulations does not always operate in terms of methodological *nationalism*, but more precisely in terms of confining problems into containers of different scales. This is the case of the *favelas* in Rio de Janeiro (Valladares 2005) or of Latin America (Hilgers and Macdonald 2017), for instance, historically framed as "problematic territories/regions" irradiating insecurities to other parts of the city/the world. The repetition of these framings of policy problems seems to constitute a symptom that merits investigation. After all, upon what assumptions our representations of specific territorial containers as anomalies rest? Under what conditions is it possible to claim a given problem as a *Colombian* one? What are the effects of confining renderings of violence as something foreign to us?

The second discomfort guiding this book is the easiness with which the Colombian "success story" brushes aside an agenda for so long vocalized by social movements in that country: that of state violence. Indeed, the Colombian "success" is confined not only within the state as a solution-bearer, but also in the Armed Forces as the protagonists of that successful formula. The credentials that came to be associated with the "success story" are, in this sense, complicit in the pacification of agendas denouncing the Colombian Armed Forces as part of the problem of violence, and not exclusively of its solution.

The third and last discomfort emerges from claims to peace. Months before the referendum of the Peace Agreement between the FARC and the Colombian government, in 2016, the campaign for the "Yes" was organized with the motto "*Por la Paz*" ("For Peace"), and the "No" was presented as the vote for the continuation of war[4]. Despite the political importance of an atmosphere of hope around the vocabulary of "peace" after so many decades of death, I hesitate towards the claim that the "Yes" circumscribes dialogue and peaceful coexistence, in contrast to the confinement of war in the "No". As a matter of fact, what is the connection between the decades-long war and the negotiations in La Habana? Under which terms dialogue is conceived as dispensable, justifying war as a mechanism for social regulation? Likewise, how can we make sense of the persistence of an institutional fabric erected in contexts of war as politically useful also for a "post-conflict"? If it is certainly relevant to reflect on the conditions under which war persists, it is also fundamental to investigate the conditions under which we claim for peace.

To approach these discomforts, the chapters to follow mobilize two analytical tools, each organizing one of the main parts of this book. In Part I, I engage the terms with which Colombia came to be constructed as a success through the concept of "problematization" (Foucault 2010). Starting from the assumption that the "success" relies on the claim that a set of problems has been overcome, Chapter 2 discusses the main processes through which Colombia came to be framed as a problematic country.

Section 2.1 excavates the encounters that made the system of problematizations constituted by the "problem of violence", the "problem of drugs", and the "problem of the guerrillas". In doing so, it exposes

---

[4] Elsewhere, I have analyzed more attentively these discursive articulations anchoring the referendum of the Colombian Peace Agreement. See: Viana (2016).

four processes emerging from that system: the expansion of the margins through which social conducts came to be framed as disturbances to public order; the consolidation of the "problem of drugs" as one of public order; the incorporation of "terrorism" in the Penal Code so as to accommodate radical otherness into the penal apparatus; and the gradual vanishing of "political delinquency" as a special category in the penal landscape. Section 2.1 thereby points to how the penal apparatus came to be expanded and strengthened to offer "solutions" to what came to be conceived as a delinquential and depoliticized "problem of violence" in the country. By its turn, Sect. 2.2 explores how such processes intersected with the problematization of drugs in the U.S. Importantly, against the portrayal of Colombia as a mere receptacle of interventionist policies of the U.S. (Crandall 2001; García-Peña 2006), Chapter 2 shows that the conditions for a delinquential and depoliticizing approach towards renderings of violence were already cemented in Colombia when such processes intersected with the war on drugs. Similarly, the inscription of delinquency in a spectrum of radical otherness through the vocabulary of "terrorism" was fermented in Colombia since the 1980s, when incorporated to the Penal Code and recurrently activated through police and military operations. From the alchemy of the processes analyzed in these two sections, Chapter 2 argues that the late 1990s witnessed the crystallization of a very specific reading of violence in Colombia: one deriving from the activity of guerrillas which found in drug trafficking the resources to fund their military power. In other words, the "problem of violence" in Colombia came to be represented by the vocabulary of "narcoguerrillas", and reframed as "narcoterrorism" in the context of the war on terror.

Chapter 3 builds on the discussion about the problematization of violence by claiming that, if the "problem of violence" reads drugs as the fuel of "narcoterrorism", then counternarcotic operations would asphyxiate the guerrillas by extinguishing the source of their military power. In this sense, it is somewhat expected that debates concerned with the performance of Colombia in solving its problems would orbit around the counternarcotic domain. By showing how the "Colombian problems" became the object of scrutiny of governmental agencies and civil society organizations, Sect. 3.1 digs into the web of criteria and performance metrics allowing for the "success story" to be told. I argue that the disputes around the more appropriate metric became increasingly insulated in a technocratic vocabulary, being less concerned with the constitutive pillars from which those "solutions" emerged, and more attentive to gains in accuracy, data compilation, and efficiency. Thus, although such a debate has constantly rearticulated the discursive field through marginal adjustments in the counternarcotic architecture, the constitutive pillars of the problematization of violence from which those policies emerged have remained intact. In contrast, Sect. 3.2 works a more confrontative kind of critique invested against the problematization of violence in Colombia, whose specific contours are expressed in the work of unionists and human rights organizations. I analyze how the lists of suspects and targets produced by the intelligence apparatus fed military and police operations, resulting in extrajudicial killings, forced disappearances and forced detentions of unionists in Colombia. These violations have constituted the work of several human rights organizations whose objective was to denounce this violence as a state crime. I further show how such denunciations came to be systematically dismissed by political officials under the claim that the information lacked credibility and accuracy. Therefore, extrajudicial killings, forced disappearances and forced detentions are both the effect through which silencing is realized and the object of silencing—a mechanism of discursive silencing that affects what is eligible to be told in the Colombian story: it is not about workers' demands or about the state as perpetrator of violence, to begin with. Based on this discussion, Chapter 3 contends that the Colombian "success story" emerges from a discursive field ordered by principles that valorize both the state as a solution-bearer and a specific (metrified) form through which claims to knowledge about policy impact are disputed. At the same time these criteria define the horizon of possibilities for claims about Colombia, they keep at bay those criticisms that confront the very ordering pillars of such a discursive field. As a result, systematic human rights violations committed by the Armed Forces fall outside the horizon of the "success story"—although coexisting with it.

Read as a whole, the ambition of Part I is to unveil the limits of the Colombian "success story"—both what it enables and what it excludes. If such story relies on a specific set of problems claimed as overcome, Part I points to the terms with which the "problem of violence" came to be historically understood in Colombia: a delinquential and apolitical violence nurtured by resources from drug trafficking. And although alternative renderings of violence constantly haunt the claim of a successful present, the political force of the ordering principles governing disputes around the "success story" keep those narratives in the discursive margins, or even condemn them to fade away.

Now, if the problematization of violence from which the Colombian "success" stems is based on the understanding that the expansion of the war on drugs would lead to the weakening of the "narcoguerrilla's" military capacity, it is a self-fulfilling prophecy that the Colombian Armed Forces would emerge as the protagonists of such story. After all, what else could the "success" be about if not a story focused on those that undertake the operations found at the core of "solutions" distilled from that very problematization? Thus, while Part I offers an account of the historical rearticulation of the "problem of violence", Part II explores the production of the military professional that came to be portrayed as one of the protagonists of such "success".

More specifically, it analyzes the transformation of the professionalization programs focusing on the Colombian Army, the branch of the military forces that receives the greatest share of the Defense budget[5] (26%) and that is found at the center of initiatives aimed at "exporting" the Colombian security expertise (Pinzón 2015). In doing so, Part II engages with the terms with which the Colombian Army has managed to capitalize their experience in the armed conflict into an expertise to be taken as a reference by other countries. To be sure, I excavate the historical making of this specific kind of knowledge, built upon the combination of doctrinal foundations with the practical lessons extracted from the experience in the terrain of operations. It is in this sense that I use the term "*savoirs*" in this book to approach the articulation between classroom and terrain in the production of a knowledge domain specific to the military. In turn, schools and training centers[6] are here read as the

---

[5] Since 2000 (Article 4, Decree No. 1512), for instance, the public budget destined to the Colombian Armed Forces has been distributed as follows: 26% to the Army, 26% to the Colombian National Police, 7% to the Navy (*Armada*), 6% to the Air Force, and 35% to other expenses (Ministerio de Defensa de Colombia 2016: 11).

[6] I concentrate on the schools constituting the center of gravity of the Army's professionalization programs. Indeed, dissecting all of the professionalization programs within the Army's schools would be an impossible task. Currently, the Colombian Army has twenty professionalization schools, without mentioning those specialized in the line of command: three formation schools (Escuela Militar de Cadetes and Escuela de Suboficiales, and Escuela de Soldados Profesionales); two training schools (Centro Nacional de Entrenamiento and Escuela de Paracaidismo Militar); and fifteen capacity building schools (Escuela de Misiones Internacionales y Acción Integral, Escuela de Equitación, Escuela

sites where these *savoirs* are reproduced in the making of the military professionals of the Colombian Army.

In this analysis, two aspects emerge as unescapable lenses through which Chapters 4 and 5 are threaded. First, that the valorization of those *savoirs* leads us to an exploration of the epistemological criteria with which they operate. Second, that it is impossible to walk through the historical production of the military professional without considering the fact that their professionalization programs stem from the transnational circulation of military *savoirs*. It is under these terms that Part II is erected upon the concept of "transnational circuit of military *savoirs*". While the latter explicitly confronts the internal–external divide with which the organization of violence came to be normalized under the discourse of modernization, Part II challenges two other fundamental boundaries in this regard: the civil-military divide, discussed more attentively in Chapter 4; and the peace-war divide, upon which Chapter 5 focuses.

To do that, I first shed light on the conditions for the emergence of this circuit in Latin America by the late-nineteenth century and, then, explore what is at stake in the rearticulation of the practices through which state violence is organized. In addition to that, each chapter investigates how Colombia is inscribed in the transnational circuit of military *savoirs*, drawing attention to the effects of such circuit to the contours with which violence is organized in the country, as well as to how the rules on the use of violence in Colombia affect the circuit. It does so by tracing the historical footprints of the *savoirs* that came to be valorized in specific contexts and by mapping the main channels through which they circulate.

This venture begins by engaging with the discursive conditions of the circuit of military *savoirs* in Latin America. Section 4.1 first turns to Norbert Elias' *The civilizing process* (2000) and Max Weber's *Politics as a Vocation* (2004) as canonic expressions of a discourse of modernization in which the civil-military boundary is produced through the entanglement

---

de las Armas y Servicios, Escuela de Infantería, Escuela de Caballería, Escuela de Ingenieros Militares, Escuela de Artillería General, Escuela de Inteligencia y Contrainteligencia, Escuela de Comunicaciones, Escuela de Aviación del Ejército, Escuela de Logística, Escuela de Policía Militar, Escuela de Derechos Humanos y Derecho Internacional Humanitario, and Escuela de capacitación en asuntos jurídicos). See: http://www.ejercito.mil.co/?idc ategoria=27. Accessed on 29 June 2021.

of civilization and professionalization in the organization of violence in a pacified social space, thereby affirming the need for the military as a technical and apolitical professional in arms. I then read Domingo Sarmiento's *Facundo* (2018) as an expression of the "problem of violence" in the post-independence Latin America to expose how this discourse locates modernity in Europe, constituting a regulative ideal whose reproduction has had profound effects both on practices of pacification and military professionalization in the region. In this regard, Sect. 4.2 discusses the late nineteenth century European military missions in Latin America—especially French and Prussian—as key to the emergence of military *savoirs* in the region. These missions aimed at producing military professionals in the host countries, ranging from the proposition of regulations to the creation of military schools and their respective curricula. This Section maps the main channels for this circulation, including the military missions themselves, as well as manuals, specialized journals, and weapons. In this process, the analysis reveals the homogenization effects of the transnational circuit operating among the armies in Latin America, reflected in similar models of conscription, regulations of the military career, and curricula implemented in military schools. When focusing on how Colombia is inscribed in such circuit, Sect. 4.3 offers us not only texture, but also tension to the ways we conceive the civil-military divide and the homogenizing effects of the transnational circuit. Indeed, to analyze the concrete contours of the work of the Chilean mission—whose claims of authority were linked to the legacy of the Prussian model—in Colombia allows us to grasp the frictions underlying the implementation of professionalization programs due to the resistance among the highest ranks towards the discourse of meritocracy, and to the constant negotiation with the civil elites for the autonomy the mission needed. Moreover, Sect. 4.3 shows how the professionalization undertaken in the Colombian *Escuela Militar* aimed at producing a "citizen-soldier" through a comprehensive pedagogical program that had the classroom as its privileged site. Chapter 4 thereby constitutes an analytical arch stemming from the discursive conditions that make the transnational circuit of military *savoirs* possible, exploring the veins through which they circulate in the region, and bringing out the frictions in their transmission. I ultimately argue that the reproduction of the civil-military boundary was, at one and the same time, the condition for the professionalization of the military and an effective impossibility. Indeed, while professionalization emerged as a solution to the "problem of the military" following the independence wars in Latin America, a systematic transit from the civil to the military domain was needed to bargain the implementation of those very professionalization programs. Breaching the civil-military boundary remained a condition for its enactment.

Chapter 5 concentrates on the peace-war boundary to reflect on the effects of the historical rearticulations in the transnational circuit of military *savoirs* in the second half of the twentieth century. By then, the U.S. had displaced Europe as the main reference for professionalization programs in Latin American armies, a move which led to placing counterinsurgency in a privileged position in the edifice of military *savoirs*. Section 5.1 traces the colonial footprints of the U.S. counterinsurgency doctrine to French and British expertise drawn from their colonies in Africa and Asia. It underlines how counterinsurgency's emphasis on tactics and plasticity offered the key to its enduring status as a "military *savoir*". Also, it sheds light on how the affinities with police work of its population-centric approach and claim to an unending task facilitated its mobilization as a war power ordering society. Such a discussion is central for Sect. 5.2, when we turn to the inscription of Colombia in the hemispheric circuit to capture the effects of the counterinsurgency-based professionalization of the Army. More specifically, I investigate how the War in Korea, in the early 1950s, came to be portrayed as inaugurating an intense and durable socialization focused on irregular warfare between the Colombian Army and their counterparts in the U.S. Section 5.2 pursues the translation of irregular warfare into architectural forms in Colombia, with special attention to the emergence of the *Escuela de Lanceros* as the center of gravity of the Army's professionalization programs. In doing so, I point to both the increasing specialization that characterizes those programs, and to the displacement of the classroom by the training center as the privileged site for the production of the military professional. By dissecting the Lancer programs, I show that, unlike the "citizen-soldier" expected to result from the *Escuela Militar*, professionalization has turned towards the large-scale production of tactically efficient bodies through short-term programs focused on the tactical level—an "expert-soldier". In this analysis, I reveal that this form is reproduced with the content of counterinsurgency, marked by an increasing mobilization of the population in tactical operations—with and without their awareness and consent—, as well as a state of permanent war.

The argument comes full circle with a discussion about the conditions allowing for the repositioning of Colombia in the transnational circuit of military *savoirs* and their relations with the "success story" in which the military professional is the main protagonist. In Sect. 5.3, I propose that we think of the decisive relevance of Plan Colombia as a catalyzer of ongoing processes with general contours stretching back to the 1950s and the U.S. as the main reference for military professionalization. Of decisive importance were the scale and speed of the new phase of specialization and training focused on counterinsurgency, as well as the correlate exponential multiplication of manpower. These are key for us to understand the relevance of the U.S. resources to the expansion of the security architecture invested against "narcoterrorism" and to the claim of a war that has been won—consequently, as key for the Colombian "success story". As such, the fact that Colombia successfully circulates in the region as a security model to be replicated speaks more about those that reproduce that formula than about Colombia itself. Indeed, if the terms of the "success story" find adherence among the counterparts of the Colombian Army—and of the Armed Forces, more generally—in Latin America and the world, we cannot grasp this process without considering the credentials with which it is purchased as a military *savoir* with a seal of excellence.

The book, therefore, invites us to come to terms with the Colombian story by reflecting on the resonance of counterinsurgency as an ordering *savoir* with elective affinities with both military and police work, and, also of an easy-to-reproduce and easy-to-apply state violence. If I start with the erasures of problematic pasts underlying the crystallization of a specific problem of violence deemed as overcome in the successful present, the wide purchase power of Colombia among its counterparts convokes us to conceive the decontextualization of renderings of violence as an indispensable condition for the circulation of military *savoirs* in the making of solutions to plastic conceptions of terrorism, insurgency, and disorder.

References

Books, Chapters, Articles

Afeikhena, J. Lessons from Colombia for curtailing the Boko Haram insurgency in Nigeria. *Prism*, v. 5, n. 2, pp. 94–105, 2015.

Almario, J. Colombia: The Genesis of the World's First Narco-Democracy. *Executive Intelligence Review*, v. 19, n. 30, pp. 41–42, 1992. Available at: https://www.yumpu.com/en/document/read/3893406/view-full-issue-executive-intelligence-review. Accessed on 05 July 2021.

Atehortúa C., A. L.; Vélez R., H. *Estado y Fuerzas Armadas en Colombia.* Cali: TM, 1994.
Carvajal C., C. La Policía Nacional en el posconflicto. *Revista Criminalidad,* v. 47, n. 1, pp. 38–48, 2004. Available at: https://www.policia.gov.co/sites/default/files/RevistaCriminalidadco.pdf. Accessed on 04 July 2021.
Casallas R. J. A. *Cooperación Técnico Militar del Ejército Colombiano al Ejército de Honduras.* Universidad Militar Nueva Granada, Programa de Relaciones Internacionales y Estudios Políticos, Bogotá, November 2015. Available at: http://repository.unimilitar.edu.co/bitstream/10654/7842/1/CasallasRu%C3%ADzJaimeAlberto2016.pdf. Accessed on 05 July 2021.
Castro, C. *O Espírito Militar: um antropólogo na caserna.* Rio de Janeiro: Zahar, 2004.
Chernick, M. *Acuerdo posible: solución negociada al conflicto armado colombiano.* Bogotá, D.C.: Aurora, 2008.
Ciro G., A. R.; Correa H., M. Transformación estructural del Ejército colombiano. Construcción de escenarios futuros. *Revista Científica General José María Córdova,* v. 12, n. 13, pp. 19–88, 2014.
Crandall R. Explicit Narcotization: US Policy toward Colombia during Samper Administration. *Latin American Politics and Society,* v. 43, n. 3, pp. 95–120, 2001.
Davis, D.; Kilcullen, D.; Mills, G.; Spencer, D. (orgs.). *A Great Perhaps? Colombia: Conflict and Convergence.* London: Hurst, 2016.
Foucault, M. Polemics, Politics, and Problematizations: An Interview with Michel Foucault. In: Rabinow, P. (ed). *The Foucault Reader.* New York: Pantheon Books, 2010 [1984].
García-Peña, R. P. Un país problema en un mundo intervencionista. In: Leal B., F. (ed). *En la encrucijada: Colombia en el siglo XXI.* Bogotá, D.C.: Norma, 2006.
Hilgers, T.; Macdonald, L. (eds.). *Violence in Latin America and the Caribbean: Subnational Structures, Institutions, and Clientelistic Networks.* Cambridge: Cambridge University Press, 2017.
Mills, G. The Door Through Which Much Follows? Security and Colombia's Economic Transformation. In: Davis, D.; Kilcullen, D.; Mills, G.; Spencer, D. (orgs.). *A Great Perhaps? Colombia: Conflict and Convergence.* London: Hurst, 2016.
Montenegro R., L. E.; Durán E., P. A. Lucha contra el narcotráfico: transferencia de una experiencia. *Revista Criminalidad,* v. 50, n. 2, pp. 57–70, 2008. Available at: https://www.policia.gov.co/sites/default/files/RevistaCriminalidadco.pdf. Accessed on 05 July 2021.
Pinzón, J. C. Colombia Back from the Brink: From Failed State to Exporter of Security. *PRISM,* v. 5, n. 4, pp. 2–9, 2015.

Pizarro L., E. La Profesionalización Militar en Colombia (1907–1944). *Análisis Político*, n. 1, pp. 20–39, 1987a.
Pizarro L., E. La Profesionalización Militar en Colombia (II): El Periodo de La Violencia. *Análisis Político*, n. 2, pp. 7–29, 1987b.
Pizarro L., E. La profesionalización militar en Colombia (III): los regímenes militares (1953–1958). *Análisis Político*, n. 3, pp. 6–30, 1988.
Ramírez, S. *Intervención en conflictos internos: el caso colombiano* (1994-2003). Bogotá: Universidad Nacional de Colombia, 2004.
Rangel, A. (org.). *Sostenibilidad de la Seguridad Democrática*. Bogotá: Fundación Seguridad & Democracia, 2005.
Rojas, D. M. Estados Unidos y la guerra en Colombia. In: Sanín, F. G.; Wills, M. E.; Gómez, G. S. (coords). *Nuestra guerra sin nombre: transformaciones del conflicto en Colombia*. Bogotá, D.C.: Norma, 2006.
Rojas, D. M. Plan Colombia II: ¿más de lo mismo? *Colombia Internacional*, n. 65, pp. 14–37, 2007.
Valladares, L. P. *A invenção da favela: Do mito de origem a favela.com*. Rio de Janeiro: Editora FGV, 2005.
Vargas V., A. *Las fuerzas armadas en el conflicto colombiano: antecedentes y perspectivas*. Medellín: La Carreta, 2012.
Villamizar, A. *Fuerzas Militares para la guerra: La agenda pendiente de la reforma militar*. Bogotá, D.C.: Fundación Seguridad & Democracia, 2003.

Documents, Reports and Studies

Cárdenas, M.; Casas-Zamora, K. *The "Colombianization" of Mexico*. Washington, DC: Brookings Institution, 21 September 2010. Available at: https://www.brookings.edu/opinions/the-colombianization-of-mexico/. Accessed on 05 July 2021.
Coordinación Colombia-Europa-Estados Unidos. *Informe Alternativo presentado por las organizaciones de la Sociedad Civil al 7mo Informe presentado por el Estado Colombiano ante el Comité de DDHH de las Naciones Unidas*. Bogotá: Coordinación Colombia-Europa-Estados Unidos, 2017. Available at: http://coeuropa.org.co/wp-content/uploads/2017/01/Informe-alternativo-al-SEPTIMO-INFORME-11-enero-2017.pdf. Accessed on 04 July 2021.
DeShazo, P.; Primiani, T.; McLean, P. *Back from the Brink. Evaluating Progress in Colombia, 1999–2007*. Washington, D.C.: CIS, 2007.
Felbab-Brown, V. Narco-belligerants Across the Globe: Lessons from Colombia for Afghanistan? *Security and Defence Working Paper*, n. 55. Madrid: Elcano Royal Institute, 28 October 2009a. Available at: http://www.realinstitutoelcano.org/wps/wcm/connect/da0e7a80401cec18ab82eb1ecbd00d37/

WP55-2009_Felbab-Brown_Narco-belligerants_Lessons_Colombia_Afghanistan.pdf?MOD=AJPERES. Accessed on 04 July 2021.

Felbab-Brown, V. The Violent Drug Market in Mexico and Lessons from Colombia. *Policy Paper* (Foreign Policy at Brookings), n. 12, March 2009b. Available at: https://www.brookings.edu/wp-content/uploads/2016/06/03_mexico_drug_market_felbabbrown.pdf. Accessed on 04 July 2021.

Isacson, A. *Colombia: Don't Call it a Model*. Washington, D.C.: WOLA, 14 July 2010. Available at: https://www.wola.org/sites/default/files/Drug%20Policy/notmodel.pdf. Accessed on 19 June 2021.

Ministerio de Defensa de Colombia. *Visión de Futuro de las Fuerzas Armadas*. Bogotá: Imprenta Nacional de Colombia, 2016. Available at: https://www.mindefensa.gov.co/irj/go/km/docs/Mindefensa/Documentos/descargas/estrategia_planeacion/proyeccion/documentos/vision_futuro_FA.pdf. Accessed on 05 July 2021.

Sweeney, J. P. Colombia's Narco-Democracy Threatens Hemispheric Security. *The Heritage Foundation Backgrounder*, n. 1028, 21 March 1995. Available at: http://thf_media.s3.amazonaws.com/1995/pdf/bg1028.pdf. Accessed on 05 July 2021.

Tickner, A. B. Colombia, the United States, and Security Cooperation by Proxy. Washington, D.C.: WOLA, March 2014. Available at: http://www.wola.org/files/140318ti.pdf. Accessed on 13 February 2021.

Velásquez R., C. A. La fuerza pública que requiere el postconflicto. *Working Papers*, n. 13. Bogotá: Fundación Ideas para la Paz [FIP], May 2015. Available at: http://cdn.ideaspaz.org/media/website/document/5547dc7eef110.pdf. Accessed on 19 June 2021.

Press Articles

Albright, M. "Colombia's Struggles, and How Can We Help", *New York Times*, 10 August 1999. Available at: http://www.ciponline.org/colombia/00081002.htm. Accessed on 05 July 2021.

Manrique Z., V. "¿Cómo debe responder la Policía a un posconflicto?", *Revista Semana*, 23 May 2013. Available at: http://www.semana.com/opinion/articulo/despues-la-habana-como-debe-responder-policia-posconflicto/344167-3. Accessed on 05 July 2021.

Ruiz B., J. "Nuestras Fuerzas Armadas en el postconflicto", *Revista Semana*, 02 March 2014. Available at: http://www.semana.com/opinion/articulo/fuerzas-armadas-en-el-postconflicto-opinion-del-general-r-jaime-ruiz/385666-3. Accessed on 05 July 2021.

Vargas V., A. "Los militares en el Postconflicto", *El Tiempo*, 09 January 2003. Available at: http://www.eltiempo.com/archivo/documento/MAM-968820. Accessed on 05 July 2021.

Viana, M. T. "A paz é mais complexa: o referendo na Colômbia e a guerra na paz", *Rede PCECS*, 14 November 2016. Available at: https://redepcecs.com/2016/11/14/a-paz-e-mais-complexa-o-referendo-na-colombia-e-a-guerra-na-paz/. Accessed on 05 July 2021.

PART I

The Colombian "Success Story" (or, What Is Allowed to Have Happened)

Introduction

A "new Colombia", built in contrast to its past: a country that is no longer taken by violence, inequality, and corruption, but by peace, prosperity, and education (Presidencia de la República de Colombia 2014a, b, c, 2015). "A new Colombia that shines today, at home and abroad, converting itself into an example to the rest of the world. It is amazing how people now say: look at Colombia, observe Colombia, do what Colombia does"[1] (Presidencia de la República de Colombia 2014c), hailed President Juan Manuel Santos in January 2014. This optimistic portrait of Colombia was crafted approximately fifteen years after Andrés Pastrana used part of the speech inaugurating his Presidency to ask for the support of the international community in his efforts to tackle the "problem of violence" in the country: "Colombia cannot do it by itself. The challenge that we now face as a nation and as part of the global community is, perhaps, the greatest challenge of our history"[2] (*Apud* Bonilla 2001: 61–62). The contrast between these two speeches is quite

---

[1] In the original: "Una nueva Colombia que hoy brilla hacia adentro y hacia afuera, convirtiéndose en un ejemplo a seguir en el resto del mundo. Es increíble como ya dicen: miren a Colombia, observen a Colombia, hagan lo que hace Colombia".

[2] In the original: "Colombia no puede sola. El reto al que nos enfrentamos como nación y como parte de la comunidad mundial, quizás, es el mayor desafío de nuestra historia".

seductive: it expresses a "metamorphosis from 'failing state' to 'success story'" (Tickner and Morales 2014: 242), the abandonment of a condition of weakness towards one of strength.

To President Juan Manuel Santos (2010–2018) and to many others mobilizing the vocabulary of a "post-conflict era" in Colombia, by the 2010s this "new" country was already in the making: 2.6 million jobs were created from 2010 to 2013 (Ministerio de Hacienda y Crédito Público 2013: 2); the country was the fourth major destination of foreign direct investment in Latin America from 2012 to 2013, behind Brazil, Mexico and Chile (UNCTAD 2014: 4); and Colombia had just become the third major economy in Latin America.[3] Economic growth is but one dimension of achievements singled out by Colombian government officials when characterizing this "new country".

Interestingly, such an enthusiasm with a "post-conflict" Colombia was manifested even before a peace agreement had been reached in La Habana (Cuba) between the government and the FARC.[4] As an illustration, Fundación Ideas para La Paz (FIP, in Spanish), a think tank established in 1999 with resources from the Colombian private sector, created a research axis especially dedicated to the "post-conflict", focused on the rearticulation of the role of the Armed Forces in this scenario (FIP 2015), as well as on transitional justice, territorial governance, and education for peace. In June 2015, while visiting Norway, one of the guarantors in the peace process in La Habana, President Santos claimed that Colombia had already entered the post-conflict period. According to him, the infrastructure and housing projects that the Colombian government was undertaking at that time were already part of the process of

---

[3] The country was officially acknowledged as the third major economy in Latin America during the World Economic Forum held in 2014, in Davos (Switzerland). See: https://bit.ly/35gHT0X. Accessed on 14 June 2021.

[4] The exploratory talks officially started in February 2012, and the main negotiation axes were announced six months later as follows: (i) comprehensive agrarian development; (ii) political participation; (iii) ending the conflict; (iv) drug trafficking; (v) victims' rights; and (vi) implementation, verification, and referendum. In August 2016, the Peace Agreement on the six pillars was announced. With the title "Final Agreement for the Termination of the Conflict and the Construction of a Stable and Durable Peace", the full text, as well as all the *communiqués* issued during the negotiation process, is available here: https://www.cancilleria.gov.co/en/node/10268. Accessed on 14 June 2021.

"addressing the very roots of our conflict, which has been particularly cruel and violent"[5] (El Espectador 2015).

Most notably, in September 2014, President Santos created the office of High-Advisor on Post-conflict, Human Rights and Security (Decree No. 1.649/2014) and appointed, to this position, General Oscar Naranjo Trujillo, former chief of the Colombian National Police (2007–2012). The new office was charged with assisting the President in the formulation, structuration, and development of policies and programs related to the post-conflict, with emphasis on security, de-mining, human rights (Article 25.2), and former combatant re-integration (Article 25.3), as well as coordinating with the Ministry of Defense issues related to citizen security (Article 25.9). Although General Naranjo only remained in the position for 11 months, it is in the very conditions allowing for his nomination that I am interested, especially if we consider that General Naranjo was voted Vice-President of Colombia in March 2017, with the task of assisting in the implementation of the peace agreement signed in the previous year with the FARC.

The choice for his name as Advisor to the President regarding the "post-conflict" is intriguing, given that the Colombian National Police was one of the main parties involved in the armed conflict. General Naranjo is known for having participated in the dismantlement of the Medellín drug cartel in the early 1990s, having been trained by the Drug Enforcement Administration (DEA) on counternarcotic operations, by the U.S. Department of State on counterterrorism, and by the Federal Bureau of Investigation (FBI) on crime prevention. He led the counter-intelligence group in the Central Division of Judicial Police and Intelligence[6] (DIJIN, in Spanish) until 2007, when Naranjo was appointed by President Álvaro Uribe (2002–2010) as the Director-General of the Colombian National Police.

When his notoriety achieved global scale, his name circulated as an expert on "citizen security"—and not explicitly on domains such as counternarcotic, counterterrorism, or intelligence. Invited to participate in the World Economic Forum (WEF) in Latin America in 2013 and 2015 (held

---

[5] In the original: "Podemos decir que, en la práctica, el posconflicto ya comenzó en Colombia y que estamos atacando las raíces mismas de nuestro conflicto, que ha sido especialmente cruel y violento".

[6] The DIJIN is now named Division of Criminal Investigation and INTERPOL.

in Peru and Mexico, respectively), he spoke as an expert on citizen security, addressing how the Colombian National Police revamped its public security policy after untangling the knot of the "drug problem" in the country.[7] On the first occasion, he attended the WEF as the director of the Latin American Citizenship Institute (*Instituto Latinoamericano de Ciudadanía*) based in Monterrey (Mexico), in addition to the two other positions he held at that time: counselor to the Inter-American Development Bank (IDB) on citizen security, and to the Mexican Presidency on security issues.

If his professional trajectory accumulates credentials of an exemplary leader, it simultaneously reveals the domains of expertise that came to enjoy a privileged status in Colombia throughout decades of armed conflict. More than an individual story, General Naranjo conciliates, on the one hand, a trajectory resulting from the combination of professional experience on intelligence, counternarcotic and counterterrorism with, on the other hand, the mobilization of "citizen security" as the key term of the "post-conflict". As we will see in this book, far from erasing the layers of expertise that made the Colombian "success story" possible, the past still pulses through discursively aseptic vocabularies advanced as fit for this "new Colombia".

This "success story" has given impulse to a series of initiatives around the vocabulary of "post-conflict", involving diverse civil society actors, from Non-Governmental Organizations (NGOs) to the private sector, as well as governmental agencies—and, among those, the Colombian Armed Forces. In this sense, that General Naranjo was chosen as High-Advisor on Post Conflict, Human Rights, and Security is actually unsurprising: since the 2010s, the National Police and, more broadly, the Colombian Armed Forces came to be repeatedly portrayed as the protagonists of a new story, one in which the country is no longer an emblematic example of the "problem of violence", but a reference to solutions in the security domain.

To be clear, their expertise after decades of armed conflict is presented by both the police and the military as a determining factor in bringing

---

[7] In 2013, General Naranjo was actually the theme of a whole session, titled "An insight, An idea with Óscar Naranjo". The video is available here: https://www.youtube.com/watch?v=vZAjekAXjKc. In addition to that, he participated on a panel titled "Drugs Policy: untangling the knot", which can be accessed here: https://www.youtube.com/watch?v=9pRHDqQ0cXs. Accessed on 14 June 2021.

Colombia back from the brink of the abyss (DeShazo *et al.* 2007). Seeing a wide range of groups in the world as particular expressions of the same phenomenon of violence that has been overcome in Colombia, the Armed Forces in this country now offer their formula as a useful and efficient expertise to the region and the world. Analogies with the Colombian guerrillas stretch from Paraguay (Diálogo 2014), Peru, Argentina (Isacson 2010), the Boko Haram in Nigeria (Afeikhena 2015), the Islamic State of Iraq and Syria (ISIS), Al Qaeda (Kelly 2015) or, more generally, transnational organized delinquency (Ministerio de Defensa de Colombia 2012). Irrespective of the plausibility of those comparisons, the "success" of the Colombian Armed Forces has found legitimacy and adherence in its counterparts. From 2010 to 2015, more than 24,000 police and military, especially—though not exclusively—from Latin American countries had been trained by the Colombian Armed Forces (Pinzón 2015: 8).

But how was it possible that a country that has been historically stigmatized as a "problematic country" came to be taken as a reference for solutions to others? Part I engages with the Colombian "success story" having as a point of departure the assumption that the claim for success relies on the idea that a specific set of problems has been overcome. By exploring the rearticulations on how the "problem of violence" has been understood, my purpose is to expose the historical sedimentation that echoes in the representation of violence claimed to be overcome in Colombia. In doing so, my point is not to contend that, in fact, specific "problem of violence" has not been overcome, nor to argue that its having been overcome came at a high human cost.

Although these analytical directions are indeed plausible and politically relevant, my objective in Part I is to pursue another path: I am particularly interested in digging into the terms upon which the Colombian "success story" was made possible and legitimate, and to expose the silencing that makes such a story audible as an important effect of its "success". If the legitimacy granted to Colombia's "success story" is strengthened by its replication as a model in other countries, the analysis in Part I aims at offering an analytical ground for us to read as both a shared diagnosis of which violence must be repressed, and which renderings of violence are marginalized and destined to fade away in the virtuous image of a "success".

This objective is pursued through three main analytical moves. In Chapter 2, I mobilize Foucault's concept of "problematization" (Foucault 2010) to investigate the processes through which Colombia came to be discursively produced as a problematic country. I argue that, by the late 1990s, these processes resulted in a very specific rendering of violence in Colombia: one deriving from the activity of "narcoguerrillas"—and, since 9/11, "narcoterrorists"—, understood as dangerous delinquents whose activities are funded by the resources from drug trafficking. Building from this analysis, Chapter 3 discusses how the Colombian performance in the implementation of counternarcotic policies became a focus of disputed claims and measuring tools. I argue that the inquiries about Colombia, the diagnoses elaborated about its problems and their correspondent treatments, as well as the disputes around the metrics with which counternarcotic operations must be assessed are all embedded in the same discursive field. By pointing to the epistemological principles that came to organize claims to truth regarding Colombia's counternarcotic performance, I show how these same principles operate as silencing mechanisms that allow for the "success story" to be told. Through an analysis focused on unions and human rights organizations, I first argue that extrajudicial killings, forced disappearances and forced detention of unionists constitute human rights violations that fall outside the horizon of disputes about Colombia's performance in tackling the "problem of violence"—and, consequently, do not resonate in the "success story". Operating as silencing mechanisms in the margins of the discursive field, the epistemological criteria governing disputes about policy impact define the limits of what the "success story" can be about: it is not about the state as part of the problem of violence, and it is not about social or land reforms.

Through the discussions developed in Part I, I argue that, far from erasing the "problematic past" of the country, the "success story" needs it: after all, claiming Colombia as a "successful" case requires a story about what problems have been overcome. Nonetheless, it is a particular past that is produced through the "success story", as well as a particular present. In the next pages, therefore, I expect to dissect the criteria of eligibility of what is allowed to be told in this story, thereby exposing the limits of what the "success story" can be about.

REFERENCES

BOOKS, CHAPTERS, ARTICLES

Afeikhena, J. Lessons from Colombia for Curtailing the Boko Haram Insurgency in Nigeria. *Prism*, v. 5, n. 2, pp. 94–105, 2015.
Bonilla, A. Vulnerabilidad internacional y fragilidad doméstica: la crisis andina en perspectiva regional. *Nueva Sociedad*, n. 173, pp. 50–64, June 2001.
Foucault, M. Nietzsche, Genealogy, History. In: Rabinow, P. (ed.). *The Foucault Reader.* New York: Pantheon Books, 2010 [1984].
Pinzón, J. C. Colombia Back from the Brink: From Failed State to Exporter of Security. *PRISM*, v. 5, n. 4, pp. 2–9, 2015.
Tickner, A. B. Morales C., M. Narrating Success: Colombian Security Expertise and Foreign Policy. In: Bagley, B. M.; Rosen, J. D. (eds). *Colombia's Political Economy at the Outset of the 21st Century*: From Uribe to Santos and Beyond. Washington, DC: Lexington, 2014.

DOCUMENTS, REPORTS AND STUDIES

DeShazo, P.; Primiani, T.; McLean, P. *Back from the Brink. Evaluating Progress in Colombia, 1999–2007*. Washington, DC: CIS, 2007.
Isacson, A. *Colombia: Don't Call it a Model*. Washington, DC: WOLA, 14 July 2010. Available at: https://www.wola.org/sites/default/files/Drug%20Policy/notmodel.pdf. Accessed on 19 June 2021.
Ministerio de Defensa de Colombia. "Combatir la delincuencia trasnacional con una visión regional es la única garantía de éxito": Ministro Pinzón. Bogotá, 03 May 2012. Available at: https://www.mindefensa.gov.co/irj/go/km/docs/documents/News/NoticiaGrandeMDN/503fce10-7277-2f10-e791-c714fff98d20.xml. Accessed on 19 June 2021.
Ministerio de Hacienda y Crédito Público. Generación de empleo 2010–2013: Superando las metas. *Reportes de Hacienda*, v. 6, año 2. Bogotá: Dirección General de Política Macroeconómica, Ministerio de Hacienda y Crédito Público, 12 December 2013. Available at: https://docplayer.es/8632435-Generacion-de-empleo-2010-2013-superando-las-metas.html. Accessed on 19 June 2021.
Presidencia de la República de Colombia. Declaración del Presidente Juan Manuel Santos en el lanzamiento de la Cátedra para la Paz. 25 May 2015. Available at: http://wp.presidencia.gov.co/Noticias/2015/Mayo/Paginas/20150525_07-Declaracion-del-Presidente-Juan-Manuel-Santos-en-el-lanzamiento-de-la-Catedra-para-la-Paz.aspx. Accessed on 19 June 2021.
Presidencia de la República de Colombia. Palabras del Presidente Juan Manuel Santos en su posesión para el período presidencial 2014–2018. Bogotá, 07

August 2014. Available at: http://wsp.presidencia.gov.co/Prensa/2014/Ago sto/Paginas/20140807_03-Palabras-del-Presidente-Santos-en-su-posesion-para-el-periodo-presidencial-2014-2018.aspx. Accessed on 19 June 2021.
Presidencia de la República de Colombia. Palabras del Presidente Juan Manuel Santos en la presentación de la segunda edición del libro '100 Colombianos'. Bogotá, 31 January 2014. Available at: http://wsp.presidencia.gov.co/Pre nsa/2014/Enero/Paginas/20140131_03-Palabras-del-Presidente-Juan-Man uel-Santos-en-la-presentacion-de-la-segunda-edicion-del-libro-100Colomb ianos.aspx. Accessed on 19 June 2021.
UNCTAD. *World Investment Report Overview 2014.* Investing in the SDGs: An Action Plan. Geneva: UNCTAD, 2014. Available at: http://unctad.org/en/ PublicationsLibrary/wir2014_overview_en.pdf. Accessed on 19 June 2021.
Velásquez R., C. A. La fuerza pública que requiere el postconflicto. *Working Papers,* n. 13. Bogotá: Fundación Ideas para la Paz [FIP], May 2015. Available at: http://cdn.ideaspaz.org/media/website/document/5547dc7eefl10. pdf. Accessed on 19 June 2021.

Press Articles

Diálogo. "Ejército colombiano entrena a soldados paraguayos para luchar contra el terrorismo y el narcotráfico", *Diálogo,* 26 August 2014. Available at: https://dialogo-americas.com/es/articles/colombian-army-trains-par aguayan-soldiers-to-fight-terrorism-drug-trafficking/. Accessed on 19 June 2021.
El Espectador. "Críticas a Santos por asegurar que 'el posconflicto ya comenzó en Colombia'", *El Espectador,* 16 June 2015. Available at: https://www.ele spectador.com/politica/criticas-a-santos-por-asegurar-que-el-posconflicto-ya-comenzo-en-colombia-article-566564/. Accessed on 19 June 2021.
Kelly, J. F. "Colombia's Resolve Merits Support", *Miami Herald,* 05 March 2015. Available at: http://www.miamiherald.com/opinion/op-ed/article20 047503.html. Accessed on 19 June 2021.
Presidencia de la República de Colombia. "Estamos creando un país distinto con oportunidades para todos los colombianos: Presidente Santos". *Presidencia de la República de Colombia,* 31 January 2014b. Available at: http://wsp. presidencia.gov.co/Prensa/2014/Enero/Paginas/20140131_02-Estamos-cre ando-un-pais-distinto-con-oportunidades-para-todos-los-colombianos-Presid ente-Santos.aspx. Accessed on 19 June 2021.

CHAPTER 2

The Problem as a Condition for Success: The Construction of Colombia as a "Problematic Country"

Most analytical efforts aimed at understanding how the image of Colombia has been transformed from one of a failing state to that of a success story focused on debating the truthfulness of this narrative. Approaches such as those adopted by DeShazo et al. (2007, 2009), and Felbab-Brown (2012) claim that there has been a net gain in Colombia when goals, achievements and costs are weighed against each other. Focusing on security, the peace process, human rights, narcotics, governance, economy, social conditions, and U.S. assistance, DeShazo et al. (2007) argue that Plan Colombia is a turning point in the repertoire of attempts aimed at addressing the problems that were leading Colombia to the brink of collapse (DeShazo et al. 2007: 9). Álvaro Uribe's (2002–2010) Democratic Security Policy, by its turn, is understood as having strengthened the main lines established by his predecessor, Andrés Pastrana (1998–2002).

As regards human rights, for instance, DeShazo et al. (2007: 24) recognize that "grave problems persist, among them extrajudicial killings, kidnapping and hostage taking, forced disappearances, recruitment of child soldiers, incidents of torture, involuntary displacement, overcrowded prisons". Nevertheless, they claim that "snapshot examinations of the human rights situation in Colombia often do not reflect that progress has been made under very difficult circumstances" (DeShazo et al. 2007: 24) and that the Colombian government has been recognized for its efforts towards improving the administration of justice (DeShazo et al. 2007: 26). By mobilizing data, building graphs, and sketching trends, the authors seem confident that should these efforts continue, the human rights situation in Colombia would be gradually transformed into a part of this success. Against analyses arguing that not only the Colombian Armed Forces but also the U.S. assistance have an active role in such a human rights picture (Human Rights Watch 1996; FOR and CCEEU 2014; Ronderos 2014), the authors claim that "the driving force behind so many of the gravest abuses of human rights has been violence from the illegal armed groups and the inability of the state to impose the rule of law more effectively" (DeShazo et al. 2007: 24).

In contrast, another group of analyses (Feldmann 2012; Isacson 2010; Tickner 2014) criticizes the "success story" on the grounds that "the correspondence between empirical facts and the stories told about Colombia has been imperfect at best" (Tickner and Morales 2014: 243). Concerned with the vocabulary of "model" orbiting around the Colombian "success story", Isacson argues that "Colombia's security gains are partial, possibly reversible, and weighed down by 'collateral damage'" (2010: 1). He exposes the scandals constituting the narrative of success, addressing the systematic involvement of the intelligence service with paramilitary groups, and of the latter with political parties, as well as the extrajudicial killings scandal known as the "false positives"[1] (Isacson 2010). In addition, he shows how the drug strategy undertaken through Plan Colombia and the Democratic Security Policy was misguided and only in more recent years seemed to recognize the failure of the strategy as a whole (Isacson 2010: 8). Based on these elements, Isacson contends that the prolonged war in Colombia has resulted in human and financial costs too high to be claimed as a "success". Underlying analyses found in this group, there is the idea that the human costs cannot be understood as a mere marginal collateral damage: bringing them to the front of the analysis implies brushing aside the vocabulary of "model" in order to refer to the Colombian experience.

---

[1] The "false positives" scandal involved the systematic killing of civilian non-combatants as combatants by the Colombian Military Forces. Their bodies were then dressed in guerrilla uniforms and presented as members of those armed groups killed in combat. In 2002, investigations led to the identification of 1,302 cases. For more information on the "false positives", see: FOR and CCEEU (2014).

The point of departure of the two perspectives identified here is considerably different, as are the conclusions they reach. Indeed, the second group highlights that the lives lost in the conflict cannot have the same analytical weight of, for instance, cocaine seizures in the debate about the Colombian performance in overcoming its problems. On the other hand, as we have seen above, studies arguing in favor of the successful character of the Colombian story do encompass human costs—in the case of human rights and social conditions (DeShazo et al. 2007), this position is made more explicitly. However, by incorporating human costs to graphs in which the variation of those categories in time is what matters, this group seems to encourage us to celebrate that Colombia went from approximately 80 massacres with at least 5 deaths each in 1999, to around 30 massacres in 2004—as reading the graph in the work by DeShazo et al. (2007: 20) suggests. In this sense, those arguing in favor of the success narrative authorize the continuity of efforts taking place and encourage the export of security policies implemented in Colombia to other countries (Pinzón 2015), while those questioning the success argue for the revision of the terms mobilized in performance assessments, as well as of the ongoing policies in Colombia.

Even if they scrutinize a different set of numbers and attribute a different analytical weight to them, these works are similar when it comes to considering numbers as windows to truth. Their disagreements rely either on the method and/or source through which indicators are obtained, or on the hierarchy built between the domains upon which cost-benefit relations are drawn. Indeed, discussing which set of indicators is most appropriate to assess the truthfulness of the Colombian "success story" can reveal much more than a pursuit of accuracy: it can expose the tensions behind the production of such metric—the politics of measuring success. But this is so only if one sees those numbers as *claims* to truth. Although moves such as these can contribute to revealing and transforming the terms of equations, to debunk peace formulae considered as harmful to specific social groups, or even to deauthorize a certain political discourse, I am more interested in exploring the Colombian narrative of success through another angle here.

Instead of diving into a fact-finding effort to inquire about the truthfulness of the "Colombian success", I propose taking one step back to explore the conditions under which this narrative is even possible. Particularly, I shall focus on how this very claim of success becomes an object of analysis and dispute. Among various disputed claims, how does a specific set of claims is raised to a privileged position, downplaying other possible readings of a given cut-out (*découpe*, in Foucault's terms) of the world? Foucault has called "emergence" this arising of a certain framing to a privileged position amid a particular play of forces. He adds a cautionary note to that: "we should avoid thinking of emergence as the final term of a historical development" (Foucault 2010a: 83). Likewise, that the narrative of Colombia's success is dominant does not imply the extinction of the forces struggling with its arising, and precisely because of this point the narrative is constantly being challenged and transformed by the confrontations in which it is continuously found. In this sense, neither the claim of a failure nor of a success should be seen as a historically natural or necessary depiction of Colombia, for they do not exist apart from the play of forces from which they have emerged. Nor should they be seen as immutable—although the translation of the "problem of violence" in Colombia into policies, edifices and piles of studies exerts resistance in this process.

Since the narrative about the "Colombian success" relies on its contrast to a problematic past, it is equally important to question the processes that made the claim of success possible as it is to investigate the processes through which Colombia came to be identified as a "problematic country", whose problems had to be dealt with by a specific set of policies. Here, I am interested in a critique on how Colombia—and the problems associated with it—came to be understood as an object of concern, debate, and search for solutions. This is a specific kind of critique, that is, "pointing out on what kinds of assumptions, what kinds of familiar, unchallenged, unconsidered modes of thought the practices we accept rest" (Foucault 1988: 154). While this Chapter mobilizes analytical elements for us to understand how a "dominant" problematization of Colombia emerged, the subsequent Chapter explores narratives challenging that specific construction of Colombia as a problem.

2.1 The Problematization of Violence in Colombia

The feature that has been most often highlighted in referring to Colombia as a problematic country is that of violence.[2] Indeed, one of the most violent confrontations in the official historiography of Colombia has come to be known as *La Violencia* (1948–1958),[3] suggesting that the level of violence observed in Colombia at that time was such that Colombians had actually witnessed the meaning of the noun "violence". Likewise, the systematic study of the phenomenon of violence came to be referred to as *violentología* ("violentology") in the country. Although the production of detailed explanations of causes and effects of violence in Colombia had already marked the 1960s, when efforts were especially invested towards explaining *La Violencia*,[4] the term *violentólogos* was coined by the late-1980s, when President Virgilio Barco (1986–1990) appointed nine academics and one military officer[5] to constitute the Commission of Studies on Violence (*Comisión de Estudios sobre la Violencia*), which was expected to elaborate a diagnosis of violence in Colombia.[6]

---

[2] For an analytical overview of the literature on violence published in Colombia during the 1990s, see Peñaranda (2003) and González et al. (2003).

[3] Periodizations such as this one are only used in this book as a general reference for the reader, for the determination of both a beginning and an end of an armed conflict is unescapably problematic. One of the main sources of inspiration for the way I see and approach armed conflicts stems from Cynthia Enloe's works, despite the differences they present in relation to this book in terms of analytical object, methodology and arguments. When did the war in Iraq end?—asks Enloe in one of the chapters in *Nimo's War, Emma's War* (2010). By discussing how the war in Iraq has affected the trajectory of Maha and her family, by killing her husband, restricting her options for jobs, and narrowing the places where safety could be found, Enloe shows that, for Maha and her children, the effects of war surely transcend the ceasefire. I hope to provide in this book elements that allow for us to be as uncomfortable as Enloe as regards sharp periodizations of numerous violent chapters in Colombian historiography, as if one had no connection with the others and, above all, as if ceasefires and other official agreements sufficed for us to understand how war carries on in people's lives even after no gun is shot.

[4] See, for instance, Sánchez G. et al. (1962), Cardona (2008), and Pizarro (1987a).

[5] The Commission was constituted by: Jaime Arocha R., Álvaro Camacho G., Darío Fajardo M., Álvaro Guzmán B., Carlos Eduardo Jaramillo, Carlos Miguel Ortiz S., Eduardo Pizarro L., Gonzalo Sánchez G. and General (r) Luis Alberto Andrade A.

[6] Intriguingly, one year before President Barco appointed the Commission of Studies on Violence, he created another, formed by his minister of Government, Fernando Cepeda, and other members of the government, as well as renowned lawyers and high-ranked

The dissection of violence undertaken by the Commission provided a taxonomy and a hierarchy of categories of violence, according to which recommendations were elaborated for Virgilio Barco's administration. This task was particularly relevant in the 1980s in Colombia. The violent chapters the country had accumulated in its historiography from the late-nineteenth century to mid-twentieth century had been written with emphasis on the two political parties. In this sense, the 1980s offered an analytical challenge, given the rising indicators of violence in Colombia, "despite" the "consortium democracy" (Pizarro 1987b) articulated between the Liberal and Conservative Parties after the Thousand Days' War (1899–1902).

In 1987, the Commission concluded that the armed conflict involving the guerrillas was not the only, nor the main source of violence in Colombia. There were multiple kinds of violence (political, economic, organized, familial etc.), and tackling them would require reforms aimed at transforming their historical causes. Implementing land reform and human rights policies and expanding the inclusive character of democracy in Colombia are some of the reforms suggested in the report presented by the Commission (Sánchez 1988).

Among its main findings, the Commission highlighted that "political violence", understood as the struggle for power and control over the state apparatus (Sánchez 1988: 56), corresponded to only 7.51% of the homicides registered in 1985 in Colombia (Sánchez 1988: 18). In addition to the "non-political" character of more than 90% of homicides registered in Colombia in 1985, the Commission argued that the urban space was the site where a greater share of violence was perpetrated, and increasingly so (Sánchez 1988: 57). In terms of crimes against life and personal integrity from 1983 to 1985, Medellin was considered the most violent city in Colombia, with 8,729 crimes of that category; Bogotá, the third, with 7,993; and Cali, the fourth, with 6,696 (Sánchez 1988: 77). According to the Commission, "delinquency" was mostly found in relations involving citizens, not in those between citizens and the state. Among the crimes

---

military officers. The mission assigned to this 1986 Commission was quite different: it was expected to study anti-terrorist legislations of England, France, Germany, Italy and Spain, given the concern of the government with mounting levels of violence (Orozco 1992: 174). Here, "terrorism" was understood in similar lines to what the Commission of Studies on Violence considered to be the most concerning kind of violence facing Colombia: one which was notably urban and non-political, and mainly perpetrated by civilians against other civilians.

registered in 1980, only 3.7% were of a citizen-state kind; and 41.5% involved private patrimonial relations (Sánchez 1988: 18).

Importantly, the report by the Commission was elaborated based on data provided by the DIJIN when referring to the crimes registered in Colombia, and on data from the National Administrative Department of Statistics (DANE, in Spanish) when referring to the population and specific characteristics of the state. This methodological option was claimed by the Commission of Studies on Violence as appropriate, for both the DIJIN and the DANE were believed to have "the most reliable data available" (Sánchez 1988: 58). By reproducing the general lines of the diagnosis about violence by the police and claiming that the report was technically accurate, the work of the Commission had the political effect of legitimizing the official narrative about that matter. One of the immediate implications of those choices is the silence of the report regarding violence perpetrated by the Colombian Armed Forces. Although the latter is mentioned in two categories of violence mapped by the Commission—state violence against ethnic minorities and social movements, and violence of the Armed Forces personnel while on duty (Sánchez 1988: 20)—excesses of violence by state forces are barely mentioned in the report and, in some of the passages, the link between victims and Armed Forces is only considered as a possible one (see, for instance, Sánchez 1988: 93).

By analyzing categories of violence, as well as ranking policy priorities anchored in allegedly accurate data and classification criteria, the Commission organized the field of knowledge about violence in Colombia. In the words of the report, it offered an "analytical flash, which, by reading what is happening, recommends something easy to digest and operate through public policy"[7] (Jaramillo 2011: 249). Given that this "digestive diagnosis" had been commissioned by the government, its claim to truth concerning violence in Colombia was invested with a considerable degree of discursive authority, strengthening the narrative constituted by the report.

By the end of the 1980s, the academics who were part of the Commission founded the Institute of Studies on Politics and International Relations (IEPRI, in Spanish) at the National University of Colombia, one of the first research centers focused on violence in the country (Pécaut

---

[7] In the original: "para producir un *flash* analítico, que a la vez que lee lo que pasa, recete algo fácil de digerir y operar en política pública."

1998; Revista Semana 2007; Jaramillo 2011). The creation of IEPRI, the report by the Commission and the sources upon which the latter relied gave impulse to the expansion of the field of *violentología* and contributed to the crystallization of the association of Colombia with violence. They became nodes around which knowledge about that topic was produced and organized through the dissemination of studies on that matter, while at the same time they stimulated the multiplication of debates, studies and research agendas, thereby channeling the visibility of certain approaches to the "problem of violence" rather than others. This circuit did not constitute the point of origin of the problematization of Colombia as a "violent country", for it has, itself, emerged from it. That is, the creation of the Commission and IEPRI, as well as the term *violentología*, were both an engine fueling this narrative and an expression of it.

As we have seen, the Commission framed the problem in accordance with a set of assumptions, categories, and data produced by the DIJIN and the DANE. Taking this into account, the findings of the Commission report based on the distinction between "political" and "non-political" violence are misleading. This is so because the Colombian National Police understood "political delinquency" differently before and after the 1980 Penal Code. When the Commission elaborated its report, in 1987, the guerrillas were recurrently framed as "regular delinquents", which implied depriving these groups from the treatment granted to "political delinquents", a legal category inherited from a classical conception of civil war, which involved rights such as access to dialogue channels and reduced penalties (Orozco 1989, n.p.). By the mid-twentieth century, the range of practices framed as "political delinquency" became narrower, and the decision processes through which a certain practice was classified as such were increasingly turned into ad hoc mechanisms[8] (Orozco 1992).

Thus, in the terms of the Commission, when the report claims that political violence was not statistically the most concerning face of violence in Colombia, it is suggesting that guerrillas were not a significant part of the problem of violence in that context. However, since the 1960s the Colombian National Police classified guerrilla warfare as a kind of *bandolerismo* (banditry), understood as an association of individuals aimed

---

[8] In particular contexts, guerrillas, drug traffickers and paramilitary groups tactically appropriated terms such as "political delinquent" depending on the benefits granted to this category, in order to obtain an advantageous position in a negotiation with the government, for instance (Orozco 1992).

at committing offenses merely for the sake of disorder. By reproducing this Police classification in its report, the Commission not only denied a political character to the guerrillas, but also erased any possibility of reading as "political agendas" issues such as land reform and labor and civil rights, which had long constituted the main demands by *campesinos* in Colombian rural areas (González et al. 2003; Pécaut 2010).

According to Orozco, the re-articulation of the boundary between "delinquent" and "political" violence towards the expansion of the former is not specific to Colombia (Orozco 1989). According to him, this process is inscribed in a broader transformation of war, whose interpretation has been increasingly based on a "punitive conception of the public international law, (…) whose main corollary is a delinquential – not political – definition of war"[9] (Orozco 1989, n.p.). In this sense, even when framing the guerrillas as an "enemy of the state" and declaring a war against these groups, they are still seen as *bandoleros* by the discourse expressed by the Colombian Armed Forces.

This was the case of the juxtaposition of *bandolerismo* and communism advanced in the state of exception issued by President Julio César Turbay Ayala (1978–1982). Operating under the logic of national security, the Security Statute (*Estatuto de Seguridad*) fused guerrillas and bandits into the same category of "enemy of the state", defined as armed groups threatening the existence of the state (Leal 2002: 21–22). By the early 1980s, the only political component attached to the guerrillas was their threatening character to the existence of the state—a move which only took shape after rights granted to "political delinquents" were aseptically removed. That the Commission report used the data produced by the DIJIN in this context can only result in declining statistics for "political violence", as any possible political character of guerrillas had already been erased through their framing as "regular delinquents" by 1987. These processes indicate that the meanings of categories such as "regular delinquent" and "political delinquent" cannot be detached from those who create and transform them—as Bonditti (2014: 193) argued in relation to the framing of terrorism as a threat.

If the report elaborated by the Commission is key for us to understand the emergence of the "problem of violence" as a distinctive feature

---

[9] In the original: "Una concepción punitiva del derecho internacional público, concebido a manera de un derecho público interno mundial, y cuyo corolario principal es una definición delincuencial – no política – de la guerra".

of Colombia, it is important to underline that it did not consider drugs a special category in the phenomenon of violence at that time. Indeed, none of the kinds of violence discussed by the Commission report (political, economic, organized, familial) connected drugs to violence indicators such as homicide rates. On the other hand, by the time the report was crafted, the Colombian National Police was already expressing concern with the delinquency indicators related to drug activity (Policía Nacional de Colombia 1980: 200–202). It is not a coincidence, in this sense, that Medellin and Cali, two of the three cities singled out by the report as the most violent in Colombia (Sánchez 1988: 77), were also the ones associated with drug cartels. Given that the report was elaborated based on data collected by the Colombian National Police's DIJIN, we must then understand how the "problem of violence" intersected the construction of the "problem of drugs" in Colombia. To do that, first we must investigate how drugs slid from a "public health problem" to one of "public order".

From the 1920s, when the first drug control legislation was passed in Colombia, to 1936, when the Penal Code was reformed for the first time, drugs were mainly framed as a "public health problem". Laws No. 11/1920 and No. 128/1928 assigned to the national government the task of updating the list of substances considered as "pernicious drugs", formulated according to the criteria established by the National Hygiene Division (Policía Nacional de Colombia 1980: 192). The discursive authority with which pharmaceutical, medical, and veterinary professionals were vested in this context could be observed not only in the specialized knowledge required in producing lists of pernicious drugs, but also in the power concentrated in these professionals to issue permissions and oversee their compliance (López 2016: 143–151). Although the police authority was evoked in the enforcement of those rules, penalties were exclusively applied to those fabricating, or commercializing without license, substances which "constitute pernicious habit", leaving to sanitary authorities the supervision of consumption. Indeed, while "drug users" had to be admitted to clinics or hospitals, the penalty for those trading such substances without permission was a 100–500 pesos fine, in addition to 1–6 months imprisonment.

The 1936 Penal Code introduces two fundamental changes in this regard. The first one refers to the penal expansion it advanced towards the "drug problem", increasing penalties[10]—both in monetary (50–1,000 pesos) and carceral terms (6–60 months)—and encompassing a wider set of modalities for these crimes, ranging from supply, to fabrication and distribution (Policía Nacional de Colombia 1980). The second major change brought by the 1936 Penal Code is one of vocabulary: instead of focusing on the individual "pernicious habit", its chapter on drug-related crimes was titled "crimes against *public health*" (my emphasis). This concern was framed in terms of a threat to society and, in this sense, involved mechanisms aimed at isolating drug users and eradicating the conditions for consumption of such substances. As argued by Holguín (2010 *Apud* Uprimny et al. 2017: 17), the 1936 Penal Code shifts the vocabulary of drug control legislation to one of "social defense" and approaches drug addiction and commercialization as a dangerous anomaly. This link was more explicitly developed in the following years, when the "anti-social conduct" of the drug-related criminal was characterized as threatening to the most cherished values in Colombian society: private property, life, and social order—as specified by the Decree No. 1669, issued in 1964 (Policía Nacional de Colombia 1980: 195).

The trajectory of the drug legislation drawn above reveals the persistence of a double rationale governing those control efforts. First, the objective of such regulations was to wipe out "pernicious substances" in order to sanitize Colombian society from a constellation of deviant conducts threatening its core values. Second, they express a logic anchored in a bifurcation between modalities of drug use, on the one hand, and modalities of production and commercialization, on the other. In the former, the specialist in charge of the problem was the sanitary/medical authority; in the latter, the police, increasingly authorized by penalties which became more severe throughout the years.

The cleavage between drug consumption and drug trafficking gradually faded in the years following the Penal Code reform. Central to this process was the 1974 National Statute on Stupefying Substances (*Estatuto Nacional de Estupefacientes*), issued by the Decree No. 1188/1974, and later substituted by the 1986 National Statute on Stupefying Substances

---

[10] Seen through this angle, the 1936 Penal Code actually inaugurated an expansion process that has never ceased in the following decades, with obvious repercussions to the Colombian penitentiary system (see, for instance, Uprimny et al. 2017).

(Law No. 30/1986), with stronger penalties[11] and an even narrower margin for a public health approach—basically reduced to some articles on campaigns against drug use.[12] But the key to understanding the crystallization of a repressive character in the whole range of modalities of drug control policies resides in the 1980 Penal Code and the sequence of states of exception starting in 1978. The reform of the Penal Code in 1980 resulted not only in the framing of drug-related crimes as "crimes against public security", but also in the incorporation of "terrorism" to the same category of crimes.

According to Article 187 of the 1980 Penal Code, terrorism is a practice by those who, "with the purpose of creating or maintaining an atmosphere of turmoil, or disturbing public order, employ means of collective destruction against persons or goods".[13] The incorporation of such a penal type to the Colombian legislation resulted from debates within a Reform Commission, integrated by Colombian jurists, whose work stretched from the mid-1970s to the approval of the new version of the Code, in 1980. Among an increasing number of strikes and students' demonstrations, as well as the multiplication of guerrillas and the consolidation of Colombia as a major drug producer and exporter, the debates in the Commission were marked by "the panic from the imminent revolution through insurrection"[14] (Orozco 1992: 166). In this context, members of the Commission such as Giraldo Marín believed that riots in the streets were the first step to insurrection. They argued for the need to punish disorder with severity and that claims for reforms had to be vocalized through democratic channels (Orozco 1992: 165). According to Marín, the rural war paradigm had been transformed into an urban insurrection one—or, in his terms, the guerrilla combat had been substituted by the general strike (Orozco 1992: 166). The final version of the Penal Code reveals a similar logic when preserving the link between "disturbances of public order" and "terrorism" (Article 187),

---

[11] Here, possession or trafficking was subjected to 3 to 12 years of imprisonment (Uprimny et al. 2017: 18).

[12] See Articles 8–13 of the 1986 National Statute on Stupefying Substances.

[13] In the original: "El que con el fin de crear o mantener un ambiente de zozobra, o de perturbar el orden público, emplee contra personas o bienes, medios de destrucción colectiva, incurrirá en prisión de diez (10) a veinte (20) años, sin perjuicio de la pena que corresponda por los demás delitos que se ocasionen con este solo hecho".

[14] In the original: "pánico a la revolución inminente por la vía insurreccional".

allowing for the association of the latter with a wide range of contestation movements. Another element contributing to this reading is the emphasis laid by Article 187 on damage caused to goods, without any further specification on what kind of damage and what kind of good was being considered. This patrimonial concern regarding public order had the effect of expanding the spectrum of possible associations of social conducts (social movements, protests, and sabotage, for instance) with terrorism.

Furthermore, Article 127 of the 1980 Penal Code established that "Rebel or seditious individuals shall not be subjected to penalty for punishable conducts undertaken while in combat only if the latter do not constitute acts of ferocity, barbarism or terrorism".[15] This move had clear implications for the guerrillas: their removal from the legal background linked to the armed conflict erased any possible association of these groups with political legitimacy. In this sense, the depoliticization of their legal framing led to the delegitimation of the guerrillas, which were thereby brought closer to the legal (criminalizing) framing of social movements, whose conduct was seen as threatening public security, under the terms of the Penal Code.

The 1980s were also marked by the increase of drug production in Colombia. By that time, the country concentrated most of the cocaine production and distribution chain and had become the main source of the cocaine consumed in the U.S. (Craig 1983; Thoumi 2002). By the mid-1980s, there were two major networks[16] concentrating the production chain in Colombia, as well as national and international distribution channels: one based in Medellín; the other, in Cali. By late-1980s, the Colombian National Police reported that drug-related crimes represented 90.75% of the "crimes against public security" in the country (Policía Nacional de Colombia 1987: 69). These crimes were concentrated in four Colombian departments: Antioquia (34.67%), Bogotá (11.07%), Quindío (10.87%) and Valle (8.18%) (Policía Nacional de Colombia 1987: 69).

---

[15] In the original: "Los rebeldes o sediciosos no quedarán sujetos a pena por los hechos punibles cometidos en combate, siempre que no constituyan actos de ferocidad, barbarie o terrorismo".

[16] According to Thoumi (2002: 108), "In reality, these were not truly cartels with the capacity to exclude and control production but rather were syndicates that improved the efficiency of distribution. Smaller syndicates remained in the shadow of the two main ones".

The core zones of the two "drug cartels" were located in two of these departments: the city of Medellin, capital of Antioquia; and Cali, capital of the department of Valle del Cauca. Similarly, Antioquia (19.35%), Valle (17.92%), Bogotá (14.34%) and Santander (12.54%) concentrated the crimes registered as "terrorism" in 1987 (Policía Nacional de Colombia 1987: 70).

Despite the innumerous triggers associated with drug-related violence, resistance to the Treaty of Extradition accounted for a significant share of assassinations perpetrated by "drug cartels". Signed in 1979, during the Turbay Ayala administration (1978–1982), the Treaty came into effect in 1984, determining that those whose crimes were also considered as an offense to the U.S. criminal law had to be judged and serve their sentence in that country. Organized as a group called *No Extraditables* ("Non-Extraditables"), some of the main drug trafficking organizations based in Colombia escalated violence in resistance to the Treaty, in what became known as *guerra sucia* ("dirty war"). The mounting levels of drug-related violence were repeatedly characterized as a form of "narcoterrorism" and were used as justification for the Decree No. 1038/1984, through which a state of exception was established.

Now, I have sketched two processes so far. First, I have shown how the framing of guerrillas was rearticulated from "political delinquency" to "regular delinquency", and from the latter to an "enemy of the state". Second, I have discussed how drugs came to be addressed no longer as a "public health problem", but as one of "public order", leading to its gradual criminalization and inscription in a vocabulary of "regular delinquency". The framings resulting from these two processes intersected in the mobilization of the category of "terrorism", allowing for, at once, the delegitimation of those framed as such and the authorization of a more intense use of violence against it.

Although the processes mentioned above were not linear, their traces make links such as guerrilla-terrorism and drug trafficking-terrorism possible. These associations can be built, abandoned, and then rebuilt in other terms. Nevertheless, a series of practices was undertaken within the terms of those links, institutions were built based upon those links, professionals were hired in order to invest their work in those links, and knowledge was produced about those links. At the same time these processes were triggered by these associations, they also reinforced them, providing them with cement, form, and political life.

An illustration can be found in the Colombian National Police's Antiterrorist Unit, created in 1991 with the objective of preventing "terrorist attacks" in the capital, Bogotá (El Tiempo 1991). Gathering police professionals from the Special Operations Group (GOES, in Spanish), the Anti-extortion and Anti-Kidnapping Special Corps (COPES, in Spanish), and from the DIJIN's Laboratory on Explosives, the Antiterrorist Unit combined the specialized knowledge that had already been developed within each of these branches. The transformation of violence since the dismantling of the "drug cartels" and the de-mobilization of guerrillas such as the M-19 in the early-1990s was translated into the re-articulation of the work undertaken by the Antiterrorist Unit in two main ways. First, the expansion of its geographical scope, from Bogotá to Medellín—when it joined the Search Bloc (*Bloque de Búsqueda*) aimed at killing Pablo Escobar—and then to urban and rural zones in general (Policía Nacional de Colombia 2009: 16). Most importantly, instead of constituting one of the branches of the Command Unit on Special Operations, terrorism came to encompass the whole special operations organizational chart—currently called Command Unit on Special Operations and Antiterrorism (Policía Nacional de Colombia 2009: 16), pointing to a privileged position of terrorism in the Colombian police architecture. Second, if special operations were initially restricted to drug trafficking (El Tiempo 1991, 1993), their scope went through a gradual expansion and is currently defined as: "high-risk operations against targets of high-value, delinquential structures and criminal organizations both in the urban and rural areas, with the objective of preserving the citizen coexistence and security across the whole national territory".[17]

These processes have resulted in the formation of specific problematizations of violence that came to be associated with Colombia, in the sense that it was through such processes that a specific set of phenomena acquired the status of problems. As we have seen, the production of knowledge by violentologists in Colombia aimed at producing a diagnosis of violence in the country—that is, the report itself resulted from renderings of Colombia as a violent country. On the other hand, the work of

---

[17] In the original: "operaciones de alto riesgo contra objetivos de alto valor, estructuras delincuenciales y organizaciones criminales tanto en ámbito urbano como rural, con el fin de preservar la convivencia y seguridad ciudadana en todo el territorio nacional". This excerpt was removed from the COPES' official institutional video, available at: https://www.policia.gov.co/especializados/copes#resena-historica. Accessed on 12 January 2021.

the Commission of Studies on Violence contributed to the crystallization of a specific reading of violence in Colombia—one which is predominantly non-political and urban. Alternative representations of violence are thereby brushed aside, as shown by the silence of the Commission report regarding the violence perpetrated by the Armed Forces or the entanglement between public and private, legal, or illegal, perpetrators.

In this sense, the portrayal of Colombia as a problem resulted from a system of problematizations. The framing of delinquential violence as a specific problem in Colombia intersected two additional processes: the problematization of drugs and that of terrorism. Their intersection contributed to the consolidation of a particular reading about violence in Colombia: that of the guerrillas as regular delinquents and that of drugs as a public order problem. When intersected with the vocabulary of "terrorism", these processes have allowed for bringing guerrillas and drug trafficking organizations closer in terms of their means (collective destruction), targets (persons and goods) and effects (disturbing public order). Most importantly, we also saw how the expansion of the margins through which a given conduct could be associated with "terrorism" dragged into that category more than guerrillas and drug trafficking organizations. In other words, the processes analyzed here show that protests, strikes, and sabotages increasingly came to be associated with disturbances of the public order.

By the 1990s, the articulation between guerrillas, drug trafficking and terrorism had been crystallized to such an extent that they came to be understood as parts of the same phenomenon. In the next section, we turn our attention to the processes that resulted in the use of the terms "narcoguerrilla" and "narcoterrorism" as conceptual formulations specific to the problematization of violence in Colombia. This move requires that we explore how the problematization of drugs in the U.S. encountered the processes mentioned above.

2.2 Fighting a Distant War: The U.S. and the Externalization of the "Drug Problem"

The "war on drugs" is often analyzed as a unidirectional intervention of the U.S. in Colombia and other Latin American countries (see, for instance, Crandall 2001; García-Peña 2006). As we have seen, however, the construction of Colombia as a problematic country was far from a foreign reading to Colombian society. The reform of the Penal Code is but one of the expressions of the gradual depoliticization of the guerrillas and the criminalization of drugs. In this sense, the mid-1980s in Colombia already offered the conditions allowing for the convergence of the discourse on drugs mobilized by U.S. agencies with that of their Colombian counterparts. Claiming that the "war on drugs" advanced by the U.S. was not imposed does not imply refusing the relevance of its effects for the construction of Colombia as a problem—on the contrary. The volume of financial and human resources involved in policies designed by U.S. agencies has given more distinctive contours to a specific problematization of violence in Colombia, as well as to a set of solutions articulated in accordance with that reading.

As we have seen, the merging of guerrillas, drug trafficking and terrorism is key for us to understand the construction of Colombia as a problem. The first conceptual articulation that contributes to this analysis is that of the "narcoguerrillas",[18] precisely because it expresses the idea that the problem of guerrillas cannot be read apart from that of drugs. The general lines of this idea are drawn in the 1986 National Security Decision Directive 221 (NSDD 221), issued during Ronald Reagan administrations (1981–1989). Before that, Richard Nixon (1969–1974) had already contended that the drug problem constituted a threat to the U.S. national security (Campbell 1992: 200) and that the consumption of illicit substances had to be exterminated from the social landscape. Notwithstanding, it was only under Reagan that the fight against drugs reached the extra-national level, based on the claim that the source of the threat facing the U.S. was in fact external to its territory. The NSDD 221 makes this move explicitly:

> While the domestic effects of drugs are a serious societal problem for the United States [...] the national security threat posed by the drug trade is particularly serious outside US borders. Of primary concern are those nations with a flourishing narcotics industry, where a combination of

---

[18] As with "narcoterrorism", the category of "narcoguerrilla" had already been fermented in Colombia. The reports published by the DIJIN in 1987, for instance, highlight that "The re-emergence of violence in rural zones as a result of the merging between guerrilla and drug trafficking, which for years has been disturbing harmony and tranquility in rural Colombia, has reached unpredictable levels" (Policía Nacional de Colombia 1987: 226). In the original: "El resurgimiento de la violencia en las zonas Rurales como resultado de la fusión de guerrilla y narcotráfico que desde años atrás viene perturbando la armonía y tranquilidad del campo colombiano, alcanza imprevisibles niveles".

international criminal trafficking organizations, rural insurgents, and urban terrorists can undermine the stability of the local government. (The White House 1986: 1)

The diagnosis made in the excerpt provides us the rationale behind what came to be known as the "supply-side approach", that is, the understanding that the most efficient way to overcome the "drug problem" was to tackle it at its source, in the "nations plagued by narcotics" (The White House 1986: 1). Upholding this claim, we can find the following discursive conditions: (i) the concrete manifestations of the problems identified in the supply-side are not found in the U.S.; (ii) the "drug problem" is irradiated from drug producing countries to the U.S., in a unidirectional flux; and (iii) the U.S. had no connection with the processes through which the "drug problem" emerged. From the 1980s to the 2000s, the supply-side approach was the formula to which the U.S. agencies invariably gave priority when designing drug policies (Crandall 2002; International Crisis Group 2005; Tickner 2007). This persistence has had at least four major implications for our discussion.

First, framing the drug problem as something external implies that the U.S. is found in a better position to elaborate solutions, for its institutions are claimed to be less corroded by that problem than the Colombian ones. The Extradition Treaty signed in 1979 between the U.S. and Colombia is an emblematic example of those assumptions and effects. Based on the claim that most drug-related crimes are also a criminal offense under the U.S. legislation, the Treaty determines the conditions for the U.S. government to claim the rights of judging and incarcerating for those crimes. Considering that the NSDD 221 highlights that "The narcotics trade threatens the integrity of democratic governments by corrupting political and judicial institutions" (The White House 1986: 2), the Extradition Treaty was presented as the best law enforcement solution to circumvent the lack of effectiveness of Colombian judicial institutions in dealing with renowned drug traffickers such as Pablo Escobar (Orozco 1990).

In this sense, the externalization of the "drug problem" allowed for the U.S. to engage with Colombia and other drug producing countries in a position of authority. By its turn, this privileged position allowed for the differentiation between the states that cooperated with the U.S. counternarcotic policies and those that did not. The creation of a certification mechanism in 1986 is inscribed in this dynamic. Every year, the

U.S. President sent a report to Congress classifying the performance of "producing countries" as regards antidrug policies in one of the following categories: (i) full certification; (ii) de-certification; and (iii) certification on the grounds of national interest.[19] The sanctions comprehended in cases of de-certification included the suspension of trade preferences and credit lines in international banks, as well as a partial suspension of the U.S. external aid to that country. Cooperating with U.S. antidrug policies implied, among many things, signing a Memorandum of Understanding with the DEA for the establishment of a representation office in the cooperating state—as it was the case in Colombia, in 1972.

The second effect of externalization is that the very position of authority mentioned above was the condition that made the objectification of "drug producing countries" possible—that is, their construction as an object of analysis, towards which U.S. agencies projected themselves in order to produce knowledge about the "problems" within that object and provide solutions to them. In the case of the establishment of a DEA office in Colombia, for instance, this meant that police investigations related to drug trafficking would incorporate the DEA into their information circuit, thereby allowing for a flux of privileged information to flow to the U.S. Needless to say, at the same time the logic of externalization of the "drug problem" allowed for the construction of "drug producing states" as an object of analysis, the position of authority allowed for expanding the flow of information to the U.S., nurturing the production of diagnoses about those "problematic countries".

Third, externalization ascribes functions and responsibilities aimed at solving the problems resulting from the diagnoses built upon the knowledge produced about such problems. As any problematization, its terms already contain the horizon of possible solutions for the problem it poses (Foucault 2010b: 389). In this sense, the repertoire of agencies in charge of U.S. counternarcotic policies cannot be detached from a specific construction of the drug problem, nor from the construction of Colombia as a problematic country. It is noteworthy that both the police and the military are explicitly framed as the protagonists of the solutions distilled by the U.S. to be implemented in "drug producing countries".

---

[19] Colombia was de-certified in 1996 and 1997, and certified on the grounds of national interest in 1998—all of them during Ernesto Samper's administration (1994–1998). For more information on the tensions involving the U.S. and Colombia during this period, see: Crandall (2001), Isacson (2005), and Chernick 2008.

According to the NSDD 221, the Secretary of Defense, in conjunction with the Attorney General and the Secretary of State, should "develop and implement any necessary modifications to applicable statutes, regulations, procedures, and guidelines to enable US military forces to support counter-narcotics efforts more actively" (The White House 1986: 3). The Central Intelligence Agency (CIA) is also mentioned in the NSDD 221 as responsible for enhancing and supporting the "drug enforcement effort targeted against international drug traffickers" (NSDD 221: 4)—that is, in support of the DEA, which was already established in Colombia since 1972. The mobilization of intelligence, military and police work indeed constitute a remarkable feature of the counternarcotic polices implemented in Colombia from the late-1980s onwards.

The fourth implication of the externalization of the "drug problem" refers to the groups most often associated with deviant conducts in the terms of this problematization.[20] As we will see in the discussion about the vocabulary of "narcoguerrilla" and "narcoterrorism", the antidrug policies advanced by the U.S. confined the "drug problem" not only to the "nations plagued by narcotics": military and police operations counternarcotic targeted specific groups. Although the idea of a "combination of international criminal trafficking organizations, rural insurgents, and urban terrorists" (The White House 1986: 1) suggests the articulation underlying the category of "narcoguerrilla" and "narcoterrorism", these specific conceptual formulations are not explicitly mentioned in the NSDD 221 or any other relevant legal instrument issued from that period.

Since the early-1980s, however, the term "narcoguerrilla" was repeatedly evoked by the U.S. ambassador in Bogota, Lewis Tambs, as well as in congressional debates. For instance, in a 1984 session in the Senate, speakers alerted that the guerrillas were connecting their activities with

---

[20] Importantly, the externalization characterizing the problematization of drugs in the U.S. also had effects inside its territory. By the early twentieth century, the prohibitionist discourse was based on the "moral degenerated habits" of specific social groups (mostly immigrants and blacks), to whom drug addiction was discursively associated (Campbell 1992: 205; Rodrigues 2008). According to Campbell, "Although they make up only 11 percent of the population, the black community's percentage of drug arrests has risen from 30 percent to nearly 40 percent since the emergence of crack" (Campbell 1992: 206). Although falling outside the scope of this book, which is concerned with how the logic of externalization affected the construction of Colombia as a "problematic country", the analysis developed by Campbell highlights this double effect of externalization: identifying the "source of the problem" both in the "drug producing countries" and in the "outsiders" within U.S. society.

drug trafficking organizations to be able to fund their operations (Rojas 2006: 40). Nevertheless, the predominant position among U.S. agencies at that time was that the guerrillas had an indirect participation in drug trafficking, mainly through the weight-based tax called *gramaje*, for the surveillance of crops and laboratories, and through the tax charged for the use of clandestine airplane landing strips in regions controlled by these armed groups (Rojas 2006: 40). In other words, the guerrillas were not found at the core of the construction of the "drug problem".

It was not before the 1990s that the term "narcoguerrilla" was used in a more systematic way. Indeed, this period is marked by an increasing presence of armed groups in almost all the strategic regions for the production of cocaine in the country[21] (International Crisis Group 2005; Echandía 2006). In 1993, the U.S. General Accounting Office (GAO) published a report aimed at informing the debates in the House of Representatives on counternarcotic policies implemented in Colombia. The document mentioned assessments produced by the U.S. Embassy and the DEA regarding the close links between insurgency and drug trafficking (U.S. General Accounting Office [U.S. GAO] 1993: 26)—which, according to the U.S. ambassador, required that the military conducted "both counterinsurgency and counternarcotic missions" (U.S. GAO 1993: 27).

It is in Plan Colombia that we can find this reading in its most explicit form. The priorities revealed through the distribution of the resources mobilized in Plan Colombia point to an emphasis on counternarcotic initiatives (Villamizar 2003; Rojas 2006; Pabón 2008; Vargas 2012: 186). Between 2000 and 2006, the U.S. foreign aid to Colombia reached US$ 4.7 billion, of which more than 80% was destined to weapons, helicopters, equipment, training, and fumigation (Isacson 2006). However, the Plan specified that the Colombian Armed Forces were not allowed to use the equipment provided for counternarcotic operations by the U.S. against the guerrillas, only for drug trafficking organizations (Villamizar 2003: 51). Months after the approval of Plan Colombia, this restriction was suspended after the FARC took over a police station in Arboleda, in July 2000 (Rojas 2006: 52). Resulting in 17 police agents killed, the

---

[21] It is noteworthy that, although the paramilitary groups were also involved in the production of cocaine (Ronderos 2014), the expression coined by the U.S. government only refers to the guerrillas—asymmetry which is also evident in the operations backed by the U.S. (Villa and Viana 2012).

attack occurred 150 km away from Bogotá, suggesting that the FARC had the military capacity to threaten the capital. From this moment on, the U.S. authorized the use of police and military equipment for counterinsurgency operations in Colombia (Villamizar 2003: 51). The creation of the Counternarcotic Battalions in 1999 within the Colombian Army is revealing on how counterinsurgency was translated into counternarcotic terms. Indeed, these battalions were responsible for eradication and interdiction operations very similar to those undertaken by the Colombian National Police's Antinarcotic Division (DIRAN, in Spanish): fumigation, destruction of processing laboratories, and detention and interrogation of "narcoterrorists" (Pabón 2008: 162–163).

Thus, rather than leading to the reformulation of the U.S. policies towards Colombia, the vocabulary of "narcoguerrilla" allowed for counternarcotic policies to be associated with the Colombian armed conflict. Based on the claim that drug trafficking was the main funding source for the guerrillas, fusing them into a conceptual formulation gave impulse to antidrug policies with the expectation that they would weaken the guerrillas' military capacity. The content of the U.S. strategy, however, had not been changed: it was still focused on eradication and interdiction operations led by military, police, and intelligence agencies. The 2002 National Security Strategy, issued during George W. Bush's administration (2001–2009), clearly expresses this rationale:

> Parts of Latin America confront regional conflict, especially arising from the violence of drug cartels and their accomplices. This conflict and unrestrained narcotics trafficking could imperil the health and security of the United States. Therefore, we have developed an active strategy to help the Andean nations adjust their economies, enforce their laws, defeat terrorist organizations, and cut off the supply of drugs (...) In Colombia, we recognize the link between terrorist and extremist groups that challenge the security of the state and drug trafficking activities that help finance the operations of such groups. (The White House 2002 *Apud* Vargas 2012: 186)

The "active strategy to help the Andean nations" mentioned in the excerpt is the Andean Counterdrug Initiative (ACI). Approved by the U.S. Congress in 2003, the program concentrated 68.6% (Veillette 2006a: 23) of its US$ 766.80 million budget (Veillette 2006b: 7) to counternarcotic operations held in Colombia, while the remaining share of these resources was distributed among Peru, Bolivia, Ecuador, Brazil, Panama, and Venezuela (Veillette 2006b).

In addition to exposing an asymmetric distribution of the resources between Colombia and other South American countries, the excerpt above and the destination of the funds to counternarcotic operations reveal that the terms with which U.S. agencies engaged with the "problem of violence" in Colombia did not change after 9/11.

Despite the contested character of the assumptions anchoring the idea of "narcoguerrillas",[22] this nexus became pervasive in Congressional debates in the U.S. and concluded the delegitimation process of these armed groups. After all, merging drug trafficking and guerrillas had an important effect of calcifying a rent-seeking portrayal of these armed groups and silenced any possibility of political claims constituting their activities. Whatever the political project these guerrillas claimed to represent or defend when they were founded, it was now considered lost by such a perspective.

On the other hand, the post-9/11 has witnessed the radicalization of the delegitimation of the guerrillas through the discursive re-articulation of "narcoguerrilla" into "narcoterrorism". Such a move was advanced by both the George W. Bush (2001–2009) and Álvaro Uribe Vélez (2002–2010) administrations under the claim that the former expression was outdated in the context of the global war against terrorism. In a session held on October 10, 2004 at the U.S. House of Representatives to discuss the country's military strategy in Latin America, Congressman Edolphus Towns (New York) read the research memorandum produced by Eleanor Thomas and Lindsay Thomas, from the Washington-based Council on Hemispheric Affairs. The document contended that, by that time, the idea of "narcoterrorism" was pervasive among U.S. high-ranked military officers within the SouthCom, quoting Lieutenant General Bantz Craddock, former Assistant Deputy Director for Strategy to the Secretary of the State, according to whom:

---

[22] Chernick (2005) and Pécaut (2006, 2010), for instance, argue that the mobilization of drug trafficking resources by the guerrillas is not a sufficient condition for us to infer that these groups have put their political projects aside. According to these authors, the resources pursued by the FARC in narco-trafficking are in service of a political project. For Chernick (2005: 205), "[t]he Colombian experience suggests that resource mobilization (greed) alone does not explain the origins or the duration of the war. Other factors – such as grievances, ideology, leadership, military strategy, and international factors – are also key".

the terms insurgents or guerrillas are less applicable today than in the past. I believe the term narcoterrorists is more appropriate, given the fact that the center of gravity for these groups is the incredible financial support they get from illicit drug trafficking. (U.S. House of Representatives 2004: 23243)

Here, the need to update the vocabulary used to refer to those armed groups does not result in the invention of a whole new vocabulary, but in the combination of specific categories in an already existent semantic field to claim a nexus between them. Indeed, "terrorism" has been the object of U.S. agencies' work well before the global war on terror, at least since the 1960s (Bonditti 2014). In this case, however, the characterization of guerrillas as a form of terrorism in Colombia, and of drug trafficking as inextricable from terrorism allowed for the geographical expansion of the U.S. "war on terror", at the same time it kept unchanged the general terms with which U.S. agencies engaged with the Colombian armed conflict. In the words of Colin Powell, Secretary of State at that time:

For a number of years, our efforts were strictly directed at narcotrafficking. Congress wanted to make sure that we didn't get involved in the other aspects of the terrorism situation in Colombia. (…) since 9/11, [the President] has increased the attention we have given to terrorism of all forms, even if they may not all be of the form of al-Qaida. (…) we really should remove this barrier between narcotrafficking activities and narcoterrorist activities. It's all linked, narco is in both terms. Financing terrorism activities through narcotics activity. It all essentially leads to the same end, and that is the destruction of the Colombian democracy. (U.S. Department of State 2002, n.p.)

Through these lines, the Colombian armed conflict came to be increasingly interpreted as the main terrorist threat in the Americas from this moment on. Furthermore, this discursive rearticulation provided the U.S. with a response to the critique mobilized against the "war on terror" on the grounds of its Islamophobic character. In this sense, the guerrillas in Colombia came to be recurrently evoked as an example of the fact that U.S. counterterrorism operations were not restricted to Islamic organizations (Rojas 2006: 54).

In Colombia, the agglutination of guerrillas, terrorism, and drug trafficking encountered expanded margins of what was conceived as a "disturbance of public order" since at least the 1980 reform of the Penal Code. In addition, the strengthening of the punitive approach towards "pernicious substances" characterizing the 1980s in Colombia resulted in the crystallization of the framing of drugs as a "public order problem"—and increasingly so. One of the main effects of the combination of these processes was that guerillas, drugs and terrorism were brought closer in the problematization of violence in Colombia. Indeed, the discussion developed in this chapter shows how the articulation of these processes during the decades nurtured the claim that the main problem of Colombia was the violence perpetrated by illegal armed groups, whose profits resulting from drug trafficking, made the continuation of their military capacity building possible, thereby corroding democratic institutions in Colombia. As we will see, this problematization of violence in Colombia is the condition under which Colombia became the object of disputed claims, and the condition under which its performance in the solutions articulated for its problems became the object of measuring tools.

2.3 Conclusion

In this Chapter, I have discussed the main processes that resulted in a specific problematization of violence in Colombia. Having walked through the system of problematizations constituted by the "problem of violence", the "problem of drugs", and the "problem of terrorism" in Sect. 2.1, I analyzed how these processes intersected with the so-called "war on drugs" advanced by the U.S. (Sect. 2.2). As we have seen, this combination was crystallized into a very specific reading of violence in Colombia: a problem deriving from the activity of guerrillas whose main funding source is drug trafficking.

Importantly, these processes converged towards a delinquential and depoliticizing approach regarding the problem of violence in Colombia, as well as towards the delegitimation of the guerrillas and a radicalized depiction of these armed groups translated into the vocabulary of "terrorism". As shown in Sect. 2.1, the conditions for this problematization were already present in Colombia by the time a supply-side approach was advanced through the work of U.S. agencies to overcome the "drug problem".

Finally, this Chapter also argued that the terms upon which the problematization of violence in Colombia was erected already define the horizon of possible solutions. Increasingly calcified as a "public order problem" derived from the activity of terrorists whose military capacity benefits from drug trafficking resources, it comes as no surprise that police, military, and intelligence came to constitute the main ingredients with which solutions were conceived. In the next Chapter, we turn to the profusion of analyses which, by the mid-2000s, aimed at measuring the impact of such policies.

REFERENCES

BOOKS, CHAPTERS, ARTICLES

Bonditti, P. Violence, 'Terrorism', Otherness. Reshaping Enmity in Times of Terror. In: Campbell, R. (ed). *Violence and Civilization: Studies of Social Violence in History and Prehistory.* Oxford: Oxbow, 2014.

Campbell, D. *Writing Security: United States Foreign Policy and the Politics of Identity.* Minneapolis: University of Minnesota Press, 1992.

Cardona, C. M. *Politicians, Soldiers, and Cops: Colombia's La Violencia in Comparative Perspective.* Dissertation presented at University of California (Berkeley), 2008.

Chernick, M. Economic Resources and Internal Armed Conflicts: Lessons from the Colombian Case. In: Arnson, C. J.; Zartman, I. W. (eds). *Rethinking the Economics of War: The Intersection of Need, Creed, and Greed.* Washington, D.C.: Woodrow Wilson Center Press, 2005.

Chernick, M. *Acuerdo posible: solución negociada al conflicto armado colombiano.* Bogotá, D.C.: Aurora, 2008.

Craig, R. B. Domestic Implications of Illicit Colombian Drug Production and Trafficking. *Journal of International Studies and World Affairs*, v. 25, n. 3, pp. 325–350, 1983.

Crandall, R. Explicit Narcotization: US Policy Toward Colombia during Samper Administration. *Latin American Politics and Society*, v. 43, n. 3, pp. 95–120, 2001.

Crandall, R. *Driven by Drugs: US Policy Toward Colombia.* Londres: Lynne Rienner, 2002.

Echandía, C. *Dos Décadas de Escalamiento del Conflicto Armado Colombiano.* Bogotá, D.C.: Universidad Externado de Colombia, 2006.

Enloe, C. *Nimo's War, Emma's War: Making Feminist Sense of the Iraq War.* Berkeley: University of California Press, 2010.

Feldmann, A. E. Measuring the Colombian "Success" Story. *Revista de Ciencia Política*, v. 32, n. 3, pp. 739–752, 2012.

Fellowship of Reconciliation (FOR); Coordinación Colombia-Europa-Estados Unidos (CCEEU). *"Falsos positivos" en Colombia y el papel de asistencia militar de Estados Unidos, 2000-2010*. Bogotá, D.C.: FOR and CCEEU, 2014.

Foucault, M. Nietzsche, Genealogy, History. In: Rabinow, P. (ed). *The Foucault Reader*. New York: Pantheon Books, 2010a [1984].

Foucault, M. Polemics, Politics, and Problematizations: An Interview with Michel Foucault. In: Rabinow, P. (ed). *The Foucault Reader*. New York: Pantheon Books, 2010b [1984].

Foucault, M. Practicing Criticism. In: Kritzman, L. D. (ed). *Politics, Philosophy, Culture: Interviews and Other Writings, 1977-1984*. New York: Routledge, 1988.

García-Peña, R. P. Un país problema en un mundo intervencionista. In: Leal B. F. (ed). *En la encrucijada: Colombia en el siglo XXI*. Bogotá, D.C.: Norma, 2006.

González, F. E.; Bolívar, I. J.; Vázquez, T. *Violencia Política en Colombia: De la nación fragmentada a la construcción del Estado*. Bogotá, D.C.: CINEP, 2003.

Isacson, A. Failing grades: Evaluating the Results of Plan Colombia. *Yale Journal of International Affairs*, pp. 138-154, Summer/Fall 2005.

Jaramillo, M. J. Expertos y comisiones de studio sobre la violencia en Colombia. *Estudios Políticos*, n. 39, pp. 231-258, 2011.

Leal, B. F. *La Seguridad Nacional a La Deriva: Del Frente Nacional a la Posguerra Fría*. Mexico, D.C.: Alfaomega, 2002.

López, R. A. *Remedios nocivos: las orígenes de la política colombiana contra las drogas*. Bogotá, D.C.: Penguin Random House Group Editorial, 2016.

Orozco, A. I. La democracia y el tratamiento del enemigo interior. *Análisis Político*, n. 6, n.p., 1989.

Orozco, A. I. Los diálogos con el narcotráfico: historia de la transformación fallida de un delincuente común en un delincuente político. *Análisis Político*, n. 11, n.p., 1990.

Orozco, A. I. *Combatientes, rebeldes y terroristas: Guerra y Derecho en Colombia*. Bogotá, D.C.: Temis, 1992.

Pabón, A. N. El papel de las Fuerzas Armadas en la política antidrogas colombiana, 1998-2006. In: Vargas, V. A. (ed). *El papel de las Fuerzas Armadas en la Política Antidrogas Colombiana, 1985-2006*. Bogotá, D.C.: Universidad Nacional de Colombia, 2008.

Pécaut, D. La contribución del IEPRI a los estudios sobre la violencia en Colombia. *Análisis Político*, n. 34, pp. 64-79, 1998.

Pécaut, D. *Crónica de cuatro décadas de política colombiana*. Bogotá, D.C.: Norma, 2006.

Pécaut, D. *As FARC: uma guerrilha sem fins?* São Paulo: Paz e Terra, 2010.

Peñaranda, R. The War on Paper: A Balance Sheet on Works Published in the 1990s. In: Bergquist, C.; Peñaranda, R.; Sánchez G., G. (eds). *Violence* in Colombia. 1990–2000: Waging War and Negotiating Peace. Wilmington (DW): Scholarly Resources, 2003.

Pinzón, J. C. Colombia Back from the Brink: From Failed State to Exporter of Security. PRISM, v. 5, n. 4, pp. 2–9, 2015.

Pizarro, L. E. La Profesionalización Militar en Colombia (1907–1944). Análisis Político, n. 1, pp. 20–39, 1987a.

Pizarro, L. E. La Profesionalización Militar en Colombia (II): El Periodo de La Violencia. Análisis Político, n. 2, 7–29, 1987b.

Rodrigues, T. Tráfico, Guerra, Proibição. In: Labate, B. C.; Goulart, S. L.; Fiore, M.; MacRae, E.; Carneiro, H. (orgs). Drogas e cultura: novas perspectivas. Salvador: UFBA, 2008.

Rojas, D. M. Estados Unidos y la guerra en Colombia. In: Sanín, F. G.; Wills, M. E.; Gómez, G. S. (coords). Nuestra guerra sin nombre: transformaciones del conflicto en Colombia. Bogotá, D.C.: Norma, 2006.

Ronderos, M. T. Guerras Recicladas: Una historia periodística del paramilitarismo en Colombia. Bogotá, D.C.: Aguilar, 2014.

Sánchez, G. G. (org). Colombia: violencia y democracia. Bogotá, D.C.: Universidad Nacional de Colombia, 1988.

Sánchez G. G.; Fals B. O.; Umaña, E. La Violencia en Colombia, volumes I and II. Bogotá: Carlos Valencia, 1962.

Thoumi, F. E. Illegal Drugs in Colombia: From Illegal Economic Boom to Social Crisis. The Annals of the American Academy of Political and Social Science, n. 582, pp. 102–116, 2002.

Tickner, A. B. Intervención por invitación: claves para la política exterior colombiana y sus debilidades principales. Colombia Internacional, n. 65, pp. 90–111, 2007.

Tickner, A. B.; Morales, C. M. Narrating Success: Colombian Security Expertise and Foreign Policy. In: Bagley, B. M.; Rosen, J. D. (eds). Colombia's Political Economy at the Outset of the 21st Century: From Uribe to Santos and Beyond. Washington, D.C.: Lexington, 2014.

Uprimny, Y. R.; Chaparro, H. S.; Oliveira, L. F. C. Delito de drogas y sobredosis carcelaria en Colombia: Documentos Dejusticia n. 37, Bogotá, D.C.: Dejusticia, 2017.

Vargas, V. A. Las fuerzas armadas en el conflicto colombiano: antecedentes y perspectivas. Medellín: La Carreta, 2012.

Villa, R. D.; Viana, M. T. Internacionalização pelo envolvimento de atores externos no conflito colombiano: atuação da OEA na desmobilização de grupos paramilitares na Colômbia. Dados - Revista de Ciências Sociais, v. 55, n. 2, pp. 403–445, 2012.

Villamizar, A. Fuerzas Militares para la guerra: La agenda pendiente de la reforma militar. Bogotá, D.C.: Fundación Seguridad & Democracia, 2003.

Documents, Reports and Studies

DeShazo, P.; Primiani, T.; McLean, P. *Back from the Brink: Evaluating Progress in Colombia, 1999–2007*. Washington, D.C.: CIS, 2007.

DeShazo, P.; Forman, J. M.; McLean, P. *Countering Threats to Security and Stability in a Failing State: Lessons from Colombia*. Washington, D.C.: CIS, 2009.

Felbab-Brown, V. Lessons from Colombia for Mexico? Caveat Emptor. *Brookings*, 24 February 2012. Available at: https://www.brookings.edu/articles/lessons-from-colombia-for-mexico-caveat-emptor/. Accessed on 14 February 2021.

Human Rights Watch (HRW). *Colombia's Killer Networks: The Military-Paramilitary Partnership and the United States*. New York, November 1996. Available at: https://www.hrw.org/legacy/reports/1996/killertoc.htm. Accessed on 13 February 2021.

International Crisis Group. War and drugs in Colombia. *Latin America & Caribbean Report*, n. 11, 27 January 2005. Available at: https://www.crisisgroup.org/latin-america-caribbean/andes/colombia/war-and-drugs-colombia. Accessed on 13 February 2021.

Isacson, A. *Plan Colombia—Six Years Later: Report of a CIP Staff Visit to Putumayo and Medellín, Colombia*. Center for International Policy, International Policy Report, November 2006.

Isacson, A. *Colombia: Don't Call It a Model*. Washington, D.C.: WOLA, 14 July 2010. Available at: https://www.wola.org/sites/default/files/Drug%20Policy/notmodel.pdf. Accessed on 19 June 2021.

Policía Nacional de Colombia. *Revista Criminalidad*, v. 23. Bogotá, D.C.: Policía Nacional de Colombia, Departamento de Información, Criminalidad y Estadística, 1980. Available at: https://www.policia.gov.co/revista/volumen-23. Accessed on 13 February 2021.

Policía Nacional de Colombia. *Revista Criminalidad*, v. 30. Bogotá, D.C.: Policía Nacional de Colombia, Dirección Central de Policía Judicial, 1987. Available at: https://www.policia.gov.co/revista/volumen-30. Accessed on 13 February 2021.

Policía Nacional de Colombia. *Manual de Operaciones Especiales*. Bogotá, D.C.: Policía Nacional de Colombia, November 2009. Available at: http://web.archive.org/web/20120603010154/http://www.policia.edu.co/policia/documentos/doctrina/manuales_de_consulta/108218_Manual%20Operaciones.pdf. Accessed on 13 February 2021.

The White House. National Security Decision Directive n. 221. Narcotics and National Security. Washington, D.C., 8 April 1986. Available at: http://www.fas.org/irp/offdocs/nsdd/23-2766a.gif. Accessed on 13 February 2021.

Tickner, A. B. *Colombia, the United States, and Security Cooperation by Proxy*. Washington D.C.: WOLA, March 2014. Available at: http://www.wola.org/files/140318ti.pdf. Accessed on 13 February 2021.

U.S. Department of State. *Press Briefing on Board Plane. Secretary Colin L. Powell* (3 December 2002). Available at: https://2001-2009.state.gov/secretary/former/powell/remarks/2002/15668.htm. Accessed on 13 February 2021.

U.S. Government Accountability Office (U.S. GAO). *The Drug War: Colombia Is Undertaking Antidrug Programs, But Impact Is Uncertain* (GAO/NSIAD-93-158). August 1993. Available at: http://archive.gao.gov/d49t13/150027.pdf. Accessed on 13 February 2021.

U.S. House of Representatives. Proceedings and Debates of the 108th Congress Second Session. *Congressional Record*, v. 150, Pt. 17. Washington, D.C.: Government Printing Office, 10 October 2004. Available at: https://www.govinfo.gov/content/pkg/CRECB-2004-pt17/pdf/CRECB-2004-pt17-Pg23242.pdf. Accessed on 13 February 2021.

Veillette, C. Colombia: Issues for Congress. *CRS Report for Congress*, RL32250, 4 January 2006a. Available at: https://www.everycrsreport.com/files/20060104_RL32250_2df02f67ff23fe997c54a61253eedc6467c89ccc.pdf. Accessed on 13 February 2021.

Veillette, C. Andean Counterdrug Initiative (ACI) and Related Funding Programs: FY2007 Assistance. *CRS Report for Congress*, RL33370, 18 April 2006b. Available at: https://www.everycrsreport.com/files/20060418_RL33370_f5d0ccd0c6e5a696c183495b4a1d0d39c4071857.pdf. Accessed on 13 February 2021.

Press Articles

El Tiempo. "Fuerza Antiterrorista en Bogotá", *El Tiempo*, 15 January 1991. Available at: http://www.eltiempo.com/archivo/documento/MAM-10076. Accessed on 13 February 2021.

El Tiempo. "Noventa minutos de búsqueda final", *El Tiempo*, 4 December 1993. Available at: http://www.eltiempo.com/archivo/documento/MAM-270373. Accessed on 13 February 2021.

Revista Semana. "Los violentólogos", *Revista Semana*, 15 September 2007. Available at: http://www.semana.com/nacion/articulo/los-violentologos/88236-3. Accessed on 13 February 2021.

CHAPTER 3

The Success and Its Monsters: Disputing the Metrics, Dodging Criticism

What are the mechanisms that differentiate what is eligible to say about the Colombian "success story" from what is not? Our point of departure in Chapter 2 was the logic that any success story is based on the idea that a set of problems has been overcome. The discussion developed therein showed that the externalization characterizing the construction of Colombia as a "problematic country" was the condition for its transformation into an object of analysis. We also saw that the diagnoses and the knowledge anchoring narratives of success cannot be detached from a specific problematization of violence in Colombia. Having walked through the terms with which "solutions" were provided to "Colombian problems", this chapter explores the main elements constituting the web of criteria allowing for the "success" to be told.

To do so, we first explore the metrics used to assess the performance of Colombian agencies in the implementation of counternarcotic policies. In 2006, when the renewal of Plan Colombia was under scrutiny, there was an abundance of efforts aimed at measuring the impact of the policies comprised in that initiative. By discussing how the Colombian "success" became the center of disputed claims and measuring tools, I argue that the proliferation of diagnoses about the "Colombian problems", solutions to tackle them, and assessments of their impact are all embedded in the same discursive field. Understood as a system of relations whose

© The Author(s), under exclusive license to Springer Nature Switzerland AG 2022
M. T. Viana, *Post-conflict Colombia and the Global Circulation of Military Expertise*, Critical Security Studies in the Global South, https://doi.org/10.1007/978-3-030-96103-9_3

constitutive elements are but its criteria of formation and (constant) transformation (Foucault 1991), the discursive field is not a coherent whole, but a dispersion of objects, operations, concepts (Foucault 1991: 54–55) and authors (Foucault 1981: 64), and they are always found in relation to one another in the discourse.

This dispersion is, nonetheless, ordered by a set of principles (Foucault 1981: 59–60)—that is, there is room for refinements, improvements and criticisms in the discursive field as long as certain requirements are met (Foucault 1981: 59). These requirements classify, separate, and hierarchize propositions, defining those which are to be preserved for their potential of truth and those which are "destined to disappear without any trace" (Foucault 1991: 60). As Foucault explains, quoting Canguilhem, "before it can be called true or false, it [a certain proposition] must be 'in the true'" (Foucault 1981: 60)—that is, in the terrain of the true.

At the same time true and false propositions are defined in the limits of the discursive field, the latter "pushes back a whole teratology of knowledge beyond its margins" (Foucault 1981: 60). Thus, more than differentiating true and false enunciations, the organization of the debate according to a set of requirements defines what is eligible to say and what is not. In this sense, the limits of the discursive field can be thought of as a frontier constituted by the tension between two kinds of deviations from the discursive norm: the "mad" and the "monster" and the respective principles of exclusion to which they are subjected, division and rejection[1] (Foucault 1981: 53).

This chapter investigates three mechanisms ordering the discursive field about the "success story" of Colombian counternarcotic performance: the rules of the game in the terrain of the true, the domestication of narratives contesting claims to success, and the outright rejection of positions confronting the pillars of the problematization upholding that discursive field. Section 3.1 focuses on "internal critique" by looking at those advocating for reforms in the measurement tools used to assess Colombia's

---

[1] Foucault explains as follows the relation between the three mechanisms ordering the discourse: "Of the three great systems of exclusion which forge discourse—the forbidden speech, the division of madness and the will to truth (…) it is towards this third system that the other two have been drifting constantly for centuries. The third system increasingly attempts to assimilate the others, both in order to modify them and to provide them with a foundation. The first two are constantly becoming more fragile and more uncertain, to the extent that they are now invaded by the will to truth, which for its part constantly grows stronger, deeper, and more implacable" (Foucault 1981: 55–56).

performance. Here, the objective is to expose the contours of the principles ordering the dispersion of positions inside the discursive field. More specifically, I show that most of the assessments of counternarcotic policies evolved towards an econometric jargon, in search of accurate data and models that made the best translation between data entry and behavior in the drug market. Insulated in their quest for accuracy, debates constituted by this modality of critique did not reveal concerns with the constitutive terms of the problematization from which the policies under scrutiny derived.

In contrast, Sect. 3.2 turns to "external critique", exploring criticisms that propose alternative terms for the problematization of violence in Colombia. Here, I draw special attention to how intelligence, police and military apparatuses were invested in unionists and human rights activists, constantly observing and differentiating the degrees of dangerousness attached to these groups, and "neutralizing" the ones framed as the most dangerous among them. Combining Foucault's account of the order of discourse (Foucault 1981) and the carceral system (Foucault 1995), we walk in the intersections of discursive policing and the mobilization of the penal-military system to expose how "monstrous" narratives about violence in Colombia were kept at the margins of the discursive field.

By shedding light on the mechanisms through which some narratives are allowed to enter the terrain of the true, while others are destined to fade away, I argue that the consolidation of the "success story" under specific terms produces a specific history about the past and the present of Colombia. Indeed, claims to success rely on particular versions of what problems have been overcome in the country. It is in this sense that the erasure of alternative problematizations of violence in Colombia pays tribute to what is allowed to have happened in Colombia's violent past.

3.1 Measuring Success: Assessing Colombia's Counternarcotic Performance

As we have seen in Chapter 2, the predominant reading of violence in Colombia has been consolidated as one deriving from drug trafficking. This activity is understood to be mainly undertaken by the guerrillas—hence the reference to "narcoguerrillas"—and, following 9/11, these armed groups came to be discursively framed as "narcoterrorists". I have also argued that this problematization of Colombia has been attached to a particular set of solutions. More specifically, the preservation of the prefix "narco" in the re-articulation from "narcoguerrilla" to "narcoterrorism" reveals the backbone of the juxtaposition of these policies. Indeed, since the 2000s, the expectation with which Plan Colombia operated was that, through effective counternarcotic policies, the guerrillas ("i.e." terrorists) were to be militarily weakened and then defeated. In other words, the defeat of "narcoterrorism" would naturally derive from an effective "war on drugs". Given the importance of the latter, here I concentrate my discussion on how the performance of Colombian agencies in counternarcotic operations under Plan Colombia has been scrutinized by a set of measurement tools.

Importantly, the implementation of Plan Colombia, in 1999, is inscribed in a broader context of the emergence of a managerial logic in the domain of public policy. Known as "New Public Management", such rationale was constituted by the absorption, in the 1970s and 1980s, of practices that were already institutionalized in the private sector, aimed at optimizing the use of public resources and improving the techniques mobilized in the assessment of public policies' impact (Ruiz V. et al. 2006: 205). The investment of this rationale in the work of governmental agencies required the translation of routine procedures and "policy problems" into "numerical representations of complex phenomena intended to render these simpler and more comparable" with other phenomena[2]

---

[2] The mobilization of numbers in government practices was not invented in the 1980s. According to Foucault, the use of statistics as a technical knowledge considered as indispensable to the exercise of power emerged in the seventeenth and eighteenth centuries in Europe, particularly in the calculation of states' resources (Foucault 2007: 274). Indeed, the administrative apparatus invested in the quantification of the strengths and weaknesses of the state allowed for a more productive ordering of the social body and, consequently, to the increase of state forces. The conditions for the emergence of this technical knowledge are not exclusively found in the state apparatus, however: universities played a major role in its development as well. One of the instances in which Foucault locates this symbiotic relation more explicitly is the police. Facing the problem of scale when disciplining societies with increasing urban populations, the police found in statistics a technique that made the abstraction of social complexities possible (Foucault 2007: 315). As an example, Foucault refers to the central role played by German universities in the development of what was by that time known as *Polizeiwissenschaft* ("the science of police") (Foucault 2007: 318). More than suggesting an osmosis between universities and the state administrative apparatus, Foucault points to the "statization" of this technical knowledge and other practices that could be useful to the ordering of the social body (Foucault 1995, 2007). Although preserving statistics as an anchor to the art of government, New Public Management does re-articulate this rationality especially as regards its mobilization to the measurement of public policies' impact.

(Davis et al. 2012: 8). In more concrete terms, this managerial logic involved a goal-oriented organization of work, the a priori definition of control and evaluation methods, and the systematic use of indicators. By the mid-1990s, these main features of New Public Management were already guiding—though with different degrees of pervasiveness—the work of governmental agencies throughout the world.

In the U.S., the approval of the Government Performance and Results Act in 1993 was an important event in this regard. Such a legal instrument aimed at avoiding "waste and inefficiency in Federal programs" (U.S. Congress 1993: Section 2.a.1), improving the provision of adequate "information on program performance" (U.S. Congress 1993: Section 2.a.2), as well as rationalizing "policymaking, spending decisions and program oversight" by privileging performance and results (U.S. Congress 1993: Section 2.a.3). With those main purposes, the Government Performance and Results Act required that U.S. federal agencies systematically incorporated strategic plans and performance reports in their bureaucratic routines. The "focus on results, service quality, and customer satisfaction" (U.S. Congress 1993: Section 2.b.3)—practices recurrently associated with private companies—suggests that its projection to the public policy domain would improve the relationship between government and citizens and would optimize the use of public resources. To be sure, it assumes that U.S. federal agencies would provide better services if their routine were guided by making sure that "customers were satisfied" with the quality of the service (Ruiz V. et al. 2006: 206). Furthermore, requiring that agencies worked with objective and measurable performance goals, as well as seeking that assessment became a regular part of their work, relied on the assumption that more efficient and effective policies would result from a decision- and policy-making process based on objective information (U.S. Congress 1993: Section 2.b.5).

Similarly, by the mid-1990s, a series of diagnoses produced inside and outside the Colombian government pointed to the need for a cultural transformation in the National Police (Ruiz V. et al. 2006: 203). In response to a poll on the citizens' perception about the police, General Rosso José Serrano, the Director-General of the Police at that time, created a technical group[3] in 1995, whose task was to identify the

---

[3] Known as *Grupo de los 30* ("Group of the 30"), this technical commission was led by a civil advisor and was integrated by numerous police professionals.

main problems in the institution. The reforms suggested by the group included an indicator-based assessment of the Police and the elaboration of performance reports—attempts that failed due to the confusing character of indicators and to the bureaucratic resistance to reorganize its routine procedures (Ruiz V. et al. 2006: 206). A second attempt in this direction was made in 1997, with strategic plans to guide the work of the Colombian National Police and to define parameters for performance assessment. However, its implementation lacked a comprehensive approach, resulting in multiple strategic plans across police units, absent of any coherence among them (Ruiz V. et al. 2006: 209). The first Strategic Plan referring to the Police as a whole was only launched after six years, in 2003 (Ruiz V. et al. 2006: 209). In this sense, although a managerial logic was already being instilled in the Colombian National Police by mid-1990s, this process was tortuous in its implementation, and heterogeneous among police units.

That the use of metrics to assess public policy performance has been increasingly pervasive in Colombia is certainly of interest to our discussion. However, I am particularly interested in how this relates to the "success story". To do that, I now explore the terms with which the metric used to assess counternarcotic policies was disputed, as well as the main effects of those disputes. My objective here is not to identify a specific metric considered to be truer or technically superior to others. Rather, I am concerned with what could be called the "politics of numbers", that is, the political struggles behind and between these metrics and the narratives constituted through them about the Colombian "success story". Following Huysmans (2006), I read the disputes for the most appropriate metric as struggles between claims to authority based on expert knowledge.[4] Since the production of knowledge about a

---

[4] According to Huysmans (2006: 8), the routine of security professionals produces crystallized framings of social phenomena as security problems that need to be solved. At the same time, the production of specialized knowledge by these professionals is the very source from which they derive authority to speak about those phenomena (Huysmans 2006: 13). Bureaucratic routine thereby embeds visions of security, providing a grid of intelligibility with which specific phenomena are rendered as security problems (Huysmans 2006: 147–148). Because the solutions to these problems are claimed to be found within that very expertise, securitization processes are always claims to power, as much as they are claims to truth. That is, advancing a specific problematization as a priority in the domain of security is inescapably also a way of promoting your own expertise to solve it. Thus, the disputes among professionals of security also reveal the technocratic competition in the institutional architecture these experts are inscribed in.

problem that needs to be solved cannot be detached from the problematization from which the identification of a need has arisen, the investment of this expert knowledge in the dispute with other metrics unescapably establishes a hierarchy between domains within that problematization.

This play of forces between different expert groups will be here referred to as a discursive field—one which emerged from the problematization of violence in Colombia we analyzed on Chapter 2. Because the solutions articulated to address the "Colombian problems" have been so emphatically translated into a counternarcotic logic, much of the disputes in this discursive field are strongly attached to the knowledge produced about drugs—although the field itself did not emerge from the objectification of drugs. As we have seen in Chapter 2, the problematization of violence in Colombia as a drug-related one has been crystallized through the intersection of numerous processes, privileging the police, military, and intelligence apparatuses as the protagonists of the solutions to this problem. It is therefore only in relation to these historical processes that drugs have been placed as one of the main objects of this discursive field. Once inscribed in this system of relations of disputed visions regarding Colombia's counternarcotic performance, the objectification of drugs is ordered through principles of dispersion—among them, the numeric representation of complex phenomena through which claims to truth are evaluated, conserved for having a potential of truth or dismissed at once.

In the primacy of numbers as a filter to the terrain of the true, there is a claim to "scientificity" which derives from individualized discourses (Foucault 1991: 54) such as the one we came to associate with Economics (econometrics and rational decision-making, in particular), Law (especially criminology) and Medicine (such as epidemiology and psychiatry) (Rodrigues 2008; Vargas 2008). In the case of the discursive field constituted by assessments of policies implemented under Plan Colombia, some of the main "solutions" provided to the "problem of violence" in Colombia rely on concepts coming from Economics: rationality, efficiency, and supply–demand. Indeed, eradication[5] and interdiction,[6] the two main axes of counternarcotic policies, aim at increasing drug prices

---

[5] That is, the destruction of illicit crops and drug processing laboratories, or the seizure of key precursor chemicals.

[6] That is, any endeavor aiming to prevent drug shipments to penetrate the U.S. territory.

in the retail market—in this case, the U.S. (Walsh 2004). In other words, eradicating coca leaf crops, destroying drug producing laboratories, seizing drug shipments, and arresting drug traffickers or leaders of drug trafficking organizations would increase the production costs. Consequently, drug producers would pass the bucket of increasing costs to the consumer, raising the price in the retail market (MacCoun and Reuter 2004: 76–78). Facing higher prices, the consumer would stop buying drugs—or so the argument goes—, and drug trafficking would become an unprofitable business (MacCoun and Reuter 2004: 76–78). This whole logic assumes a chain of events involving rational actors: based on those assumptions, policy makers work to create incentives and constraints to modify that behavior and achieve the expected outcome (Rasmussen and Benson 2003: 679–683; MacCoun and Reuter 2004: 76–78).

When Plan Colombia was launched, in 1999, it had only one specific goal: "to reduce the cultivation, processing and distribution of narcotics by 50%" within six years, that is, from 1999 to 2005.[7] On the other hand, the six objectives constituting Plan Colombia do suggest the metric through which the main goal was expected to be achieved. Among the key actions established in the Objective No. 1 ("Strengthen the fight against drug trafficking and dismantle the trafficking organizations through an integrated effort by the armed forces"), the Plan mentioned the destruction of "processing structures and improve land, air, ocean and river interdiction of drugs and illegal precursor chemicals"—indicating that both the destruction of processing laboratories and the seizure of drugs and precursor chemicals shipments would compound an appropriate metric to assess the impact of Plan Colombia. Importantly, the concern for violence is only timidly mentioned in the text, and in strict connection with "drug-related violence", as we read in Objective No. 4, titled "Neutralize and combat violence agents allied with the drug trade".[8]

---

[7] The full text of "Plan Colombia: Plan for Peace, Prosperity, and the Strengthening of the State" is available here: https://www.usip.org/sites/default/files/file/resources/collections/peace_agreements/plan_colombia_101999.pdf. Accessed on 20 January 2021.

[8] Although Objective No. 4 did not present any specific goal, it did suggest that the number of arms seized was to be considered a key indicator when mentioning, among its lines of action, to "halt the acquisition of arms by those groups that profit from drug trafficking". Contrastingly, Objective No. 4 did not set any guideline so that "increase security for citizens against kidnapping, extortion, and terrorism" could be achieved. As for Objectives No. 2 and 3 (respectively, "Strengthen the judicial system and combat

In addition to these two indicators, the assessment of any progress in counternarcotic operations was also based on hectares fumigated; drug traffickers/combatants arrested or killed; and number of weapons seized. These were not new parameters: they were extensively used in the 1980s, when the "war on drugs" was intensified against the main drug cartels in Colombia (DEA, n.d.: 31–32, 36–37). However, the development of technologies and the production of knowledge about drug markets have allowed for the expansion of data collection horizons, as well as for the refinement of those numbers (Walsh 2004: 4). In this sense, the incorporation of specific indicators to a measurement matrix and the development of methodological criteria through which such indicators were formulated is both a cause and an effect of an increasing specialized knowledge on drugs.

In Colombia, the branch of the police specialized in the implementation of eradication policies is the DIRAN. As an illustration of that claim to precision, in its 2005 report, the DIRAN highlighted three record-breaking achievements in its performance during that year: the seizure of 74.418 kilos of cocaine, "the greatest volume registered since 1975" (Policía Nacional de Colombia 2005: 15); the eradication of 172.946 hectares of coca leaf crops, "the greatest area fumigated since 1974" (Policía Nacional de Colombia 2005: 15); and the destruction of 910 laboratories, "the highest number since 1990" (Policía Nacional de Colombia 2005: 15). The DIRAN's report illustrates not only how the debate about the performance of counternarcotic policies was based on numbers, indicators, and goals—hence the repeated mention of "record breaking"—, but also the level of accuracy of the numbers evoked in the debate—with each unit of measurement counted. This particular way of

corruption" and "Neutralize the drug trade's financial system and seize its resources for the state"), words such as "strengthen" (institutions, for instance), "reinforce" and "support" (e.g., anti-corruption groups) were mentioned without any further specification regarding how that would be assessed. Likewise, Objective No. 5 ("Integrate national initiatives into regional and international efforts") lacked specifications on how or what kind of "information and intelligence [would be shared] with other security agencies in the country", much less how Colombian agencies could "Contribute to and coordinate with regional and international operations and efforts". Following a series of actions related to interdiction and eradication, only Objective No. 6 presented a contrasting approach: "Strengthen and expand plans for alternative development in areas affected by drug trafficking". It was expected that this would be achieved through the provision of "job opportunities and social services to people living in the cultivation zones" and promotion of "public information campaigns on the dangers of illegal drugs".

attesting the effectiveness of drug policies has been not only normalized throughout the first six years of Plan Colombia, but also strengthened.⁹

In 2005, the U.S. Congress was expected to give its verdict on the renewal of Plan Colombia. As the assessment of public policies was itself marked by a metrified goal-oriented logic, the main questions driving the discussions on the counternarcotic performance included: how were the impacts of Plan Colombia measured? At what costs they were achieved? Has Plan Colombia met its goals? By that time, the puzzle facing the U.S. government was the following: although U.S. and Colombian agencies had registered record-breaking numbers in most of the interdiction and eradication indicators, the retail price remained stable in the U.S. market, and Colombia still provided 90% of the cocaine entering the U.S. territory (U.S. Government Accountability Office [U.S. GAO] 2005). Instead of triggering the reformulation of the approach on drugs, this diagnosis has led to debates on how to improve the metrics used to assess the impact of counternarcotic policies. According to a report prepared by the U.S. GAO to inform a Congressional Session about Plan Colombia held in 2005, such a refinement could be achieved if agencies shared their data and harmonized the indicators they used (U.S. GAO 2005: 25–26).

Indeed, this challenge is an inescapable effect of the specialization increasingly characterizing the production of knowledge and numbers about drugs. In this context, the effectiveness of operations was often considered within a broader chain of initiatives constituting Plan Colombia: to prove their relevance in the antidrug architecture, agencies started to draw the connection between their achievements and Plan Colombia's main goal—i.e., to reduce the cultivation, processing, and distribution of narcotics by 50% within six years. The Colombian National Police, for instance, reported that, "Considering that the estimation of cocaine production based upon cultivated area is 4.7 kilos per hectare, the amount eradicated in 2005 implies that 812.8 metric tons of cocaine

---

⁹ The Colombian Army also started to publish the numbers of its own counternarcotic performance—although their systematic presentation only came to constitute a regular practice by the mid-2010s, years after the Colombian National Police. The achievements of military operations are regularly reported with focus on the seizure of war material, the destruction of drug trafficking infrastructure, the seizure of drugs and precursor chemicals, and the capture or surrender of illegal armed groups members—that is, basically the same indicators used by the Colombian National Police. See, for instance: https://www.ejercito.mil.co/informes_noticias/noticias/importante_balance_operacional_387289#. Accessed on 21 January 2021.

were prevented from entering the distribution chain"—corresponding to a US$80 billion loss in revenue for drug trafficking and illegal armed groups, according to the report[10] (Policía Nacional de Colombia 2005: 15). By situating these achievements within the whole production chain, the Colombian National Police highlights not only its participation in the reduction of drug consumption, but also its contribution to alleviate interdiction policies undertaken in the U.S.

Agencies directly involved in the implementation of counternarcotic initiatives were not the only ones taking part in the debate about the metrics used to assess such policies. In the context of the renewal of Plan Colombia, criticism regarding its effectiveness became particularly intense. An expression of that was the profusion of studies (Rasmussen and Benson 2003: 682, fn. 12; Trace et al. 2004; MacCoun and Reuter 2004; Thoumi 2005; Bewley-Taylor 2012) but also of think tanks especially dedicated to monitoring public spending with drug policies, and/or developing assessment criteria, indicators, and tools. How this criticism resonated in the discursive field, however, was intrinsically related to the principles ordering this system of relations. As a matter of fact, many of the critical engagements towards the metrics used in the assessment of counternarcotic policies operated within the rules of the game of the discursive field. In other words, they do not confront the pillars upon which the grid filtering and hierarchizing claims to truth is built, such as the assumption on the rationality of actors, the pursuit of efficiency as a normative driver for public policy management, and the primacy of numeric representations.

In a paper published in 2003, for instance, Rasmussen and Benson (2003), two renowned scholars in the domain of drug policy, criticized the "war on drugs" for its lack of rationality. Enforcing the seizure of drugs, destroying processing laboratories, and increasing interdiction of drug and precursor chemical shipments do lead to increasing costs in the drug supply. However, the authors argue that drug suppliers adapt

---

[10] In the original: "Si se tiene en cuenta que la producción estimada de cocaína por hectárea cultivada es de 4.7 kilos, quiere decir que, con la cantidad erradicada en 2005, 812.8 toneladas métricas de cocaína dejaron de entrar a la cadena de distribución. Se evitó así la comercialización de aproximadamente 812 millones de dosis personales y 80,000 millones de dólares dejaron de ingresar a las arcas de los narcotraficantes y los grupos armados ilegales".

to these rising costs in multiple fronts.[11] According to them, since the dismantling of the Colombian cartels, drug production was re-articulated into a more dispersed processing: "Suppliers created labs processing cocaine in many Latin American countries, and greatly increased the number of transshipment points (...) making subsequent interdiction efforts much more costly and ineffective" (Rasmussen and Benson 2003: 699). Other kinds of adaptation mentioned by the authors include the geographic displacement of production (Rasmussen and Benson 2003: 698); the so-called "outcome substitution", that is, sliding to the production of a different drug (Rasmussen and Benson 2003: 699); and the substitution of the workers demanding higher payments for others, for "there is no scarcity of people prepared to enter the drug business to replenish the personnel needs for suppliers" (Rasmussen and Benson 2003: 697).

Rasmussen and Benson (2003) contend that these adjustments make the expectation that such policies lead to increasing drug prices implausible. Further, the authors claim that, after years of evidence piled up against the effectiveness of antidrug policies, keeping intact the theoretical propositions upon which the whole drug architecture is erected constitutes a matter of faith, not facts (Rasmussen and Benson 2003: 696). Aiming at "rationalizing drug policy", the authors recommend its de-centralization so that local officials are "more likely to be held accountable for their actions and therefore are more likely to carefully consider the full costs of a largely ineffective drug policy" (Rasmussen and Benson 2003: 733–734). In this sense, the key to a rational drug policy lies in its institutional design: through de-centralization, constraints over the preservation of inefficient policies become stronger, and the costs for keeping them, higher. Their analysis suggests that this institutional dynamic will lead to a more factual analysis—perhaps even to the change in the approach adopted by U.S. drug policies, from a supply-side to a public health one.

Even strong critics of counternarcotic policies work within the epistemological requirements of the discursive field under analysis. A good

---

[11] Rasmussen and Benson claim that the same rationality ascribed to actors in the legal markets must be incorporated in any analysis aimed at understanding the behavior of actors in the illicit market: "there is no reason to believe that entrepreneurs in illicit drug markets are any less likely than those in legal markets to engage in these efforts [technological change and product development]"—terms used by the authors in order to describe rational responses to changing incentives and constraints in the market (Rasmussen and Benson 2003: 700).

example can be found in one of the various texts published on that matter by the Washington Office on Latin America (WOLA). Created in the 1970s, the NGO defined as one of its three major goals for the 2000's "to shift U.S. aid for Colombia, Mexico, and Central America away from military assistance and toward economic and social development programs".[12] While in the position of WOLA's Drug Policy program coordinator, John Walsh criticized the engulfment of the U.S. counternarcotic policies by a "flood of numbers" (Walsh 2004: 1) under the argument that it only expresses a "mirage of success" (Walsh 2004: 9). According to him,

> The array of indicators traditionally presented as measures of progress in international drug control (...) undoubtedly convey a sense of action and accomplishment, and give us a sense of the pace at which overseas drug control activities are being conducted. But the number of drug control operations conducted and their immediate accomplishments do not tell us anything about whether progress has been made toward the fundamental U.S. policy goal of making supplies scarce enough to drive up cocaine and heroin prices in the United States. (Walsh 2004: 8–9)

For Walsh, most of the metrics used by counternarcotic agencies are not reliable because they can be used both as evidence of successful operations and an expression of increased drug production and trafficking—as in the case of drug seizure (Walsh 2004: 9). In other words, that greater volumes of drugs are being seized can either mean that interdiction operations are being effective or that the whole network of counternarcotic policies is inefficient in decreasing the volume of drugs trafficked. In addition, Walsh argues that eradicated crops must not be considered as an appropriate metric for assessing the impact of drug policies, for two main reasons. First, because coca farmers have adapted to aerial fumigation by "planting in smaller plots in remote zones, interspersing their coca with other crops, and taking advantage of taller vegetation to hide their coca from aerial surveillance" (Walsh 2004: 10). Second, eradicating coca crops has little impact on the profits of drug trafficking organizations, for leaves respond for a tiny fraction of cocaine's ultimate retail price in the U.S. Walsh uses data from the DEA to show that "For less than US$1000, traffickers can purchase the coca leaf needed to produce a kilogram of cocaine

---

[12] Available at: http://www.wola.org/history_of_wola. Accessed on 20 January 2021.

that retails for about US$150,000 in the United States (when sold in US$100 units of one gram each, two-thirds pure)" (Walsh 2004: 15). Furthermore, he points to the unreliable character of numbers regarding aspects such as crop yield and refining capabilities when it comes to illegal activity. Due to this inescapable inaccuracy, the author argues that a good methodological starting point would be to work with a range, rather than with a numerical estimate as a single figure (Walsh 2004: 10).

In support of a "factual debate about how to improve drug policy" (Walsh 2004: 19), Walsh suggests that policymakers focus on price trends instead of eradication, seizures, and arrests in order to measure progress in supply-side drug control policies—that is, the wrong numbers are being looked at. If price trends were taken "not as an afterthought, but as the point of departure" (Walsh 2004: 18) for assessing the effectiveness of such policies, these would certainly be considered as an inefficient approach. Walsh mentions the same RAND 1994 report cited by Rasmussen and Benson in order to argue that, in fact, evidence points to a solid efficiency of a public health approach to the drug problem. He writes:

> the effectiveness of drug treatment in reducing drug use is supported by three decades of scientific research and clinical practice (...) every dollar invested in treatment saved the state's taxpayers seven dollars in future costs, primarily by preventing crime. (Walsh 2004: 18)

These two samples of assessments regarding the U.S. counternarcotic strategy reveal how even analyses advocating for the reformulation of antidrug policies operate within the formal requirements distributing positions in this discursive field. They preserve both an ontology and epistemology based upon the rationality of actors, associated with a language anchored in numeric representations of phenomena and efficiency as a normative driver. In those critical engagements, the problem is presented in terms of method: it is either found in the design of drug policies, which are not yielding the expected outcomes, or in the data resulting from the implementation of these policies, which is claimed to be inaccurate or analytically misplaced. In both cases, problems are identified as resulting from imperfections or misinterpretations regarding the numeric raw material with which counternarcotic agencies work, from the misfunction of incentives and constraints channeled through these institutions; and/or from the lack of coordination between them—which is often reduced to a problem of information management and, consequently, of inefficiency in the use of resources. Despite the differences in the recommendations made within the discursive field, debates have concentrated on finding the most appropriate metric to assess the impact of antidrug policies, improving the accuracy of the numbers resulting from its implementation, and reducing the costs with which agencies perform achievements.

The insultation of disputes around "problems of method" has been so pervasive in this discursive field that agencies directly engaged in counternarcotic policies reacted to criticisms with technical adjustments in the components of such policies. From the Fiscal Year (FY) 2003[13] to the FY 2004, for instance, the U.S. Office of National Drug Control Policy (ONDCP) removed from its federal drug-related budget the spending on prosecution and incarceration of drug offenders. Importantly, these activities responded to a US$4.4 billion request during the FY 2003. Consequently, the ONDCP was able to concentrate a more significant share of resources to supply control and demand reduction initiatives—which corresponded to one of the most recurrent criticisms towards the U.S. counternarcotic strategy.

The political implications of technical responses to criticism are also clear in the texts we have walked through. As Rasmussen and Benson put more explicitly, that which is not measurable—"such as civil and economic liberties"—is placed outside the scope of the analysis (Rasmussen and Benson 2003: 684), for there must be no subjective footprint in the production of knowledge. The same move underlies Walsh's claim on the need for a "factual debate about how to improve drug control policy" (2004: 19). Here, the key is not only a fact-based analysis, but one built upon a specific representation of facts: numbers, indicators, rates, ranges, estimations.

As a requirement organizing the dispersion of claims in the discursive field, this fact-based imperative anchored in numeric representations produces the need to "speak numbers" as the epistemological condition for enunciations to dispute the status of "true" in the discursive field. Simultaneous to the stimulus created by this mechanism to crystallize representations of violence in Colombia into numeric molds, representations that escape or refute this epistemological format, are pushed outside

---

[13] The US federal government's "Fiscal Year" (FY) is the budget approved by the Congress for a 12-months period, starting on October 1. The FY 2003, for example, stretches from October 1, 2002 to October 1, 2003.

the limits of the discursive field. As Aaron Haspel reminds us in the epigraph of Muller (2018), "Those who believe that what you cannot quantify does not exist also believe that what you can quantify, does".

In this sense, the analysis above is part of the general ambition of this chapter, interested in grasping the limits of what the "success story" can be about. As we have seen in this section, the disputes about the metrics anchored in the criteria mentioned above resulted in marginal adjustments in antidrug policies, but kept intact the problematization of violence from which it emerged. In the following pages, we turn to external criticisms, that is, those challenging the ordering principles of the discursive field.

3.2 The Silencing That Makes the Success Audible

As shown in the previous section, it is necessary to speak numbers and to master the language of rationality to participate in the conversation—although this does not guarantee the status of true to a certain proposition. At the same time these requirements establish the credentials allowing for enunciations to dispute the status of "true", they push beyond the margins of the discursive field those propositions that defy its ordering principles. This section turns to the division and rejection operations located in the margins of the discursive field, separating what is possible to say from what is not. To do so, first I want to lay down the terms that make the combination of Foucault's accounts of the order of discourse (1981) and the carceral system (1995) an insightful starting point for our analysis of the "monsters" haunting the Colombian "success story".

The metaphor of the "madman" and that of the "monster" have something in common in their relation to the order of discourse, according to Foucault (1981): either as speech rejected by an external cut or speech domesticated through its transformation into an object of analysis, they both remain in an underprivileged position. The value and circulation of the speech of the madman derives from what is taken out from it: it is one among various raw materials for knowledge to be produced about deviations of the norm (thereby reinforcing the norm), how dangerous they are or can be and how to keep the norm safe (by curing the mad or isolating him from the social body). In this sense, the speech of the madman only circulates when tamed: it must be brought in under a set of conditions and principles according to which knowledge about this social pathology is produced. There, in madness, where there seems to be disorder, a system of classification, separation, and hierarchy of different kinds of madness operates.

But the taming of the speech of the madman is as much revealing of the anguish for order as it is of the fear of disorder. As Foucault suggests, "It is just as if prohibitions, barriers, thresholds and limits had been set up in order to remove from its richness the most dangerous part, and in order to organize its disorder according to figures which dodge what is most uncontrollable about it" (Foucault 1981: 66). The "monster", contrastingly, is that which has not been tamed, that which lies outside the discourse; the monster is the imaginary, the belief—as opposed to scientific knowledge (Foucault 1981: 60). At the same time, it is an extreme deviation of the norm, the most dangerous form of disorder, for it is the negation of the order built within the discursive field.

Foucault refers to "discursive 'policing'" when thinking about the constraints resulting from the rules operating in the limits of the discursive field: "It is always possible that one might speak the truth in the space of a wild exteriority, but one is 'in the true' only by obeying the rules of a discursive 'policing' which one has to reactivate in each of one's discourses" (Foucault 1981: 61). Rather than suggesting that this discursive control stems from the work of a centralized apparatus, the metaphor of a discursive policing emphasizes the constraining effect of rule enforcements that are found dispersed in practices that reactivate the ordering principles of the discursive field.

Now, as we have seen, divisions (as the one operating in relation to the madman) and exclusions (as the one operating in relation to the monster) are the conditions under which these very rules operating in the true are possible. For this reason, policing must concentrate on divisions and exclusions, for these are the sites from which the unexpected is expected to come. Although this attention is even more emphasized in the frontier separating the ordered discourse from the monsters, it is important to remember that the division upon which the analysis of the speech of the madman relies always operates on a silent alert (Foucault 1981: 54)—that is, under the suspicious gaze that madness can, anytime, subvert the taming impinged upon it.

In the case of the discursive field emerging from assessments of the counternarcotic performance of Colombian agencies, the system of exclusion relies on a set of institutionalized practices that express the encounter of discursive policing and what Foucault called the "carceral system"

(Foucault 1995). Indeed, it is through surveillance and detention that delinquent narratives about the "success story" are controlled. To be clear, "delinquency" is a population which is analyzable because it is understood as potentially dangerous to social order, that is, to the mass of disciplined and productive bodies. In Foucault's terms, delinquency is "a politically or economically less dangerous—and on occasion, usable— form of illegality" (Foucault 1995: 277). The knowledge built from the examination of the delinquent is, therefore, also useful to the social body, for it is only by mapping the profiles considered as "prone to crime" and by knowing the resistances against disciplining practices that the techniques of government can be re-articulated in order to circumvent, tame or even repress them. The system of records and permanent surveillance produce and constitute a grid of knowledge against which delinquency is classified, separated, and hierarchized. Operating as a kind of "political observatory" of the social body, delinquency (Foucault 1995: 277) allows for disorder to be tamed.

In this section, the metaphor of the "madman" and of the "monster" allow us to grasp the mechanisms that keep some discourses at bay from the circuit through which narratives of success are disputed, criticized, and reformulated. Despite the vast array of social groups affected by silencing mechanisms in Colombia (see, for instance, Human Rights Watch [HRW] 1996; Colectivo de Abogados 2005; Coordinación Colombia-Europa-Estados Unidos [CCEEU] 2016a), I focus on unionists and human rights NGOs because they reveal with more explicit contours the two principles of exclusion I mentioned earlier. Since my objective in walking through those cases is to expose the mechanisms of discursive division and rejection operating therein, my expectation is that this analysis can also shed light on silencing dynamics towards other social groups.

When thinking about the conditions affecting the circulation of discourse, it is in the Colombian intelligence apparatus that we find a key site for the intersection of discursive policing and the carceral system. Indeed, it compiles information and translates it into "intelligence" that feeds counternarcotic operations undertaken by the police and the military in Colombia. Although Foucault understands the carceral system as constituted by police, prison, and delinquency (1995: 282),[14] any analysis devoted to understanding the connection between counternarcotic operations in Colombia and its silencing effects to the discursive field cannot afford leaving the military aside—especially the Army—, given its privileged position in the security architecture in that country.

A key intelligence resource fed into police and military operations is the production of lists classifying suspects across a spectrum of dangerousness. This was one of the main responsibilities of the Administrative Department of Security (DAS, in Spanish), the national central agency for intelligence in Colombia. First created in 1953 (Decree No. 2872) as the Administrative Department of Intelligence Services (SIC, in Spanish), the agency had its name changed to DAS in 1960 and was directly linked to the Colombian Presidency (Decree No. 1717). Until its dismantlement[15] in 2011, the DAS had been in charge of collecting biographical information, mapping the social network, analyzing personal habits, routine and displacement routes, as well as building political and psychological profiles of people considered to be "disturbing the security or threatening the integrity of the constitutional regime" (Article 6 of Decree N. 2110/1992).

It is also possible to find practices related to intelligence in the Armed Forces—although diffusely distributed across different branches. Indeed, since the escalation of violence in the 1990s, the Colombian National Police and the Army developed their own intelligence units.[16] While the DIJIN concentrates the police operations of this type, the Military Forces

---

[14] According to him, "Police surveillance provides the prison with [law] offenders, which the prison transforms into delinquents, the targets and auxiliaries of the police supervisors, which regularly send back certain number to prison" (Foucault 1995: 282). Although Foucault does not explicitly contemplate the intelligence apparatus in his analysis of the carceral system, its relevance to the latter echoes in the central analytical position that the production of knowledge about the social body have in his account of ordering practices and the knowledge-power nexus in government practices.

[15] Following a series of scandals related to systematic phone interceptions of court magistrates, journalists, and activists, and to the involvement of the DAS with paramilitary groups, the intelligence agency was dismantled in 2011, and its functions were redistributed among different branches of the Colombian National Police and Military Forces.

[16] The creation of multiple intelligence systems suggests that intelligence information does not circulate evenly among the different agencies inscribed in the Colombian security architecture. If we consider the pressure for efficient results over these agencies and

have an Intelligence Unit attached to the Central Command, as well as a series of intelligence services dispersed across its divisions and brigades.

Moreover, in 2003, the Democratic Security Policy launched by President Álvaro Uribe's administration (2002–2010) institutionalized the practice of using citizens as informants in order to assist the Colombian Armed Forces in the fight against terrorism. In the first years of Uribe's Presidency, 1.5 million citizens were incorporated to a network of informants (International Crisis Group [ICG] 2003: 5), expected to provide the military and the police with information on any suspicious activity, and were paid for information that contributed to the arrest of members of the armed groups or to the prevention of a hostile action (ICG 2003: 15).

The information nourishing this whole intelligence apparatus stems from informants, infiltrated personnel, interception of phone calls and e-mail communications, as well as from the interrogation and torture of detainees. Analogous to the speech of the madman, the value of "human resource exploitation"[17] derives from that which is extracted from it. In this sense, both the silent compilation of information based on infiltration and informants and the extraction of information from detainees feed the typologies used by the intelligence apparatus regarding disturbances of the public order. Based on collected information, intelligence separates leaders from followers within a "cell" and hierarchizes their actions between suspicious and threatening.

This apparatus targeted unions and other social movements in Colombia on the grounds of their alleged links to insurgency. As we have seen in the previous chapter, the historical processes that resulted in the crystallization of a specific problematization of violence in Colombia included the expansion of the margins within which phenomena came to be framed as a disturbance to public order. Thus, if categories such

---

intensified by the competition among them, the restrictions over the circulation of intelligence information may have created the need for these agencies to search for short-term solutions in the domain of intelligence.

[17] This is the technical jargon used to refer to the extraction of information from human sources for intelligence purposes. Importantly, during the 1980s, most of the training for Latin American countries on "Human Resource Exploitation" was based on manuals produced by the U.S. CIA and the U.S. Army Special Forces (Gill 2004). The 1983 version of the CIA intelligence manual was developed in cooperation with British military officers (CIA 1983: n.p.) and preserved the emphasis laid by the renown Kubark Intelligence Manual on "coercive questioning" (CIA 1983: K-1).

as "narcoguerrilla" and "narcoterrorism" were central to the construction of Colombia as a "problematic country", other social movements that contested ordering practices in that country were also dragged into the process. Associated with the vagueness characterizing the penal type "terrorism", this problematization of violence offered the conditions that made the association of social movements with insurgency not only possible, but one that came to constitute a regular object of surveillance in Colombia.

This was particularly the case for labor unions (Atehortúa C. 2010; Urrego A. 2013). In one of the military manuals disclosed by Human Rights Watch (HRW) in 1996, soldiers were instructed to infiltrate houses as workers or visitors, dressed in civilian clothes. In these covert operations, soldiers classified the reaction of civilians towards the troops as indicators of alignment with subversives (HRW 1996, chapter 3). Based on this information, the military built different lists organizing suspects according to the degree of dangerousness they allegedly represented: those highly suspected of cooperating or being part of guerrilla movements had their names registered on a "black list"; those whose alignment was uncertain were kept on a "grey list" (HRW 1996: 19).

The step that resulted from the elaboration of lists classifying different degrees of dangerousness to additional detentions in search of more information, or even extrajudicial killings connects the intelligence apparatus to the operational level of the police or the military, focused on "neutralizing" specific targets. It is on these grounds that we must read the striking levels of violence registered in Colombia. According to Colectivo de Abogados, a renowned Colombian NGO of human rights defenders, between 1991 and 1999, 1336 unionists were killed in the country (2005: n.p.). From 2001 to 2005, Colombia registered 33 disappearances, 37 kidnappings, 90 forced detentions of unionists, in addition to 1,276 death threats to unionists and 14 bombings of unions' headquarters (Colectivo de Abogados 2005: n.p.).

One of these cases took place in Arauca, in 2004, when the Army reported a confrontation with the National Liberation Army (ELN, in Spanish) during a military operation that resulted in the death of three "insurgents" and the detention of two others. The operation was heavily criticized by human rights NGOs for aiming at unionists, not guerrillas. The three people killed on that occasion were Leonel Goyeneche, who worked in the financial department of the Central Workers' Union (CUT, in Spanish) in Arauca; Jorge Eduardo Prieto, the president of the hospital workers' union; and Héctor Alirio Martínez, a known leader among *campesinos*. Those detained by the Army had a similar profile: Samuel Moreno was the president of CUT in Arauca; and Raquel Castro, the director of the teachers' local union. Responding to criticisms, the Minister of Defense, Jorge Uribe, contended that the operation was in accordance with the law. It was backed by detention warrants for rebellion issued by the local Fiscalía, and the lethal outcome of the operation was actually in self-defense, as the military personnel involved only responded to the gunshots coming from the "insurgents"—argued the Minister. By that time, the Vice-President, Francisco Santos, who also headed the Presidency's Human Rights Office, did recognize that those people were leaders of social movements, but added that they were also "involved, according to the intelligence reports, in activities which were not related to their work" (El Tiempo 2004).

As this case reveals, the intelligence apparatus reproduces the historical associations of unions with insurgency—that is, although the processes leading to the crystallization of this link had emerged long before the implementation of Plan Colombia (Atehortúa C. 2010; Urrego A. 2013), they persist until the present (Archila 2012; González R. et al. 2012; Pereira F. 2012). The reproduction of such discourse is anchored in a claim of authority with which the work of intelligence agencies is legitimated. More specifically, the intelligence value taken out of the surveillance of unionists is revealed by the alleged accuracy with which followers are put aside, while leaders are singled out as the central concern of police and military operatives. It is in this alleged precision with which different degrees of "insurgents" are dissected that the claim of authority of the intelligence apparatus resides.

At the same time, the fear unleashed by the striking numbers of extra-judicial killings of comrades, the threats made to unionists and their families, the arbitrary detentions based on "secret intelligence reports", and the extrajudicial killings themselves are all silencing mechanisms with profound effects over the terms of the Colombian "success story". Indeed, the dismantlement of labor unions resulting from these practices is also a dismantlement of their political agendas, such as the protection of workers' rights, and the confrontation of the framing of those groups as insurgents. If the articulation of the police, military and intelligence apparatuses operates towards silencing unionists, demands that would emerge from these movements fade away and ultimately do not resonate in the content of the "success story". In this sense, the effects of these persisting practices are directly related to what the "success" can be about: it cannot encompass workers' rights—nor land reform, if we extend the analysis to the leaderships of *campesinos* who are also often framed as insurgents and targeted by police and military operations, as illustrated by the case of Héctor Alirio Martínez, in the 2004 Arauca case.[18]

With the objective of shedding light on the striking levels of violence against unionists and social movements in general in Colombia, NGOs such as CCEEU, Lawyers' Collective (*Colectivo de Abogados*), Movement of State Crime Victims (MOVICE, in Spanish), Research and Popular Education Center (CINEP, in Spanish), HRW, and Amnesty International have been key in exposing dynamics and perpetrators of human rights violations in Colombia. Through regular reports, conferences and hearings with victims, these NGOs seek in international organizations the support they are not able to earn in the Colombian government. The CCEEU, for instance, regularly organizes workshops where victims and other human rights activists gather to discuss issues such as extrajudicial killings and forced disappearances (FOR and CCEEU 2014; CCEEU 2016a). Their reports are presented to institutions like the Inter-American Commission on Human Rights (IACHR) and the United Nations High Commissioner for Human Rights (UNHCHR), as an attempt to hold the Colombian state accountable for human rights violations, to push for judicial investigations in those cases and for the reparation of victims.

Similarly, NGOs such as the HRW have been placing the Colombian Armed Forces in the center of debates about violence in Colombia at least since the 1990s. In a report published in 1996, HRW revealed that it had:

> obtained evidence (…) that shows that in 1991, the military made civilians a key part of its intelligence-gathering apparatus. Working under the direct orders of the military high command, paramilitary forces incorporated into intelligence networks conducted surveillance of legal opposition political figures and groups, operated with military units, then executed attacks against targets chosen by their military commanders. (HRW 1996: n.p.)

---

[18] According to a report published by the Coordination Colombia-Europe-United States (CCEEU, in Spanish) (2016a), the number of forced disappearances of leaders of *campesinos*' movements is impressively high in Colombia. While singling out the case of Henry Pérez, a *campesino* leader in Tibú (Northern Santander), a region disputed by the military forces, the FARC and paramilitary groups, the document reports that, since his disappearance, seven additional leaders were threatened.

According to the NGO, the Military Forces worked in partnership with paramilitary groups in intelligence gathering and extrajudicial killings of "anyone perceived as supporting the guerrillas, but also members of the political opposition, journalists, trade unionists, and human rights workers" (HRW 1996: n.p.). In Barrancabermeja, one of the regions where these networks operated, a former intelligence agent reported to HRW that Navy Captain Juan Carlos Alvarez Gutiérrez and Lieutenant Coronel Rodrigo Quiñones "would identify the targets, which included the membership and leaders of the Oil Workers' Union (…), the San Silvestre Transportation Workers' Union, the Regional Committee for the Defense of Human Rights (…) and the UP [Patriotic Union Party]" (HRW 1996: n.p.) and would communicate these names to paramilitary commanders. According to the same report, this partnership made no mention of drugs: "Instead, the Colombian military (…) presented a plan to better combat what they call 'escalating terrorism by armed subversion'" (HRW 1996: n.p.).

The synergies between the Military Forces and paramilitary groups are often observed in territories of great economic relevance—most notably for extractivism purposes (Ronderos 2014). For example, Barrancabermeja, the stage of several human rights violations in the department of Santander, hosts the Magdalena River Port and the largest oil refinery in Colombia, operated by Ecopetrol. Furthermore, both Arauca and Santander departments are traversed by the most important oil pipeline in the country: Caño Limón-Coveñas.[19] In addition to suggesting the complicity of the private sector regarding the military-paramilitary cooperation (Franco R. 2009; Ronderos 2014), the concentration of their activities in regions of economic prominence reveals that this connection is far from restricted to a few random cases (CINEP 2004; Franco R. 2009; FOR and CCEEU 2014; CCEEU 2016b; Project Counselling Service et al. 2014; Ronderos 2014).

---

[19] The concern with protecting the infrastructure used for extractivism is so central to military operations that, in the context of Plan Colombia, the Army created Brigades specialized in the protection of Caño Limón-Coveñas (Rojas 2006: 54; Vargas V. 2014). The oil pipeline stretches across the territories of the following departments: Córdoba, Sucre, Bolívar, Magdalena, Cesar, Norte de Santander and Arauca.

According to testimonials from paramilitary combatants, the tactical usefulness of this cooperation lies in the fact that they are not as accountable as the Colombian military for human rights violations. For Ramón Isaza, former paramilitary leader,

> the Army cannot do things because it is straightjacketed by human rights. For this reason, I plea with the national government that it offers support to the Army and that it makes this human rights thing disappear because this is giving result to the guerrillas, not to us.[20] (apud Franco R. 2009: 375)

That the paramilitary groups are tactically useful does not imply that the Colombian Military Forces have full control over these groups. Still, the absence of legal brakes to their actions against the guerrillas[21] and the economic interests permeating their operations can be read as contemporary expressions of what Foucault called "useful delinquency" (Foucault 1995: 280) when discussing government practices in nineteenth century Europe.[22] That is, a form of illegalism "which one manages to supervise, while extracting from it an illicit profit through elements, themselves

---

[20] In the original: "Hoy en día, así el Ejército quiera hacer las cosas, no puede porque está maniatado por los derechos humanos. Por eso yo le digo al gobierno nacional que le preste apoyo al Ejército y que desaparezca eso de los derechos humanos porque eso le está dando resultado a la guerrilla pero no a nosotros".

[21] Two observations are noteworthy here. The first one is that the paramilitary action is not naturally absent of legal brakes: it is *made* so. In other words, there is a selectivity running through the functioning of the Colombian penal system that results in making most of paramilitary operations a blind spot to these institutions. Needless to say, this reveals a systemic complicity of judicial institutions with paramilitary action, in addition to that of the military and the private sector to which I have already called the attention. Secondly, paramilitary operations are far from exclusively focused on the guerrillas. Although it falls outside the argumentative scope of this book, we could even go further and show that massacres against civilians constituted a regular paramilitary practice and also yielded economic gains to the private sector. These violent practices often resulted in the expulsion of local inhabitants, who either abandoned their properties or sold them at very low prices, benefiting land grabbing and the formation of large rural estates in Colombia to be used for agribusiness purposes. For more on this, see: Viana (2018).

[22] According to Foucault, the use of specific delinquencies is a historically persistent feature of practices of government, dating back at least to the nineteenth century. In this sense, it does not refer to a problematic specificity of Colombia, nor a "new" phenomenon. According to Foucault, "Arms trafficking, the illegal sale of alcohol in prohibition countries, or more recently drug trafficking show a similar functioning of this 'useful delinquency' (…). The political use of delinquents—as informers and *agents provocateurs*—was a fact well before the nineteenth century. But, after the Revolution, this

illegal, but rendered manipulable by their organization in delinquency" (Foucault 1995: 280). Thus, far from adding on to the portrayal of a complete chaos in Colombia, paramilitary action provides order to territories deemed economically strategic. In this sense, despite all the accusations of human rights violations perpetrated by the paramilitary and its characterization as an "illegal armed group", they are detached from the guerrillas when it comes to the penal outreach often invested towards "disturbances of public order" in Colombia.

The exposure of the military-paramilitary links in Colombia advanced by human rights NGOs have two main implications for our purposes. The first one refers to the boundary between legality and illegality upon which the "success story" is erected. As we have seen, the initiatives developed to tackle the "problem of violence" in Colombia are centered on the strengthening of the Armed Forces and other governmental institutions, so as to give impulse to an increased presence of the state in regions that have been taken by illegal armed groups—hence the title of Plan Colombia, "Plan for Peace, Prosperity, and the Strengthening of the State". In other words, solutions to the "Colombian problems" must reach out to "ungoverned regions" and vest them with law. In contrast to the clear differentiation between legality and illegality this rationale is anchored in, the historically persistent cooperation between the Military Forces and the paramilitary groups points to a blurred boundary between these two dimensions. As a consequence, the causal relation between legality and peace is destabilized and can no longer uphold narratives about the "Colombian success".

The second implication is the stigmatization of those often portrayed as the protagonists of the Colombian "success story". Instead of reinforcing the image of protectors of citizens, the denunciations of human rights violations—with and without the paramilitary groups—paint the Colombian Military Forces as perpetrators of the violence they claim to combat. This vision of the military stands in deep contrast to the terms anchoring the problematization of violence in Colombia. As I have argued

---

practice acquired quite different dimensions: the infiltration of political parties and workers' associations, the recruitment of thugs against strikers and rioters, the organization of a sub-police—working directly with the legal police and capable if necessary of becoming a sort of parallel army—a whole extra-legal functioning of power was partly assured by the mass of reserve labour constituted by the delinquents: a clandestine police force and standby army at the disposal of the state" (Foucault 1995: 280).

in Chapter 2, the whole architecture of "solutions" to the "Colombian problems" was focused on the construction of "narcoguerrilla" and "narcoterrorism" as the sources of that violence. Recognizing the Military Forces as perpetrators does not only lie outside such a problematization: it requires another one, in which the state is not exclusively part of the solution. My point is that the military-paramilitary link and the human rights violations exposed through the work of NGOs could not be accommodated within the problematization upon which all the initiatives aiming at solving the "Colombian problems" relied. In other words, human rights organizations offered an alternative problematization which concurred with the one analyzed in Chapter 2: one in which the Colombian state was part of the "problem of violence".

The "monstrosity" of the discourse reproduced through the activities of NGOs was brushed to the margins of the discursive field about the performance of Colombian agencies under Plan Colombia. This process operated through two main mechanisms. First, the content of the work undertaken by these human rights organizations was inscribed in the discursive field as the "speech of the madman". By mid-1990s, the incorporation of "human rights workers" to intelligence lists in Colombia (HRW 1996: n.p.) suggests that the "madness" of their speech was already under the gaze of that apparatus. Indeed, threats and other forms of intimidation to human rights activists were so pervasive that the UNHCHR dedicated a special section to cover that topic in its regular reports. In the 2012 version of that document, the United Nations agency notified 107 threats to human rights defenders in Colombia from September 2011 to January 2012 (UNHCHR 2012: 5).

The second mechanism involves the full refusal of the discursive "monstrosity" expressed by the problematization underlying the reports produced by human rights NGOs. As an illustration, in 1996, when HRW issued its report about military-paramilitary links in Colombia, its full content was discredited by Juan Carlos Esguerra, Minister of Defense at that time, on the grounds that it was based on outdated information[23]

---

[23] A recurrent argument for the rejection of human rights reports is the "lack of credible evidence", which is mostly related to the form they present the denunciations. Anticipating these accusations, a report prepared by FOR (2010: 6) underlined that: "reports of extrajudicial executions that result in the Prosecutor General's office or Inspector General's office opening a formal investigation constitute credible evidence that the military committed the violation. We also are aware of the strict standards used by the human rights organizations that constitute the Working Group on Extrajudicial Executions, and

(El Tiempo 1996). By his turn, Military Forces Commander, General Harold Bedoya, contended that the work of some organizations aimed at de-legitimizing the Armed Forces and keeping them from fighting drugs and terror in Colombia (El Tiempo 1996). During Álvaro Uribe's administration, the work of human rights NGOs was classified as a form of "terrorism": in 2003, the president dismissed the human rights violations reported by 80 NGOs, arguing that it had been produced by those engaged in "politicking" (*politiqueros*) who are "in service of terrorism" and "hide themselves behind the human rights flag" (El Tiempo 2003).

Such an outright rejection does not mean that confrontative criticisms invested against the "success story" had no effect whatsoever over the discursive field. The terms of their critique did push for a re-articulation of the discursive regime with which agencies had their role in Plan Colombia justified. One such re-articulation was the approval of the "Leahy Amendment" by the U.S. Congress, in 1997, determining the blockage of foreign aid to countries with military officers involved in human rights violations. During the same period, the U.S. Presidency created a certification on human rights, authorizing the Embassy to investigate the respect for human rights in the Colombian military troops.[24] Responding to these pressures, the Colombian Military Forces have increased the certification on human rights and humanitarian law for its officership and insisted on a "rotten apples" narrative (FOR and CCEEU 2014: 71–78), as an attempt to show that administrative actions were being taken to tackle the problem of violations.

Importantly, however, these criticisms were not translated into the re-configuration of the ordering principles of the discursive field, nor into the transformation of the pillars upon which the problematization of violence relied. Given the impossibility of denying the existence of human rights violations, the critique that could be accomodated in the dominant problematization of violence was filtered, at the same time the confrontative part of that critique was kept at bay from the discursive field. As we have seen in this section, the mechanisms of exclusion operating in the limits of the discursive field had the effect of silencing "madmen" and "monsters"

contend that reports of extrajudicial executions from these organizations also constitute credible evidence".

[24] Chernick (2008: 133) and Isacson (2005: 141–142) argue that these concerns with human rights were merely apparent, given the continuous flux of U.S. foreign aid to Colombia despite a series of scandals of abusive violence involving the Armed Forces.

through their transformation into an object of the Colombian intelligence apparatus, the annihilation of activists and the outright rejection of their confrontative speeches.

These dynamics have had profound consequences for the content of the "success story", whose conditions of possibility came to exclude themes such as labor rights, social and land reform, state violence, and associations across the legal-illegal spectrum in the perpetration of systematic violence against citizens. As Colombian history shows, threatening and killing the messengers did not result in the full erasure of the message: critical engagements have coexisted with claims to success in the limits of the discursive field, challenging it to re-articulate the terms with which the Armed Forces would be advanced as the protagonists of a sucessful performance in Plan Colombia.

3.3 Conclusion

In this chapter, we built on the discussion about the construction of a specific problematization of violence in Colombia and explored the emergence of this country as an object of analysis of experts engaged with "solutions" to its problems. Since the debates, diagnoses and cures produced in this context cannot be detached from the terms of that problematization, the emphasis placed by the latter on the "narcoguerrilla" and "narcoterrorism" as the main perpetrators of violence is reflected in the repertoire of "solutions" to the "Colombian problems"—hence the privileged position of counternarcotic policies in this debate.

In Sect. 3.1, I have shown that the implementation of Plan Colombia was inscribed in a context when governmental agencies were guiding their bureaucratic routine by a "performance measurement" logic. In this sense, I argued that the disputes around the Colombian counternarcotic performance came to be ordered through a grid of intelligibility, according to which the pursuit for "the most appropriate metric" was framed in terms of accurate numeric representations, technical adjustments, and institutional/policy design, while preserving the pillars of the problematization from which those "solutions" emerged.

Section 3.2 shed light on another modality of critical engagement: the "external critique", that is, those confronting the constitutive pillars of the discursive field. Using the metaphor of "discursive monstrosities", I discussed how the lists of suspects produced by the intelligence apparatus fed military and police operations, pointing to unionists as targets on the grounds of their alleged links to insurgency. This circuit has historically resulted in striking numbers of extrajudicial killings, forced disappearances, and forced detention of unionists in Colombia. I argued that, in this process, not only were the political agendas of labor unions dismantled, but also their confrontations of de-legitimizing classifications of unionists as insurgents. Although these and other human rights violations were systematically denounced by NGOs, the content of their reports was repeatedly rejected under the claim that they lacked credibility and accuracy. Further, I contended that these denunciations offered an alternative problematization of violence in Colombia—one in which the state was a perpetrator of violence and, consequently, part of the problem of violence.

The silencing mechanisms operating towards the "monstrosities" expressed by unionists and human rights NGOs have profound impacts on the horizons of discursive possibilities for the "success story". It cannot be about state violence, social or land reform, for these problematizations of violence are kept beyond the margins of the discursive field. In this sense, read as a whole, Chapters 2 and 3 discuss the conditions under which the "success" is claimed, as well as the silencing mechanisms allowing for a specific story to be told. I thereby expect to have provided elements for us to understand the limits of what the "success story" can be about, and under which terms it produces a specific past and present of Colombia.

References

Books, Chapters, Articles

Archila, M. Luchas laborales y violencia contra el sindicalismo en Colombia, 2002–2010. ¿Otro daño "colateral" de la Seguridad Democrática? *Controversia*, n. 198, pp. 161–218, June 2012.

Atehortúa C., A. L. El golpe de Rojas y el poder de los militares. *Folios*, n. 31, pp. 33–48, Primer Semestre 2010.

Bewley-Taylor, D. R. *International Drug Control: Consensus Fractured.* Cambridge: Cambridge University Press, 2012.

Centro de Investigación y Educación Popular (CINEP). Del Batallón Charry Solano a la Brigada 20 una continuidad paramilitar. *Noche y Niebla* (Dossier: Deuda con la Humanidad: Paramilitarismo de Estado en Colombia 1988–2003). Bogotá, D.C.: CINEP, 2004.

Chernick, M. *Acuerdo posible: solución negociada al conflicto armado colombiano.* Bogotá: Aurora, 2008.

Davis, K. E.; Kingsbury, B.; Merry, S. E. Introduction: Global Governance by Indicators. In: Davis, K. E.; Fisher, A.; Kingsbury, B.; Merry, S. E. (eds.). *Governance by Indicators: Global Power Through Quantification and Rankings*. Oxford: Oxford University Press, 2012.

Fellowship of Reconciliation (FOR); Coordinación Colombia-Europa-Estados Unidos (CCEEU). *"Falsos positivos" en Colombia y el papel de asistencia militar de Estados Unidos, 2000–2010*. Bogotá, D.C.: FOR and CCEEU, 2014.

Foucault, M. The Order of Discourse. In: Young, R. (ed.). *Untying the Text: A Post-structuralist Reader*. Boston, London and Henley: Routledge, 1981 [1971].

Foucault, M. Politics and the Study of Discourse. In: Burchell, G.; Gordon, C.; Miller, P. *The Foucault Effect: Studies in Governmentality*. Chicago: University of Chicago Press, 1991.

Foucault, M. *Discipline and Punish*. New York: Second Vintage Books, 1995.

Foucault, M. *Security, Territory, Population*. New York: Palgrave Macmillan, 2007.

Franco R., V. L. *Orden contrainsurgente y dominación*. Medellín: Siglo del Hombre, 2009.

Gill, L. *The School of the Americas: Military Training and Political Violence in the Americas*. Durham and London: Duke University Press, 2004.

González R., J. D.; Masullo J., J.; Sánchez M., C.; Restrepo T., J. A. Registrar, cuantificar y debatir. ¿Cómo se ha medido la violencia contra trabajadores sindicalizados en Colombia? *Controversia*, n. 198, pp. 57–110, June 2012.

Huysmans, J. *The Politics of Insecurity: Fear, Migration and Asylum in the EU*. London: Routledge, 2006.

Isacson, A. Failing Grades: Evaluating the Results of Plan Colombia. *Yale Journal of International Affairs*, pp. 138–154, Summer/Fall 2005.

MacCoun, R. J.; Reuter, P. *Drug War Heresies: Learning from Other Vices, Times, and Places*. Cambridge: Cambridge University Press, 2004.

Muller, J. Z. *The Tyranny of Metrics*. Princeton and Oxford: Princeton University Press, 2018.

Pereira F., A. Violencia en el mundo sindical. Un análisis cualitativo sobre una práctica persistente en Colombia, 1986–2011. *Controversia*, n. 198, pp. 13–56, June 2012.

Rasmussen, D. W.; Benson, B. Rationalizing Drug Policy Under Federalism. *Florida State University Law Review*, v. 30, n. 679, pp. 679–734, 2003.

Rodrigues, T. Tráfico, Guerra, Proibição. In: Labate, B. C.; Goulart, S. L.; Fiore, M.; MacRae, E.; Carneiro, H. (orgs.). Salvador: UFBA, 2008.

Rojas, D. M. Estados Unidos y la guerra en Colombia. In: Sanín, F. G.; Wills, M. E.; Gómez, G. S. (coords.). *Nuestra guerra sin nombre: transformaciones del conflicto en Colombia*. Bogotá, D.C.: Norma, 2006.

Ronderos, M. T. *Guerras Recicladas. Una historia periodística del paramilitarismo en Colombia*. Bogotá, D.C.: Aguilar, 2014.
Ruiz V., J. C.; Illera C., O.; Manrique Z., V. *La tenue línea de la tranquilidad. Estudio comparado sobre seguridad ciudadana y policía*. Bogotá, D.C.: Universidad del Rosario, 2006.
Thoumi, F. E. The Numbers Game: Let's All Guess the Size of the Illegal Drug Industry! *Journal of Drug Issues*, pp. 185–200, Winter 2005.
Trace, M.; Roberts, M.; Klein, A. Assessing Drug Policy Principles and Practice. *Drugscope Report*, n. 2. London: Beckley Foundation Drug Policy Programme, 2004.
Urrego A., M. Á. El movimiento sindical, el período de la violencia y la formación de la nueva izquierda colombiana, 1959–1971. *Diálogo de Saberes*, n. 38, pp. 135–145, 2013.
Vargas, E. V. Fármacos e outros objetos sócio-técnicos: notas para uma genealogia das drogas. In: Labate, B. C.; Goulart, S. L.; Fiore, M.; MacRae, E.; Carneiro, H. (orgs.). Salvador: UFBA, 2008.
Vargas V., A. The Profile of the Colombian Armed Forces: A Result of the Struggle Against Guerrillas, Drug Trafficking and Terrorism. In: Mares, D. E.; Martínez, R. (eds.). *Debating Civil-Military Relations in Latin America*. Brighton: Sussex Academic Press, 2014.

Documents, Reports and Studies

Central Intelligence Agency (CIA). Human Resource Exploitation Training Manual (DRV HUM 4082). Fairfax: CIA, 1983. Available at: http://nsarchive.gwu.edu/NSAEBB/NSAEBB122/CIA%20Human%20Res%20Exploit%20A1-G11.pdf. Accessed on 15 February 2021.
Colectivo de Abogados 'José Alvear Restrepo'. *Libertad sindical y derechos humanos en Colombia*. Bogotá, D.C.: Colectivo de Abogados, 13 June 2005. Available at: https://www.colectivodeabogados.org/libertad-sindical-y-derechos-humanos-en-colombia/. Accessed on 14 February 2021.
Coordinación Colombia-Europa-Estados Unidos (CCEEU). *Informe Alterno sobre la Situación de las Desapariciones Forzadas en Colombia Presentado ante el Comité Contra la Desaparición Forzada de Naciones Unidas*. Bogotá, D.C.: CCEEU, September 2016a. Available at: http://coeuropa.org.co/wp-content/uploads/2016/10/Informe-Desaparici%C3%B3n-forzada-arreglado-10-oct-ilovepdf-compressed.pdf. Accessed on 14 February 2021.
Coordinación Colombia-Europa-Estados Unidos (CCEEU). *Informe Alternativo al Septimo Informe Presentado por el Estado de Colombia al Comité de Derechos Humanos de las Naciones Unidas*. Bogotá, D.C.: CCEEU, October 2016b. Available at: http://coeuropa.org.co/wp-content/uploads/2017/01/Inf

orme-alternativo-al-SEPTIMO-INFORME-11-enero-2017.pdf. Accessed on 14 February 2021.

Drug Enforcement Administration (DEA). A History of the DEA: 1975–1980. *The DEA Museum & Visitors Center*, n.d., pp. 24–42. Available at: https://www.deamuseum.org/deahistorybook/1975-1980.html. Accessed on 15 February 2021.

Drug Enforcement Administration (DEA). A History of the DEA: 1980–1985. *The DEA Museum & Visitors Center*, n.d., pp. 43–57. Available at: https://www.deamuseum.org/deahistorybook/1980-1985.html. Accessed on 15 February 2021.

Fellowship of Reconciliation (FOR). *Military Assistance and Human Rights*: Colombia, U.S. Accountability, and Global Implications. Bogotá, D.C.: FOR, July 2010. Available at: https://peacepresence.org/2010/09/22/report-military-colombia-us/. Accessed on 15 February 2021.

Human Rights Watch (HRW). *Colombia's Killer Networks*: The Military-Paramilitary Partnership and the United States. New York, November 1996. Available at: https://www.hrw.org/legacy/reports/1996/killertoc.htm. Accessed on 13 February 2021.

International Crisis Group (ICG). Colombia: President Uribe's Democratic Security Policy. *Latin America & Caribbean Report*, n. 6, 13 November 2003. Available at: https://d2071andvip0wj.cloudfront.net/06-colombia-president-uribe-s-democratic-security-policy.pdf. Accessed on 14 February 2021.

Policía Nacional de Colombia. *Revista Criminalidad*, v. 48. Bogotá, D.C.: Policía Nacional de Colombia, Dirección Central de Policía Judicial, 2005. Available at: https://www.policia.gov.co/sites/default/files/RevistaCriminalidad2005.pdf. Accessed on 15 February 2021.

Project Counselling Service, Comisión Intereclesial de Justicia y Paz, Corporación Colectivo de Abogados José Alvear Restrepo y Fundación Comité de Solidariedad com Presos Políticos. *El desmantelamiento del Paramilitarismo: Aprendizajes y Recomendaciones desde las Víctimas*. Bogotá, D.C.: Project Counselling Service, November 2014. Available at: https://issuu.com/cajar/docs/201411_desmantelamiento_-_final. Accessed on 15 February 2021.

United Nations High Commissioner for Refugees (UNHCR). Report of the United Nations High Commissioner for Human Rights on the situation of human rights in Colombia (A/HRC/19/21/Add.3). New York: Human Rights Council, 31 January 2012. Available at: http://www.hchr.org.co/documentoseinformes/informes/altocomisionado/report2011.pdf. Accessed on 15 February 2021.

U.S. Congress. An Act to Provide for the Establishment of Strategic Planning and Performance Measurement in the Federal Government, and for Other Purposes. Washington, D.C.: U.S. Congress, 5 January 1993. Available at:

http://govinfo.library.unt.edu/npr/library/misc/s20.html. Accessed on 15 February 2021.

U.S. *Government Accountability Office* (GAO). Drug Control. Agencies Need to Plan for Likely Declines in Drug Interdiction Assets, and Develop Better Performance Measures for Transit Zone Operations (GAO-06–200). November 2005. Available at: http://www.gao.gov/new.items/d06200.pdf. Accessed on 15 February 2021.

Walsh, J. M. Are We There Yet? Measuring Progress in the US War on Drugs in Latin America. *WOLA Drug War Monitor*. Washington, D.C.: WOLA, December 2004.

Press Articles

El Tiempo. "Ejército rechaza informe de Human Rights Watch", *El Tiempo*, 26 November 1996. Available at: http://www.eltiempo.com/archivo/documento/MAM-601138. Accessed on 15 February 2021.

El Tiempo. "Fuerte réplica de Uribe a ONG", *El Tiempo*, 9 September 2003. Available at: http://www.eltiempo.com/archivo/documento/MAM-1006587. Accessed on 15 February 2021.

El Tiempo. "Grave lo de Arauca", *El Tiempo*, 8 September 2004. Available at: http://www.eltiempo.com/archivo/documento/MAM-1532348. Accessed on 15 February 2021.

Viana, M. T. Colombia's New Presidency: Peace as Business (as Usual). *e-IR*, 31 July 2018. Available at: https://www.e-ir.info/2018/07/31/new-presidency-in-colombia-peace-as-business-as-usual/. Accessed on 15 February 2021.

PART II

The Transnational Making of the Military Professional in Latin America

Introduction

Part I discussed how the discursive production of the "problem of violence" in Colombia has fueled renderings of a country at war, thereby authorizing the mobilization of the military in internal order. This persistent call of duty cannot be disassociated from the protagonism of the military in the pacification of Colombia and, consequently, from the "success story" with which the country currently circulates internationally. In this sense, while Part I digs into the historical articulation of the "problem of violence" that is claimed to have been overcome through the "success story", Part II explores the production of the military that came to be portrayed as the professional without which the "success" would not have been possible. Here, I am particularly interested in grasping how the formation of these professionals is related to the criteria upon which the use of violence is admitted in the Colombian society.

Such a topic has been widely explored by the literature in Colombia as a puzzle stemming from the "strange coexistence" of democracy and violence in that country. Indeed, during the second half of the twentieth century, Colombia was repeatedly noted as one of the most stable democracies in the region, in contrast to the concerted emergence of military regimes in South America (Atehortúa and Vélez 1994; Gómez-Suárez 2010: 152; Pizarro 1987a). According to Mainwaring *et al.* (2006: 8), "In 1976–1977, they [Venezuela and Colombia] were exceptional cases in the region; along with Costa Rica, they were two of three islands of democracy in a sea of authoritarianism".

This may be surprising, if we consider that the Thousand Days' War (1899–1902) and *La Violencia* (1948–1953) were still echoing in the country, after having resulted in 300,000–400,000 deaths (Bushnell 1993: 151, 205)—the first, a civil war led by the Conservative and Liberal Parties disputing the federative regime (centralist *vs.* federalist) to be implemented in the country; the second, a civil war unleashed by the assassination of Liberal presidential candidate Jorge Eliécer Gaitán. By the 1980s, the strengthening of drug cartels had led to corruption scandals involving the justice system during the *guerra sucia* (Orozco 1990) and presidential campaigns in the early 1990s, such as in the case of Ernesto Samper's (Gutkin 1994). Although the claim of an enduring democracy in Colombia continued to be repeated from the 1990s onwards, this could not be done without some degree of discomfort.[1] After all, the galloping levels of violence persisted in many forms throughout those years,[2] contributing to the consolidation of the image of a problematic country that irradiated insecurity to its population, the region and the world (García-Peña 2006; Tickner 2007).

---

[1] Created in 2012, with the objective of promoting the Colombian culture to its citizens and to the world, boosting exports, and stimulating tourism and investments in the country, "Brand Colombia" (*Marca País Colombia*, in Spanish) dedicates a specific section of its website to the democratic status of Colombia. Acknowledging the claim of the "most enduring democracy in Latin America" as "polemic", the section highlights three reasons why Colombia merits such a title: (i) the long period for which the country has had elections (since 1810); (ii) an uninterrupted electoral legacy since 1830; and (iii) the institutional stability, having had only one military government in the twentieth century, from 1953 to 1958. The discomfort mentioned above is reflected in the fact that the website invites visitors to compare those three elements found in Colombia with other countries in the region since the 1950s. But it is also reflected in the careful—and narrow—institutionalist approach towards "democracy", basically understood in terms of peaceful changes of government every four years, and with scarce occasions of military officers leading the Presidency. See: https://www.colombia.co/pais-colombia/historia/por-que-se-dice-que-colombia-tiene-la-democracia-mas-antigua-de-america-latina/. Accessed on 20 June 2021.

[2] In that period, violence had reached unprecedented levels in Colombia (Echandía 2006). As I argued in Section 2.1, the expression *violentología* ("violentology") emerged in the late 1980s to designate a profusion of analyses trying to make sense of the phenomenon of violence in the country. In the trajectory of *violentología*, no decade has been as violent as the 1990s, however.

The claim that Colombia is one of the most enduring democracies in Latin America was only possible through the argument that, since its independence, it witnessed military officers leading the Presidency for only seven years: the governments of Rafael Urdaneta (1830–1831) and José María Melo (1854) in the nineteenth century, and those of Gustavo Rojas Pinilla (1953–1957) and the Military Junta (1957–1958) in the twentieth century. This exceptional character was especially evoked from the 1960s to the 1980s, when most Latin American countries went through military regimes.

Nonetheless, the absence of military officers in the Colombian Presidency has coexisted with their pervasive participation in politics (Pizarro 1987b). In this sense, if Colombia was an "island of democracy in a sea of authoritarianism", the excessive presence of the military in the civil domain—either formally, such as a head of the Ministry of Defense, or informally, as a political force in the management of public order (Pizarro 1987b)—deserved attention. As such, the systematic breach of the civil-military divide in Colombia was turned into an object of investigation aimed at destabilizing its democratic status. Here, the institutionalist unease was invested towards the coexistence of democracy and violence, since the active participation of the military in internal ordering practices was considered to be intimately connected to the levels of violence in the country. After all, how is it possible that such a solid democracy came to historically coexist with pervasive violence?

Intrigued by this specific understanding of Colombia's exceptional character, a growing group of scholars in the 1980s started to advocate for more studies on the history of the military forces in the country. Some of these works have taken up this puzzle by examining how the professionalization of the Colombian military, especially of the Army, was linked to their persistent mobilization in party politics and public order (Pizarro 1987a, b, 1988; Atehortúa and Vélez 1994; Leal 2016). The concern with what they interpreted as a pervasive breach of the civil-military boundary stemmed from the historical production of the military as a technical and disciplined professional, whose expertise on war derived from a particular socialization inside the barracks (Atehortúa and Vélez 1994; Bushnell 1993; Pizarro 1987a, b, 1988; Rouquié 1984). In this sense, the problem with which such analysts grappled is presented as the contamination of the military with politics, which was both seen as an obstacle to their proper professionalization and the reason why more professionalization was necessary—that is, better military professionals remain in the barracks, developing their mastery of war and discipline.

La Violencia is often referenced in these works as a watershed regarding the professionalization of the military (Rouquié 1984; Pizarro 1987a, b, 1988; Atehortúa and Vélez 1994). For Atehortúa Cruz and Vélez Ramírez (1994: 23), the insurrection that followed the assassination of the political leader Jorge Eliécer Gaitán, in April 1948 (known as *Bogotazo*), marks the transition from a period of insulation to an active role of the military in the civil domain. Prior to the 1950s, the Military Forces oscillated as a priority in the political agenda according to the disputes between the Conservative and Liberal parties: whenever frictions exacerbated, the military were appropriated for particularistic purposes by the dominant party in that context (Atehortúa and Vélez 1994: 211–212). For Pizarro Leongómez (1987a), the halt in the disputes between Liberals and Conservatives was the very condition that made possible a consistent professionalization of the Colombian Military Forces. At the same time, this process coexisted with the persistent and increasing interference of the military in public security, especially after their role in the repression of *Bogotazo* (Pizarro 1987a, b). The pervasive presence of the military in internal ordering practices has had major implications on how "democracy" was realized in that country.

As we can see from the brief discussion on the studies devoted to understanding the "strange coexistence" of democracy and violence in Colombia, the military were justified as an object of investigation either because they left the barracks (politicization as a problem), and/or because war was mobilized in internal ordering practices (war in the making of public security as a problem). In addition, and similar to the problematizations of violence analyzed in Chapter 2, here also the irregularities identified in the role of the military in Colombia have been framed as a national idiosyncrasy. In other words, just as the "problem of violence", the "problem of the military" also came to be interpreted through methodological nationalism. Even when some of these studies look at the participation of Europe or the U.S. in the professionalization of the Colombian military, they are often restricted to how these external actors impacted the national container we came to call "Colombia". In doing so, they do not emphasize the transnational and epistemological edifice upon which military operations undertaken in Colombia's territory rely—that is, how they are expressions of *savoirs* that are transnationally valorized by military professionals.

To take such elements seriously, Part II unfolds into two boundaries that came to govern our imaginaries of the organization of the use of violence by the modern state: civil-military; and peace-war—all the while exploring the internal-external mirage revealed by the transnational circulation of military *savoirs*.

Taking the civil-military boundary as its center of gravity, Chapter 4 explores how the military professional is an expression of the discourse of modernization, particularly regarding the entanglement between pacification, civilization, and professionalization as conditions for progress to flourish. Based on this discussion, Chapter 4 excavates the emergence, by the late-nineteenth century, of a circuit of military *savoirs* in Latin America that had Europe—France and Prussia, most notably—as the main reference for the production of military professionals in the region. We then turn to how Colombia is inscribed in that circuit, allowing for us to grasp the effects of such a transnational circulation of military *savoirs* in that country. On the one hand, the analysis shows that the reification of the civil-military boundary advanced the professionalization of the military—or a "better" professionalization— as the solution for the "problem of the (politicization of the) military". On the other hand, I also expose how the very condition for professionalization programs to be undertaken in Colombia lay in the crossing of the civil-military boundary, as military foreign missions often bargained with civil elites for budget, regulation, and autonomy.

In turn, Chapter 5 sheds light on the peace-war boundary while walking through the rearticulation in the hemispheric circuit of military *savoirs* in the second half of the twentieth century. That particular period was marked by the emergence of counterinsurgency as the privileged *savoir* in the military epistemological edifice, as well as by the U.S. as the main reference for professionalization programs of the military in Latin America. Attentive to the elective affinities between counterinsurgency and social control practices, the analysis unfolds into a discussion on how these reconfigurations in the circuit affected the production of the military professional in Colombia. Two aspects are underlined in this regard. First, that a more systematic implementation of professionalization programs in the 1950s was simultaneous to the privileged position the military came to enjoy in internal ordering practices in Colombia, along with the police. Second, that the center of gravity for the production of military professionals slid from military schools to highly-specialized training centers in the second half of the twentieth century, allowing for not only a rapid multiplication of manpower, but of troops manned by expert-soldiers—especially after Plan Colombia.

Such analysis has relevant implications for our readings of the Colombian "success story". As an assumption governing the civil-military boundary, the need to push the military away from politics so as to preserve them as professionals of war leads to an unavoidable claim: that war does not belong to the domain of politics. Mirroring such a claim is the assumption of a pacified social space under the authority of the police: it is their work, not the military's, to control social deviances. Thus, the civil-military boundary determines not only the proper space for the military and the police, but also the proper space for war and control. The development of a "profession" for two different kinds of "men in arms"—the military and the police—implies the inscription of a specific *savoir* into the realm of the police, and of another specific *savoir* into the realm of the military. In doing so, the reification of the civil-military boundary does not allow us to grasp how military tactics have been key to the *savoirs* mobilized in the organization of the social body by the police (Foucault 1995: 168) and, therefore, how the knowledge of war making is constitutive of peace.

What I propose, then, is to look at the military as political actors inside the barracks, and to military schools and training centers as sites in which we can understand professionalization as articulated *within* society, not apart from it. After all, in the making of a "modern Colombia", the Military Forces were a central piece in the production of the ideal citizen, in the building of the infrastructure that would connect the territory as a national one, and in the production of *savoirs* on social order. Read as a whole, Part II invites the reader to think of war power as a rationality invested in ordering practices *across* three fundamental boundaries that came to operate as regulative ideals for the organization of violence by the state: inside-outside, civil-military, peace-war.

If Part II aims at showing that such boundaries do not exist, that does not mean that they are nothing. As the Colombian "success story" teaches us, the reification of such boundaries allows for promises of reconfigurations of the military and the police in accordance with this "new Colombia": a police force focused on citizen security, a military doctrine anchored in human security. As I expect to show in the next pages, nonetheless, these promises carry the layers of expertise that allowed for their offer as a solution to other countries. In this sense, they must be interpreted as new guises amid discursive continuities regarding the conditions upon which the use of state violence is admitted in the regulation of societies. As the transnational circuit reminds us, neither the problem, nor the solution are a Colombian idiosyncrasy.

REFERENCES

BOOKS, CHAPTERS, ARTICLES

Atehortúa C., A. L.; Vélez R., H. *Estado y Fuerzas Armadas en Colombia*. Cali: TM, 1994.
Bushnell, D. *The Making of Modern Colombia: A Nation in Spite Itself*. Berkeley (CA): University of California Press, 1993.
Echandía, C. *Dos Décadas de Escalamiento del Conflicto Armado Colombiano*. Bogotá: Universidad Externado de Colombia, 2006.
Foucault, M. *Discipline and Punish*. New York: Second Vintage, 1995.
García-Peña, R. P. Un país problema en un mundo intervencionista. In: Leal B., F. (ed.). *En la encrucijada: Colombia en el siglo XXI*. Bogotá, DC: Norma, 2006.
Gómez-Suárez, A. US-Colombian Relations in the 1980s: Political Violence and the Onset of the Unión Patriótica Genocide. In: Esparza, M.; Huttenbach, H. R.; Feierstein, D. (eds.). *State Violence and Genocide in Latin America. The Cold War Years*. New York and London: Routledge, 2010.
Leal B., F. *Estudios sobre el estado y la política en Colombia* (Tomo II). La contribución de Francisco Leal Buitrago. Bogotá: Universidad de los Andes, 2016.
Mainwaring, S.; Bejarano, A. M.; Pizarro L., E. An Overview. In: Mainwaring, S.; Bejarano, A. M.; Pizarro L., E. (eds.). *The Crisis of Democratic Representation in the Andes*. Stanford: Stanford University, 2006.
Orozco A., I. Los diálogos con el narcotráfico: historia de la transformación fallida de un delincuente común en un delincuente político. *Análisis Político*, n. 11, n.p., 1990.
Pizarro L., E. La Profesionalización Militar en Colombia (1907-1944). *Análisis Político*, n. 1, pp. 20-39, 1987a.
Pizarro L., E. La Profesionalización Militar en Colombia (II): El Periodo de La Violencia. *Análisis Político*, n. 2, pp. 7-29, 1987b.
Pizarro L., E. La profesionalización militar en Colombia (III): los regímenes militares (1953-1958). *Análisis Político*, n. 3, pp. 6-30, 1988.
Rouquié, A. *El Estado Militar en América Latina*. Buenos Aires: Emecé, 1984.
Tickner, A. B. Intervención por invitación: claves para la política exterior colombiana y sus debilidades principales. *Colombia Internacional*, n. 65, pp. 90-111, 2007.

Press Articles

Gutkin, S. "DEA Agent attackes Colombia as 'narco-democracy'", *Washington Post*, 1st October 1994. Available at: https://www.washingtonpost.com/archive/politics/1994/10/01/dea-agent-attacks-colombia-as-narco-democracy/410189e6-0878-48b9-925a-127ce47148f1/. Accessed on 20 June 2021.

CHAPTER 4

"Technical, not Political": The Military Professional as the Citizen-Soldier

If the discussion opening Part Two underlined how professionalization is key to the organization of violence running through the claim of a "modern Colombia", this chapter aims at understanding what is at stake in the claim for the need to professionalize the military forces and what are the effects of such a claim. The chapter is organized in three main analytical moves. Section 4.1 digs into the discourse of modernization by engaging with Elias' *The Civilizing Process* (2000) and Weber's *Politics as a Vocation* (2004). Read as expressions of the discourse of modernization, these works reveal how civilization and professionalization are both a condition and an effect of the pacification of the social space. In other words, these texts expose how central the organization of violence is in the discourse of modernization.

The final part of Sect. 4.1 mobilizes Sarmiento's Facundo (2018) as a canonic expression of how the discourse of modernization has been reproduced in Latin America. Examining Sarmiento's account of *caudillismo* and the problem it posed to the monopolization of violence and civilization in the Argentinian nation allows us to capture two aspects of central importance. First, that the *caudillo* came to be understood as a problem not only because of the pulverization of violence it represented, but also because his refusal to subject to civil authority was read in terms of its rural—"hence", uncivilized—origins. This incivility was at the core of the image of an uncontrolled violence that came to be attached to the *caudillo,* thereby providing the cement for the regime of justification that came to govern attempts to tame the military as an imperative for the modernization of states in Latin America. Second, the discourse expressed by Sarmiento's Facundo (2018) reinforces the framing of Europe as a regulative ideal of modernity, with concrete effects in Latin American countries.

Sections 4.2 and 4.3 explore some of the main effects of such a discursive position of Europe. We start with a discussion on how solutions articulated to the "problem of the military" came to be translated into professionalization programs in 19th-century Latin America. Here, I am especially interested in exposing the recurrence with which the boundary separating what is "civil" from what is "military", and what is "technical" from what is "political" appeared as an inescapable feature of modern nations. In this context, I show that Latin American governments turned to Europe as the reference for what a military professional had to be: subjected to civil authority, disciplined in the barracks and in times of war, and regular in his professional character. The analysis in Sect. 4.2 unfolds into the military circuit that emerges in Latin America during the second half of the nineteenth century, with the intense transit of European missions—most notably, French and Prussian—and the implementation of professionalization programs across the region.

While Sect. 4.2 analyzes the homogenizing effects of the reproduction of the discourse of modernization in Latin America, Sect. 4.3 observes how Colombia is inscribed in the circuit of military *savoirs.* To be clear, I look at the professionalization programs articulated by the Chilean missions, hired by the Colombian government in the first years of the twentieth century, as the most affordable "messenger" of the Prussian Army in South America. Here, I am mostly attentive to the negotiations that took place across the political-technical and civil-military boundaries as a condition for the preservation of the technical ("i.e." apolitical) and military character of the Chilean mission and its professionalization programs. In doing so, I expect to provide elements for us to see, through the limits of the work of the Chilean mission, the limits of the discourse of modernization.

4.1 Organizing Violence: The Regulative Ideal of Modernization and the Civil-Military Divide

In this section, I turn to the intricate relation between peace and violence in the discourse of modernization and argue that the fabrication of a "pacified social space" implies the organization of violence, rather than its extinction, within such a discourse. To be sure, I look at how the professionalization of the armed forces is claimed as both a condition for modernization and an effect of pacification. I am aware of the diversity of discourses of modernization across different social groups, as well as across distinct historical and geographical contexts. Nonetheless, here I am more interested in how its constitutive pillars are played in dominant expressions of the discourse of modernization both in Colombia and in Latin America, most notably in the 1850s.

Indeed, it is during this period that we can observe the emergence of a military circuit in the region, whose discursive engine is found in the reproduction of Europe as a reference for what history "had to be" for those recently-independent Latin American states. As I argue further in this section, the resonance of such discourse throughout Latin America was the condition for the circulation of *savoirs* on how to deepen the professionalization of the public force,[1] allowing for a certain homogenization of their regulations, schools, formations, and functions among Latin American countries.

To develop this argument, I explore the conditions under which modernization is understood to be possible regarding the organization of violence, by looking at how pacification, civilization, and professionalization are played in such discourse. As we will see, no modernization is conceived without the organization of violence, which, by its turn, assumes the monopolization of violence as an imperative for the claim

---

[1] The professionalization of the police is also a fundamental aspect of the organization of violence in the modern state. As we will see further in this chapter, if the production of the military professional came to articulate a specialized function (war making) and space (outside the state boundaries), the police professional came to be associated with law and order inside the state. However, since the nineteenth century, there are several cases of police professionals taking part in the circuit of military *savoirs* in Latin America. Such juxtaposition invites us to consider an underlying logic shared by these professionals—a discussion I begin to explore elsewhere (see Viana and Peixoto 2019). On the professionalization of the police in Colombia, see Castaño Castillo (1947) (one of the first works about the history of the Colombian National Police); Llórente (1999) and Ruiz V. et al. (2006).

of a pacified social space, the crystallization of socially accepted conducts in that space, and the legitimation of professionals in charge of handling the use of violence under specific conditions and rules.

It is on these grounds that I turn to the close reading of Elias' *The Civilizing Process* (2000) and Weber's *Politics as a Vocation* (2004) as canonic texts expressing a dominant discourse of modernization[2] While Elias (2000) explores how the diffusion of norms of social conduct is related to the organization of violence in "pacified social spaces", Weber (2004) focuses on the rationalization constituting the consolidation of the modern state, allowing us to grasp how it relates to the professionalization of the public force. In more general terms, my objective is to provide elements for us to think about the terms anchoring claims on the need to separate war from peace, as well as what is civil from what is military, and what is technical from what is political in such discourse.

That I am not mobilizing these texts as sources of historical sociology does not mean that we must ignore the fact that these two works are centered on Europe. On the contrary: by giving central importance to the organization of violence, the discourse expressed by these texts produces "Europe" not as an empty spatial category, but as a political entity representing a regulative ideal for historical processes. As an illustration, Elias' analysis about the civilizing process in the French court society does operate towards an analytical framework of what he calls a "sociogenesis" of the modern state in Europe (Elias 2000: 257–362). At the same time, it pays tribute to a political imagination of Europe as a historical ideal, towards which other historical processes must converge. It is through these lines that we must read his interpretation of Peru and Saudi Arabia, for instance: claimed as difference because having Europe as a reference, their contrasting social structure is described as "nearer to that of Western medieval society than that of the West today" (Elias 2000: 391)—that is, their difference can only be interpreted as "Europe's past". By mobilizing Elias (2000) and Weber (2004) as discourse, I am interested in what conditions are defined as indispensable for modernization to take place, and the political strength of such discourse exposes what

---

[2] This implies that I will not address aspects which are of fundamental importance if one is reading them as sources of historical sociology about the formation of the modern state, as is the case of Elias' concept of "sociogenesis" (Elias 2000: 257–362) or Weber's account of the historical processes that led to the rationalization characterizing the ideal type of the modern state's bureaucratic apparatus (Weber 2004: 34).

practices are authorized in the name of the imperative to be where one must be: in "Europe".

With that in mind, the idea of a "pacified social space" in Elia's work (2000: 373) is a good starting point, for it is a fundamental condition triggering a chain of discursive articulations about how violence must be organized in the modern state. According to the author, the consolidation of "pacified social spaces" resulting from the monopolization of violence in sixteenth-eighteenth century Europe (Elias 2000: 276) is marked by the erasure of abrupt oscillations of emotions and actions from the social landscape[3] (Elias 2000: 372).

Several historical processes account for the stability that comes to characterize social life in Europe, he argues. The scarcity of wars during that period creates the conditions for durable institutions to be built and ideas of socially accepted conducts to become crystallized. At the same time, the immersion of individuals in increasingly populated and interdependent societies stimulates the specialization of functions and the control over their social conducts. Furthermore, it gives impulse to the formation of "an automatic, blindly functioning apparatus of self-control" (Elias 2000: 367–368). It is in this sense that Elias claims that the battlefield has moved within: "Part of the tensions and passions that were earlier directly released in the struggle of man and man, must now be worked out within the human being" (Elias 2000: 375). According to him, the joint effect of durable institutions and the self-constraint molding individuals' behavior is the harmonization of social conducts towards their gradual predictability. In times marked by the imperative to strengthen trade as the means to strengthen the state (Elias 2000: 372–395; Foucault 2007: 314–315), keeping social conducts within a moderated range of expectations makes easier the task of governments to optimize the circulation of goods and persons—the sociogenesis of the modern state cannot be dissociated from this rationality, argues Elias. In his own words, "fluctuations in behaviour and affects do not disappear, but are moderated" (Elias 2000: 372).

---

[3] Here, Elias is referring mainly to the medium and upper social strata. According to him, "the lower strata, the oppressed and the poorer outsider groups at a given stage of development, tend to follow their drives and affects more directly and spontaneously, that their conduct is less strictly regulated than that of the respective upper strata" (Elias 2000: 382).

The monopolization of violence and the pacification of the social space claimed through this discourse are, therefore, more than two sides of the same coin. They set the bases for the organization of modern social life, creating the conditions for durable institutions, regulated social conduct, and self-constraint to be possible. All these processes imply the absence of violence as a mechanism regulating social relations, just as they require that oscillations in social conduct operate towards a middle line. Here, we see an important line being drawn: the one differentiating deviant from normal social conduct, which is also key in the organization of violence, as we will see further in this section.

What Elias calls the "civilizing process" does circumscribe the diffusion of norms of conduct and the self-constraint of individuals. There is, however, an additional fundamental element constituting Elias' understanding of the civilizing process: the continuous social differentiation through the polishing of conducts (Elias 2000: 424). The author contends that the nobles who used to derive their social status from the use of violence gradually lost their privileged position in the organization of society. As violence was no longer as frequent and necessary in pacified social spaces, the noble's main source of monetary gain had waned (Elias 2000: 393). Also, in this emerging historical context, customs and traditions (such as land titles as the prize for their participation in wars) had lost strength to capital accumulation as a parameter of social prestige (Elias 2000: 394–395). Nobles had a social function but no occupation (Elias 2000: 388), in profound contrast to the bourgeoisie, which was "less free to elaborate their conduct and taste; they have professions. Nevertheless, it is at first their ideal, too, to live like the aristocracy exclusively on annuities and to gain admittance to the court circle" (Elias 2000: 424).

The king himself had lost strength to the bourgeoisie in this context. Despite its lack of economic relevance, the court had a critical political use for the king[4] (Elias 2000: 396): preserving the position of the court in

---

[4] According to Elias, the central ruler is key in upholding the tense balance of society in a context still marked by monopolies with a private and personal character (Elias 2000: 388). This is why he refers to "royal mechanism" (Elias 2000: 396) to describe the expansion of the rules of *civilité* from the court to other social strata, as well as the differentiation of courtly manners from those of the bourgeoisie. For him, these were continuous processes that simultaneously assured the preservation of the nobility as a counterweight to the bourgeoisie, and stimulated the tensions between nobility and bourgeoisie, "to allow neither estate to grow too strong or too weak" (Elias 2000: 396).

this society meant counterbalancing the bourgeoisie and all that its ascension would mean to customs and traditions as the condition for kings, nobles, and knights to hold themselves in the upper social strata. Elias suggests that:

> It is the necessity to distinguish themselves from anything bourgeois that sharpens this sensitivity; and the particular structure of court life – under which it is not professional competence or even the possession of money, but polished social conduct, that is the main instrument in the competition for prestige and favour – provides the opportunity for the sharpening of taste. (Elias 2000: 422)

Read together, these processes have both led to the incorporation of knights as dependents on the king in the court—what Elias refers to as the "courtization" of the warriors (2000: 387–397)—, but also to another feature of the civilizing process: the continuous refinement of habits of the court, social conventions on gestures, speech, on how to behave at the table, how to dress etc. The constant update of rules of etiquette operated as a permanent mechanism of differentiation between the court society and the bourgeoisie: irrespective of the monetary power of a bourgeois, there was always something he could not reach so as to be recognized as part of the upper social strata.

In this sense, the civilizing process analyzed by Elias is, at once, the unceasing refinement of human conducts within the court as a mechanism of social differentiation; the continuous transformation of social conducts as an effect of the consolidation of durable institutions; and the harmonization of social conducts towards a middle line allowed for the optimized circulation of persons and goods in the pacified social space. Constituted by the assimilation of socially accepted behaviors and by the repulsion of this approximation through the refinement of manners, the civilizing process walked "hand in hand with an increase in the social power of that class [the bourgeoisie], and a raising of its standard of living to that of the class above it, or at least in that direction" (Elias 2000: 429). This attraction-repulsion movement was a condition for social order to be kept: indeed, the social control produced through the civilizing process is key to the optimal circulation of goods in those urban, pacified spaces, and the accumulation of capital resulting from that trade feeds the government structure through taxes and charges. The civilizing process is, therefore, a dynamic through which power relations were organized

(Elias 2000: 431), a central instrument to social ordering and a condition that made the government of the pacified social space not only possible, but also strong.

Now, if the discourse of modernization expressed by Elias' analysis places the pacification of the social space as the ignition of the civilizing process, his account of the latter transpires the rationality of social ordering practices in the modern state. On one hand, the criteria that produces the line differentiating deviant and normal social conducts are guided by the concern for increasing the productivity of society (Foucault 1995, 2007; Malaguti 2011). This suggests that the durable institutions, the regulation of social conducts and the naturalization of self-constraint made possible by the pacification of the social space all operate within this rationality—that is, they are governed by expectations towards historical processes that are tied to a logic of accumulation. On the other hand, power relations are not only mediated by monetary power: lineage, tradition and customs also take a fundamental part in this social dynamic. Here, the eurocentric character of this dominant discourse of modernization produces an imaginary of "Europe" as a political entity circumscribing these two sources of social prestige: monetary accumulation and polished manners. As we will see, that Latin American societies took "Europe" as a reference for their modernization processes gained discursive traction irrespective of their considerably different historical conditions for the formation of both a bourgeoisie and a court society, among other aspects. At the same time, these contrasting historical trajectories reminded Latin American highest social strata that even their monetary power could not provide them the social prestige to be recognized as part of "Europe".

There is yet another dimension of the civilizing process that is of fundamental importance to our discussion about how the organization of violence is understood in the discourse of modernization. Particularly, I am interested in the claim of a transition from war to control. In order to explore what is at stake in this process, I suggest that we take a closer look at the "courtization of the warriors" (Elias 2000: 387–397). As we have seen, war making was central to the formation of increasingly complex human agglomerations and to the pacification of the social space. But what happens to war makers once the monopolization of the use of physical violence is found in an advanced stage?

According to Elias, as the control over the instruments of physical violence is centralized and the functional interdependence of the nobility and the bourgeoisie grows, physical violence is no more a central mechanism regulating social relations (Elias 2000: 423). Through courtization,[5] the warrior nobility is gradually replaced "by a tamed nobility with more muted affects" (Elias 2000: 389). Violence within the pacified social space is thereby tamed by an internalized self-control (both conscious and unconscious), by rules of socially accepted behavior and by other control mechanisms of the state apparatus.

In the discourse expressed through Elias' analysis, the civilizing process is a key instrument in dealing with internal conflict. On one hand, *civilité* marked the differentiation of the behavior, refinement, and social manners of the court from the conducts of the lower social strata. On the other hand, the civilizing process also circumscribed the whole range of processes operating towards the harmonization of behaviors towards the middle line. For social order to be possible, it could not rely solely on the repulsion dynamic involving the court and the bourgeoisie, nor on the self-constraint of individuals: the state apparatus had to actively mold conducts in the pacified social space.

Revolving archives about the historical use of the term "civilization", Lucien Febvre argues that the word "civilization" was used interchangeably with "police" until the mid-eighteenth century (*Apud* Neocleous 2014: 128–131). Indeed, the diffusion of ideas of socially accepted behavior is set as the condition for government to be possible, as well as its effect. That said, the connection between civilization and policing is found on the assumption that there are always people whose conduct, manners and language had to be polished for society to be ordered—"well-policed" (Neocleous 2014: 133). There lay the work of the police: the fabrication of order in the pacified social space through the enforcement of laws crystallizing understandings of conducts deviating from the norm. In this discourse of modernization, the claim that the monopolization of violence produces peace inside the social space implies that the police must not use violence. Here, we find an important line differentiating peace and war, drawn right in the boundary between the inside and the outside of the pacified social space.

What does it change in the terms of this discursive regime with the rise of the bourgeoisie as the ruling class in Europe? According to Elias,

---

[5] Elias understands "court" as the home of a large number of people and whose ruler achieved a position of predominance over other warriors in battles, allowing for him to concentrate a greater share of lands and military power (Elias 2000: 389).

the monopolization of the means of violence, the deepening of functional specialization within societies, the monetization of social relations (as tradition is downplayed as a parameter of prestige), the diminishing contrasts between social strata, and the internalization of norms of socially accepted behavior created the conditions for the bourgeoisie to emerge as the privileged social strata by the eighteenth century, and for absolutist-courts to gradually disappear from the political landscape in Europe by the nineteenth century.[6] The spread of civilized conducts in this context still operates according to the movements of assimilation-repulsion that had characterized the previous period (Elias 2000: 428, 430), but with a different logic. "[F]rom now on profession and money are the primary sources of prestige, and the art, the refinement of social conduct ceases to have the decisive importance for the reputation and success of the individual that it had in court society",[7] argues Elias (2000: 425). The functional specializations are now reflected in an increasingly professional compartmentalization within society—domains in which the wealth accumulated by individuals resulting from their work defines their social status, not hereditary or other customary criteria.

In this social context, the courtiers have to work in order to make a living, and the monopolization of the physical force is not anymore personalized, that is, attached to the person of the king: it is now considered as a profession within the bureaucratic apparatus of the state. These transformations analyzed by Elias reveal not only the taming of violence through the pacification of social spaces and the courtization of the warriors: they also indicate the conditions under which legitimate violence is organized as a profession whose political character derives from its connection to the modern state. In other words, no other kind of political violence is allowed within that durably pacified social space.

---

[6] In this sense, Elias did not conceive the French Revolution as a rupture with the Ancient Regime: the conditions for this bourgeois "revolution" were already under a maturation process, which, though not historically predetermined, pointed to a historical direction. As the author argues when referring to the general problem of historical change, "nothing in history indicates that this change [represented by the civilizing process] was brought about 'rationally', through any purposive education of individual people or groups. It happened by and large unplanned; but it did not happen, nevertheless, without a specific type of order" (Elias 2000: 365).

[7] In this process, expressions of good taste, etiquette or courtly-like rituals are relegated to the sphere of private life, argues Elias (2000: 426).

It is not hard to recognize Weber's classic definition of the modern state through these lines: "a state is a human community that (successfully) claims the *monopoly of the legitimate use of physical force* within a given territory" (2004: 33, emphases in the original). In other words, it is not only the use of physical force, but the monopoly of its legitimate use that defines the modern state in Weber's terms. In his understanding, the monopolization of the means of violence is the condition for the consolidation of a whole bureaucracy erected in response to the technical needs of the public administration (Weber 2004: 46). As in Elias, the pacified social space is key for Weber, for the rationalization characterizing the organization of domination in the modern state is only possible in the context of the monopolization of the means of violence. In this pacified space, "force is certainly not the normal or the only means of the state (...) but force is a means specific to the state" (Weber 2004: 33). In this sense, Weber's analysis echoes not only some of the main categories mobilized by Elias, but also the relations Elias draws between them.

As we have seen, one of the aspects emphasized by both authors is the organization of violence constituting the formation of the modern state. Weber underlines a fundamental implication of this process: that legitimacy is locked-in in the use of political force by the modern state. Weber contends that "the right to use physical force is ascribed to other institutions or to individuals only to the extent to which the state permits it. The state is considered the sole source of the 'right' to use violence" (Weber 2004: 33). The monopolization over the means of violence in the modern state is, therefore, also the monopolization of political violence: in other words, as the modern state monopolizes the use of violence, political violence is founded.

Under these terms, the use of violence by institutions or individuals other than the state—or other than those authorized by the state—is not only outside his understanding of political violence, but also illegitimate. Importantly, Weber's account reinforces the claim that without the monopoly of legitimate violence, there cannot be rationalization and bureaucratization in the modern state. In this sense, the joint reading of Elias and Weber creates a discursive framework that authorizes the mobilization of violence against breaches in the monopolization of political violence. Pacification thereby operates as a regulative ideal in this discursive articulation: it is through pacification that the legitimate monopolization of violence is re-instantiated; and only in a pacified social space there is room for the state to function.[8]

Weber's formulation expresses a circularity that is constitutive to the discourse of modernization. As formulated by Bartelson in his analysis about political authority and the use of force/right to war in the Western discourse, "[s]overeign states have the right to defend themselves and their citizens with violent means against internal as well as external enemies, yet the very source of this legitimacy is nothing but the ability to do so successfully" (Bartelson 2010: 86). For Bartelson, it is in fact this "double-bind" that "makes contemporary efforts to relocate legitimate authority to agents other than the states difficult" (2010: 83). In this discourse, pacification is always understood as legitimate.

There is yet an additional aspect regarding the organization of violence which is extremely relevant for us to understand how professionalization is related to the discourse of modernization. As we have seen in Elias, the courtization of the warrior has constituted a process towards the taming of violence: as members of the court, these former warrior nobles were tied to the king. The state's wealth and lands were still considered as properties of the king—he who personified the state—and the bureaucratization of the modern state in Weberian terms was not found on an advanced stage by then. As the absolutist regimes gradually faded away in Europe throughout the mid-nineteenth century, tradition decreased in importance as a reference for social prestige, as work—and money accumulated through it—and knowledge emerged as the main parameters according to which social prestige would be assessed.

The state apparatus was not immune to these social transformations. More than that: it was also their catalyzer. According to Weber (2004), bureaucratization was one of the most important processes in the consolidation of the modern state. The creation of specialized and technical institutions in what we have come to associate with the "public domain" dates back to the fifteenth century, when the financial tasks of the prince were placed under the responsibility of a specialized administrator. Later, jurists were also incorporated to the state apparatus as the protection

---

[8] Take, for instance, the following passage in Elias (2000: 428–429): "Classes living permanently in danger of starving to death or of being killed by enemies can hardly develop or maintain those stable restraints characteristic of the more civilized types of conduct. To instill and maintain a more stable super-ego agency, a relatively high standard of living and a fairly high degree of security are necessary".

of private property became a key function of the state. As both Elias and Weber claim, the monopolization of the use of violence is also immersed in this more comprehensive process of institutional capillarization of the modern state. Functions increasingly seen as indispensable for the preservation and strengthening of the state apparatus are thereby gradually detached from a familial or personal logic of control. Instead, politics is taken over by the de-personalized vocabulary of "administration". For Weber, one of the main implications of the bureaucratization of the modern state is the complete separation between ownership and administration. In his words:

> No single official personally owns the money he pays out, or the buildings, stores, tools, and war machines he controls. In the contemporary "state" (…) the "separation" of the administrative staff, of the administrative officials, and of the workers from the material means of administrative organization is completed. (Weber 2004: 38)

The de-personalization of the state—which also defines the boundary between public and private[9]—marks the transition from Weber's "charismatic authority" to the "legal" one (Weber 2004: 34). The "Political Man" of the modern state emerges as the administrator of a bureaucratic apparatus whose resources he does not possess and whose legitimacy derives from an authority anchored in the "belief in the validity of the legal statute and functional 'competence' based on rationally created rules" (Weber 2004: 34). For Weber, the emergence of such an "ideal type"[10] of political authority resulted from long-term transformations in the relations of social groups and in the material conditions negotiated through the tensions amongst such groups.

---

[9] A very similar argument is advanced by Elias, for whom the absence of any distinction between the expenses of the prince or the king and those related to the administration of the realm (Elias 2000: 272) faded away throughout the eighteenth and nineteenth centuries. By that time, a gradual separation between the administrative staff from the material means of the public administration took place.

[10] Weber is aware that these categories are not found in their homogeneous and coherent forms in reality. In his own words, "These conceptions of legitimacy and their inner justifications are of very great significance for the structure of domination. To be sure, the pure types are rarely found in reality. But today we cannot deal with the highly complex variant, transitions, and combinations of these pure types, which problems belong to 'political science'" (Weber 2004: 34).

Both Elias and Weber do not see these processes as linear ones: the steps constituting the rationalization and the expansion of the bureaucratic web of the state apparatus were taken in the context of specific practical challenges.[11] According to Weber, by the nineteenth century, the appointment of persons to positions in the state bureaucracy was made in accordance with one's mastery of a specific domain of knowledge considered as necessary to the administration of the state. Importantly, the rationalization of politics as an organization which required training in the struggle for power led to

> the separation of public functionaries into two categories, which, however, are by no means rigidly but nevertheless distinctly separated. These categories are "administrative" officials on the one hand, and "political" officials on the other. The "political" officials, in the genuine sense of the word, can regularly and externally be recognized by the fact that they can be transferred any time at will, that they can be dismissed, or at least temporarily withdrawn. (...) Even under the old regime, one could be the Prussian minister of education without ever having attended an institution of higher learning; whereas one could become *Vortragender Rat* [Advisor to the Emperor], in principle, only on the basis of a prescribed examination. The specialist and trained (...) *Vortragender Rat* were of course infinitely better informed about the real technical problems of the division than was their respective chief (...). Consequently, in all routine demands the divisional head was more powerful than the minister, which was not without reason. (Weber 2004: 52)

Although "faceless", these highly specialized bureaucrats provide and systematize the information upon which the creation of (rational) rules relies. Bureaucracy is, thus, the condition for the modern "Political Man"

---

[11] According to both Elias and Weber, it was facing practical problems that princes have delegated key functions to technical administrators—processes which have triggered a centuries-long and increasing rationalization of the state apparatus. Many of these "practical solutions", however, were not taken as definite solutions in a first moment: even taxes, found at the heart of the extractive function of the modern state, were created and dissolved on an ad hoc basis before made regular (Elias 2000: 353–354). The *Chambre des Aides*, for instance, was recurrently established and then dismantled in France during the fourteenth and fifteenth centuries, until it was turned into a regular branch of the state apparatus (Elias 2000: 354). For Elias, these fluctuations "make it clear how little all these functions and formations resulted from the long-term, conscious plans of individuals, and how much they arose by small, tentative steps from a multitude of intertwining and conflicting human efforts and activities" (Elias 2000: 354).

to emerge, for the management of public affairs and the "technical functions of the state apparatus would be endangered" without them, argues Weber (2004: 48). This differentiation between political and administrative officials within the state apparatus is key for our discussion about the professionalization of the military as a central process in the organization of violence in the discourse of modernization.

As other branches of the administrative bureaucracy, the military must serve the political officials leading the management of public affairs. Here, we find a fundamental imperative underlying the discourse of modernization and its differentiation between the civil and the military domains. The distinctive element of the professional of violence within the state apparatus is not the passion invested in combat, but the knowledge on war doctrine and strategy, as well as the fighting skills developed through disciplined training. It is within this context that we must interpret the building of military schools by the end of the eighteenth century and mid-nineteenth century.[12]

The connection drawn by Elias and Weber between the monopolization of political violence and the bureaucratization of the state apparatus reveals two aspects that are relevant for our analytical purposes. First, it creates the condition for the claim that the taming of violence in the modern state requires the professionalization of the military. If monopolization and bureaucratization are mutually reinforcing processes, there can be no professionalization in a space that has not been pacified. Under these terms, the modern organization of violence confines the military in specialized schools so that they can prepare for war while in times of peace. Second, to claim the existence of a pacified social space implies the primacy of civilized conducts over "warlike actions" (Elias 2000: 161) therein. This means that, for progress to flourish, the use of violence cannot be the mechanism through which social coexistences are regulated. According to Elias,

---

[12] The creation of the Prussian War Academy is an emblematic expression of this discourse of military professionalization. Founded in 1653 as a cavalry school and dismantled shortly thereafter, it was inaugurated as the Prussian War Academy in 1765 with an expanded curriculum, comprehending areas such as History, Geography, Philosophy, Geometry, Rhetoric, Grammar, French, Dance and Equitation. As others of the kind throughout Europe, this military academy was dissolved a few years later. In the context of the Prussian military reform, by the early-nineteenth century, the Military Academy was once more established as the main school in charge of the military professionalization in Prussia.

opportunities that previously had to be won by individuals through military or economic force, could now become amenable to planning. From a certain point of development on, the struggle for monopolies no longer aims at their destruction; it is a struggle for control of their yields, for the plan according to which their burdens and benefits are to be divided up, in a word, for the keys of distribution. (Elias 2000: 275)

In this sense, the discourse of modernization of which Elias and Weber are expressions is based on the claim that violence is not extinguished, but organized in the context of the primacy of civilization. The pacified social space is the civil space, whose authority corresponds to the domain of politics—not the domain of warfare. Amid the decreasing relative importance of the pursuit of the monopolization of the means of violence (Elias 2000: 275), the "Political Man" emerging from these social transformations is the administrator of the terms and material conditions under negotiation for the distribution of the yields resulting from the web of interdependent and productive functions of this society. As we have seen with Weber, however, the domain of politics is constituted by both the political and the administrative officials. If, on one hand, the professionalization of the military is placed in the latter, as one bureaucratic branch among others in the state apparatus, on the other hand, its position within this bureaucracy is a very specific one though.

As Weber insists, the specific means peculiar to the modern state is the use of political force (2004: 33). Ultimately, it is the possibility of the use of physical violence—and not its recurrent use—that constitutes the sociological specificity of the modern state, according to Weber (2004). As we have discussed, the formation of the modern state cannot be dissociated from the monopolization of political violence. But, through Weber, this must be read as a claim that every violent attempt competing with the state is considered illegitimate. Following this logic, the political content of military violence derives exclusively from its linkage with the modern state bureaucracy. As such, this violence must also follow the imperative of the primacy of civilized over warlike actions (Elias 2000: 161). This implies, firstly, that these wielders of political violence are subjected to the domain of politics; and secondly, that both the professionals of war and the political officials are expected to fulfill their respective functions, in their own domains, under the precepts of what "civilized conduct" was understood to be—each in their own professional domain, nonetheless.

It is in this sense that the professionalization of the military is taken as a central process in the taming of violence. The once-upon-a-time-knight-turned-courtier, now called the military, is part of the bureaucratic apparatus: he is a professional specialized in warfare, whose authority derives from the technical knowledge resulting from his training in and for war. Moved by this discourse are all the military schools conceived as the sites where professional soldiers and commanders are taught the rules on the use of violence. The mobilization of the military inside the pacified social space, so the discourse goes, must be exceptional and determined by political officials—who are, by their turn, trained in the struggle for power (Weber 2004: 52). In other words, despite the privileged position of the professionals of violence in the bureaucratic apparatus of the modern state, they are subjected to the professionals of politics—those occupying the civil offices in the state apparatus.

On the other hand, it is precisely the privileged position of the military in the state bureaucracy—that which is peculiar to the modern state—that creates the condition for the authorization, in specific moments in history, of discourses (not exclusively vocalized by the military officialdom) on the need for the military to take a leading role in politics. Indeed, the "courtization of the warrior" and the professionalization of the military must not be read as processes operating towards the extinction of violence: rather, they both re-articulate, in different ways, the terms under which violence is to be used inside the pacified social space.

Although the works by Elias (2000) and Weber (2004) are based on the formation of the modern state in Europe, they are expressions of a dominant discourse of modernization whose terms have been widely reproduced in post-independence Latin America. As we will see on Sects. 4.2 and 4.3, the professionalization of the military in the region and in Colombia, respectively, were anchored in the separation between civil and military, and technical and political. It is precisely in this regard that the relevance of mobilizing Weber and Elias resides: their works express the terms under which the "European history" has been taken as a norm, according to which the trajectory of Latin American countries has been assessed and adjusted. It is, therefore, within the terms with which this discourse has been reproduced in Latin America that deviations from the European parameter came to be interpreted as historical pathologies that had to be corrected.

Particularly interesting is how the reproduction of the discourse of modernization offered the conditions for the emergence of military professionalization programs and for the consolidation of a circuit of professionals of violence which had Europe as its regulative ideal. As wars have gradually resulted in the formal independence of different states in Latin America, the pursuit of the "promises of modernization" was endorsed by the expectation that these newly independent countries would be considered as equals to European states in international politics if they reproduced a certain story of progress. Indeed, the narratives emerging in the nineteenth century around the nation in Latin America revealed a vision of modernity which was profoundly dependent on the "European optics" (Pamplona 1997, 1998: 32), making the renderings apart from this grid of intelligibility as unthinkable. In this sense, the discursive elements expressed by the works of Elias (2000) and Weber (2004) echoed in the efforts that aimed at purging anything resembling a "relic of colonialism incompatible with notions of republican equality before law" (Bushnell 1993: 85). Likewise, the repulse of social deposits considered as inheritances from colonialism and the praise of liberal values as the pillars for these "new" societies have impregnated the narratives of modernization regarding how violence was to be organized in these states emerging from the independence wars (Rouquié 1984; Bushnell 1993; Loveman 1999).

Thus, if we have walked through Elias (2000) and Weber (2004) so as to grasp how they express a dominant discourse of modernization, we now turn to an expression of how such a discourse came to be appropriated in 19th-century Latin America: Sarmiento's *Facundo*.[13] Published in 1845 and originally titled *Civilización y Barbárie* ("Civilization and

---

[13] Elias' account of the civilizing process is attentive to colonization, explicitly drawing a parallel between the European nations and their colonies, on one side, and the upper- and lower-classes, on the other (Elias 2000: 385–386). Nonetheless, despite his efforts to incorporate the colonies into his analysis, Elias' historical sociology remains remarkably Eurocentric in denying the social dynamics in the colonies a constructive role in the affect-control structure of the metropole. Read as a historical claim, this has been contested by those critically thinking how the colonial alterity was and still is a constitutive element of the production of European modernity (see, for instance: Kapoor 2003; Inayatullah and Blaney 2004; Fernández and Esteves 2017). However, read as part of a discourse, the location of modernity in Europe can be seen as constructing a regulative ideal whose reproduction in Latin American discourses is not so much something to be negated as something whose concrete effects must be specified. It is in this spirit that, having read Elias and Weber as referential works expressing the discourse of modernization, I turn to Sarmiento's *Facundo* to explore some of the effects of the reproduction of that same regulative ideal.

Barbarism"), the book was named after Juan Facundo Quiroga, a federalist *caudillo* in Argentina who had defeated unitarist military troops,[14] including the one Sarmiento was part of. *Facundo* is considered as one of the canonical texts about the Argentinian nation—or how it came to be narrated (Pamplona 1997, 1998). In this work, Sarmiento expresses the problem of violence as an obstacle to the realization of civilization in Argentina. More specifically, he argues that *caudillismo* was the main challenge to the monopolization of the means of violence and, in his terms, also to the modernization of Argentina. As such, it hindered the formation of a pacified social space—one of the conditions for progress to be achieved, as we have seen in the discussion above.

The way independence wars were fought against the Spanish crown intensified the pulverization of arms in what was roughly considered as "national territories" by then. Indeed, the defense system adopted by the independent states in Latin America was characterized by militia warfare (Loveman 1999; Morelli 2007: 138), that is, a de-centralized organization of violence that came to be known as *caudillismo*. Loveman (1999: 39) defines the *caudillo* as a ruler whose authority over a limited area derives from his personal control over the means of violence and around whom a network of loyalty revolves. In other words, it is more a form of authority deriving from a personal ability than from the rule of law (1999: 39). This conception circumscribes a vast range of trajectories: the *caudillo* can be a professional officer in the command of regular army units, a militia officer, or a civilian leading a militia. The element connecting these contrasting trajectories is the absence of a formal institutional bond and the political influence of these *caudillos* over a specific group within a given territory. If we were to read this phenomenon in Weberian terms, the *caudillo* is far from the "legal authority" not only because he lacks a bureaucratic state apparatus attached to his ruling, but

---

[14] The independence wars in Latin America were fought in several axes. The main ones include loyalists to the Spanish Crown against independentists, all of which were part of the *criollo* elite i.e. a land-owning elite and nobility; monarchists against republicans, who, amongst the independentists, disputed the political regime that would be created after independence; and federalists against unitarists, who, amongst the republicans, disputed the federal regime that would be established. The disputes characterizing the wars of independence and the period thereafter cannot be summarized in these lines, however. For a more in-depth analysis on this historical context, see Bushnell (1993), Loveman (1999), Safford and Palacios (2002), Lynch (2004) and Safford (2004).

also because his leadership is remarkably personalized, once based on his charisma.

To Sarmiento, *caudillismo* was a rural phenomenon and threatened the civilized character of life in the city and the progress represented by the latter:

> Such is the character of the *montonera* [troops of mounted rebels], since its beginning; a singular kind of war and justice making (...) which must never be mistaken with the habits, ideas, and customs of the Argentinian cities, which were, as every American city, a continuation of Europe and Spain. The Argentinian War of revolution has been double: first, war led by the cities, waged within the European culture, against the Spanish, aiming at giving a wider reach to this culture; second, war led by the *caudillos* against the cities, aiming at avoiding any subjection to civil authority and developing its character and hatred against civilization[15] (Sarmiento 2018: 93)

The dualism built by Sarmiento between the urban and the rural is based on the association of each of these environments with a specific and contrasting character. While the city was characterized by Europeanized, civilized, educated and productive social relations; the countryside was marked by brutality, disorganization, and laziness. The city represented all that which the civilizing process had managed to achieve as an effect of modern life, as well as the condition for its reproduction (Sarmiento 2018). In this sense, *caudillismo* was more than a threat to the amalgamation of a coherent territory that could be considered as "national": it also challenged the consolidation of a space where civilized conducts could be nurtured, thereby hindering the development of a rational and institutionalized government. Not surprisingly, Sarmiento associated *caudillismo* with barbarism, an obstacle to civilization and modernization.

According to Sarmiento, the disorganization of violence expressed by the *caudillos* went against the "European culture" in the sense that it

---

[15] In the original: "Tal es el carácter que presenta la montonera desde su aparición; género singular de guerra y enjuiciamiento (...) que no ha debido nunca confundirse con los hábitos, ideas y costumbres de las ciudades argentinas, que eran, como todas las ciudades americanas, una continuación de la Europa y de la España. (...) La Guerra de la revolución argentina ha sido doble: 1°, guerra de las ciudades, iniciadas en la cultura europea, contra los españoles, a fin de dar mayor ensanche a esa cultura, y 2°, guerra de los caudillos contra las ciudades, a fin de librarse de toda sujeción civil y desenvolver su carácter y su odio contra la civilización".

implied the absence of any subjection to civil authority. Under these terms, *caudillismo* challenged the realization of civilization in Argentina in two main directions. First, the recurrence of attacks promoted by *caudillos* in both urban and rural areas imposed a logic of violence to the regulation of human coexistences, hindering the consolidation of a pacified social space. Such pattern of violence rendered the primacy of *civilité* over "warlike actions" impossible, as well as the establishment of the "good government". Second, the fracture in the rural–urban axis characterizing the distribution of violence in Argentina made impossible for the civil elites to create a set of stable institutions and rules aimed at optimizing the circulation of goods and allowing for progress to flourish.

By evoking terms such as "brutal ferocity" and "terrorist spirit" (Sarmiento 2018: 92) to refer to and condemn the *caudillo* way of governing, Sarmiento contends that the virtues of a republic cannot flourish from the character he identifies in *caudillismo*. This is so because he sees civilization as the appropriate content of republican governments—the "good government". Sarmiento's objection to *caudillismo* is, thus, also a claim of a proper character of politics—the civilized one—, which implied, by its turn, a demarcation of a "domain of politics" that had to be tackled by "political men" (in his words, "civil authority"), not uncivil men whose use of violence is irrational.

Importantly, when analyzing the two different kinds of war taking place in Argentina—the one led by the cities against the Spanish crown, and the war led by the *caudillos* against the cities—, Sarmiento does not claim that violence exists in opposition to civilization. To him, the wars led by the cities were fought "within the European culture". The richness of details in the depictions drawn by Sarmiento about the brutality of the *caudillos* (see, for instance, Sarmiento 2018: 92–93) finds no equivalent when he addresses the "European culture" of waging war. This contrast suggests that the civilized way of war is more aseptic, more calculated, and proportionate—rational. The violence wielded by the *caudillos* is barbarian not only because it is excessive, "sanguinary" (Sarmiento 2018: 93) and unpredictable—as it is not based on established rules—, but also because it leads to dictatorial, despotic governments. In contrast, the violence wielded by the sculptors of civilization in Argentinian cities is unleashed only to the extent it leads to freedom. More than justified, it is a *necessary* violence.

The discourse expressed by Sarmiento's *Facundo* sheds light on two key elements regarding the imperatives governing the organization of violence. The first one is that violence is constitutive of civilization in this discourse, but not any kind of violence. Sarmiento draws a hierarchical relation between the civilized violence—wielded "within the European culture"—and the barbarian violence of the *caudillos*. The former is considered superior to the latter because it is rational and civilized— "therefore", subjected to civil authority. According to Sarmiento, the war of the *caudillos* against Argentinian cities "deforms the words of the civil dictionary"[16] (Sarmiento 2018: 86), corrupting the values and purposes of the civilization that had been erected in the Argentinian cities throughout the years (Sarmiento 2018: 86). This leads us to the second aspect I would like to underline: ultimately, what differentiates the civilized violence from that of the *caudillos* is the absence, in the latter, of a power superior to that of the arms (Bedregal 1971: 23 *Apud* Rouquié 1984: 63). At stake in this discourse, therefore, is the foundation of a civil space—a pacified social space, governed by rules of socially accepted behaviors. Under the terms of civilization, violence must be tamed and subjected to a civil authority, so that a republic can be established.

Bridging the historical processes observed in Europe with the ones taking place in Argentina does not seem a strange move to Sarmiento. Indeed, the author makes no differentiation between Europe and the Argentinian cities in the post-independence context: for him, the cities in Argentina were a "continuation of Europe and Spain" (Sarmiento 2018: 93). Sarmiento does not read the independence wars as an attempt to deny Europe: rather, he sees it as a necessary violence which, inspired by the European culture, aimed at breaking the European ruling over the colonies in Latin America.

Now, Sarmiento conceives two kinds of *caudillo*: Facundo and Juan Manuel Rosas. The latter was the Governor of the United Provinces of Rio de la Plata and the Argentine Confederation from 1835 to 1852 and advanced a federalist organization of the state, repressing political opposition, especially unitarists—such as Sarmiento. Writing from his exile in Chile, Sarmiento considers Rosas a sanguinary bureaucrat: a *caudillo* who became the head of state and impregnated the state bureaucracy with his sanguinary character. He is portrayed as a bureaucrat murderer,

---

[16] In the original: "Doy tanta importancia a estos pormenores porque ellos servirán a explicar todos nuestros fenómenos sociales y la revolución que se ha estado obrando en la República Argentina; revolución que está desfigurada por palabras del diccionario civil, que la disfrazan y ocultan, creando ideas erróneas".

who had others to murder for him: "Rosas never goes into a fury; in the quiet and seclusion of his office, he calculates and, from there, the orders are sent to his hired assassins"[17] (Sarmiento 2018: 206–207). To Sarmiento, Juan Manuel Rosas represents the opposite character of that which the Argentinian nation had to be made of. For his barbarianism was destroying the civilization that had been built in Buenos Aires throughout the years. Under the ruling of Rosas, cities had "their spirit, government, civilization" (Sarmiento 2018: 87) devastated and watched the formation of the "central, unitary, and despotic Government of the *estanciero* (rancher) Juan Manuel Rosas, who hammers, in the civilized Buenos Aires, the *gaucho*'s[18] knife and destroys the work that took centuries to accomplish—civilization, laws and freedom"[19] (Sarmiento 2018: 87).

Although Sarmiento associates any kind of *caudillismo* with brutality, he contrasts Rosas' cowardliness with Facundo's bravery. The latter is, according to the author, the "faithful expression of a way of being of a people, of their preoccupations and instincts; Facundo, in short, being who he was, not by an accident of his character, but by unavoidable antecedents (…), is the most singular historical character"[20] (Sarmiento 2018: 43). Through this specific angle, Sarmiento seems to forgive Facundo, for he "was not cruel, was not bloodthirsty; he was just a barbarian who did not know how to contain his passions, which, once irritated, knew neither measure nor limit"[21] (Sarmiento 2018: 205).

---

[17] In the original: "Rosas no se enfurece nunca; calcula en la quietud y en el recogimiento de su gabinete, y desde allí salen las órdenes a sus sicarios".

[18] *Gaucho* is the expression used to describe *mestizos* who inhabited the rural region surrounding Rio Grande do Sul in Brazil, and Rio de la Plata in Argentina and Uruguay during the eighteenth and nineteenth centuries. Although this expression is used in these regions until the present day, at that time, it was attached to a racialized migratory horseman, whose main economic activity was related to cattle work.

[19] In the original: "en Facundo Quiroga, últimamente triunfante en todas partes, la campaña sobre las ciudades, y dominadas éstas en su espíritu, gobierno, civilización, formarse al fin el Gobierno central, unitario, despótico, del estanciero don Juan Manuel Rosas, que clava en la culta Buenos Aires el cuchillo del gaucho y destruye la obra de los siglos, la civilización, las leyes y la libertad".

[20] In the original: "Facundo, expresión fiel de una manera de ser de un pueblo, de sus preocupaciones e instintos; Facundo, en fin, siendo lo que fue, no por un accidente de su carácter, sino por antecedentes inevitables y ajenos de su voluntad, es el personaje histórico más singular".

[21] In the original: "Facundo no es cruel, no es sanguinario; es el bárbaro, no más, que no sabe contener sus pasiones, y que, una vez irritadas, no conocen freno ni medida".

Facundo's problem is his lack of civility: being a *gaucho* turned *caudillo*, he threatened the realization of civilization in Argentina just as Rosas. Nonetheless, Sarmiento nurtures a certain nostalgia for his bravery and authenticity, a passionate conduct that is gradually effaced with the rationalization characterizing the modernization process.

Sarmiento's contrasting attitude towards Rosas and Facundo points to the limits of the author's quest for civilization in Argentina, once revealing the tensions between tradition and reason and a certain appreciation for the former. However, the message of *Civilización y Barbárie* is clear: civilization is the path to be pursued (Sarmiento 2018). If the portrayal of Rosas as a tyrant defined the destiny that Sarmiento envisaged for him—annihilation—, what would be then the attitude towards what Facundo represented? Sarmiento looked at the United States, whose cities he characterized as the "continuation of Europe and Spain" (Sarmiento 2018: 93), and highlighted that there he found "the only people in the world that massively reads, and uses the writing for each of its necessities (…) and where education and welfare are diffused in every corner"[22] (Sarmiento 1981: 454, 471 *Apud* Pamplona 1997/1998: 40).

In search for interventions aimed at constraining the effects of nature in the constitution of Argentina as a nation, Sarmiento saw in education the vaccine against the barbarism characterizing a society resulting from the mixture of "indigenous, primitive, and pre-historical races, without any basic element of civilization and government"[23] (Sarmiento 1915: 454 *Apud* Pamplona 1997/1998: 42–43). The United States served as an example to Sarmiento in yet another aspect: he observed that half a million immigrants arrived each year from different parts of the world to the United States and pondered that Latin American states had to open towards the exterior and stimulate the immigration of "races which were naturally inclined to progress" (Sarmiento 1915: 454 *Apud* Pamplona 1997/1998: 42). Sarmiento thereby identified in both education[24] and

---

[22] In the original: "el único pueblo del mundo que lee en masa, que usa de la escritura para todas sus necesidades (…) y donde la educación como el bienestar están por todas partes difundidos".

[23] In the original: "[sociedades] mezcladas a nuestro ser como nación, razas indígenas, primitivas, prehistóricas, destituidas de todo rudimento de civilización y gobierno".

[24] The implementation of an educational system inspired in Europe was one of the veins he explored while President (1868–1874), years following the publication of *Civilización y Barbárie*, in 1845 (Pamplona 1997/1998: 40–41).

immigration two complementary paths leading to the consolidation of civilization in Argentina. Both operated towards the assimilation and filtering, through a Europeanized lens, those "races" which were considered as "naturally unmodern", gradually breeding civilized values and conducts into the Argentinian society through schools and the interaction with "races" considered as "prone to progress".

The discourse expressed by Sarmiento's Facundo (2018) reveals a problematization of *caudillismo* that reproduces the constitutive elements of a dominant discourse of modernization, as expressed in the works of Elias (2000) and Weber (2004). To be clear, these elements are marked by: (i) the monopolization of the means of violence as the condition for both the foundation of the civil space and the claim on the legitimacy of the state; (ii) the centrality of civilization as a condition for and an effect of modernization; (iii) the central position of professionalization processes in both civil and military domains; (iv) a specific organization of violence, marked by its subjection to the civil authority, as an imperative of modernity; and (v) Eurocentrism, that is, the position of Europe as the regulative ideal for post-independence Latin American societies.

Facundo's propositions to correct what he considered as an inferiority of specific groups in Argentina echo in different policies adopted across the region by the late-nineteenth century. Although immigration promotion was widely adopted by governments of that time, the next section turns its attention to an appropriation of education as a correction mechanism to a particular problematization of violence: that of the military. More specifically, it explores how the reproduction of the discourse of modernization in Latin America came to be translated into professionalization programs crafted by European missions focused on taming the military in the post-independence context. In doing so, we walk through the discursive conditions that led to the emergence of a circuit in which specific *savoirs* circulated among military professionals in the region.

4.2 The Circuit of Military *Savoirs* and the Modernization of Post-independence Armies (or, Europe is Where Latin America is Supposed to be[25])

The independence wars in Latin America[26] resulted in the strengthened position of the military in terms of their share in the national budget in many states in Latin America (Bushnell 1993: 87; Loveman 1999: 41; Rouquié 1984: 62). The centrality of violence in those independence processes also contributed to a privileged position of the military in political disputes about the government to be built. Indeed, military officers who had participated in war campaigns during the independence wars in Mexico, Venezuela, Bolivia, Peru, and Uruguay dominated post-independence politics until the late-nineteenth century (Loveman 1999: 28; Rouquié 1984: 72). At the same time, the multiple fronts with which those wars were fought resulted in the diffusion of arms throughout the territory. Either framed as *caudillismo*, rebellion or banditry (Loveman 1999: 37), the characterization of widespread violence offered the grounds for claims on the need to pacify internal disturbances. In this context, extraordinary powers were granted to the military by the Constitution, allowing practices such as the confiscation of property and the preservation of the *fueros* (special courts for the military), as well as the neutralization or annihilation of "internal enemies" (Loveman 1999: 38).

---

[25] Here, I borrow from Walker's (2000) provocation in "Europe is not where it's supposed to be" that we are better off understanding "Europe"—and, therefore, also "Latin America"—as discursively produced political entities, instead of geographical categories.

[26] If the reader finds scarce mentions of Central-American cases, this is mainly due to the particularities of the discourses on state formation in this region, especially with regard to their relation with the United States. According to Loveman (1999: 28), "In Central America, independence came virtually without war, although civil-military *caudillos* created the new nations that fragmented from the failed Central American Federation (1824–1838)". This rendering of state formation in Central America contrasts with the tensions between the civil elites and the military that came to mark analyses about post-independence South America. This points to a set of questions that cannot be developed in this study; one of them refers to the repeated characterization of Central America as a terrain of undisputed politics, absent of any tension between the *caudillos* and other social groups in a first moment, and as a "zone of influence to the United States" (Loveman 1999: 204–205), in a second moment.

This picture of mid-nineteenth century Latin America made the monopolization of the means of violence one of the main concerns regarding the "security of the Republic" in these countries—as expressed in the wording of the 1821 Constitution of Gran Colombia (*Apud* Loveman 1999: 38). In addition to that, what to do with the military emerged as a problem to be dealt with by the civil elites engaged in the establishment of republican governments in these newly independent states. In this section, we walk through some of the main practices working with this specific problematization. As we will see, at the same time that the military forces were invested in the pacification of states in Latin America, the "problem of the military" was the fuel for the invitation of several European missions to the region. Among the most recurrent cases are French and Prussian military missions expected to assist in the professionalization of the military. My argument is that the reproduction of the discourse of modernization has allowed for the emergence of a circuit of military professionals in Latin America, operating towards their homogenization. As we will see with the Colombian case in Sect. 4.3, however, the particularities through which the discourse of modernization is filtered expose the limits of its universalizing pretense.

Amidst the attempts to tame the military in the post-independence context in Latin America, a decision often made was to dismantle the Army so as to build another, almost from scratch. In Chile, for instance, the official historiography refers to the years following independence wars as "anarchy" (Rouquié 1984: 65)—in sharp contrast to the order allegedly established by later governments. Indeed, in 1830, the claim for the need to pacify Chile was mobilized by the Conservative government of José Tomás Ovalle—the first president of the Chilean republic—when purging the military officials identified as Liberals from the army, as well as those who had participated in mutinies. Aiming at putting an end to factions disturbing order in the new republic, the Minister of the Interior at that time (1830–1831; 1835–1837), Diego Portales, reduced the size of the Chilean Army to 3,000 members and created militarized civil militias, which reached 25,000 men (Rouquié 1984: 65–66).

A similar project was implemented by Rafael Reyes (1904–1909) in Colombia, when the Army was dismantled almost in its entirety after the civil war known as the Thousand Days' War (1899–1902) (Atehortúa 2009: 21). Much earlier, the tension between the civil elites and the military was already constituting political discourses in New Granada. Particularly, the dispute between the civil elites and the military by that time was framed as one involving, on one side, the "men of Law", and on the other, "the men in arms". In this tension, the "men of Law" represented an authority whose legitimacy derived from rationally created rules, as illustrated by the educational background in Law of Francisco de Paula Santander, one of the main exponents of this characterization of the civil elites (Bushnell 1993: 55). Contrasting to Simón Bolívar, whose professional trajectory had been based on military campaigns, Santander represented the promise of the primacy of *civilité* over violence in the regulation of human coexistences in New Granada[27]

According to the historian José Manuel Restrepo, who occupied several public offices in New Granada from 1819 to 1860, the military were seen as representing a threat to republican ideals—a "cancer that is devouring the people's substance" (Restrepo 1858 *Apud* Bushnell 1993: 71). On the other hand, the military considered to be an outrage that lawyers "are in open war with an army to whom they owe their very existence", declared the Venezuelan General José Antonio Páez (Safford and Palacios 2002: 116–117). The persistent suspicion towards the military led to successive reductions in its outlays, for its share in the national budget was the largest one during that period. According to Bushnell, "[t]he size of the military establishment was kept under strict control, with the authorized force level hovering around 3,300 men, or one for every 500 inhabitants, more or less" (Bushnell 1993: 87). At stake in these disputing narratives, there was the claim for the need to subject the military to civil authority, a simultaneous move to the demarcation of a domain which is specific to politics. These processes were portrayed as a necessity so that the republican ideals could flourish in New Granada.

---

[27] The social ascension of the military due to their achievements in battle added another component of tension here, once the elites in New Granada complained about the lack of good manners and education in the military establishment (Safford and Palacios 2002: 116). While the empiricism that nurtured the heroic self-portrait of the military was discursively guided by merit, effectiveness and courage; the discourse of education as a source of social prestige magnified lineage, protocol and etiquette. Importantly, the concentration of literacy and education in the *criollos* since the Spanish rule revealed education not as a means for social ascension, but as a mechanism for the reaffirmation of social distinctions. As for the military rank achieved through the experience in battle, it sought in merit the substance for the claim of social ascension. As argued in Sect. 4.1, however, social differentiation is not incompatible with merit in the discourse of modernization. The fact that social distinction involved etiquette, protocols, and ways of speaking and acting in public allows us to understand how, even after social ascension, the military still faced barriers in terms of manners and customs.

Rouquié considers these tensions between the civil elites and the military as a constitutive feature of the formation of Latin American states—hence his expression "state building against the military" (Rouquié 1984: 65). Indeed, similar cases could also be observed in Peru, Ecuador, and Mexico, for instance (Rouquié 1984: 64–68; Loveman 1999: 57–58). In each context, the play of forces between civil elites and the military resulted in specific contours of the bureaucratization and professionalization of the military. The claim that the pulverization of violence across the national territory was reflected in the composition of the military personnel led to the dismantling of the armies in different Latin American countries, not only in Chile and New Granada. Purging off the opposition and reducing the personnel to the minimum necessary—a recurrent motto throughout the region in the post-independence context.

Now, the dismantling of the armies coexisted with the claim for the need to pacify the internal space. But how to dispense with violence if warlike actions were considered as indispensable to this emerging national order? There were multiple concrete "solutions" articulated to address that puzzle, but governments often chose to create "militarized civil militias" in contexts that the military themselves were not trustworthy (Palau 1907: 32; Rouquié 1984: 65–66). In this sense, we must read Rouquié's "state building against the military" as attempts both to tame the armies in the region and to pacify the nation.[28] Under these terms, "state building" reveals a fundamental aspect of the organization of violence: the search for a politically aseptic army mobilizes a logic which is similar to that of the search for a politically aseptic society.

The historical context of the late-nineteenth century was also marked by wars among Latin American states—such as the War of the Triple

---

[28] These pacification practices undertaken in Latin American countries cannot be separated from their pursuit for a place in the global market as independent states. Indeed, the global political economy in which the Latin American states were found after the independence wars reaffirmed the position they occupied while colonies, as providers of commodities to Europe and the United States (Bushnell 1993; Safford and Palacios 2002). In this context, one of the main effects of the mobilization of the discourse of modernization in Latin American states was that it authorized the monopolization of the means of violence through the pacification of the social space, aiming at optimizing the circulation of goods and services, both inside and outwards. This extrovert growth (Rouquié 1984: 74) requires, under the terms of this discourse, "political stability" and "social peace" and goes hand in hand with a legislation specifically devoted to optimizing the circulation of persons and goods, as well as with the building of an infrastructure connecting the territory and the bureaucratization of the state apparatus.

Alliance (1864–1870) and the War of the Pacific (1879–1884). Considered to have revealed "the cost of unpreparedness, military weakness, and poor political leadership" (Loveman 1999: 48), these wars resulted in the incorporation of an additional element to the claim on the need to professionalize the military. If the regime of justification of such an effort was first focused on pushing the military away from the domain of politics, creating a specific domain for the professional of violence, and subjecting it to the civil authority, this justification also came to encompass the claim that the formation of regular armies was the condition for a more efficient use of violence in international wars. In other words, regular armies were considered to fight better. The dismantling of the armies was, thus, only a preliminary stage of a more comprehensive project: the professionalization of the military forces, understood as key to the modernization of Latin American states. As a matter of fact, this process was two-fold: it referred to the de-politicization of the military, at the same time it involved the build-up of an army that made an efficient use of violence.

Here, European armies were the main reference for this military professional in the making. This was the case even before the creation of military careers in Latin American countries, when *caudillos* travelled to Europe to improve their abilities in war through the pursuit of a military career in Europe back in the eighteenthcentury[29] (Rouquié 1984: 69). In the other direction, European military officers and mercenaries also worked as advisors, and in some cases even participated in wars in Latin America (Loveman 1999: 63). Once these participations were made on an ad hoc basis and in specific campaigns, they did not result in the formation of permanent and regular armies. As Rouquié argues, "in the majority of the cases, the commanders of the independence armies had never known a regular army, nor had they pursued military studies"[30] (1984: 70). They were more empiricists, deriving their expertise on the military affairs from their direct participation in battles. Therefore, even those considered as career officers by that time were not professionals in the terms of the

---

[29] The Argentinian General San Martín, for example, joined one of the regiments in Spain in 1789, where he pursued his military studies until 1812. Upon his return to Argentina, he organized the *Ejército de los Andes* (Army of the Andes) as a regular force: with a command hierarchy, the creation of specialized divisions based on arms or services, and uniform troops in terms of equipment (Rouquié 1984: 69).

[30] In the original: "Pero en la mayoría de los casos, los jefes de los ejércitos de la independencia jamás han conocido un ejército regular ni realizado estudios militares".

discourse of modernization: they were not part of a stable bureaucracy, nor were they schooled on war as a domain of knowledge, much less permanently trained to be disciplined. Taming this instability was framed as a need for the preservation of republican values.

Not surprisingly, the first attempts to create a modern army in post-independence Latin America sought regularity in the professional character of the military. Under this logic, taming the military forces required disciplinarization mechanisms such as rules and criteria governing their career and a rigorous control over their routine inside the barracks. In this context, different states in Europe were invited to send official missions aimed at contributing to the building of professional and "apolitical" public forces in Latin America. With contrasting levels of scope and functions, foreign military missions were charged with supervising the reform of military laws and regulations defining the terms for the creation of a military career; the establishment of military schools; the elaboration of new curricula; the diffusion of military doctrine, strategy and tactics; and the implementation of routine drill and maneuvers (Rouquié 1984: 90–98; Pizarro L. 1987a; Loveman 1999: 64, 66; Atehortúa 2009: 43–44, 51). Despite the contrasts among, for instance, the Spanish, the French and the German organization of troops and strategy, professionalization was generally understood as the formation of an elite corps of academy-educated officers and a consistent career system.

The "de-politicization" of the Latin American military personnel was expected to be achieved through the creation, perfecting and valorization of what was considered specific to the military: warfare, not politics. Indeed, the work of these foreign missions reproduced the boundary between what was specific to the domain of politics (the civil) and that which pertained exclusively to the military domain. From the creation of a Penal Code and Tribunal especially for the military professional to the creation of journals exclusively dedicated to the debate and diffusion of military doctrine, strategy, and tactics—all these practices aimed at demarcating the specificity of the function and knowledge of the military ("hence", also special duties and rights). It is through these lines that we must interpret declarations such as the one given by the Peruvian General Pedro Pablo Martínez, in 1935:

> The twelve years in which General Clément and Colonel Dogny presided over the Military School as its directors marked the 'golden age' of our Army. Only military ideas were heard in its classrooms. Political interests

dared not intrude on its grounds. (...) the Chorrillos School was a temple of military science. (Martínez 1935 *Apud* Loveman 1999: 63)

In this excerpt, we see the celebration of both the military domain and the legacy of the French mission. The former is expressed through references such as "golden age" and "temple", attached to the Chorrillos School, the Peruvian military school built at the end of the nineteenth century with the assistance of the French mission. The demarcation of a domain specific to the military acquires concrete contours when the school is presented as the site where "only military ideas were heard"—indicating the impenetrability of "political interests" in the "temple of military science".

Most notable, however, is the disdain towards "political interests", which "dared not intrude" in the school. There is more than the separation of the domain of politics from that of the military at stake here: there is a clear attitude of superiority of the latter towards the former. Conceived as the main site for the production of the military professional, the military schools offered a "totalizing" experience (Rouquié 1984: 118; Loveman 1999: 70; Castro 2004; Gill 2004), operating in a boarding-school format and with an all-encompassing curriculum (stretching from the most basic writing and reading skills to classes on history and geography), the military schools provided a self-sufficient infrastructure, including dorms, health clinic, chapel, as well as priests, doctors, musicians, hairdressers and veterinaries—most of them, also military (Rouquié 1984: 87). By introducing the military professionals in the making to a socialization that is different from that of the "rest of the society", the military schools aim not only at mimicking the conditions of a military campaign, but also isolating them in an environment where "virtues, expertise, and patriotic values" are superior to those of civilians (Rouquié 1984: 118; Loveman 1999: 70; Castro 2004: 46). This isolation allows for the military professionals to develop, under the specific regime operating within the military school, a disciplined conduct which would later be diffused as an example of obedience and efficiency to various instances outside the military schools (from the practice of sports, to regular schools and prisons). It is in the combination of the isolation of the military and the belief in the superiority of the procedures and values nurtured within the military schools that the disdain towards "political interests" in the excerpt above must be interpreted.

Furthermore, General Martínez's declaration associates the French mission with the Chorrillos School's "golden age", suggesting that the French contribution to this "temple" of military science was key to the consolidation of that which is specific to the military. More than a French footprint that cannot be erased from the Peruvian military historiography, such a declaration points to the superior position enjoyed by the French mission in relation to the Peruvian military officers. This is not a particularity of Peru, neither of France: in many cases, the leaders of the European missions invited to work in the professionalization of the military in Latin American countries formally occupied chief positions in military schools, ministries, and even in the police. In Chile, for instance, Captain Emil Körner was named Chief of Staff (*Jefe del Estado Mayor*) by the end of the nineteenth century (Ejército de Chile 1924: 117; Rouquié 1984: 91); in Bolivia, the Prussian mission's director, Colonel Hans Kundt, was named Minister of War (Loveman 1999: 67); and in Colombia, the French Commissioner Jean-Marie Marcelin Gilibert was named the first Commander of the National Police (Castaño C. 1947: 58–59).

The recurrent mentions to French and Prussian military professionals in Latin America should not come as a surprise, for they were considered as the most prestigious of the world at the end of the nineteenth century. Indeed, they responded for a significant share of the military missions sent to Latin America at that time. For instance, French military missions were sent to Argentina in the 1860s, Peru in the 1890s, Bolivia in the 1900s, and Brazil in the 1910s; and Prussian missions were sent to Chile in the 1880s, Argentina and Brazil in the 1900s, and Bolivia in the 1910s (Rouquié 1984: 90–97; Loveman 1999: 70–96; Atehortúa 2009: 35–42).

Importantly, the French and the Prussian armies were taken as a reference for different reasons. After its victory in the Franco-Prussian War (1870–1871), the German army became a synonym of efficiency in waging war: its officers participated in military missions whose scope ranged from the organization of war games and codes to the elaboration of curricula and military codes of conduct, in addition to a direct engagement with training and teaching in the military schools (Nunn 2001: 16). In the war against the French Empire, the Prussian troops revealed a well-trained and consistent leadership, in addition to an efficient mobilization of troops. The latter resulted, first, from a rail network that made the logistic support not only possible, but efficient; second, from a conscription system that was able to assure wide reserves of personnel

(Scalercio 2015: 94). Of course, these characteristics must be inscribed in the context from which the material conditions for such a military efficiency emerged: the colonial relations that allowed for the concentration of capital by Prussia; and the technological advances—especially rail and arms industries—without which victories in the strategic and tactical levels would be unthinkable.

As for the French army, it is noteworthy that it remained as a reference even after its defeat to the German troops: indeed, French missions were sent to Bolivia, Brazil, and Peru during the 1890s and 1900s. Known for the victorious campaigns characterized by the *levée en masse* since the late-eighteenth century, the French army acquired notoriety for its professionalism only after the Franco-Prussian War. Interestingly, some of the officers who were part of the French military mission sent to Peru in 1890s had served in Northern Africa, in French colonies (Nunn 2001: 16). The curriculum of the Peruvian military school reformed by these French officers included the texts *Du role social de l'officier* ("On the social role of the officer") and *Du role colonial de l'armée* ("On the colonial role of the army"), written by Hubert Lyautey and published in 1891, after his time serving in Algeria. In his works, Lyautey argued that officers and colonizers had to realize their "civilizing mission" towards, respectively, the lower-ranked military and the colonial population: to educate them and to be their moral and cultural mentors was at the core of the mission of the military (Nunn 2001: 20). Indeed, in the years following the publication of the essays mentioned above, Lyautey's military expertise relied on his very experience in the colonial administration in Algeria, Madagascar, Indochina, and Morocco. In this sense, if the hallmark of the Prussian army was efficiency through discipline and leadership through the effective use of infrastructure and weaponry, what distinguished the French army seemed to be more attached to what was considered as an efficient management of colonial order—the transformation of manners and human conduct in general being a key part in this process.

Nevertheless, it would be misleading to claim that Latin American states adopted a "French model" or a "Prussian model" for the professionalization of their armed forces. In fact, it was often the case that missions from different nationalities were invited by the same country within a short period.[31] In 1901, for instance, a Prussian mission was sent

---

[31] Hiring a foreign military mission relied on a complex equation. As we will discuss ahead in this Section, the provision of arms was often part of the contract—as it still

to Bolivia to direct the War College and the Military School. Six years later, French officers visited Bolivia (1907–1910) with the same objective, followed by a German mission in 1911 (Loveman 1999: 67). In Brazil, the change from a Prussian (1906) to a French mission (1919) occurred in less than fifteen years. In Colombia, this was no different: right after the end of the Thousand Days' War (1899–1902), Colombia received military missions from Chile (1907; 1909–1911; 1911–1913; and 1913–1915), Switzerland (1924–1933), Germany (1929–1934) and France (1939) (Bushnell 1993: 157, 193; Safford and Palacios 2002: 283). With a few exceptions, the most common configuration of military professionals in Latin America resulted from successive attempts to build modern military forces with the assistance of foreign missions from a few European states, and from the juxtaposition of parts of different professionalization programs in the same curriculum.

Chile is an interesting case in this regard, for it was not only a state whose military professionalization was more consistently developed in reference to a specific model—Prussia—, but also because Chile was itself invited to send military missions to other states in Latin America (namely, Ecuador, Colombia, El Salvador and Venezuela) as it was considered as the closest to the Prussian mission that could be found in the region. Chile was the first Latin American country to establish, in 1817, a military school—the *Academia Militar* (Military Academy). As the War of the Pacific (1879–1884) was close to an end and the Chilean forces defeated Peruvian and Bolivian armies, a commission of military officers was created to assess the needs of the Chilean army and its errors in the war[32] (Loveman 1999: 80). Moved by the idea that professionalizing the military forces was key for Chile to not be vulnerable to Peru or Bolivia in case of another armed confrontation, or to Argentina, whose military campaigns aiming at expanding its territory could affect Chile (Rouquié

---

is. At the same time, the range of options was narrowed during World War I due to the involvement of European great powers therein. Also, the choice for a specific foreign military mission derived from what the hiring country could afford.

[32] Despite the relatively easy Chilean occupation of Lima in 1881, the War of the Pacific was extended for almost three years due to the Peruvian and Bolivian resistance through guerrilla warfare. This led to the assessment that the Chilean victory did not result from its undeniable military superiority, but from the relative poor capacity of its opponents. According to Loveman (1999: 56), the Chilean Army was criticized in the Congress and the press for "The lack of strategic plans, poor tactics, and needless loss of life".

1984: 90; Loveman 1999: 80; Atehortúa 2009: 36), the commission was sent to Berlin in early 1880s to negotiate the establishment of a Prussian mission.[33]

Sent to Santiago in 1885, the Prussian mission was led by Captain Emil Körner and was integrated by thirty officers who worked as instructors both in the military schools in Chile and in the troops (Ejército de Chile 1924: 117). Körner had participated in the Franco-Prussian War (1870–1871) and, by the 1880s, taught tactics, military history and ballistics in the School of Artillery and Engineering of Charlottenburg[34] (Ejército de Chile 1924: 116). During his time in Chile, Körner reorganized the Chilean army from the highest to the lowest ranks through the proposition of laws focused on the structuration of the military career, such as one on mandatory conscription. He also deepened the specialization of the army branches and worked on the improvement of its mobility. To do so, the Prussian mission reformed the curriculum of the *Escuela Militar*, which had been established in 1863, and created the War Academy (*Academia de Guerra*) in 1887, an institution dedicated to the formation of the high-ranked officers, as well as the officers of the General Staff (*Estado Mayor*) (Ejército de Chile 1924: 116). As the head of the mission, Körner created specialized support-functions within the Military Forces, such as health, veterinary and supply branches. Another important front of the mission's work involved the development of an infrastructure allowing for the troops to be rapidly deployed and communications to be made. In this regard, the Prussian mission created battalions specialized in building railroads (1909) and telegraphs (1910) (Loveman 1999: 81).

The Prussian mission worked in the professionalization of the Chilean Army from 1885 to 1914. According to the internal documents of the Chilean Army, Körner was key to the professionalization of the military. In the 1924 *Memorial del Ejército de Chile* (*Memorial of the Chilean*

---

[33] Importantly, the expansion of nitrate and copper reserves resulting from the Chilean victory in the War of the Pacific allowed for the funding of the mission—a condition that many states in Latin America lacked at that time.

[34] Körner had himself participated in another military circuit of *savoirs* by that time, having travelled to France, Italy, Spain, and Russia to develop studies in the areas mentioned above (Ejército de Chile 1924: 116).

Army), not only Körner[35] but the Prussian mission in general, are celebrated for their legacy to the Chilean Army: at the core of this legacy was the consolidation of the *Escuela Militar*, where most of the officers considered as professionals at the outset of the twentieth century started their military career (Ejército de Chile 1924: 116). As the 1924 *Memorial* celebrates the achievements of professionalization, it contrasts it with the previous organization of the Chilean Army:

> The achievements of the Army (...) since the end of the war of the Pacific are numerous (...). The discipline of this Army was magnificent and each of its members was motivated by the purest patriotism; however, neither the organization in times of peace, nor the way with which instruction was developed corresponded to the requirements of war, for the campaign itself (...) revealed both that improvisation was its characteristic and that it was necessary to create everything simultaneously to the deployment of the operations.
>
> In the work undertaken by General Körner in our Army, one can highlight the fact that he formed a homogeneous officialdom, enthusiastic about its service and motivated by a great spirit of work. As a whole, this officialdom passed, almost without exception, by the *Escuela Militar*, which constitutes one of its most remarkable differences from the past organization, in which officers formed by this institution only corresponded to a reduced number.[36] (Ejército de Chile 1924: 118)

---

[35] When he first arrived in Chile, Emil Körner held the rank of Captain. His engagement and political projection in Chile were so expressive that, by the late-nineteenth century, he was named Chief of Staff (*Jefe del Estado Mayor*) and granted the rank of General.

[36] In the original: "Los progresos realizados por el Ejército (...) desde la terminación de la guerra del Pacífico son numerosos (...). La disciplina de ese Ejército era magnífica y cada uno de sus miembros estaba animado del más puro patriotismo; sin embargo, ni la organización de tiempo de paz, ni la forma como se desarrollaba la instrucción correspondían a las exigencias de la guerra, pues la campaña misma (...) demostró que la improvisación había sido su característica y que hubo necesidad de crearlo todo durante el transcurso mismo de las operaciones. De entre la obra realizada por el General Korner en nuestro Ejército se destaca en forma muy especial el hecho de haber formado una oficialidad homogénea, entusiasta por el servicio y animada de grande espíritu de trabajo. Toda ella, casi sin excepción, ha pasado por la Escuela Militar, lo que constituye una de las diferencias más marcadas con la organización antigua, en que los oficiales salidos de ese establecimiento solo constituían un reducido número".

The excerpt portrays the Prussian mission as a watershed in the professionalization of the Chilean Army. Underlining the effects that the mission had on its officialdom, the *Memorial* claims a transformation from "improvisation" to "preparedness" and from "heterogeneity" to "homogeneity". The Army's officialdom is herein presented as the mirror of this new military corporation, whose professionals are not only mobilized in the context of war: it is in times of peace that more rational uses of the resources and personnel are conceived, taught, and trained. Both preparedness and homogeneity operate in this direction: the latter is the condition for the former, as it allows for a more predictable and efficient use of forces.

As it concentrates the achievements of professionalization in "times of peace", the Army's *Memorial* reveals an understanding of "peace" that does not comprehend the numerous operations led by the Chilean Army in the repression of strikes in ports, mines, and cities—operations aimed at pacifying the social space. From the 1890s to 1924, that is, while the Prussian mission was still in Chile, the Army was recurrently mobilized in operations against "disturbances of the public order". From 1911 to 1920, for instance, the Chilean Army intervened in almost three hundred strikes (Loveman 1999: 84). As President Carlos Ibáñez del Campo (1927–1931) often highlighted, the Chilean Army held an "honorable mission"[37] of "healing the body politic and saving the nation" (Loveman 1999: 85). Under these terms, and with an emphatic association of labor movements with "the dangers of communism", the Chilean Army was systematically mobilized in the repression of strikes in nitrate plants (Rouquié 1984: 115; Loveman 1999: 82, 84).

The investment of social ordering functions to the military was not a particularity of Chile. In Colombia, the Army was often engaged in

---

[37] A few years later, Ibáñez invited an Italian mission to work in the professionalization of the Chilean national police force. The mission was formed by *Carabinieri* officers (Loveman 1999: 85)—which, though existing since 1814, had been turned into the first national police force in 1861, following the Italian unification. In this context, the *Carabinieri* were responsible for repressing the political opposition (Nunn 2001: 21). The Chilean option for the *Carabinieri* indicates a persistent logic with which violence was organized in Chile. After all, the effect expected through the production of the professional military was very similar to the function that the police professional was being polished to undertake: to cope with the "internal gangrene" in Chile (Ibánez 1927 *Apud* Loveman 1999: 84)—mostly associated with leftist labor movements (Loveman 1999: 82, 85).

the repression of protests organized by workers in the fruit industry (Fonnegra 1986) and coffee crops (Bergquist 1989); in Argentina, the focus of military operations corresponded to metallurgical workers (Rouquié 1984: 115), in Guatemala, the fruit industry (Chapman 2007); and in Peru, mining plants (Loveman 1999: 86)—just to mention a few examples. The similarities observed in the operations with which the different armies were engaged in Latin America is one of the aspects pointing to the emergence of a circuit of military *savoirs* in the region. Importantly, at the same time the homogenization of military operations can be read as an effect of the circuit of military *savoirs*, it can also be interpreted as the condition allowing for this very circuit to emerge. As we have seen, the reproduction of the discourse of modernization in Latin America authorized the pacification of "disturbances to public order" so that modernization could be realized.

The intense transit of European military professionals in Latin America since the second half of the nineteenth century is certainly one of the main elements characterizing this circuit of military *savoirs*. The work advanced by these missions was not only invested in the regulation of the military career and in the establishment of military schools, nonetheless. The creation of military archives and specialized reviews, as well as the translation of manuals and textbooks,[38] corresponded to an additional vein in which these missions worked (Rouquié 1984: 93; Loveman 1999: 73–74; Castro 2001: 67; Nunn 2001: 18–20). Here, Europe also enjoyed a privileged position, once constituting both the object of the experiences addressed in these texts, and, in many cases, the source from which they were translated. As an example, in Chile, the Prussian mission created a military archive in 1903 for the storage of documents, manuals and issues of military journals such as the *Revista Militar de Chile*—which had been created in 1885 (Loveman 1999: 80–81). In Argentina, where a Prussian mission worked in the professionalization of the military officers from 1899 to 1914, and then from 1921 to 1930 (Atkins and Thompson 1972: 257, 259, 261), half of the 120 articles published between 1918 and 1930 in the *Biblioteca del Oficial* were translated from German[39] (Rouquié 1984: 93).

---

[38] Given that illiteracy was pervasive among soldiers across all Latin American countries at that time (Rouquié 1984: 111–113), these texts were mainly used by military officers.

[39] It is noteworthy that the book by Colmar von der Goltz, *Das Volk in Waffen* (*The People in Arms*), published in 1883 in Prussia, has been translated to Spanish and

Among the conditions that made the establishment of archives and specialized reviews possible was the enduring character of the knowledge produced for and by the military. As with the archive, the military specialized reviews created in most of Latin American states from the 1880s to the 1920s[40] were both an expression of the professionalization of the military and what allowed this professionalization to be consolidated and reproduced. By exchanging impressions on operations, stimulating discussions on doctrine, strategy, and tactics, and discussing "disturbances of order" that were the object of their concerns, military officers systematized their knowledge within a specific domain, transmitted this knowledge to their counterparts, and learned from the other military officers' texts. Such dynamic relies on the assumption that military officers, in the same state and across different states, are taught similar subjects, engage in similar operations, and face similar challenges—they are all military professionals.

Finally, it is important to highlight that the circuit of military *savoirs* is not solely constituted by the transit of military professionals, nor by the transnational diffusion of manuals, textbooks, and articles in the region: weapons are a fundamental element in this circuit. Indeed, it is almost impossible to dissociate the fluxes of European military professionals from the circulation of arms in Latin America. The technological development of the arms industry is the condition for a specific *savoir* to be thinkable—there is no operation for which a corresponding weapon does not exist. At the same time, the demand for arms in Latin American states stimulated the formalization of contracts for the establishment of military missions. Needless to say, it was not any weapon that was offered as part of a package comprehended in the work of a given foreign military mission. The Prussians emphasized the use of Mauser, Schneider and Krupp rifles and canons, for instance: seven years after the Prussian mission was established in Chile, 100,000 Mauser rifles were imported in 1892 (Loveman 1999: 81). The dependence cycle created through the foreign missions is exemplified again in the Chilean case, where ammunitions and gunpowder

---

widely used in the curricula of the military schools reformed by Prussian missions in Latin America (Nunn 2001: 18–19).

[40] As previously mentioned, in Chile, the military specialized review was created in 1885 (Loveman 1999: 80). In the cases of Peru and Venezuela, official military periodicals were created in the early-twentieth century (Loveman 1999: 74).

factories were established in 1894 with the objective of supplying the military use of the weapons that had been procured from Prussia (Loveman 1999: 81). In this sense, transmitting military *savoirs* to Latin American states was part of a broader development strategy, one that found elective affinities with the arms industry. More than a military counterpart, Latin American hosts of Prussian and French missions were a consumer market for weapons—not to mention the construction of rail networks, which was also part of Krupp's business in the region, to mention but one example.

In this section, we have seen that the emergence of the circuit of military *savoirs* in Latin America in the second half of the nineteenth century must be inscribed in the context of the independence wars in the region. Although the relation between newly-independent states and European states was based on the principle of equality among sovereign units, we saw that the reproduction of the discourse of modernization by Latin American countries positioned Europe as a reference for the professionalization of the military in the region. Once the organization of violence was a key element in such discourse, Latin America looked up to Europe as the future it wanted to be part of, and to the Prussian and French military, as what it needed to be in order to leave its political past behind. In this context, French and Prussia were the states in Europe often invited to assist in the creation of a military career, as well as to work in the establishment of military schools and the implementation of its curricula.

Two aspects are noteworthy regarding the political dynamic of this circuit. First, that it was connected to Europe in very specific terms: the latter represented models to be replicated in the production of military professionals in Latin America. As such, whenever European missions were hired to assist in this process, they established a hierarchical relation with their host countries. Second, even among Latin American states there were asymmetries: those with more capital could invest more in the build-up of their military apparatus—hiring a foreign mission and negotiating the acquisition of arms, for example.

This circuit of military *savoirs*, therefore, emerges within a specific historical context and is constituted by intense fluxes of military professionals, which are not unidirectional. Although the French and Prussian missions were systematically invited to assist in the professionalization of Latin American military, there were specific cases in which the latter attended courses in Europe to polish their knowledge and skills. However, the asymmetries characterizing the circuit imply that some fluxes are more remarkable than others—in this case, from France and Prussia to Latin American states.

As we have seen, the professionalization of the Chilean Army allowed for this state to position itself within the circuit of military *savoirs* as a reference for the "Prussian model". Indeed, in the first decades of the twentieth century, Venezuela and Colombia hired Chilean officers to work in the creation and reform of military schools. Interestingly, these missions encouraged the procurement of Prussian weapons. This leads us to another trait of the circuit of military *savoirs*: that fluxes of weapons cannot be dissociated from those of *savoirs*. Such a circuit is the condition for and the effect of the transmission of military *savoirs*.

The textual edifice erected upon the circuit of military *savoirs* constituted a set of mechanisms through which knowledge was diffused among military professionals. Its content reflected the lines of asymmetry within the circuit, as discussed above in reference to manuals, textbooks, and specialized reviews. Both the fluxes of military professionals and the textual repertoire characterizing the circuit are mechanisms that point to the *savoirs* that are valorized in a specific historical context. That several Latin American military officers were being taught the same courses allowed for them to exchange *savoirs*; at the same time, such a practice reinforced the circuit. In this sense, the circuit made the endurance of military *savoirs* possible.

Two additional effects of this circuit deserve our attention. By claiming the need to consolidate a domain specific to the military and away from the domain of politics, the reproduction of the discourse of modernization enabled and catalyzed practices such as the adoption of the mandatory conscription for the military, the establishment of similar rules for the military career, the translation of manuals and texts from Europe, as well as the diffusion of certain conducts and manners. By the first half of the twentieth century, in contrast to the previous century, the military in Latin America were significantly similar in terms of uniforms, textual references, conduct and discourse, despite the different historical and geographical contexts in which their professionalization was being or had been undertaken (Rouquié 1984: 86; Loveman 1999: 63).

The second effect refers to the similarity in the operations for which the armies were mobilized in Latin America. Despite the differences between the French and Prussian missions, the examples mentioned above reveal that the armies in Latin America were systematically engaged in the pacification of the internal space. That strikes and protests repeatedly constituted the object of military operations points to the mutual reinforcement between concerns with pacifying the internal space and those with stimulating the production and commercialization of commodities. Thus, in the history of Latin America, the domestication of the military did not only mean that they had to be brought to the rule of civil authority and disciplined through professionalization programs, but also that they were repeatedly deployed in the pacification of the domestic space.

In the next section, we examine how Colombia was positioned in the circuit of military *savoirs* by analyzing the main axes guiding the work of the Chilean military mission in the country. As we will see, their work faced several frictions with the Colombian military officers. In exposing these tensions, my objective is to discuss the effects and the limits of the discourse of modernization within the circuit of military *savoirs*.

4.3 The Frictions and Fictions of the Civil-Military Boundary in the Colombian Army

When the first Chilean military mission arrived in Colombia, in 1907, the Presidency of General Rafael Reyes (1904–1909) had its efforts concentrated in recovering the country from the devastating impacts of the Thousand Days' War (1901–1903). Placing emphasis on the reconstruction of infrastructure and the integration of the national territory, as well as on social order, Reyes' government came to be framed as a centralized project of modernization in Colombia (to mention but a few, see Pizarro L. 1987a; Bergquist 1989: 225; Bushnell 1993: 158–159; Aterhortúa and Vélez 1994: 56–58; Atehortúa 2009: 19–20). Considered as one of the turning points in the trajectory of the professionalization of the Colombian Army (Pizarro L. 1987a; Atehortúa and Vélez 1994: 56–58; Atehortúa 2009: 19–20), the Reyes' administration is key for us to understand how the reproduction of the discourse of modernization was translated into the production of the military professional in Colombia.

In this section, I examine the scope of the Chilean mission invited by Reyes to develop the first systematic professionalization program of the military in Colombia. In particular, I look at the center of gravity of the work of the Chilean mission: it was in the *Escuela Militar* (Military School) that a specific profile of a disciplined, hygienic, and literate soldier was expected to be produced—the Colombian "citizen-soldier". Drawing from a discussion on the profile of the students in the *Escuela Militar* and its curriculum, I explore the tensions between the Chilean and Colombian military officers regarding the work of the mission. Here, I am especially interested in what these frictions tell us regarding the limits of the discourse of modernization: what it enables, but also what it precludes. To do that, we first need to walk through the mottos mobilized by the Reyes' administration so as to grasp the context from which the work of the Chilean mission emerged.

In reaction to "politics"—which he considered as an obstacle to the modernization of Colombia—, Reyes' motto "more administration and less politics" (*"mucha administración y menos política"*) (Palau 1907: 27; Atehortúa 2009: 19) aimed at building a government above the disputes of the two main political parties, which had characterized the 19th-century Colombia. In this sense, "administration" was conveyed as that which would allow modernization to be actualized—different from the political disputes that, for decades, had hindered the monopolization of the means of violence and the consolidation of infrastructure in the country, for instance. An illustration of how the discourse on administration was understood by the Reyes' government is found in the formation of his staff based on a technical and practical profile, not on political party affiliation (Pizarro L. 1987a; Atehortúa 2009: 20). Following these lines, Reyes not only assigned ministries to both Liberal and Conservative parties: he also named one of the main leaders of the Liberal party at that time, General Rafael Uribe Uribe, for the position of plenipotentiary Ambassador for South America.

These measures were said to aim at reinforcing the technical and downplaying the political as the privileged criterion for the organization and management of a government whose task was to modernize the state.[41]

---

[41] Interestingly, however, the condition for any choice based on "technical" criteria was an even distribution of political offices among the Conservative and Liberal Parties—what Pizarro Leongómez (1987a) called a "consortium democracy". That is, what is celebrated as a technical decision—the choice of a political opponent because of his expertise in a given area—also serves as a bargain based on the balanced distribution of political offices among the two main Parties in Colombia.

Importantly, however, both Reyes and Uribe were military.[42] The presence of both Reyes and Uribe in leading positions in civil offices of the government points to the continuous authority enjoyed by the military in Colombia since independence wars (Pizarro L. 1987a, 1987b; 1988; Bushnell 1993: 50–73; Atehortúa and Vélez 1994). Furthermore, it suggests that the mobilization of the discourse of modernization in Colombia was, by that time, emphatic for "technicality" and for the need of professionalizing the "Political Man", but not for the need of separating what is civil from that which is military.

Considered as a condition for the establishment of this technical administration, the pacification and the monopolization of violence were at the center of another motto of Reyes' government: "peace, harmony and work" (*"paz, concordia y trabajo"*). As for the pacification of the country, Reyes created special commissions to collect guns, ammunitions, and other reminiscences of wartime from the hands of civilians (Atehortúa 2009: 21). By its turn, the use of "work" in Reyes' motto refers to an indispensable condition for the modernization of the country, as well as to one of the expected effects of pacification. In other words, the pacification of the social space would constitute a fruitful environment for a productive labor force and a modern Colombia to be built. At the same time, pacification and the modalities of violence it implied were considered as necessary for the disciplinarization of this labor force—hence the intolerant disposition of the Reyes' administration towards strikes and other forms of social protest, framed as "seditious" (Atehortúa 2009: 21).

Pacification was, thus, seen as a door through which other promises of modernization would ensue. One of the main obstacles to this virtuous cycle was the politicization of the public forces, which had been intensified after the Thousand Days' War (1901–1903)—often portrayed as a civil war between the two political parties in Colombia (Liberal and Conservative), despite the multiplicity of regions and social groups involved in the confrontations (Bergquist 1989). The internal disputes in the public forces and their mobilization during the Thousand Days' War put into question the assumption that more army necessarily meant more peace. In this context, the professionalization of the military undertaken during

---

[42] While Rafael Reyes was granted the military rank of General after his participation in the repression of a Liberal rebellion in Panama in 1885, Rafael Uribe Uribe was ranked General after having led the Liberal rebel army during the Thousand Days' War.

the Reyes' government sought, at once, a strong army to conduct pacification operations and disciplined troops, obedient not only to hierarchy, but also to the civil authority.

It is through these lines that we must read the dismantling of the Colombian Army in the first year of the Reyes' administration. While the Army had 50,000 men from 1901 to 1902—that is, during the Thousand Days' War—, in 1903 this number was reduced to 5,000 men (Pizarro L. 1987a; Atehortúa 2009: 21; Rey 2008: 163). Such an expressive dismantling of the Army shows that the "politicization" of the military was considered irreversible: the professionalization of the Army would have to start almost from scratch. As for the remaining group, the Ministry of War (*Ministerio de Guerra*) ordered that entire battalions of *zapadores* turned to civil construction projects, such as bridge- and road-building, in the capital but especially in remote areas (Pizarro L. 1987a; Rey 2008: 163). According to a communiqué issued in 1907 by the Presidency,

> The national army, in the present peace era, has been reduced to its minimum expression, with a remaining troop which is strictly necessary for the service, and the majority of the soldiers constituting the national militia have been assigned to work as *zapadores*, and are currently working in the public streets for the benefit of trade, industry and progress.[43] (Palau 1907: 32)

On one hand, the threatening character attached to the Colombian Army was evoked to justify its reduction to the "strictly necessary for the service". On the other, the remaining 10% of the Army were assigned the task of engineering the nation and fostering progress. A threat to the nation and what the nation needed in order to prosper: this tenuous line allegedly separating the risk from the need is permanently haunting discourses about military professionalization. Reyes' administration did not escape this logic.

In times of war, the function of the *zapadores* is crucial: they are responsible for facilitating the mobility and defense of troops, as well as

---

[43] In the original: "El ejército nacional en la presente era de paz ha sido reducido a su mínima expresión, dejando un pie de fuerza armada estrictamente necesario para el servicio, y aun la mayor parte de los soldados que constituyen la milicia nacional han sido destinados a trabajos de zapadores, y trabajan en las vías públicas en beneficio del comercio, de la industria y del fomento".

for creating obstacles to the enemy's mobility (by laying or clearing minefields and demolishing strategic buildings, for instance). Under the Reyes' government, the *zapadores* were mobilized in times of peace, in the physical integration of this modern-to-be Colombia.[44] Connecting the territory was essential to the production of the nation in two main senses. First, it provided concreteness to the idea of the nation as a "connected whole"—the territory and the population both under the jurisdiction of a central government. Second, the constitution of this whole allowed for the rationalization—as well as an aspired optimization—of the production and circulation of goods. The latter was also a condition for the increase in exports of key products—such as tobacco and coffee, which had been registering decreasing numbers since the end of the nineteenth century (Palacios 1980: 7, 19). Using the *zapadores* for the development of infrastructure was also justified as a means of saving resources in times of economic crisis, especially considering that Colombia had just gone through a three-year war.

But above all, using the *zapadores* for the development of the national infrastructure was a way of making those military productive men. In the words of the Minister of War at that time, Manuel Sanclemente: the work of the *zapadores* had a "double effect, considering that the investment in constructions of public utility reduces the cost of the troops; at the same time that arms which, in the barracks, would remain deprived from working, are kept in the social economy"[45] (Sanclemente 1907: 313–314). Instead of idle bodies in the barracks, active arms were invested in the "social economy". Work was, according to this view, not a natural disposition of those soldiers but a disposition made natural through the training of their bodies. Furthermore, Reyes considered work to be an activity that allowed for moral regeneration: "Today, the soldier has once again acquired the habit of morality and work and can be offered as

---

[44] This was not an exclusive feature of Colombia. Brazil, Argentina and Chile are among the cases in which the military played an active role in public work projects. During the 1960s–1970s, this concern with engaging the military in "national development" projects, as framed by the vocabulary of National Security Doctrine, became even more prominent.

[45] In the original: "para hacer tanto menos sensible a la Nación el sostenimiento del Ejército cuanto sea el incremento que la industria y el comercio obtienen con la mayor facilidad de las vías de comunicación, el Gobierno lo ha aplicado a trabajos de zapadores; medida de doble efecto, puesto que si se invierte en obras de pública utilidad el costo de las tropas disminuye; también se le conservan a la economía social brazos que en los cuarteles permanecerían secuestrados del trabajo".

an example of strength and correction"[46] (Reyes 1906: 19). Reyes' was not the first[47]—nor the last—presidential administration in Colombia in which work was thought as a disciplining and regenerating mechanism to both the body and the morale of the soldier.

In addition to the mobilization of *zapadores* in civil construction projects, the Reyes' administration proposed a comprehensive, systematic and institutionalized approach towards the "regenerative mission" of the military to tackle the problem of how to discipline the military and make them obedient to the civil authority. More professionalization—and a better one—was thus claimed as the solution to the lack of discipline associated with the Army. To do this, the plenipotentiary Ambassador for South America, General Rafael Uribe Uribe, was sent to visit Latin American states, aiming to understand how the best military forces in the region were organized. In 1905, he visited Panamá, Ecuador, and Chile with this mission (Atehortúa 2009: 24–25). The fact that Ecuadorian forces had been trained by Chilean military missions and that some Chilean instructors were still working in Ecuador while Uribe visited the country suggests a consistent interest in the Chilean model in the region–or, as a more distant legacy, in how the Prussian model was being incorporated to professionalization programs in Latin America. In this sense, it is unsurprising that it was about Chile that Uribe provided a more detailed description of his visit to the Colombian Presidency (Atehortúa 2009: 25–27).

In Chile, Uribe visited the Military School (*Escuela Militar*), the Schools of Application (*Escuelas de Aplicación*), the War Academy (*Academia de Guerra*), the General Inspection, the Archives, the Administrative Department, and the Direction of Arsenal, Parks and Cavalry Training (*Dirección de Arsenales, Parques y Maestranza*) (Atehortúa 2009: 28). His impressions were registered in a document titled *Memoria sobre*

---

[46] In the original: "Hoy el soldado ha vuelto a adquirir hábitos de moralidad y trabajo, y puede ser ofrecido como ejemplo de fortaleza y corrección".

[47] As a matter of fact, these elements constituted the discourse on military professionalization since the late-nineteenth century in Colombia. In the period known as *Regeneración* (Regeneration), for instance, President Miguel Antonio Caro (1892–1898) adopted several measures aimed at establishing discipline among the military, ranging from religion to literacy, cooking and hygiene. Under the motto "*Regeneración o catástrofe*" (Regeneration or catastrophe), Caro's administration also intensified the enforcement of anti-vagrancy and anti-beggary laws (Castro B. 2011; Botero J. 2012), and promoted a central role for the Catholic Church in social education.

las instituciones militares de Chile (Memoir on Chile's military institutions). The emphasis on the "complete transformation" of the military as a result of the work upon each individual reveals one of the main effects expected to result from the professionalization of the military: the production of the "ideal citizen", reflected in the image and substance of the soldier once he leaves the school. According to the Uribe's memoir:

> Pictures have been taken in order to illustrate how torn the Chileans are when they enter the barracks and how they leave it: it is a complete transformation in their clothes, in the way they present themselves, in their expression and appearance, in their habits and in their moral orientation.[48] (Uribe *Apud* Atehortúa 2009: 29)

In another passage of the same document, Uribe claims that the organization of the Chilean Army "corresponds to the requirements of the modern military art and that in its ranks not only soldiers are formed, but also citizens are educated through the instillation of ideas of civism, respect for authority and intellectual culture"[49] (Uribe *Apud* Atehortúa 2009: 29). In both declarations, it is clear that the purpose of Uribe's official mission went beyond the reproduction of a building, a regulation or a procedure that would result in the amelioration of military skills in battle or in the arrangement and deployment of troops. At the core of the official mission was the concern on how to establish and to consolidate a complex of institutions and professionals aiming at producing not only a soldier who mastered the "modern military art", but also a citizen who mastered the principles of civism. The description Uribe provides of the pictures taken in his official mission suggests that this civism comprehended the appearance ("their clothes, in the way they present themselves"), as well as the "habits" and "moral orientation". The military school gave architectural form and pedagogical purpose to this project: a "school of citizens". The transformative experience expected to

---

[48] In the original: "Se han tomado fotografías ilustrativas del modo como los rotos chilenos llegan al cuartel y del modo como salen: es una transformación completa en el vestido, en la manera de presentarse, en la expresión de la fisionomía, en las costumbres y en la orientación moral".

[49] In the original: "De lo expuesto se deduce que la organización del Ejército de Chile corresponde a las exigencias del arte militar moderno y que en sus filas no sólo se forman soldados sino que se educan ciudadanos, infundiéndoles ideas de civismo, respeto a la autoridad y cultura intelectual".

result from the period soldiers spent therein was therefore both visible and inner.

A remarkable feature of this project lies in the differentiation made between "instruction" and "education" in the schools' schedule. When describing how the Chilean Army was organized, Uribe highlighted that, in the Military School, the Cadet

> does not only receive a perfect military education, but also knowledge that is useful to men in his search for life (...). It is common sense that the other Chilean Institutes *instruct*, but that the Military School *educates*, once autonomous men are physically, morally and intellectually formed through knowledge, character and honor.[50] (emphasis in the original; Uribe *Apud* Atehortúa 2009: 29)

The excerpt reveals that "education" was considered to be more comprehensive, ranging from physical preparation to moral and intellectual formation. Although neither "instruction" nor "education" were conceptually defined by Uribe, this differentiation was invested in the Military School curriculum through two kinds of professionals. According to Uribe's notes on the organization of the Military School in Chile, the "educator" was the key figure in the formation of "citizen-soldiers": his work was not only focused on perfecting skills, but also on moral and intellectual development.

Once implemented, the curriculum of the *Escuela Militar* in Colombia was based on two different kinds of professional: the instructor, whose role was strictly related to training the soldier's body; and the teacher, whose work had an intellectual and moral content. Although part of the instruction-related activities was developed inside the classroom, the characteristic environment of the instructor was the training field. In contrast, most of the curriculum taught by the teacher (such as Literacy, History, Geography, and Doctrine) was transmitted in the classroom. It was precisely the combination of these two professionals that built up a

---

[50] In the original: "Todo el personal del ejército se ha formado en la Escuela Militar, establecimiento donde recibe el Cadete no sólo una perfecta educación militar, sino todos aquellos conocimientos útiles al hombre en su lucha por la vida (...). Es opinión común la de que en los demás Institutos de Chile se *instruye*, pero en la Escuela Militar *se educa*, por cuanto física, moral e intelectualmente se forman hombres dueños de sí mismos por el saber, por el carácter y por el pundonor".

comprehensive character to the project of forming disciplined soldiers and civilized citizens—the "citizen-soldier"—in the military schools.

One of the main challenges to the consolidation of this "new army" in Colombia was not specifically how to build military schools that reflected the purposes of such project, but how to build durable ones. Indeed, the first military schools established after independence had existed for a considerably short period, having had their activities interrupted by violent confrontations. For instance, the School of Civil and Military Engineering (*Escuela de Ingeniería Civil y Militar*), created by the Decree 632 of 1880, was extinguished five years later due to a civil war; and the Military School of Cadets (*Escuela Militar de Cadetes*) was created in 1896 and closed in 1899 due to another civil conflict. In the expectation that the middle- and long-term effects of disciplinarization and civilization over the military personnel could be harvested, the concern with the durability of this complex of military institutions turned its attention to the strategic role of the high-ranked military in this project. They would have a position of command in future military campaigns and were the main candidates for the positions of teachers and instructors.[51] As we will see, the high-ranked officials were indeed one of the focal points of the professionalization program advanced by the first Chilean mission. A few years after the mission had been established, however, they were also the group from which the strongest resistance to implementation of the program emanated.

Importantly, the production of a "citizen-soldier" involved different practices according to the military rank of the student. For soldiers, serving under a specific regime of mandatory conscription, literacy, hygiene, and discipline were at the core of the transformative process of their professionalization. For officers, the professionalization involved a comprehensive palette of courses, from Topographical Drawing to German and History. These contrasts are related to the social fracture separating the military officer (*oficial*) from the enlisted personnel (*suboficial y soldados*) (Rouquié 1984: 97). This mechanism of social differentiation among these categories of the military personnel occurs in

---

[51] In this sense, Uribe's *Memoir* not only recommended that the Reyes' administration hire a Chilean mission to structure military professionalization programs and elaborate the necessary regulations to implement them, but also that Colombian military officers be sent to the Chilean Army for two or three years, with the objective of transmitting what they had learned once back in Colombia (Atehortúa 2009: 29).

two main directions. In the context of universal conscription, the social cut results from a series of criteria allowing for the higher social strata to circumvent the mandatory character of the military service—a diploma, a document proving an experience as pilot, or as a member of a shooting club are but a few examples (Rouquié 1984: 111). Second, requirements such as a specific level of education or even literacy automatically excluded from the military officialdom the lower social strata, whose access to education was considerably restricted at that time (Rouquié 1984: 99). Deprived from the access to the military officer career and facing a narrow range of exceptions to the "universal" character of the military service, the lower social strata came to historically form the frontline of military campaigns, battles, and operations. This does not imply the absence of disciplinarization and civilization mechanisms operating towards military officers, but a different set of practices circulating in this specific social circle.

After the invitation of the Chilean military mission was formalized, in 1907, the Prussian General Emil Körner appointed two Chilean Captains to lead the mission: Arturo Ahumada Bascuñán and Diego Guillén Santana[52] (Pizarro L. 1987a; Rey 2008: 169; Atehortúa 2009: 45). Their main objective in Colombia was to consolidate a new rationale in the military personnel through the elaboration of an organic regulation of the military career; the reorganization of the high-ranked military; and the re-organization of how the troops were operatively deployed (Pizarro L. 1987a; Rey 2008; Atehortúa 2009: 44). The privileged position granted to the Chilean mission in the professionalization of the Colombian Army authorized an all-encompassing role for their members, ranging from the definition of the uniform to be used (Atehortúa 2009: 51) to the organization of the whole military career system (Atehortúa 2009: 44). The focal point of this work was the *Escuela Militar*, created on April 13, 1907 (Decree No. 434). The head of the Chilean mission, General Ahumada, was appointed as the director of the *Escuela Militar* by the Ministry of War (Resolution No. 38). The first group of students was formed by

---

[52] Both had consolidated careers in the Chilean Army and complementary areas of expertise: the former, infantry; the latter, artillery. While the former had developed his studies in Germany, where he was also an aggregate in the Infantry Regiment for two years, Guillén Santana was chosen as the best Captain of the Chilean Army in the early-twentieth century (Atehortúa 2009: 45).

38 Cadets (*Cadetes*) and 20 military officers—among which, 3 Captains (*Capitanes*) and 13 Second Lieutenants (*Subtenientes*) (Rey 2008: 170).

The profile of these students was remarkably from the higher social strata—and this was expected, considering the application requirements defined by the Chilean mission. Indeed, establishing secondary education as a criterion for eligibility in the nineteenth-century Colombia meant restricting access to the military career to the higher social strata (Rouquié 1984: 99; Bushnell 1993: 55; Safford and Palacios 2002: 116; Atehortúa 2009: 46–47). Physical requirements such as a minimum stature were added to the list of mechanisms of exclusion: the minimum height determined by the *Escuela Militar* for its students kept certain indigenous populations out of the eligibility horizon, for instance (Rouquié 1984: 99; Atehortúa 2009: 47).

The fact that the selection process was concentrated in the capital, Bogota, was itself a constraining condition—not to say impeditive—for those living in remote areas. This was especially significant in the case of Colombia because the transportation and communication networks were scarce, in a territory traversed by a *cordillera* ("Colombian Andes"). As an illustration, one of the 38 Cadets in the first group of students of the *Escuela Militar* took 27 days to arrive in Bogota for the selection; for another 4 Cadets, the trip took from 14 to 17 days (Atehortúa 2009: 47–48). Such constraints operated towards the homogenization of the students in the *Escuela Militar*: many of them spoke at least one language in addition to Spanish, studied at the university and resided in Bogota (Atehortúa 2009: 48). Among the university courses they were attending before having enrolled in the *Escuela Militar*, one can find Law, Medicine and Odontology—a clear sign that they were part of the higher social strata in the Colombian society.

As previously mentioned, the Chilean mission encountered resistance from the students and military officers of the highest ranks in its first years. To stimulate obedience and discipline in the Colombian Army, one of the paths pursued by the mission involved the consolidation of rigorous criteria and procedures to organize the ascension within the military career. Although meritocracy had been initially accepted as a formal principle, the mission's insistence on a meticulous evaluation of merit resulted in frictions when it came to be translated in the revision of ranks granted to some of the military officers.

One of the instances in which such tensions emerged was related to the distribution of the Army personnel across the different ranks. According to the "Guide for military organization instruction" (in Spanish, *Guía para la enseñanza de organización militar*), elaborated by the Chilean mission and used as the basis for courses taught in the Colombian Military School, the recommended composition of the military forces had 400–500 officers, and around 6,000 sub-officers and soldiers (Atehortúa 2009: 71). The Chilean's disposition to revise the rank-system in the officialdom of the Colombian Army stemmed from the assessment that the composition of its personnel was far from what the mission considered as the modern military formation. There were 4,000 high-ranked officers for a significantly lower number of low-ranked officers and soldiers in the Army by that time (Atehortúa 2009: 54), revealing both the social cut with which the dismantling of the Army by Reyes had been undertaken, and the difficulty in changing the criteria organizing the ranks related to the higher social strata.

The grading system implemented by the Chilean mission in the *Escuela Militar* was another instance in which tensions with the Army's officialdom emerged. In the first year, the average grade granted in 1907 to the students was 6.8 (Atehortúa 2009: 46). Considered as too severe, the grading system revealed the gap between the Chilean and the Colombian military regarding the quality and consistency of their background. Along with the meritocracy discourse, it made explicit the distance separating military professionals from those whose promotions were still too connected to patronage (*padrinazgo*) and whose formation was still based on empiricism and improvisation. The rigor with which students from the Colombian elite were evaluated exposed those who did not meet the standards set by the Chilean mission to embarrassment. In the case of the officers, the grading system exposed them to questions regarding the criteria through which they were granted their military rank. In this sense, it is no surprise that the resistance towards the Chilean mission grew as its work advanced in the *Escuela Militar*.

The educational program was formed by two main domains of knowledge: a military and a civil one. The former included courses such as "Infantry Tactics", "Artillery Tactics", "Topographical Drawing", "Fortification" and "Knowledge on Weapons". The civil domain comprehended courses such as "Spanish", "German", "Universal History and Geography" and "National History" (*Historia Patria*) (Atehortúa 2009: 46). These courses were taught in the first four years of the Cadets course, and one additional year was especially dedicated to the military formation (Atehortúa 2009: 46).

The relative balance with which the civil and military domains were distributed in the curriculum of the *Escuela Militar* reveals a central feature of the professionalization of the low-ranked. As we have seen, the profile of the students selected by the Chilean mission was characteristic of the higher social strata in Bogota. Within this group, building "citizen-soldiers" did not involve teaching how to read and write—for they were already literate—, nor habits of hygiene—for their conducts were already in accordance with socially accepted norms of hygiene. Rather, it involved a comprehensive curriculum, indicating that the "citizen-soldier" was expected to be built from far more than the key areas of the military domain. In addition to the main spheres of the Prussian military tactics and other complementary military techniques, students had to learn how to speak proper Spanish, for instance. The military professional emerging from the *Escuela Militar* also had to learn German—a sign of Prussia's relevance to the professionalization program led by the Chilean Army. Furthermore, the mandatory character of history classes ("Universal History and Geography" and "National History") points to a curriculum whose objective is to produce an illustrious citizen.

In light of the differences regarding the soldiers and the officers, narratives on the transformative effect of the *Escuela Militar* acquire a different meaning from that of the "complete regeneration" of the military through its professionalization. When the Chilean diplomat based in Colombia, Eugenio Rodríguez Mendoza, highlighted that many of the young Cadets "belonged to the best society of this country"[53] (Rodríguez M. 1908 *Apud* Atehortúa 2009: 49), he was not only shedding light on the privileged social status that came to characterize the students of that school, he was also fighting the negative image with which military institutions had been associated in Colombia until that time. In a document sent by the Chilean diplomat to the Minister of Foreign Relations of Chile in 1908, Rodríguez Mendoza reports that:

> Before the mission arrived, (the army) was incredibly distant not only from a scientific and modern organization, but from any organization at all: the soldier was recruited by force, he lacked any of the most basic habits regarding civilized life, he slept on the floor, in the demoralizing company of his indigenous companion and he was kept in the military ranks through

---

[53] In the original: "El resto lo forman jóvenes cadetes, muchos de los cuales pertenecen a la mejor sociedad de este país".

the brutal discipline of the whip. This deplorable state has already been considerably changed: they begin to acquire new habits, the uniforms are not the same, nor are the instruction methods. (Rodríguez M. 1908 *Apud* Atehortúa 2009: 51)[54]

As we have seen in this section, the problem of discipline in the military was partially interpreted as resulting from the lack of quality in the leadership, but it was also considered as deriving from the indiscipline of the troops. This view is clearly expressed in Rodríguez Mendoza's report: before the arrival of the Chilean mission, the Colombian soldier was described as uncivil, immoral, and lacking the manners of a "civilized life". This portrayal justifies the importance of the Chilean mission, by demarcating its positive effect on the Colombian military: according to him, the pedagogical project and the instruction methods mobilized by the Chilean mission were able to transform the manners and habits of those soldiers.

By emphasizing the civilizational effect of the work undertaken by the Chilean military, the diplomat's report reinforces the hierarchy between the two Armies. Interestingly, however, this asymmetry is not expressed in terms associated to warfare (for instance, equipment, weaponry, or strategy). Although it can ultimately result in a superiority that manifests itself in warfare terms, the fundamental character of this hierarchy is discipline—by its turn, associated to the manners and social conducts of the "civil life". Under such reading, discipline is the condition for the development of strategy and tactics: without discipline, every Army is "distant not only from a scientific and modern organization, but from any organization at all", as reported by Rodríguez Mendoza.

The depiction made by the Chilean diplomat about the professionalization program reveals yet another important element: what he considered a transformation achieved by the military mission regarding the civility of the Colombian soldier was in fact the elitization of the Army – now formed by "the best society of this country", according to Rodríguez

---

[54] In the original: "Hasta el arribo de la misión (el ejército) estaba increíblemente distante no solo de una organización científica, moderna, sino en general de toda organización: el soldado era reclutado por fuerza, carecía en absoluto de los hábitos más rudimentarios en materia de vida civilizada, dormía en el suelo, en la desmoralizadora compañía de su camarada indígena y era mantenido en filas mediante la disciplina brutal del azote. Este estado deplorable ha cambiado ya considerablemente: empiezan a ganarse nuevos hábitos, los uniformes no son los mismos, ni tampoco los métodos de instrucción".

Mendoza. When contending that the military mission had transformed the habits and manners of the Colombian soldiers, his ideas of "before" and "after" are not commensurable, for they do not refer to groups of individuals with the same social profile.

According to Rodríguez Mendoza, this "deplorable state" had been considerably changed by 1908. As we have seen, however, the eligibility criteria defined by the Chilean mission for the Military School were difficult to meet for a significant part of the Colombian population at that time. Operating as a mechanism of social exclusion, these criteria produced what was conceived as a superior Army in terms of civility. In this sense, the transformation in the civility of the Colombian military claimed to be achieved by the Chilean mission had, as its condition of possibility, the mechanism of social exclusion. The civilization aspired by the Chilean mission in the short period established in the contract was only considered to be possible in the higher social strata, for their manners and habits were already seen as superior.

Importantly, "the best society of this country" also had to be civilized, given their inferior position in relation to the Chilean military. For instance, the use of the whip and other punishment techniques persisting since the colonial period among teachers and instructors was considered barbaric and, therefore, had to be substituted by more rational punishment methods (Rouquié 1984: 76). Nonetheless, the higher the military rank, the stronger was the resistance against the civilizing work of the Chilean mission. In this context, when the Chilean mission had its contract renewed, in 1909, and the focus of its activities was turned to the professionalization of the line of command (Atehortúa 2009: 51), the resistance against its work increased. After having established the Superior War College (*Escuela Superior de Guerra*) and the General Staff College (*Escuela del Estado Mayor*) (Decree No. 453/1909), the Chilean mission witnessed the narrowing of its scope.

At the same time, newspapers in the Colombian capital published articles signed by self-proclaimed "republicans" or "civilists", defending the Chilean mission. An editorial published in *La Fusión* in October 1909, for instance, condemned "The speed with which in our wars high-ranked military are fabricated, ignoring most of the most elementary principles of the honorable military career" (*Apud* Atehortúa 2009: 58). According to the same editorial, the persistence of such a practice put in evidence "not the warrior who will sustain the national flag with the pride and dignity that it deserves, but the eternal chieftain who the contingencies of our political resentments have transformed into a fearful *caudillo* of much machete and very little civilization"[55] (La Fusión 1909 *Apud* Atehortúa 2009: 58–59).

The Chilean mission also complained about the lack of respect those high-ranked officers had towards the criteria, parameters and rules structuring the professionalization program implemented in the *Escuela Militar*. According to a letter sent by the heads of the mission to the Chief of Staff of the Chilean Army (Díaz and Charpín 1909 *Apud* Atehortúa 2009: 60), officers graduated from that program were dispensed from service by high-ranked officers, and their positions were filled with those who were loyal to the Minister of War or recruited without attending the courses in the *Escuela Militar*. The same document claimed that there was a systematic promotion of Generals (*Generales*), Colonels (*Coroneles*) and Majors (*Mayores*) without any regard to their virtues and merits, nor to the rules and criteria legally established for the military career (Atehortúa 2009: 60). Such attitudes had clear impacts towards the pedagogical schedule with which the Chilean mission was working in the *Escuela Militar*. In one of the cases reported, almost all the officers with the highest ranks were removed from the two groups with the best preparation in the capital one day after the instruction course had started (La Fusión 1909 *Apud* Atehortúa 2009: 61). In this sense, the Chilean mission not only faced resistance to changing the criteria guiding the organization of the high-ranked military career: this very difficulty impacted the work undertaken in the *Escuela Militar* towards the low-ranked.

Under these circumstances, the Chilean mission formally requested to the Ministry of War an expressive reduction in the group of senior officers, so that those concluding the professionalization program of the *Escuela Militar* could better express the meritocratic criteria the mission aimed at consolidating in the Colombian Army. The request faced increased resistance after the creation of a course specifically dedicated to the General Staff (*Estado Mayor*), whose first selection process had

---

[55] In the original: "La rapidez con que en nuestras guerras se fabrican militares de alta graduación que ignoran la mayor parte los más elementales principios de la noble carrera militar, nos impele a ver en ellos, no el guerrero que sostendrá el pabellón nacional con la altivez y la dignidad que se merece, sino el eterno gamonal a quien las contingencias de nuestros rencores políticos han convertido en medroso caudillo de mucho machete y muy poca civilización".

only one Colombian high-ranked officer approved (Atehortúa 2009: 58). In a letter sent in September 1909 to the Chief of Staff of the Chilean Army, the two heads of the Chilean mission, Francisco Díaz and Pedro Charpín, explained that they had submitted to the Colombian Executive bills on manpower (*planta y pie de fuerza*); organization of military divisions; career progression criteria; recruitment; wages; and retirement, but after months, none of these bills had been presented to the Colombian Congress (Atehortúa 2009: 59).

Soon it became clear that the reorganization of the military forces aspired by the Chilean mission required the support of both the Minister of War and the Colombian Congress. Indeed, the changes proposed by the mission relied on military internal decisions that had to be made official through the *Military Official Bulletin* (*Boletín Militar*), as well as on rearrangements in the existing regulation of the military career. Ironically or not, General Luis Enrique Bonilla, the Minister of War at that time, had the exact profile that the Chilean mission was confronting. In an editorial published on October 10, 1909, the newspaper *El Domingo* commented with irony:

> General? Yes, gentlemen. Of division. Observe, gentlemen, how he has divided, or more appropriately, how he has partitioned the backbone of the scientific organization of the Army. (…) And when at his desk in the Capitol, he demolishes with decrees based on party lines what the Mission has founded. Mister Bonilla does not aspire to a National Army, entirely of the nation. His ideal is a Conservative Army, the Army who deliberates, the Army of a party.[56] (El Domingo 1909 *Apud* Atehortúa 2009: 58)

The Minister of War is here portrayed as a reminiscence of a historical past in Colombia. Instead of a professional whose work was devoted to the construction of a "National" and "scientific" army, the Minister was immersed in the disputes between the Liberal and Conservative parties. On the other hand, the work of the Chilean mission is here presented as the foundation of what the trajectory of a modern Army must be: an

---

[56] In the original: "¿General (Luis Enrique Bonilla)? Sí, Señores. Y de división. Vean Ustedes cómo ha dividido, mejor dicho, cómo ha partido por el eje la organización científica del Ejército. (…) Y cuando funciona en su pupitre del capitolio, demuele con decretos partidistas lo que la Misión ha fundado. El Señor Bonilla no aspira a un Ejército Nacional, enteramente de la patria. Su ideal es el Ejército Conservador, el Ejército que delibere, el Ejército de un partido".

a-political and scientifically organized Army, in service of a whole nation—and not a specific political party. Importantly, the superiority with which the Chilean mission regarded the Colombian military in general, and most notably the high-ranked officers, had to be negotiated with its reliance on a certain level of support in the political game in Colombia.

The intricate tensions involving the mission, the Colombian Presidency, the Minister of War, and their counterparts in Chile regarding the reach and depth of the authority that would be granted to the mission in the professionalization program reveal the limits of the boundary between the technical and the political. More specifically, they point to the unavoidability of an active engagement of the Chilean mission with party politics in Colombia, aiming at building a favorable play of forces for its program.

This was made even more explicit in the fourth Chilean mission in Colombia. On one hand, it proposed a universal mandatory recruitment as the best system to strengthen the formation of national armed forces in service of the homeland (Atehortúa 2009: 100–103). To gather support for the idea, they sided with internal interests in Colombia, such as the Minister of War José Medina Calderón, whose similar demand was meant to avoid the need to attract recruits by raising wages. On the other hand, local forces managed to include exceptions in the recruitment through payment, effectively reducing recruitment to poor urban and rural populations who could not afford to dodge the draft—a situation the Chilean mission strongly objected. Increasingly entangled in these political disputes, the Chilean mission finished its contract with an eroded mandate.

Two dynamics are made bare in this tension. First, the Chilean mission's aim—and, more broadly, the boundary authorized in the modern discourse analyzed above—of keeping the Armed Forces "technical" and away from the "political" could only be accomplished through the active participation in politics. Likewise, and inversely, the political purity of the Armed Forces could only be achieved by turning political disputes into "technical matters" of how to most effectively achieve a (non-politically) given set goals. Hence, the condition of possibility of the boundary between the political and the technical is shown to lie, paradoxically, in its crossing.

Second, the Chilean mission's constant meddling in Colombian "politics" led to the erosion of its position in the country, ultimately leading to the Presidential opposition to its continuation and, soon after, to its departure from Colombia. It is noteworthy how such departure has been justified in the press: "the Chilean pullout must not be accorded the importance of a conflict between States" since the responsibility for the failure of the Mission was attributed to "the lack of experience and military knowledge of the Colombian agent charged with contracting, in Santiago, the latest Mission"[57] (La Sociedad 1915 *Apud* Atehortúa 2009: 103)—another instance of the preservation of the distinction of "technical" and "political" through a depoliticizing claim to what is technical (lack of experience), aimed at preserving a technical definition of what is political (State conflict).

4.4 Conclusion

This chapter explored the conditions of emergence of the military professional in Latin America and, more specifically, in Colombia. To do that, it sought to inscribe the creation of military professionalization programs in discursive articulations of how violence had to be organized so that modernization could flourish.

Reading Elias' *The Civilizing Process* (2000) and Weber's *Politics as Vocation* (2004) as canonic expressions of a discourse of modernization, Sect. 4.1 analyzed how monopolization/pacification, civilization, and professionalization are connected in this discourse. In particular, I explored how civilization and professionalization are entangled in the process of organizing violence within the pacified social space to grasp the main stakes in the claims for the need to professionalize the military— among them, the boundaries between the "civil" and the "military", and the one between the "technical" and the "political". By bringing Sarmiento's Facundo (2018) as a discursive expression about the "problem of violence" in the context following independence wars in Latin America, I showed how this discourse locates modernity in Europe, constituting a regulative ideal whose reproduction has had profound effects both on pacification and on military professionalization programs in the region.

Considering these elements, I discussed the emergence of a circuit of military *savoirs* in nineteenth-century Latin America, having mainly France and Prussia as references for solutions to the "problem of the military". Looking at this circuit, Sect. 4.2 mapped the main fluxes of

---

[57] In the original: "la inexperiencia y falta de conocimientos militares del agente de Colombia encargado de contratar en Santiago la última Misión venida al país".

military professionals and the main veins through which military *savoirs* circulated therein. In doing so, I analyzed the main aspects allowing for us to identify the homogenization of the armies in Latin America as one of the main effects of the reproduction of the discourse of modernization through this circuit of military *savoirs* in the region.

If Sect. 4.2 offered a general landscape of the circulation of military professionals and *savoirs* in Latin America, Sect. 4.3 brought texture to this picture by shedding light on Colombia's position within this circuit. More specifically, I discussed the work of the Chilean mission invited to assist in the professionalization of the Colombian military, as well as the main frictions deriving from the civilizational traits of the mission work towards the Colombian Army.

With this move, my objective was to challenge two claims recurrently operating in studies about the professionalization of the military. First, the inescapable need to engage with "politics" so as to preserve the "technical" character of the Chilean mission blurs, at once, two boundaries that are constitutive of the discourse of modernization: the political-technical and the civil-military ones. This invites us to think about them not as hermetic containers, but as domains operating with the same underlying logic.

Second, I argued that despite the homogenizing effects of the circuit of military *savoirs*, the discussion about the professionalization of the Colombian military points to the tensions deriving from residues of tradition amid a claim for rationality; of patronage amid a claim for meritocracy; of politics amid a claim for the technical; of particularity amid a claim for universality. Since we cannot understand the professionalization of the military in Colombia away from the circuit of military *savoirs*, my argument is that this is not an exclusive feature of that country, but an unavoidable fracture constituting the discourse of modernization.

References

Books, Chapters, Articles

Atehortúa C. A. L. *Construcción del Ejército Nacional en Colombia, 1907–1930.* Reforma Militar y Misiones Extranjeras. Medellín: La Carreta, 2009.

Atehortúa C. A. L.; Vélez R. H. *Estado y Fuerzas Armadas en Colombia.* Cali: TM, 1994.

Atkins, G. P.; Thompson, L. V. German Military Influence in Argentina, 1921–1940. *Journal of Latin American Studies*, v. 4, n. 2, pp. 257–274, November 1972.
Bartelson, J. Double Binds: Sovereignty and the Just War Tradition. In: Kalmo, H.; Skinner, Q. (eds.). *Sovereignty in Fragments—The Past, Present and Future of a Contested Concept*. Cambridge: Cambridge University Press, 2010.
Bedregal, G. *Los Militares en Bolivia. Ensayo de interpretación sociológica*. LaPaz, p. 23, 1971.
Bergquist, C. *Coffee and Conflict in Colombia, 1886-1910*. Durham, NC: Duke University Press, 1989.
Botero Jaramillo, N. El problema de los excluidos. Las leyes contra la vagancia en Colombia durante las décadas de 1820 a 1840. *Anuario Colombiano de Historia Social y de la Cultura*, v. 39, n. 2, pp. 41–68, Jul–Dic. 2012.
Bushnell, D. *The Making of Modern Colombia: A Nation in Spite Itself*. Berkeley, CA: University of California Press, 1993.
Castaño, C. A. *La Policía*. Su origen y su destino. Biblioteca Escuela de Policía "General Santander", Vol. VIII. Bogotá: Cahur, 1947.
Castro, C. The Army as a Modernizing Actor in Brazil, 1870–1930. In: Silva, P. (ed.). *The Soldier and the State in South America: Essays in Civil-Military Relations*. New York: Palgrave Macmillan, 2001.
Castro, C. *O Espírito Militar: um antropólogo na caserna*. Rio de Janeiro: Zahar, 2004.
Chapman, P. *Bananas: How the United Fruit Company Shaped the World*. Edinburgh: Canongate, 2007.
Elias, N. *The civilizing process*. Oxford: Blackwell, 2000.
Fernández, M.; Esteves, P. Silencing Colonialism: Foucault and the Modern International. In: Bonditti, P.; Bigo, D.; Gros, F. (eds.). *Foucault and the International: Silences and Legacies for the Study of World Politics*. New York: Palgrave Macmillan, 2017.
Fonnegra, G. *Las Bananeras*. Un testimonio vivo. Bogotá: Círculo de Lectores, 1986.
Foucault, M. *Discipline and Punish*. New York: Second Vintage, 1995.
Foucault, M. *Security, Territory, Population*. New York: Palgrave McMillan, 2007.
Gill, L. *The School of the Americas: Military Training and Political Violence in the Americas*. Durham and London: Duke University Press, 2004.
Inayatullah, N.; Blaney, D. L. *International Relations and the Problem of Difference*. New York: Routledge, 2004.
Kapoor, I. Acting in a Tight Spot: Homi Bhabha's Postcolonial Politics. *New Political Science*, v. 25, n. 4, pp. 561–577, 2003.

Llórente, M. V. Perfil de la Policía Colombiana. In: Deas, M.; Llórente, M. V. (eds.) *Reconocer la guerra para construir la paz*. Bogotá: UniandesCerec-Norma, 1999.

Loveman, B. *For la Patria: Politics and the Armed Forces in Latin America*. Wilmington, DE: Scholarly Resources Books, 1999.

Lynch, J. As origens da independência da América Espanhola. In: Bethell, L. (org.). *História da América Latina:* da Independência a 1870, vol. III. São Paulo: EDUSP, 2004.

Malaguti, V. *Introdução Crítica à Criminologia Brasileira*. Rio de Janeiro: Revan, 2011.

Morelli, F. Entre el antiguo y el nuevo régimen. La historia política hispanoamericana del siglo XIX. *Historia Crítica*, n. 33, Enero-Junio, pp. 122–155, 2007.

Neocleous, M. *War Power, Police Power*. Edinburgh: Edinburgh University Press, 2014.

Nunn, F. M. Foreign Influences on the South American Military: Professionalization and Politicization. In: Silva, P. (ed.). *The Soldier and the State in South America: Essays in Civil-Military Relations*. New York: Palgrave Macmillan, 2001.

Palacios, M. *Coffee in Colombia, 1850–1970. An Economic, Social, and Political History*. Cambridge: Cambridge University Press, 1980.

Pamplona, M. A. Nação e modernidade nos escritos de Sarmiento e Nabuco. *Letterature d'America*. Anno XVII–XVIII, n. 75–76, pp. 25–65, 1997/1998.

Pizarro, L. E. La Profesionalización Militar en Colombia (1907–1944). *Análisis Político*, n. 1, pp. 20–39, 1987a.

Pizarro, L. E. La Profesionalización Militar en Colombia (II): El Periodo de La Violencia. *Análisis Político*, n. 2, pp. 7–29, 1987b.

Pizarro, L. E. La profesionalización militar en Colombia (III): los regímenes militares (1953–1958). *Análisis Político*, n. 3, pp. 6–30, 1988.

Rey, E. M. F. La educación militar en Colombia entre 1886 y 1907. *Historia Crítica*, n. 35, pp. 150–175, Enero-Junio 2008.

Rouquié, A. *El Estado Militar en América Latina*. Buenos Aires: Emecé, 1984.

Ruiz V. J. C.; Illera C. O.; Manrique Z. V. *La tenue línea de la tranquilidad. Estudio comparado sobre seguridad ciudadana y policía*. Bogotá, D.C.: Universidad del Rosario, 2006.

Safford, F. Política, Ideologia e Sociedade na América Espanhola do Pós-Independência. In: Bethtell, L. (org.). *História da América Latinai:* Da Independência a 1870, vol. III. São Paulo: EDUSP, 2004.

Safford, F.; Palacios, M. *Colombia—Fragmented Land, Divided Society*. Oxford: Oxford University Press, 2002.

Sarmiento, D. F. *Facundo – o civilización y barbarie*. Buenos Aires: Biblioteca del Congreso de la Nación, 2018.

Scalercio, M. A. *As armas e as consciências*. Tese de Doutorado, Instituto de Relações Internacionais, Pontifícia Universidade Católica do Rio de Janeiro. Rio de Janeiro, 2015.

Viana, M. T.; Peixoto, G. Brasil: um novo 'caso de sucesso' para a segurança pública na América Latina?, *Revista Cult*, n. 244, pp. 11–18, 2019.

Walker, R. B. J. Europe Is Not Where It Is Supposed to Be. In: Kelstrup, M.; Williams, M. C. (eds). *International Relations and the Politics of European Integration: Power, Security and Community.* London and New York: Routledge, 2000.

Weber, M. Politics as a Vocation. In: Owen, D.; Strong, T. B. (eds.). *The Vocation Lectures.* Cambridge: Hackett, 2004.

DOCUMENTS, REPORTS AND STUDIES

Castro Blanco, E. El Derecho como positivación fáctica de exclusión a los vagos en Colombia. In: *Diálogo de Saberes*, No. 34 (Ene-Jun. 2011), pp. 163–196.

Ejército de Chile. La llegada al país de los restos del General de División don Emilio Körner. *Memorial del Ejército de Chile.* Santiago (Chile), Talleres del Instituto Geográfico Militar, Año XIX, Ago. 1924, pp. 115–118.

Palau, L. *Colombia en 1907* – bajo la administración del Sr. General Rafael Reyes. Bogota: Imprenta Nacional, 1907.

Reyes, R. Exposición de Rafael Reyes. Presidente de la República de Colombia a sus compatriotas. In: *Gaceta de Santander*, No. 3764 (January 23, 1906).

Sanclemente, M. (Ministro de Guerra). Informe de los Ministros del Despacho efectivo dirigidos a la Asamblea Nacional Constituyente y Legislativa en 1907. In: *Diario Oficial,* No. 12.913 (April 3, 1907).

CHAPTER 5

"All They Understand Is Force": The Military Professional as the Expert-Soldier

This chapter looks closely at the peace-war boundary to reflect on the effects of the historical transformations in the transnational circuit of military *savoirs* during the second half of the twentieth century. By that time, counterinsurgency occupied a privileged position among military *savoirs* and was increasingly translated into professionalization programs for Latin American armies, having the U.S. as the main reference points for military professionals. With this analysis, this chapter seeks to grasp the historical conditions for the repositioning of Colombia in the transnational circuit of military *savoirs* by the late 2000s.

To explore the stakes in the emergence and durability of counterinsurgency as a valorized *savoir* in the region and its effects on the peace-war boundary, my point of departure is the discussion on the colonial imprints in the making of the U.S. counterinsurgency doctrine. Section 5.1 goes

---

This is a statement by Fred Halliday, quoted in Brown (2008: 443), used in reference to the Iraqi population. To Halliday, either the enemy or the population in Iraq only understands the use of force. Here, I am appropriating Halliday's phrase to refer to one of the remarkable characteristics of the "expert soldier", discussed in this chapter, i.e. the emphasis on tactically efficient bodies in the making of the military professional.

© The Author(s), under exclusive license to Springer Nature Switzerland AG 2022
M. T. Viana, *Post-conflict Colombia and the Global Circulation of Military Expertise*, Critical Security Studies in the Global South, https://doi.org/10.1007/978-3-030-96103-9_5

back to the mid nineteenth century to unveil the terms within which conventional warfare coexisted with the so-called "small wars", a modality of warfare upon which later versions of counterinsurgency were based. In this discussion, I show that the circulation of "small wars" was confined to the European colonies in Africa and Asia—where the brutality of armies was not restrained by so-called rules of civility of conventional warfare. I analyze the main terms upon which the competition between these two *savoirs* relied and discuss the conditions for and implications of the acknowledgement of counterinsurgency as a military *savoir*. Then, I explore the mechanisms through which counterinsurgency travelled from Europe to the U.S. and later to Latin America.

Section 5.2 builds on this discussion by inscribing Colombia in the hemispheric circuit of military *savoirs* and by looking at the systematic interaction between the U.S. Army and the Colombian Army in the development of counterinsurgency-based professionalization programs since the early 1950s. In doing so, I show that the center of gravity of those programs slid from the Military School to the Lancers' School (*Escuela de Lanceros*), focusing on tactical and physical training through short-term courses. As a consequence, I argue that, unlike the "citizen-soldier" envisioned in the Military School, professionalization turned towards the production of "expert soldiers".

In line with those features, Sect. 5.3 analyzes the relevance of Plan Colombia to the repositioning of Colombia in the transnational circuit of military *savoirs*. More specifically, I discuss the main axes structuring the Plan and show how it intensified the reproduction of the expert soldier, authorizing the claim that the war against "narcoterrorism" had been won in the country—and, thus, making the Colombian "success story" possible. The chapter lands in a discussion on the reorganization of the Colombian Army in the "post-conflict" context, while also shedding light into the main characteristics of the Colombian expertise which many countries in the region and the world have been looking up to.

5.1 The Re-articulation of the Circuit Around Counterinsurgency, an Old New Military *Savoir*

"Quasi-professionals". These were the terms with which military officers who advocated for the superiority of conventional warfare referred to military engaged in "small wars" (Porch 2013: 2). The differentiation between these two *savoirs* was anchored in their degree of "civility". On one hand, the civilized character of conventional war was read as the effect of principles and rules guiding war fighting, as well as a remarkable characteristic of those who waged war—both the soldiers and the sovereign state on behalf of which they fought (Rouquié 1984: 87–89; Keene 2004: xi, 6–7, 126; Porch 2013: 21). In contrast, those who engaged in "small wars" were considered uncivilized soldiers especially because the rules of conventional war could not apply against uncivilized insurgents (Keene 2004: xi, 7). In other words, the incivility of the enemy meant that the scientific knowledge pursued by conventional war, as well as the limits on the use of violence established through the *jus ad bellum* and the *jus in bello* were only justifiable when the two warring parties were civilized—"that is", when they were nineteenth century European modern states (Keene 2004: xi, 7).

The category "small"/"irregular" itself reveals the privileged position of conventional war in the architecture of military *savoirs* at that time. Indeed, its status of norm makes all kinds of warfare that are not symmetric nor regular a deviation from what war should be. Through these lines, the British Major General Sir Charles Callwell, founder of one of the first schools dedicated to the professionalization of small warriors in the late-nineteenth century, conceptualized "small wars" as operations of regular armies against irregular forces (Porch 2013: 4). Importantly, both his noble title "Sir" and his military rank indicate that, despite having a career inscribed in the underprivileged domain of small wars, Callwell was neither outside the military ranking system, nor outside the criteria through which social prestige was attributed.

If civility was so central to the differentiation between conventional and small warfare, we can infer that tensions would emerge from attempts to professionalize "small wars" as a discrete category of warfare. First, because this would imply a certain validation of small wars and, consequently, the possibility of a competition with conventional wars for legitimacy, prestige, and resources. Second, the discourse of professionalization cannot be dissociated from the civilizing process, as we discussed in Chapter 4. In this sense, the professionalization of "small warriors"—a civilizing battle with an uncivilized character—would undermine the civilization of the modern military soldier himself. Given the incivility to which the practice of "small wars" was invariably associated, its validation as a discrete category of warfare would require the re-articulation of the regime of justification for the professionalization of the military. After all, if the ideal citizen was expected to emerge from the specific socialization of the soldiers inside the barracks, what kind of "ideal citizen" would result from professionalization schools specialized in "small wars"?

The challenge for those who advocated a position for "small wars" in the edifice of military *savoirs* (Wasinski 2012) was to crystalize a set of principles and rules that could constrain excesses of violence in "small wars" and avoid their association with brutality. More specifically, through such an effort, massacres that could easily slide into accusations of barbarism could instead "be explained as anomalies inflicted by stressed-out conscripts, by conventional soldiers untutored in the hearts and minds fundamentals of war among the people (...) rather than as patterns of racialized violence endemic to small wars" (Porch 2013: 3).

If the British military are considered as those who first advanced towards the professionalization of "small wars" through the creation of specialized schools in the last decades of the nineteenth century, the historiography of this *savoir* stretches back to the French colonial experience in Africa, in the first half of that century (Porch 2011: 246, 2013; Draper 2019: 1022). Therefore, for us to dissect the professional code built around "small war" as a discrete category of modern warfare, we must take a close look at the most prominent figures in the French colonial trajectory to understand the principles consolidated in reference to this emerging military *savoir*.

The names often mentioned in this context include the French General Louis-Gabriel Suchet, who came to be linked with the conception of information campaigns aimed at winning the "hearts and minds" of Aragonese and Catalans in French-occupied Spain from 1808 to 1812 (Porch 2011: 246). In particular, the project comprised infrastructure and institutional improvements, presented as materializations of the Napoleonic modernization project. Suchet built hospitals, orphanages and schools and addressed values such as liberty, fraternity, and equality in his speeches (Few 2010). This concern with disseminating information about the benefits and legitimacy of the occupation government was gradually translated into what we came to know as "psychological operations"—which were to be found at the core of small wars years later.

Here, I am not particularly interested in presenting a counter-narrative to the regime of justification of colonial enterprises, nor questioning the position of military officers such as Suchet in the historiography of small wars. Rather, I want to explore the conditions that made their circulation as references within the edifice of modern military *savoirs* possible—or, more specifically, the criteria that rendered their expertise not only legitimate among their counterparts, but efficient in the terrain.

The context of Revolutionary France is key in this regard. The operations that characterized the territorial occupations during the Napoleonic wars and in the following period aimed at building a friendly image of French imperialism. The discursive focus on persuasion and clemency was portrayed as a less brutal form of war, claimed as contrasting with those of the Ancient Regime (Few 2010). Reading resistance to the French occupation as necessarily deriving from misinformation, Suchet sought to make the Spanish aware of the benefits of the French administration, expecting that this would enhance the legitimacy of their occupation.

However, the privileged position of conventional war was based on a validation test (Wasinski 2012), according to which the combination of military technology with the subordination of a set of tactics to a grand military strategy had to prove its efficiency in the battlefield, through a "decisive victory". Its scientific character was precisely the refinement of that combination so as to achieve victory through the optimization of resources applied in war. In this sense, "small wars" needed more than a "hearts and minds" program to earn a position in that edifice: it had to adjust to the criteria according to which validation was granted.[1] More specifically, it needed to provide tactical answers to eventual resistance against the French colonial administration in Algeria. At the same time this validation test posed a challenge to "small wars", it offered an opportunity.

It is in this regard that General Thomas-Robert Bugeaud acquired prominence, especially in the development of a tactical *savoir* that proved to be efficient in "small wars". When sent to Algeria in 1840 to take the position of Governor General, the bulk of Bugeaud's Napoleonic wars experience had been spent fighting *partidas* in Spain (Gildea 2019: 19), guerrilla formations disputing the control of the Iberian Peninsula with the French army in the 1800s. Because the French professional soldiers

---

[1] According to Porch (2013: 13), it was only by the late-nineteenth century that one could observe the remarkable contrast between conventional and small warfare. Indeed, the intensification of the Industrial Revolution not only made the differentiation between the two more explicit, but also gave it technological contours—especially with the development of weaponry in line with the agility required by "small wars". Thus, technological advances in military weaponry walked hand in hand with the development of the edifice of military *savoirs*: actually, one was the condition for the other.

of that time were not taught guerrilla warfare in military schools, the tactics lapidated by Bugeaud had mainly the battleground as its source of inspiration.

The French conquest of Algeria puzzled European strategists for failing to fit the "decisive battle" paradigm (Rid 2009: 618). The sequence of confrontations in a never-ending conflict was closer to what they considered a "pre-modern" warfare dynamic (Porch 2013: 22). According to Bugeaud, the technology developed for conventional wars could not be adjusted to the conditions of armed confrontations in Algeria. Once irregular warfare was mostly characterized by the avoidance of great armed confrontations and by the attraction of the enemy army to one's own territory, oversized expeditions and heavy weaponry were not only less agile, but also easy targets for the enemy. Believing that mobility was the key for the success of the French occupation in Algeria, Bugeaud created small military formations, equipped with light weaponry, and nurtured by an intelligence network (Porch 2013: 20). The agility with which French forces operated in Algeria soon became the core of the "scientific" refinement with which European tacticians of "small wars" would engage in the following years. In Bugeaud's terms, such effort resulted in military forces "even more Arab than the Arabs" (*Apud* Porch 2013: 20)—that is, for him, the French are better at being Arabs when mimicking them.

Given that the conflict between the French forces and the "insurgents" had mobility as the fundamental principle of their tactical operations, grand strategies such as the ones governing the planning and the organization of conventional wars were of little use, for the transformation of the scenarios was remarkably accelerated. Importantly, when highlighting the centrality of tactics, Bugeaud was advocating for an operational edge of "small wars" over conventional ones, taking into consideration the particularities of the conditions found in Algeria.

Thus, rather than denying the criteria which constituted the validation system of military *savoirs*, Bugeaud and other proponents of "small wars" as a discrete category of modern warfare aimed at refining the military edifice, so that it also encompassed a *savoir* specialized in another type of enemy. The opportunity identified by Bugeaud was, therefore, related to the absence of a category of *savoir* built upon the idea of an enemy with an inferior, savage nature. The development of such a tactical knowledge did not emphasize constraints in the use of violence: in contrast to the multiplication of international mechanisms focusing on the legitimacy and proportionality in the use of force in conventional wars, there was a regulatory silence in this regard towards "small wars" during the nineteenth century.

A remarkable example of how the tactics designed by Bugeaud relied on the assumption of the inferior nature of the enemy are the *razzias*. Distilled by Bugeaud while Governor General in Algeria, the *razzias* aimed at suffocating the resistance against French occupation through the eradication of anything that could be used as food, shelter, and clothing (Gildea 2019: 19). Speaking in defense of Bugeaud's *razzias*, Marshal de Castellane wrote: "how do you act against a population whose only link with the land is the pegs of their tents? (…) The only way is to take the grain which feeds them, the flocks which clothe them. For this reason, we make war on silos, war on cattle, the *razzia*" (1852 *Apud* Porch 2013: 21–22). Intensified by the narrative of the racial inferiority of the enemy, by the end of the 1840s, the *razzias* had unfolded into an excessive brutality aimed at eliminating any economic and psychological condition of resistance (Porch 2013: 25).

The racial pillars constituting Bugeaud's *razzias* relied on an information apparatus built even before he arrived in Algeria. In 1833, the French colonial administration had created the *bureaux arabes* with the objective of gathering intelligence on politics and specific individuals of the "Algerian tribes" through a network of agents, spies, and informants. A similar information apparatus was built by the British in India: initially formed by civilians admitted through a rigorous test in native languages, history, and law, by the 1830s, the Indian Political Service was mainly integrated by military personnel (Porch 2013: 32). The system of information collection in Algeria was directly linked to the *goum*, local soldiers who served in auxiliary units attached to the French Army of Africa, who were in charge of undertaking the *razzias*, punishing the treacherous, terrorizing neutrals, and giving incentives to those who were loyal to the French troops (Porch 2013: 31).

As the symbiosis between the intelligence apparatus and the activities of the *goum* reveal, information gathering was turned to the identification of suspects and to the division of the population according to degrees of dangerousness. An illustration of these practices is found in 1871, when the British issued the "Criminal Tribes Act", whereby "entire castes, communities, and tribes were registered (…) as 'habitual offenders' requiring constant surveillance and control" (Porch 2013: 37). In this sense, mechanisms justified as contributing to a better understanding of the intricacies of the local culture, the *bureau arabe* and the Indian Political Service used information to control and repress the Algerian and Indian populations.

It is particularly to this use of cultural intelligence that the military refer to when they mobilize the expression "to weaponize culture" (Brown 2008), that is, to instrumentalize the cultural aspects of the population so as to optimize the efficiency of the military mission, both through the amplification of its acceptance by the locals and through the better identification of the enemy. In this process, the locals were seen as having no capacity of critical thinking whatsoever nor political discernment: they were either manipulable by the French "hearts and minds" programs so that they could be "safely" considered as friends; or they had to be rescued by the French forces from the manipulation of the enemy.

As we have seen, the information apparatus, the *razzias,* and the emphasis on mobility were the three main pillars of the tactics designed by Bugeaud based on his experience on the Algerian terrain. All these operational axes were grounded on the claim of inferiority of the Algerians, as well as on the irregular character of the combat. Bugeaud's place in the edifice of military *savoirs* stems from the mobilization of this tactic as an efficient answer to the challenges facing colonial order. More than that: Bugeaud and his supporters advocated that the French way of waging war in Algeria merited recognition as a *savoir* as modern as the conventional warfare. Indeed, the "efficiency card" was played as an attempt to translate the "small wars" into the validation terms sustaining the edifice of military *savoirs*. A similar movement was made in the identification of a gap in that edifice, which provided no tactical contribution to wars involving an inferior, uncivil enemy.

Suggesting a gradual acknowledgement of its efficiency, the tactic of *razzia* was replicated by Russia, Great Britain, the U.S. and Prussia during the nineteenth century (Porch 2013: 26) in variated forms, such as internment, resettlement, curfew, house demolition and food control (Porch 2013: 22). Despite its colonial foundations, the circulation of this *savoir* was ultimately wider than in populations colonized by European states. In the U.S., for instance, it was applied during the nineteenth century wars against the Indians (Grove 2016).

However, it was only decades later, that "small wars"—now called counterinsurgency—started to enjoy a more privileged position in the edifice of military *savoirs*. To be sure, it was only after World War II that it came to be more systematically incorporated to the curriculum of military professionalization schools in Europe and in the U.S. If, on one hand, Bugeaud's footprint in the trajectory of counterinsurgency derives from his tactical contribution, he never translated his experience in Algeria into a counterinsurgency doctrine[2] (Porch 2013: 165).

In the absence of a doctrinal framework, there were no structured channels through which experience and lessons could be transmitted from one colony to another. Indochina is an emblematic example: there, no intelligence apparatus analogous to the *bureaux arabes* in Algeria had been built, although both coexisted as French colonies in that period of the nineteenth century (Porch 2013: 165). Having served in Algeria almost a hundred years after Bugeaud, Galula (2006: v) explained: "In my zone, as everywhere in Algeria, the order was to 'pacify'. But exactly how? The sad truth was that, in spite of all our past experience, we had no single, official doctrine for counterinsurgency warfare".

It is in this regard that the French Army Major David Galula is considered a central figure, for he was one of the first who attempted to condense the French experience into a set of prescriptions and to crystalize a counterinsurgency doctrine. Galula is also known for having bridged the French experience with the U.S. Army (Porch 2013: 163, 175). When assigned to the 45th Colonial Infantry Battalion in the 1950s, he adopted a systematic approach aimed at the development of a counterinsurgency doctrine.[3] The Battalion was initially responsible for the colonial order in an experimental area, where methods would be tested, and, if successful, later applied in other parts of Algeria (Porch 2013: 179).

In his two books *Pacification in Algeria 1956–1958* (1963) and *Counterinsurgency Warfare* (1964), Galula articulates what he considers as the main lessons from the French experience in small wars into a set of prescriptions that would come to constitute a counterinsurgency doctrine, specifying tactical and operational routines and translating them to the

---

[2] Porch defines "doctrine" as a "trailing indicator of inherited practices and a receptive intellectual environment, combined with tactical and operational routines developed by units to meet current contingencies" (Porch 2013: 179).

[3] It is at least intriguing that Galula's name reached such a projection, considering that the Algerian War in which he participated terminated in 1962 with the Algerian independence. According to Galula, however, the absence of a counterinsurgency doctrine was a key factor in the outcome of the War, as it allowed for a heterogeneous distribution of tactics in that French colony—a dynamic that turned out to be favorable to the resistance.

context of a "communist threat"—or a "revolutionary war", in the words of Colonel Charles Lacheroy, a French military officer known for his theorization on this kind of warfare (Villatoux and Villatoux 2012) as "the conflict scenario of the future" (Porch 2013: 173). In general terms, he preserved the three main characteristics of the operations conducted by Bugeaud in nineteenth century Algeria. By emphasizing tactics rather than strategy, Galula gave central importance to mobility and to psychological operations, and incorporated a derivation of the *razzias* to the doctrine (Galula 1964).

For us to understand the links between the counterinsurgency doctrine developed by Galula and the circuit of military *savoirs* in the Americas, we must explore how the "revolutionary war" was conceived by Lacheroy and Galula. After having served in the Indochina War (1946–1954), Lacheroy insisted that, in the future, the pattern of conflicts would be more accurately characterized as a "communist conspiracy" than as a colonial war. One of the specificities of the revolutionary wars was the difficulty to distinguish friend from foe—which both Galula and Lacheroy associated with the unlimited character of this kind of conflict. For Galula (1964, 2006), it was precisely this aspect that made the early identification of the insurrection a necessity for the military: according to him, neutralization would turn even more difficult once the insurrection penetrated in the population. In other words, the more the conflict lingered, the more vulnerable the military forces would become before the public opinion in their home countries (Galula 1964).

In this "new" context, Galula re-appropriated one of the main effects of the *razzias*—curfews and resettlements—and developed a doctrinal component aimed at separating the population from the rebels. In Algeria, for example, facing difficulties in stabilizing villages, the French military displaced Algerians from their lands towards camps so that they could better control them—what the Army referred to as *regroupement* (Porch 2013: 187). Since every friend could indeed be a foe, other practices were added to the *regroupement*, such as the issuing of identity papers, food rationing, house searches, curfews, and the creation of self-defense groups (Porch 2013: 187). Although the possible infiltration of enemies risked de-authorizing *regroupement* as an inefficient operation, its continuous use by the French was justified for other positive effects it yielded. Above all, *regroupement* enabled another kind of control: the creation of "free-fire zones" in the villages that had been cleared through the resettlement, that is, anyone found in those zones was taken as insurgent and, therefore, was a target (Porch 2013: 188).

All the aspects analyzed thus far operate within a population-centric approach: a logic in which the population was the key for victory in revolutionary wars. Drawing from his experience in Indochina, Colonel Lacheroy claimed that the French failed to counter the insurgent's propaganda that manipulated the population against the French forces (Porch 2013: 174). He believed that, in addition to the *regroupement* operations, the French needed a propaganda campaign to build a positive image of the French, convincing the population that the war was not about colonialism, but about liberating Algerians from the communist threat (Galula 1964: 99). With this objective, in 1956, psychological operations units were created in each division of the French Army in Algeria (Porch 2013: 186).

According to Galula (2006: v), the French military had to "Outwardly treat every civilian as a friend; inwardly you must consider him as a rebel ally until you have positive proof to the contrary". This prescription had two main effects. On one hand, it displaced to the Algerians the burden of proving that they did not support the insurgents. On the other, it authorized practices such as the *quadrillage* (the segmentation of a zone in search of insurgents), the *ratonnades* (an army sweep of areas to arrest "suspects"), and the "swarming tactics" (multiple units attack from all sides of a target), as well as the arbitrary arrests, interrogations, torture, and decapitation of the insurgent organization—that is, the detention or killing of its leaders—that derived from those operations.

Read together, the burden of proof and these "rat-chasing operations" met Galula's prescription that the ideal moment for the counterinsurgents to initiate the "purge" (Galula 1964: 89–92) was "not when the cell members have been positively identified—a process that would take much time and leaves much to chance—but instead, when enough information has been gathered on a number of suspected villagers" (Galula 1964: 91). Privileging the arrest and interrogation of villagers rather than the cell members as a first step of the "purge" was an approach based on the belief that "every villager normally knows who the cell members are, or at least knows who is screening them" (Galula 1964: 91). In this sense, the arrest and interrogation of villagers[4] was a moment when their

[4] For Galula, one of the main concerns of counterinsurgents when undertaking a propaganda campaign was "to minimize the possible adverse effects produced on the population

collaboration with the counterinsurgent forces was tested: either an informant to the counterinsurgents or a supporter of the insurgents. As for the cell members, once captured, leniency was conditioned to the "sincerity of his repentance", which had to meet two criteria: "a full confession of their past activity and a willingness to participate actively in the counterinsurgent's struggle. Another advantage of a policy of leniency is to facilitate the subsequent purges" (Galula 1964: 91). This need that either the "suspect" or the "repentant rat" actively reveal the side he was on and concretely collaborate with the "right side" relied on a political binary that left no room for hesitation: with or against "us".

Indeed, there was no room for indifference towards the military mission goals during the revolutionary war. In an excerpt from *Counterinsurgency Warfare*, Galula explains that:

> The administrator in peacetime has to preserve a politically neutral attitude toward the population, has to let 'a hundred flowers blossom, a hundred schools of thought contend', but not in counterinsurgency, where his duty is to see that only the right flower blossoms and not the weed, at least until the situation becomes normal again. (Galula 1964: 70)

Divergence was only possible among the "right flowers", but within the terms considered as acceptable by the counterinsurgent forces. In times of war, the mission needed the consent of "friends" to be rendered legitimate, and proactive collaboration to be rendered effective. In doing so, friends proved that they were the "right flowers", not the "rats" to be swept away.

In this sense, the population circumscribed both a source of information and legitimacy, on one hand, and a source of resistance to be countered, on the other. It was this ambiguous potentiality that made population so central to counterinsurgency as a military *savoir* useful for revolutionary wars. As systematized by Galula, counterinsurgency doctrine offered a framework for pacification to be achieved through a population-centric approach.

---

by the arrests. He will have to explain frankly why it is necessary to destroy the insurgent political cells, and stress the policy leniency to those who recognize their error" (Galula 1964: 92).

Importantly, the very distinctive character of counterinsurgency—the claim of an impossible "decisive victory"—made the discursive differentiation between peace and war blurred. Despite Galula's effort to draw this line of demarcation (Galula 1964: 70), he himself emphasized that pacification did require waging war against insurgents, but "civic action" was the central work to be undertaken for a durable pacification (Porch 2013: 191). In similar lines, Kilcullen's account of contemporary counterinsurgency doctrine frames the challenge of "armed social work" as "an attempt to redress basic social and political problems while being shot at" (Kilcullen 2006: 33).

As we have seen, this civic/social work acquires civilizational contours when read through the practices of the population-centric approach. Actions such as the development of local infrastructure and the provision of service to "natives" were repeatedly evoked in counterinsurgency operations, but always under the condition that the beneficiaries behaved according to the norms of conduct defined by the occupation forces—among them, to actively collaborate whenever requested. Civic work is, thus, a legitimation component of counterinsurgency whereby the population is called to support the mission goals and to defend them as their own.

If the image of bringing progress to villagers while being shot at invests the counterinsurgent soldier with a martyr mantle, those who resisted this work were read as an obstacle to progress. In other words, the enmity character of "insurgency" was its threat to the civilizing mission undertaken by occupying forces. For this reason, social ordering in the terrain of counterinsurgency was actually not seen as an imposition, for pacification was undeniably legitimate in the eyes of counterinsurgents. Peace is, under these terms, the absence of any resistant organized violence.

The impossible discursive differentiation between war and peace in counterinsurgency reveals a shared rationality of order that organizes the use of violence across a spectrum of dangerousness. As argued by Neocleous (2014: 30–32), if every peace already contains the terms within which war will be activated—peace as coded war—, peace must in fact be understood as pacification of those social conducts deemed unacceptable. This leads us to an unescapable discussion on what Neocleous (2014) calls "war power" and "police power":

> The war power and the police power need to be grasped alongside, as part of and in conjunction with one another. Now, this process was worked out

in different ways in different states, but the general tendency is clear: the process as a whole facilitated a functional integration of the powers of the modern state operating under the sign of peace and security. The process concerns not just the violent crushing of opposition (though it certainly involves that), nor just a question of which 'force' does the crushing (military, paramilitary, police?), but is also very much about the shaping of the behavior of individuals, groups and classes, and thereby ordering the social relations of power around a particular regime of accumulation (...). If peace is a coded war, it is coded as pacification. (Neocleous 2014: 31–32)

His point echoes the discussion developed in Chapter 4 regarding the civilizational disposition that characterizes the production of durably pacified social spaces in the discourse of modernization—especially as expressed in the work of Elias (2000). As I have argued, the engine of such a discourse works through the imperative of social order as a condition for the optimization of the circulation of goods and persons in the pacified social space. And, in doing so, it authorizes pacification through use of violence whenever control is no longer understood as a valid mechanism for the regulation of social relations.

Not surprisingly, when Galula claimed that "civic action" was the central condition for a durable pacification, he phrased it in terms of less waging war and more policing (Porch 2013: 191). In concrete terms, however, this "change of approach" did not result in a transformation of the scope of ordering practices: given the scarce availability of police personnel in Algeria at that time, "civic action" was basically undertaken by military personnel wearing police uniforms (Porch 2013: 191). Using Neocleous' (2014) terms, the fabrication of social order in the Algerian context revealed an understanding that war power was needed, irrespective of "which 'force' does the crushing", whether the police or the military professionals.

It is worth mentioning that the colonial order in Algeria provides a special meaning to the association we came to naturalize between "police" and "law and order". One of Lacheroy's three rules for victory to be achieved in counterinsurgency campaigns was precisely not fighting "revolutionary wars" within the legal framework (Porch 2013: 180). Indeed, the "lawless character" of counterinsurgency as it had been practiced in the colonies derived from the claim of an inferior nature of the enemy. As we will see further in this Chapter, these terms governed the framing of enmity in social contexts far more than exclusively in terrains formalized as colonies.

The problematization of violence that came to generally characterize the second half of the twentieth century—one which emphasizes irregular warfare as the main pattern of conflict—had significant elective affinities with counterinsurgency doctrine. At the same time, the rationality of counterinsurgency gave shape and breath to this problematization of violence, fusing different social contexts into the label of "insurgency" and investing a similar tactical repertoire to pacify it. Through these lines, the second half of the twentieth century witnessed not only the acknowledgement of counterinsurgency as a doctrine for irregular warfare, but also saw it raised to a privileged position in the edifice of military *savoirs*. With some discursive and tactical re-articulations, the constitutive pillars that we have walked through are still part of counterinsurgency in the present days. In a document addressed to military officers to discuss the fundamentals of counterinsurgency,[5] Kilcullen claimed that

> Your role is to provide protection, identify needs, facilitate civil affairs and use improvements in social conditions as leverage to build networks and mobilize the population. Thus, there is no such thing as impartial humanitarian assistance or civil affairs in counterinsurgency. Every time you help someone, you hurt someone else—not least the insurgents. So civil and humanitarian assistance personnel will be targeted. Protecting them is a matter not only of close-in defense, but also of creating a permissive operating environment by co-opting the beneficiaries of aid—local communities and leaders—to help you help them. (Kilcullen 2006: 34)

---

[5] By doing so, Kilcullen is not denying the pillars that we have discussed so far. When setting the scene he wanted to explore in the document, he did reinforce the position of Galula as a referential theoretical reference. It is in perfectioning the tactical repertoire of counterinsurgency that Kilcullen is more interested, mostly by providing tactical responses to the lack of pertinence of some of the counterinsurgency fundamentals in the terrain. In his words, "Your company has just been warned for deployment on counterinsurgency operations in Iraq or Afghanistan. You have read David Galula, T.E. Lawrence and Robert Thompson. You have studied FM 3-24 and now understand the history, philosophy and theory of counterinsurgency. (...) But what does all that theory mean, at the company level? How do the principles translate into action—at night, with the GPS down, the media criticizing you, the locals complaining in a language you don't understand, and an unseen enemy killing your people by ones and twos?" (Kilcullen 2006: 29). The plasticity of counterinsurgency resides in its emphasis on tactics, allowing for its constant re-articulation through the preservation of its constitutive pillars.

Reading what the population "needs" and providing protection and civil work in order to address those needs is part of the quest for improvements in social conditions with the objective of mobilizing the population to "the right side". Further in the same document, Kilcullen recommends that "For your side to win, the people do not have to like you but they must respect you, accept that your actions benefit them, and trust your integrity and ability to deliver your promises" (Kilcullen 2006: 29). Disagreement must give way to respect so that the "right side" can achieve victory and the population can harvest the benefits of pacification once the insurgency is defeated—contends Kilcullen (2006). The respect for counterinsurgent forces is related to its ability to see beyond what the population is able to see—"hence" its superiority and leading role.

As in Galula, Kilcullen conditions the effectiveness of counterinsurgency to a submissive position of the population, to whom the silent roles of beneficiary, protected and collaborator (whenever requested) are the key to success. As important as this voiceless position, is the responsibility transferred to the population for its own protection. Algerians, as Afghanis and Iraqis, must help counterinsurgents to help them—in other words, proving that they merit the protection to be delivered by the military is a burden to bear by the population itself.

That the general characterization of French and U.S. counterinsurgencies is very similar is not a coincidence. During the 1960s, professionals from the French Army who had directly participated in the Algerian War attended symposiums and taught courses in military schools in the U.S. Galula was himself among the participants of a symposium held at the RAND Corporation Office in Washington in 1962. The objective of that event was "to distill lessons and insights from past insurgent conflicts that might help to inform and shape the U.S. involvement in Vietnam and to foster the effective prosecution of other future counterinsurgency campaigns" (Hosmer and Crane 2006: vii). Since its foundation, in 1948, RAND has been working hand in hand with the U.S. government in the development of research and models that spoke directly to the priorities of the security agenda (Jardini 2013).

By that time, armed conflicts in Korea and Vietnam were referred to as "limited wars" (Jardini 2013: 136) and were not a priority in the RAND agenda, comparable to the projects dedicated to nuclear strategy.[6]

---

[6] Through a historical analysis of the RAND Corporation and its main research projects from 1945 to 1975, Jardini contends that "While the Korean experience did stimulate a

It was only after 1964 that the attention to research on counterinsurgency was expanded, having mainly conflicts in Southeast Asia as an object for the validation of that expertise. In that year, RAND's President Frank Collbohm created a committee in the Corporation to assess "RAND's competence to address U.S. security problems in Southeast Asia and to make recommendations concerning RAND's Southeast Asia research program" (1965: i *Apud* Jardini 2013: 144). According to the Director of that committee, the economist Charles J. Zwick:

> We are convinced that there is a great opportunity for RAND once again to enter into an area of national policy in which there is today a considerable vacuum—that of policy, doctrine, and techniques related to countering and discrediting revolutionary warfare as a Communist strategy (...) A significant opportunity to influence policy and techniques is there (1965: 1–2 *Apud* Jardini 2013: 144–145)

It is in this context, marked by an "opportunity" seized by RAND, translated into an expanded research program on counterinsurgency, with strong adherence to the U.S. government's agenda, that the 1962 symposium held in RAND's Washington Office must be read. The participation of British and French military officers in this event—among them, Lieutenant Colonel David Galula (Hosmer and Crane 2006: xi)—is key for us to grasp the connections between their counterinsurgency practices and those being developed in the U.S. in the context of the Cold War.

Although the participants' trajectories all reveal a footprint in former European colonies[7]—from Philippines, to Malaya, India, and Algeria—, the presentation of their short-bios in the report resulting from the 1962 symposium does not evoke the vocabulary of colonialism—nor the content of the report itself. On the other hand, the silence about

---

small amount of interest in limited warfare at RAND, its analysis and research remained geared almost exclusively to strategic nuclear conflict. Counterinsurgency research was especially distasteful to the Air Force since that service seemed to play no independent role in anti-guerrilla operations. Not surprisingly, then, in 1961 RAND devoted just two percent of its Project RAND work (...), approximately five man-years, to limited warfare" (Jardini 2013: 143).

[7] However, it is important to highlight that, by the time the RAND symposium took place, Algeria was still a French colony in formal terms. As a matter of fact, the Algerian independence was only declared in July 1962, three months after the event held by RAND.

colonialism speaks through the "deeds" associated with some of the participants. Galula, for instance, is presented as an officer with a "wide variety of experience in a number of theaters of revolutionary warfare" (Hosmer and Crane 2006: xix). His campaign in Algeria is referred to as a succesful accomplishment in "clearing militarily and returning to governmental control in the two years of his command [in the district of Kabylie]" (Hosmer and Crane 2006: xx). According to Porch, it was this very sanitization of the French military experience in Algeria "from its context of racism, brutality, and the implosion of French civil-military relations" (Porch 2013: 175) that made Galula a palatable reference for the U.S. counterinsurgency.

In the context of his participation in the symposium, Galula was commissioned to elaborate a detailed study of his experience in Algeria for RAND (Hoffman 2006: vii). Titled *Pacification in Algeria, 1956–1958* and published in 1963, it only uses the word "colonial" between quotation marks (for instance, Galula 2006: 14, 49, 86, 232) or when referring to the name of the Battalion he commanded (the Colonial Infantry Battalion) and other branches of the French apparatus in Algeria (to mention but a few, Galula 2006: 1, 65, 200). A footnote suggests that this was far from a random semantic preference, however:

> The French colonial troops, from the seventeenth century to the end of the nineteenth, were Marines, employed and supported by the Navy. As our colonial empire grew, so did they, until the Navy complained that the Marines were using too large a share of appropriations. At the turn of the century, the Marines were separated from the Navy, attached to the Army as an independent force, and called the Colonial Army. The government realized recently that "colonial" has become a bad word, and in May 1958 we were given back our old name of "Marines", and the 9th R.I.C. [Régiment d'Infanterie Coloniale] became the 9th R.I.M. (Régiment d'Infanterie de Marine) (Galula 2006: 213)

Thus, although the whole experience of Galula in Algeria merited longevity through the publication of his *memoirs*, the vocabulary mobilized in reference to decades of French presence in Algeria had to adjust to the "new times". In the context of the Cold War, Lacheroy's "revolutionary war" terminology offered an alternative. "Pacification", on the other hand, was not only kept in the title of Galula's *memoirs*, but also preserved as a motto of counterinsurgency campaigns during the "revolutionary wars". More than pointing to the durability of counterinsurgency in time, this constant adaptation of its tactical repertoire while preserving its constitutive pillars reveals the plasticity of this military *savoir* across different contexts of social ordering.[8]

Now understood as a modern military *savoir*, counterinsurgency incorporated to military schools and research centers linked to defense policy making. To mention but a few cases, the British Lieutenant Colonel Frank E. Kitson taught at the British Army Staff College at Camberley and at the U.S. Armed Forces Staff College at Norfolk (Virginia) in the 1950s and 1960s (Hosmer and Crane 2006: xx). His courses were based on the work of police forces with intelligence in Kenya, and with antiterrorist campaigns in Malaya (Hosmer and Crane 2006: xx). Galula, by his turn, taught courses on unconventional warfare and on the war in Algeria in the National Defense Headquarters in Paris from 1958 to 1962 (Galula 2006: ix). After having attended the Armed Forces Staff College at Norfolk (Virginia) for a six-month period, Galula joined the Center of International Affairs at Harvard University as a research associate in 1962 (Hosmer and Crane 2006: xx).

Other French military officers who also taught in U.S. military schools at that time include Lieutenant Colonel Roger Trinquier, a specialist in psychological warfare, who commanded a battalion in Indochina during the 1940s and another in Algeria in the 1950s; and General Paul Aussaresses, who worked with intelligence in Algeria under the command of General Jacques Massu, also in the 1950s. Hosted by the U.S. Army Special Warfare School at Fort Bragg in the 1960s (Porch 2013: footnote n. 40, 371–372), both Trinquier and Aussaresses are known for the systematic use of torture in the operations they were part of. During their season at Fort Bragg, they provided detailed accounts of the "techniques" used in their operations, as well as a regime of justification for such a use[9]—"a Cartesian rationale for the use of torture", in the

---

[8] In the British case, for instance, the experience in colonies such as Malaya and Kenya was understood as useful for a re-articulated version of counterinsurgency against the Irish Republican Army (IRA) since the early-twentieth century (Porch 2013: 112–119, 246–265). Above all, the operations undertaken by the British government against the IRA were marked by an intelligence apparatus deeply penetrated in the insurgency, which also gave shape to a systematic civil-military cooperation (McFate 2005: 27).

[9] Trinquier, for instance, claims that interrogations must be "conducted by specialists perfectly versed in the techniques to be employed" (Trinquier 1985: 23), and then identifies a set of action-reaction sequences that may take place during an interrogation and what kind of information is expected to be extracted in such situations (Trinquier 1985).

words of Bernard Fall in the Introduction to the 1985 English version of Trinquier's *Modern Warfare*, translated by the US Army Command and General Staff College at Fort Leavenworth (Fall 1985: xv). In 1961, Aussaresses became France's military *attaché* in Washington, while he was also instructor of counterinsurgency tactics at Fort Bragg (Porch 2013: 176). In the 1970s, he also instructed Brazilian and Chilean military officers on "subversive warfare" and counterinsurgency techniques (Porch 2013: 176).

That U.S. military schools quickly absorbed the experience of the 1960scolonial wars is directly linked to the emergence of Vietnam as a puzzle to the military doctrine of that time (Krepinevich 1986). Indeed, the re-articulation of the main pillars constituting the French counterinsurgency into a *savoir* proclaimed as a doctrine "made in USA" aimed at offering tactical responses to the challenges deriving from the impossibility of a decisive victory (Salamone 2008; Porch 2013). As we have seen, such a re-articulation involved an aseptic removal of the colonial vocabulary from the French experience in Algeria and its re-reading into the terms of "revolutionary wars" and the fight against communism. On one hand, Galula's systematization of his experience in Algeria into "lessons" and tactical guidelines is a remarkable point in these transformations. On the other, although the crystallization of a *savoir* on counterinsurgency "made in USA" certainly intensified in the 1960s, France had already appeared as a reference for the U.S. back in the nineteenth century, when Bugeaud's experience in Algeria came to be understood as useful in the wars against the Indians (Grove 2016), as previously mentioned.

The persistent claim of an inferior nature of the enemy allowed for re-articulated versions of the colonial pillars of counterinsurgency from the nineteenth century—if not before[10]—to the twentieth century, and

---

Aussaresses, by his turn, narrates in rich details specific cases of torture and execution, under the basic logic that "Some prisoners started talking very easily. Others only needed some roughing up. It was only when a prisoner refused to talk or denied the obvious that torture was used. (…) They would therefore either talk quickly or never" (Aussaresses 2010: 128).

[10] The Carlisle Barracks were originally established in the mid-eighteenth century for the preparation of British and Provincial troops to fight against the Indians. At that time, the motto of the Carlisle School was "Kill the Indian and save the man". Closed only in 1918, the barracks served as the basis for the establishment of the U.S. Army War College in Carlisle in 1973. Despite the change in the name, the preservation of its facilities symbolizes an enduring component of that brutality. Indeed, a testimonial given

then to the twenty-first century. Hence the preservation of the main tactical lines developed by Bugeaud under different names: no longer the "colonial wars", but the "revolutionary wars"; no longer the French *regroupement,* but the "strategic hamlets". The connection of the wars against the Indians and the war in Iraq, for instance, is made explicit in Bass' account of a seminar on counterinsurgency he attended at the US Army War College, in Carlisle, where a Colonel reportedly declared that "We used to be real good at dealing with tribes. Back in the days of Manifest Destiny, we were geniuses at setting one group of Indians against another. This is what we need to do in Iraq. Get some Sunnis on our side, to block the crazy Shi'a" (Bass 2008: 233).

The 1962 RAND symposium must not be interpreted as a watershed, therefore. Rather, it is an expression of the emergence of counterinsurgency to a privileged position within the edifice of military *savoirs*. Importantly, this was the result of a set of processes that did not only involve military officers, but also economists, politicians and other professionals informed by and informing the U.S. security agenda. The increased relevance of counterinsurgency in the U.S. was also stimulated and justified by the effervescence of guerrilla movements based on a combination of doctrines ranging from Mao to Guevara. Amalgamated by French and U.S. counterinsurgency theorists as "revolutionary wars", the irregular warfare represented by these guerrillas was repeatedly evoked as the "conflict scenario of the future" (Jardini 2013: 136; Porch 2013: 173). Finally, as we have seen, the making of a counterinsurgency "made in USA" cannot be understood away from the close interactions among French, British and American military officers since the 1950s. In this regard, the institutionalization of these *savoirs* in military schools was an effect of the consolidation of counterinsurgency as a privileged military *savoir*, and also a condition for its constant reproduction and re-articulation.

---

by a Colonel to Bass (2008) during his field work suggests that the Carlisle School is more than an abandoned fragment in the debris of the wars against the Indians: "Back in the days of Manifest Destiny, we were geniuses at setting one group of Indians against another. This is what we need to do in Iraq. Get some Sunnis on our side, to block the crazy Shi'a. Then, when things calm down, we start introducing the poison blankets" (Bass 2008: 233). Celebrating the eighteenth and nineteenth centuries as a time when the U.S. knew how to handle tribes militarily, the connection drawn between the expertise of the past with that of the present also reveals a persistent claim of inferiority projected towards those against whom counterinsurgency is mobilized.

Its incorporation into a web of schools, training programs and instruction manuals is what particularly interests me here. If that movement already existed by the 1950s,[11] counterinsurgency took the fore of military professionalization from the 1960s onwards. In this process, the brutality once evoked by conventional warfare strategists in order to refuse the status of "professional military" to "small warriors" faded away as it was gradually covered with a theoretical sophistication façade.[12]

The web of US military schools built around counterinsurgency contributed to the diffusion of this *savoir* far beyond the colonial circuit that had characterized the circulation of the expertise on counterinsurgency in the nineteenth century. Decades later, in 2002, Amnesty International estimated that there were around 275 military schools and facilities in the U.S., and more than 4,100 courses offered through this institutional fabric, through which approximately 100,000 foreign police and military, from more than 150 countries, were trained per year (Amnesty International 2002: iii–iv). In addition to the thousands that were trained in these programs, many more received U.S. training in their own states (Amnesty International 2002: iii).

As we will see in the next section, this dense web of U.S. military schools came to be taken as the main reference in the circuit of *savoirs* on counterinsurgency—similar to the position Prussia and France had to Latin America in the nineteenth century. Schools such as the U.S. Army War College and the U.S. Army Special Warfare School were among the

---

[11] The 1950 "Operations Against Guerrilla Forces" is considered the first manual on counterinsurgency in the U.S. The manual does not mention Latin America in the section about the main concerns regarding "guerrilla warfare" in the world: it concentrates the diagnosis of the problem under those terms in the Soviet "zone of influence" and in Asia (especially Philippines) (The U.S. Infantry School 1950).

[12] To be sure, this did not imply the erasure of brutal practices such as the ones associated with the French colonial legacy. In the case of torture, brutality was vested with a set of "interrogation techniques" that suggested precision and provided a regime of justification for the interrogation (CIA 1963: 3, 82–85). The first U.S. manual for this kind of operation was produced in 1963 by the Central Intelligence Agency (CIA). Titled *Kubark Counterintelligence Interrogation*, the manual used the terminology of "coercive counterintelligence interrogation of resistant sources" (CIA 1963: 52) instead of torture. It also included categories of interrogated, situation-specific categories of coercion, and professionals that would join the military in the interrogation, such as the doctor, whose participation in the process aimed at turning the escalation of the pain of the interrogated into an object of scientific observation (CIA 1963: 82–85).

main hubs through which the *savoirs* on counterinsurgency were transmitted to the Latin American military. Part of this institutional fabric, the School of the Americas (SoA) was the destination of numerous military professionals in Latin America, especially from the 1960s to the 1980s. Indeed, during the military regimes in the region, the SoA mobilized counterinsurgency *savoirs* through a variety of courses focused on matters related to "national security"—irregular warfare, internal security, civil-military action, intelligence and counterintelligence and interrogation techniques (Gill 2004).

This web of schools anchored in the "U.S. military expertise" contributed to the gradual homogenization of military practices across Latin American countries. In the discussion to follow, we will inscribe Colombia in this hemispheric circuit and discuss how counterinsurgency came to be understood as the most appropriate military doctrine for the "problem of violence" in Colombia. To do so, our attention will turn first to the conditions under which Europe was displaced by the U.S. as the main reference for the professionalization of the Colombian military.

5.2 (The Imperative of) Winning Hearts, Minds, and Populations in the Never-Ending Colombian War

Discussions about the professionalization of the Colombian military often evoke its close ties with the U.S. in the second half of the twentieth century as a determinant factor for their prominent role in internal ordering practices (Rouquié 1984; Pizarro L. 1987; Atehortúa C. and Vélez R. 1994; Leal B. 2002; Rodríguez H. 2006; Vargas V. 2014). Indeed, if *prusianización* ("Prussianization") is used to illustrate the centrality of Prussia in the professionalization of the Colombian military during the early-twentieth century, *norteamericanización* ("Americanization") (Rouquié 1984: 153) refers to the switch from Prussia to the U.S. as the military model for professionalization programs since the 1940s in Colombia.

Importantly, the *prusianización* of the Colombian Army must not be interpreted as the projection of every rule, procedure, doctrine, curriculum, and operation characterizing the Prussian Army—or, as we have seen in Sect. 4.3, the Chilean Army, which led the Prussian-inspired professionalization of the Colombian military for almost 30 years. As previously argued, the negotiations and tensions around the Chilean mission's authority in the professionalization program resulted in the gradual corrosion of the scope initially planned for their work. At the same time, the *norteamericanización* of the Colombian Army did not mean the erasure of the Chilean footprints from the procedures and rules reproduced in the routines of military schools in Colombia. Nor did it mean that the close interaction with the U.S. military faced no resistance regarding the incorporation of certain procedural or doctrinal aspects. Rather, the characteristics of the Colombian military professional reflect the historical sedimentations of durable socializations with their counterparts.

This Section analyzes the systematic interaction between the Colombian and the American military since the mid-twentieth century. As we will see, although the "Prussian traits" sedimented through the works of the Chilean military mission in Colombia have not been completely erased, the center of gravity of the professionalization process was transferred from the *Escuela Militar* (Military School) to the *Escuela de Lanceros* (Lancers' School). The objective of this Section is not to explain why conventional war lost its privileged position as a military *savoir* in the Colombian Army—or in the Americas. I am mostly interested in how the Colombian military officers themselves justified the importance of counterinsurgency for their terrain, how that *savoir* was operationally translated to the specificities of Colombia and with what effects.

The 1950s provide us a good starting point, for this period was marked by an incipient interaction with the U.S. Army that gradually acquired a systematic character, as shown by the profusion of assistance frameworks, instruction materials, and training programs emerging thereafter. The War in Korea (1950–1953), more specifically, came to be portrayed by Colombian military officers as a watershed in this regard. For General Álvaro Valencia Tovar, the relevance of the War in Korea in fact spoke to modern warfare in general, not exclusively to Colombia. In his own words, it was "a source of extraordinary experiences (...) which divides the modern history [of the army] in two eras: before Korea and after this experience, when the army was modernized and learned how to fight accordingly to modern concepts" (*Apud* Pizarro L. 1987).

The importance of the War in Korea to the Colombian Army seems puzzling if we look at the precarious preparation of the troops deployed in May 1951. According to Atehortúa Cruz (2008, 66), some of the volunteers joined the "Colombia Battalion No. 1" right before it departed to

Korea: although they were formally enlisted, many of them did not have any previous military instruction. Another group from the Battalion was selected among those who their superiors considered to be supportive of the Liberal Party in Colombia (Puyana G. 1993: 64 *Apud* Atehortúa C. 2008: 66). In 1951, the Conservative Party holding the Presidency was still under *La Violencia*,[13] and emphasizing the enlistment of military professionals with "Liberal inclination" was seen as a way of isolating them from the internal turmoil (Atehortúa C. 2008: 66). In addition to that, the participation of the Colombian Army in the War in Korea was capitalized as an opportunity in two main directions: to negotiate the procurement of arms with the U.S. in a more favorable position (Atehortúa C. 2008: 67–70); and to build a consistently close relation with the U.S. Army (Rodríguez H. 2006: 41–56).

Indeed, that Colombia had been the only Latin American country to support the UN forces led by the U.S. in Korea was insistently mentioned by the Colombian Presidency and Ministry of War when attempting to negotiate the provision of arms and equipment to strengthen the military forces in the context of *La Violencia* (Atehortúa C. 2008: 67–70). Given that the Conservative Party controlled a significant share of the public forces with "political police" powers, the bulk of the armed resistance was formed by liberals and communists, organized as guerrilla warfare (Pizarro L. 1987; Pécaut 2010). The regime of justification used by the Colombian government for the provision of arms framed the internal turmoil as a particular manifestation of the Western fight against communism (*El Tiempo* 1952 *Apud* Atehortúa C. 2008: 69). In a 1952 public conference held in Bogota, the Minister of War at that time, José María Bernal, conflated communists and liberals into a general problem of "communist *bandolerismo*" ("communist banditry") threatening democracy in Colombia[14]:

---

[13] For analyses about the political tensions that led to *La Violencia*, see Sánchez G. et al. (1962), Pizarro L. (1987), Cardona (2008), andPécaut (2010). For an interpretation of that period focused on the tensions between the civil elites and the Colombian Army, see Atehortúa C. and Vélez R. (1994).

[14] This problematization of violence would change significantly in 1956, with the Benidorm Agreement. Signed by the leaders of the Conservative and the Liberal Party (respectively, Laureano Gómez and Alberto Lleras Camargo), the Benidorm Agreement established the rules for a peaceful coexistence between the two main political parties in Colombia, creating the *Frente Nacional* (National Front), dissolved only in 1974. This

> Communism, the universal enemy, operates in the whole world with an unabated activity and through identical systems, but adjusting itself in each site to the particularities of the terrain and adopting the name which is more suitable for the achievement of its goals. In each country, it holds the flag of the opposition in order to sow chaos in every crisis. [In Colombia] at least apparently, communism widely operates under the flag of liberalism. And liberalism, consciously or not, serves the Soviet plans of international domination.[15] (Bernal 1952: 15 *Apud* Atehortúa C. 2008: 69)

Such discourse allowed for three interwoven political effects. First, it provided an alternative reading to the context of widespread repression in Colombia, whereby the massive mobilization of violence, censorship, and espionage were claimed as legitimate once inscribed in a struggle to preserve "democracy" in the country. Second, just as the U.S. portrayed the fight against communism as a war waged by the "free world" and "civilized world", the Colombian participation in the War in Korea was presented by the Presidency as a manifestation of the "defense of the Christian civilization", aimed at avoiding that "inequity dominated the world" (Atehortúa C. 2008: 73). Conflated with the Western fight against communism, the repression of political opposition in the context of *La Violencia* was also read under these terms. Finally, it suggested that *La Violencia* and the War in Korea were symptoms of the same problem, i.e. communism—which, irrespective of the particularities of each terrain, contributed to "Soviet plans of international domination". In this sense, if the first U.S. Army manual on counterguerrilla, dated 1950, did not mention any example of communism or guerrilla warfare in the Latin American region (The US Infantry School 1950), the discourse running

---

Agreement is a fundamental moment in the construction of the "problem of the guerrillas" in Colombia because it de-coupled members of the Liberal Party not only from the problematization of communism (Pécaut 2010), but also of violence. In this sense, it cleared the ground for the association of "guerrilla warfare" with leftist armed groups, which became the basis of the counterinsurgency doctrine emerging in the following years, as we will see further in this Section.

[15] In the original: "El comunismo, enemigo universal, opera en todo el mundo con incesante actividad y con sistemas idénticos pero ajustándose en cada sitio a las peculiaridades propias del terreno y adoptando la denominación más adecuada para el logro de sus propósitos. Echa mano en cada país de la bandera de la oposición para sembrar el caos a todo trance. (En Colombia) al menos en las apariencias, el comunismo opera a sus anchas bajo la bandera del liberalismo. Y el liberalismo, consciente o inconscientemente, sirve los planes del dominio internacional soviético".

through the Colombian government provided the U.S. Army with such an example, as well as with a justified need for their cooperation.

In 1952, one year after the "Colombia Battalion No. 1" was sent to Korea, a bilateral agreement for the provision of arms was signed with the U.S. Army under the Military Assistance Program—a framework aimed at assisting countries engaged in the fight against communism (Atehortúa C. 2008: 67). The text reinforced the discursive elements mentioned above even when underlining Colombia's commitment that the arms, equipment, and training provided by the U.S. were only to be used for the purposes of the agreement: i.e. "to maintain peace in the Western hemisphere" (*Apud* Atehortúa C. 2008: 68). As we have seen, these terms could be easily accomodated in the claim that the guerrillas in Colombia were a particular expression of the threat to Western democracies posed by the problem of communism more generally.

There was yet another angle through which the participation of "Colombia Battalion No. 1" in the War in Korea was taken as an opportunity: it also marked the intensification of the professionalization of the Army through "U.S. lines"[16] (Rodríguez H. 2006: 54; Atehortúa C. 2008), and consequently the inscription of Colombia in the hemispheric circuit of military professionals that had the U.S. as its main reference. In this context, the return of the "Colombia Battalion No.1" from Korea,

---

[16] To be sure, there had been ad hoc bilateral interactions before. Military officers from both countries participated in a series of meetings that culminated in the creation of the Inter-American Defense Board, in 1942, for instance. Also, in 1938 representatives from the U.S. Army made an official visit to Colombia. Studies about the scope and effects of this mission are scarce, nonetheless. According to Rodríguez Hernández (2006: 47), that particular visit was focused on Naval and Air Forces and did not involve the Colombian Army. However, a campaign manual on war in the jungle (*La Guerra en la Selva, Manual de campaña*) suggests otherwise. Published in 1944 by the Colombian Military Forces General Staff and mostly used in professionalization programs of the Army, the manual reads "translated and adapted by the Military Mission from the U.S." in its opening pages (Estado Mayor General de las Fuerzas Militares 1944: 3).

in 1954, was capitalized by the government as a remarkable contribution to the technical and professional character of the Colombian Army[17] (Pizarro L. 1987: 32; Leal B. 2002: 20; Rodríguez H. 2006).

To be clear, the high-ranked military officers that commanded the Battalion in Korea were not only the main vocalizers of such a narrative: they were also the ones who led the translation of the "valuable contributions" of the experience in Korea into doctrinal and operational terms—among them, General Alberto Ruiz Novoa. Having commanded the "Colombia Battalion No. 1" from July 1952 to June 1953, General Ruiz Novoa registered in three different books what he considered as the main contributions of the "Colombia Battalion No. 1".[18] With regard to the tactical domain, he emphasized the role of infantry and of patrols in small-units in a context of guerrilla warfare and pointed to the need of replacing the heavier and costlier artillery used in conventional war campaigns for portable weapons, such as bazookas, assault rifles and mortars (Rodríguez H. 2006: 64–65). In addition, General Ruiz Novoa considered that propaganda and information campaigns could be useful in the demoralization of communist guerrillas in Colombia—as had been the case with the psychological operations in Korea (Rodríguez H. 2006: 65–66).

Thus, although the War in Korea was fought by a combination of conventional and irregular warfare, the lessons that General Ruiz Novoa underlined from the experience of "Colombia Battalion No. 1" privileged the elements characterizing the latter. By identifying affinities between the U.S. Army expertise and the needs of the Colombian Army for a

---

[17] In the words of General Rojas Pinilla, President at that time: "Repeat to your brothers the lesson learnt in Korea: organization of the troop, unified command, cooperation while in service, arms stretched to the comrade under the most acute torments, greatness of the soul when defeated, and serene rejoicing when victorious. Discipline, patient preparation, methodic training, loyalty, agile mobility towards the objective, without letting the spirit to be intimidated nor the muscle to be weakened"(Rojas P. 1954: 243-244 *Apud* Rodríguez H. 2006: 56). In the original: "Repetid a vuestros hermanos la lección aprendida en Corea: organización de las fuerzas, unidad de mando, cooperación en el servicio, brazos tendidos al camarada en las supremas angustias, grandeza de alma en la derrota y sereno regocijo en el triunfo. Disciplina, paciente preparación, entrenamiento metódico, lealtad, ágil movilización hacia el objetivo, sin que el espíritu se amilane ni el músculo flaquee".

[18] These works were titled: *El Batallón Colombia en Korea: 1951-1954* (published in 1956); *Enseñanzas militares de la campaña de Corea aplicables al Ejército de Colombia* (1956); and *El Gran Desafío* (1965).

successful pacification of "the problem of communism", this narrative offered a regime of justification for the position of the U.S. as a reference for the professionalization of the Colombian military. Importantly, General Ruiz Novoa's pursuit to strengthen the ties with the American Army was not undertaken without friction.

The reduced availability of economic resources in Colombia at that time posed a problem to the costs that redirecting the contours of military professionalization programs would require (Rodríguez H. 2006: 63). Further, the re-articulation of the military *savoirs* which would result from this process implied the displacing of positions of authority that stood on decades of footprints left by the Chilean missions on the schools and training centers of the Colombian Army. The strongest resistance, however, referred to the development component of military campaigns prescribed within John F. Kennedy's Alliance for Progress in the 1960s (Leal B. 2002: 44). Although these frictions did not hinder the alignment of the Colombian Army with its American counterpart in the following decades, they set the limits on how development was to be incorporated to military campaigns.

The first concrete attempt to invest a development lens on military operations was "Plan Lazo", launched in 1962 while General Ruiz Novoa was Minister of War. According to him, "the philosophy of the Plan was 'to remove the water from the fish', that is, to remove the peasant's support to the guerrilla"[19] (Ruiz N. 1992 *Apud* Leal B. 2002: 44) through a set of social and economic policies that would be supplementary to military operations.[20] In a speech published in *Revista de las Fuerzas Armadas* in 1964, General Ruiz Novoa drew the connection between the military and development as follows:

> As there has been astonishment towards the fact that the Minister of War copes with such issues, I have to explain the reasons why: (...) it is evident that social and economic injustices lead to the generation of violence as much as *bandolerismo* emerged as an effect of the political violence, and that this situation of unbalance significantly affects public order, whose

---

[19] In the original: "La filosofía del Plan era 'quitarle el agua al pez', o sea, quitarle el apoyo campesino a la guerrilla".

[20] For this reason, General Ruiz Novoa became known as one of the first *desarrollistas* ("developmentalists") among the Colombian military officers (Leal B. 2002: 45; Rodríguez H. 2006: 61).

preservation is the responsibility of the Minister of War[21] (Ruiz N. 1964: 240).

Here, General Ruiz Novoa understands violence in Colombia as an effect of poverty: that is, social and economic underdevelopment meant insecurity and, therefore, had to be tackled by the military. At the core of this intervention mechanism was the concept of "civil-military action" (*acción cívico-militar*), a comprehensive engagement of civil and military institutions focused on the poorest, most notably Colombian peasants (*campesinos*) (Ruiz N. 1964: 247).

Under the argument that this was not a task for the Army, a group of Generals refused to incorporate civil-military action initiatives in their respective jurisdictions (Leal B. 2002: 44). This play of forces led to a narrow component of "civil action" by the military, often translated into the distribution of pamphlets with general information about the mission of the Colombian Army, in addition to specific services offered by the military in small villages. Importantly, those services coexisted with armed confrontations and with psychological "techniques", such as infiltration and torture, aimed at obtaining information from the insurgents.

In these circumstances, it comes as no surprise that General Ruiz Novoa is indeed silent about social and economic concerns when presenting his account of one of Plan Lazo's main operations:

> The operation Marquetalia resulted in the extinction of the "independent republic". This was achieved with the support of operations of the psychological kind. We were helped by former liberal *guerrilleros*, such as "Peligro". We entered Marquetalia without the peasants having to be evacuated. In December 1965, the last operation in El Pato and Guayabero was undertaken[22] (Ruiz N. 1992 *Apud* Leal B. 2002: 44)

---

[21] In the original: "Como se ha mostrado cierta extrañeza porque el Ministro de Guerra trate estos temas, debo explicar las razones: (...) es evidente que las injusticias sociales y económicas son tan generadoras de violencia como el bandolerismo aparecido como secuela de la violencia política y que esta situación de desequilibrio incide fundamentalmente sobre el orden público cuyo mantenimiento, corresponde al Ministro de Guerra".

[22] In the original: "Con la operación Marquetalia desapareció la 'república independiente'. Se hizo con el apoyo de operaciones de tipo psicológico. Nos ayudaron antiguos guerrilleros liberales como 'Peligro'. A Marquetalia entramos sin que salieron los campesinos. En diciembre de 1965 se gestó la última operación en El Pato y Guayabero".

Marquetalia was the region where the "independent republic" was founded by a group of *campesinos* who had fought as part of the Liberal guerrillas during *La Violencia* (Pécaut 2010). After the agreement reached by the elites of the Conservative and Liberal Parties in Benidorm (1956), the "independent republic" came to be discursively reframed as a "communist guerrilla". The portrayal built by General Ruiz Novoa of a surgical military intervention ("without the peasants having to be evacuated"), backed by former Liberal *guerrilleros* as informants, contrasts with narratives of Operation Marquetalia as marked by widespread violence, torture, and looting (Olave 2013: 155–156). Interestingly, this particular operation is taken as a central event in the narrative constructed by the FARC about its foundation (Arenas 1966; Marulanda V 1973). In this sense, General Ruiz Novoa's silence about the persistence—or even intensification—of the armed resistance following Operation Marquetalia is a key condition for Plan Lazo to be claimed as a success among the Colombian military.

The forces participating in the operations constituting Plan Lazo had been trained in irregular warfare in the Lancers' School, established in 1955 as a specialized unit of infantry. Months before the foundation of the School, a commission formed by Colombian high-ranked military officers visited the facilities at Fort Benning (Georgia) to attend the "Ranger Course" (Leal B. 2002: 44; Rodríguez H. 2006: 77). The rangers had been formalized as a specific force of the U.S. Army Infantry School in 1951, and their skills were mobilized in the War in Korea. The rangers are agile and flexible small-unit soldiers engaged in irregular warfare, whose formation was based on short-term courses about counter-guerrilla doctrine for jungle and urban terrains, instruction on how to perform ambush and infiltration, in addition to a set of exercises focused on physical preparation and resistance (Rodríguez H. 2006: 77).

With the assistance of U.S. Army's Captain Ralph Puckett, the Lancers' School was built as a mirror of the Rangers School. In an article coauthored with Captain John Galván and published in 1959 in the official review of the U.S. Army Infantry School (*Infantry Review*) and then in the Colombian *Revista Militar*, Captain Puckett claimed that the Colombian Army interest in the "Ranger Course" derived from the massive presence of guerrillas and *bandoleros* in specific regions of the country:

> These irregular groups have been, for a long time, a continuous threat to the peace and security of the Colombian people; experts on the paths in

the mountains and jungle, they are very difficult to find and defeat, and the Army has not been so successful in dominating them. To overcome this difficulty, it was necessary to advance a specific training in this special kind of operation, and since small units were used to combat the anti-socials, the solution was evident: selected officers and non-commissioned officers had to be trained in order to fight the enemy on his own terrain and with the same methods. The Lancers' School took this mission and did it very well. (Puckett and Galván 1959: 94 *Apud* Rodríguez H. 2006: 78)[23]

Under these terms, the creation of the Lancers' School was considered a concrete response to a security problem, for it offered not only the agile mobility such an irregular warfare required, but also a specialized *savoir* on the terrains for which the guerrillas and *bandoleros* were experts: the mountain and the forest. The whole training provided by the Lancers' School is claimed to be based on previous study on where and how the "anti-socials" fight. According to a campaign manual dated 1944, translated and adapted by the U.S. military mission to the Colombian Military Forces, "In the war in the jungle, the soldier fights two different enemies: man and nature. Among these two, nature is often the most impressive one"[24] (Estado Mayor General de las Fuerzas Militares 1944: 5). To make the soldiers more familiar to the hostile conditions of the jungle, the manual instructs troops to count on local guides, "carefully selected, [and] whose loyalty and integrity are undisputable"[25] (Estado Mayor General de las Fuerzas Militares 1944: 50). However, in the words of the manual, the "native population" is both necessary for

---

[23] In the original: "Estas bandas irregulares han sido desde hace mucho tiempo una continua amenaza para la paz y seguridad del pueblo colombiano; expertas conocedoras de los caminos en la montaña y la selva, son muy difíciles de descubrir y vencer, y el Ejército ha tenido muy poco éxito en su misión de dominarlas. Para obviar esta dificultad, fue lógicamente necesario adelantar un entrenamiento específico en este tipo especial de operaciones, y desde que pequeñas unidades se emplearon para combatir a los antisociales la solución fue evidente: oficiales y suboficiales seleccionados debieron ser entrenados para combatir al enemigo en su propio terreno y usando sus mismos métodos. La Escuela de Lanceros llevó a cabo esta misión y lo hizo muy bien".

[24] In the original: "En la guerra en la selva el soldado combate contra dos enemigos: el hombre y la naturaleza. De estos dos, la naturaleza es con frecuencia el enemigo más formidable".

[25] In the original: "guías cuidadosamente seleccionados, cuya lealtad e integridad sean indiscutibles".

the military to feel safer on a terrain they are not familiar with, and suspicious, for they may be the enemy infiltrated in the troop. It is by means of a more sophisticated selection process and the constant surveillance over the selected "natives" that the risk of infiltration can be minimized. The manual contends that the work of instructing the native troops is compensated by the benefits gained with their knowledge of the local inhabitants and language: "The use of organized native troops (…) will not only help to dissipate any objection to the presence of our troops, but also strengthen the solidarity against a common enemy"[26] (Estado Mayor General de las Fuerzas Militares 1944: 51).

The population is thereby portrayed as either the enemy to be defeated or an asset to be explored so that the operation succeeds—constituting a source of knowledge about the terrain which is foreign to the non-"native", as well as a source of intelligence and legitimacy. Here, we see a clear expression of the ambiguity with which the population came to be approached by counterinsurgency warfare, as discussed in Sect. 5.1. On one hand, the "foreign" character of the terrain makes the collaboration of "natives" indispensable to the success of military missions. On the other, it reveals the very reason why the work of the military is deemed necessary on that particular terrain: to bring that population "back in" the Colombian territory and away from the anti-sociability allegedly characterizing insurgency.

With this purpose, the professionalization program built with the assistance of the U.S. military for the Lancers' School dedicated a significant part of its training program to the familiarization of the soldiers with the hostile environmental conditions of the jungle. Its main course comprised a twelve-week instruction for low-ranked military professionals (Rodríguez H. 2006: 79), structured in four stages. The first aimed at preparing the soldier physically, through physical training, fencing with bayonet, personal defense, swimming, and survival skills. During this 6-week program, the soldier was also instructed on intelligence and tactics, as well as on how to read aerial-photographic maps, to work with explosives, and to lead. In the next 2.5 weeks, instructions focused on

---

[26] In the original: "La familiaridad de estas tropas con el terreno y su conocimiento de los habitantes y del idioma compensarán ampliamente el trabajo de instruirlas. El empleo de tropas nativas organizadas y controladas por el comandante de la fuerza expedicionaria. No solamente ayudará a disipar cualquier objeción a la presencia de nuestras tropas sino que fortalecerá la solidaridad contra un enemigo común".

patrolling on a flat, jungle terrain, where soldiers were given different counter-guerrilla missions. In the 2 weeks corresponding to the third stage, the soldiers patrolled on mountainous terrains, participated in technical and tactical exercises on how to prepare and protect from an ambush, and engaged in combat simulations. In the final week of the Lancers' Course, the soldiers went through several tests on command, patrol, and physical resistance (Rodríguez H. 2006: 80). As for the commanders of those small-units, 200 military officers graduated in 1959, all of them also low-ranked (Rodríguez H. 2006: 81).

That the Lancers' School came to constitute the center of gravity of the military professionalization in Colombia exposes a re-articulation of these programs towards training facilities. If the analysis developed in Chapter 4 revealed the classroom as the main site for the production of the military professional and the authority of the teacher in this process, here we see the training facility and the instructor as the main site and authority in the professionalization of the military. While this intensive training was being provided to Colombian low-ranked military personnel in the Lancers' School (Rodríguez H. 2006), the high-ranked officers were participating in the discussion, consolidation, and refinement of military doctrine with their counterparts in the U.S. Army (Gill 2004). This means that the re-articulation of the professionalization program was made more explicit in the lower ranks, for it was in this layer that the production of tactically efficient bodies through short-term immersion courses was concentrated, allowing for its reproduction in large scale.[27]

Through these lines, the first groups who graduated from the Lancers' School were attached to the brigades operating in regions considered to be "infested with guerrillas", in the words of two Colombian captains who published an article on *Revista Militar,* the Colombian official military review (Vásquez and Negret V. 1960: 60 *Apud* Rodríguez H. 2006: 81). The 1960 *memoirs* of Rafael Hernández Pardo (1959–1960), Minister of War at that time, celebrated the efficiency of the *lanceros* in controlling "subversion" *foci* in those regions. A few years later, this infantry specialization already constituted the backbone of Plan Lazo.

---

[27] As we will see in the next Section, these characteristics of professionalization programs would become key to the intensification of military campaigns in the context of Plan Colombia. Indeed, the fact that the military preparation could be undertaken through short-term courses and in large scales allowed for the fast multiplication of the Colombian Army's manpower when pacification operations were intensified in the country.

In addition to the U.S. mission that assisted the Colombian Army in the creation and implementation of the Lancers' School training program, a group of military officers from the U.S. Army Special Warfare School at Fort Bragg (North Carolina) visited Colombia in 1962 to participate in the design of Plan Lazo (Human Rights Watch 1996: n.p.). Led by General William P. Yarborough,[28] Commander of the U.S. Army Special Warfare School at that time, the mission emphasized counterinsurgency tactics and psychological operations, most especially intelligence,[29] and recommended the creation of a "civil defense" force that would give direct support to the military troops. According to a supplement to his report presented to the Chief of Staff, General Yarborough argued that a

> concerted country team effort should be made now to select civilian and military personnel for clandestine training in resistance operations in case they are needed later. This should be done with a view toward development of a civil and military structure for exploitation in the event the Colombian internal security system deteriorates further. This structure should be used to pressure toward reforms known to be needed, perform counter-agent and counter-propaganda functions and as necessary execute paramilitary, sabotage and/or terrorist activities against known communist proponents. It should be backed by the United States. (Yarborough 1962 *Apud* McClintock 1992: Chapter 9)

[28] Known as "the father of the Green Berets", General William P. Yarborough commanded the U.S. Army Special Warfare Center (later renamed JFK School) at Fort Bragg (North Carolina) from 1961 to 1965. During this period, he reviewed training programs and doctrine material, and expanded the special warfare curriculum, creating additional groups and courses, such as the "Unconventional Warfare Course" and the "Counter-Terrorism Course". He is also known for his contribution to intelligence operations against black protesters in Detroit and Newark in 1967. Named "Continental United States Intelligence" (Conus Intel), the federal operation General Yarborough was part of was created to monitor "subversive groups" inside the U.S., having classified thousands of civilians according to their "potential to cause trouble". For more information, see Bernstein (2005).

[29] In the same period, the U.S. Army Special Warfare School hosted courses with Lieutenant Colonel Roger Trinquier and General Paul Aussaresses—French military officers whose "acknowledged expertise" on psychological warfare and counterinsurgency tactics derived from their experience in Algeria. Although this does not imply that Trinquier and Aussaresses' expertise was flowing directly to Colombia, it does point to the domains that were valorized in the U.S. Army Special Warfare School at that time. And it was to that particular school that Colombia was turning its attention when rearticulating the professionalization of its military personnel in the second half of the twentieth century.

The use of self-defense groups for tactical purposes was a constant component of the U.S. Army *modus operandi* during the Cold War[30] (Human Rights Watch 1996): to train "civilian irregulars" was considered as "most effective when they included army reservists, retired officers predisposed to a fierce anticommunism, and men familiar with local residents, customs, and terrain" (Human Rights Watch 1996: section II). Such a use of illegality with a tactical purpose drew from practices of the German and Japanese Armies during the World War II and was replicated by the U.S. in the Philippines, Korea, and Vietnam, and by the British in Malaya (McClintock 1992)—to mention but a few cases.

Similarly, the Colombian Army often made an instrumental use of anti-subversive armed groups (Ronderos 2014: 35)—terms that I consider to be more accurate so as to build the contrast with the "self-defense groups", formed by *campesinos* in reaction to violent incursions by the armed forces. After the Colombian Army defeated guerrillas in specific regions, these anti-subversive groups kept their armed presence therein, serving as security personnel to land owners and, on many occasions, engaging in massacres (Human Rights Watch 1996; Guzmán B. and Moreno Q. 2007; Ronderos 2014). The Army provided intelligence and logistical support to such groups in the form of guides and "leaked" lists of those considered suspects of being members of guerrillas (Human Rights Watch 1996: section III).

Another important effect of the 1962 U.S. mission was the selection of a group of Colombian military officers to attend an intelligence course—one of Yarborough's main expertise—at Fort Holabird[31] (Maryland).

---

[30] As mentioned in Sect. 3.2, it is important to highlight that this relation with illegality is not an invention of the U.S., an exclusive feature of Colombia, nor a specific trait of the Cold War. Moreover, the sequence of armed confrontations that marked the trajectory of Colombia since independence resulted in the proliferation of arms across the territory and in its use for "self-defense" purposes long before the creation of "organized self-defense groups" was stimulated as a military tactic. As the play of forces in the armed conflict increased in complexity, different paramilitary groups orbited around the Colombian Armed Forces, oscillating between partners and enemies depending on the context. In other words, despite the usefulness of such groups, the Colombian Armed Forces never had full control over them—as it has been also remarked in Sect. 3.2.

[31] The U.S. Army Intelligence School and Counter-Intelligence Records Facility operated at Fort Holabird until 1971, when they were transferred to Fort Huachuca (Arizona). Both the U.S. Army Intelligence Center and the 111th Military Intelligence Brigade, based in Fort Huachuca, conduct training programs on human intelligence (interrogation and counterintelligence, for instance) and imagery intelligence, among other courses.

Among the selected officers was Lieutenant Coronel (*Teniente Coronel*) Ricardo Charry Solano,[32] who came to be known as "the artificer of military intelligence in Colombia". By the time he was sent to the U.S., he was teaching irregular warfare in the Superior War College (*Escuela Superior de Guerra*).[33] Ranked Colonel (*Coronel*) upon his return from the U.S., Solano articulated the first intelligence networks of the Colombian Army and organized, with the other officers who had visited Fort Holabird, the first "Intelligence and Counterintelligence Course for Military Officers" and "Intelligence Course for Sub-Officers" in 1963. In addition, the Command of the Army created the Intelligence and Counterintelligence Battalion (BINCI, in Spanish) in 1964 (Resolution No. 20), whose facilities were based in the Military School (*Escuela Militar*).

The BINCI not only formalized the entanglement between intelligence and irregular warfare at the operational level: it incorporated anti-subversive armed groups as a regular component of the operations undertaken by the BINCI. According to a 1979 report from the US Embassy in Bogota on the human rights situation in Colombia,[34] the BINCI had created the American Anti-Communist Alliance (also known as "Triple A") in 1979, a branch of the Battalion (U.S. Department of State 1979) to which missions such as exploding "apparatuses" considered as strategic to the enemy, as well as torturing and assassinating

---

[32] See https://esici.edu.co/index.php/historia-de-la-esici/. Accessed on 18 May 2021.

[33] Before taking that position, he had already commanded the Artillery Battalion No. 6 "Tenerife", where the instruction on counterinsurgency tactics was invested against the "independent republic". For more information, see https://esici.edu.co/index.php/charry-solano/. Accessed on 18 May 2021.

[34] The document was sent to the U.S. Department of State. Labelled as "classified" in 1979 (i.e. confidential information), the full content of the report was only disclosed in 2007. Available at: http://static.iris.net.co/semana/upload/documents/Doc-1474_2 007630.pdf. Accessed on 18 May 2021. The report is evidence that Colombian high-ranked officers were not only aware but commanded "para-terrorist operations" (Evans 2007). As it has been discussed in Chapter 3, the countless accusations of human rights violations were repeatedly dodged through the evocation of the "bad apples" narrative or the change in the name of the command unit accused of "deviant conduct". It was no different with the BINCI, which had its name changed to "20th Brigade" (*Brigada 20*). As the accusations of abuses in the use of violence continued to flow towards the Brigade, the latter was extinguished in 1998. For more information, see CINEP (2004) and Evans (2007).

members of "leftist-groups" in Colombia were assigned[35] (El Día 1980; CINEP 2004; Evans 2007).

The fact that the U.S. government was aware of massive human rights violations in Colombia did not hinder the continuous exchange between military professionals from the two countries. On the contrary, the durability of their socialization remained throughout the following decades, finding legitimacy and breath in the institutional fabric of the hemispheric circuit of military *savoirs*. As we have seen, the interaction between American and Colombian professionals has only grown since the 1940s, with an increasing depth and diversity in its scope.

The case of the Lancers' School shows that this socialization was not only aimed at crystalizing a *savoir* on irregular warfare in the form of a specialized school, but also generating the conditions for the transmission of that *savoir*—and, consequently, for its multiplication. Another characteristic of this dynamic was an increasing number of visits of Colombian high-ranked military officers to the U.S., aimed at making sure that they were in the position to teach a specific technique, operational domain, or doctrine upon their return to Colombia.

The durability of their socialization reveals, simultaneously, the durability of the U.S. as a reference for professionalization programs for the Colombian military. This privileged position of the U.S. survived decades through an adaptation to the "rise and fall" of problematizations of violence in the region.[36] At the same time, the *savoirs* circulating in the hemisphere molded the operational and doctrinal terms with which violence would be tackled by military professionals. In this sense, while an institutionalist perspective classified the countries in South America as democracies or dictatorships from the 1960s to the 1980s, focusing

---

[35] Suspects of collaborating with "leftist-groups" were also targeted by the "Triple A". In July 1980, for instance, five military officers who used to integrate the Battalion denounced the BINCI for planning and carrying out, through the "Triple A", the explosion of the headquarters of the magazine *Alternativa*, as well as of the newspapers *El Bogotano* and *Voz Proletaria*. See El Día (1980).

[36] As I hope to have shown in the previous pages of this book, the re-framing of threats both in Colombia and in the hemispheric circuit of military *savoirs* must in fact be interpreted as discursive re-articulations of the "problem of violence". These versions stem from the combination of a claim to novelty with sedimentations of how violence was historically understood. The fact that a military *savoir* such as counterinsurgency came to be understood as valid throughout the decades expresses this very persistence of historical deposits in problematizations of violence presented as fit for "new times".

on the circulation of military *savoirs* provides us a shared understanding among those professionals regarding problematizations of violence and the expertise needed to repress it—across the democracy-dictatorship spectrum.

A closer look at one of the main hubs in this hemispheric circuit of military *savoirs* in that period, the SoA, illustrates this point. Between 1970 and 1979, Bolivia, Chile, Colombia, Honduras, Panama, and Peru sent between 1,100 and 1,800 students each, accounting for 63% of the total enrollment in the school (Gill 2004: 78). Colombia was the only country on the list above that did not have a military in the Presidency at that time. Indeed, because the country was not formally identified as a military regime in the context of Operation Condor, Colombia was often claimed as the most "enduring democracy" in South America (Pizarro L. 1987; Atehortúa C. and Vélez R. 1994; Gallón G. 2007; Gómez-Suárez 2010: 152). Nonetheless, the Colombian military were attending the same courses as those attended by their counterparts from countries under military regimes.

When Colombia did have a formal military government, in the context of *La Violencia*, the mobilization of the military was considered by part of the political elites and the private sector as useful for the pacification of the turmoil in the country. With the establishment of *Frente Nacional*, this very "solution"—namely, the "eruption of the armed forces as political actors in the national life" (Pizarro L. 1987: 28)—came to be framed as a problem for civil elites. Similar to the terms constituting the problematization of the military by the end of the nineteenth century, the question on what to do with the military was again a major concern, this time expressed in what would later be known as "Lleras doctrine". In a 1958 speech addressed to the military, the first President of the *Frente Nacional* laid out the terms of such doctrine as follows:

> All of your life has been dedicated to obey and, as a consequence, to know how to command, when the time is appropriate, but to command people who do not ponder over your orders, nor discuss them. This is an exercise radically different from the command within the civil life. (…) Politics is the art of controversies, by excellence. Militia, of discipline. (…) Keeping them [the Armed Forces] away from the public deliberation is not a whim of the Constitution, but a necessity of their function. If they engage in a deliberation, they do so with their arms. (…) This is the reason why the Armed Forces (…) must not deliberate in politics. Because they have been

created by the whole nation, because the whole nation (...) has given them arms (...) with the mission of defending its common interests, (...) and all of this with a condition: that they do not invest all of their weight and force over innocent citizens in the name of others. (...) I do not want the Armed Forces, instead of the people, to decide on how the nation must be governed, but I do not want, in any way, that the politicians decide how they must manage the Armed Forces, as regards their technical function, their discipline, their regulations, their personnel (Lleras C. n.d. 211–214 *Apud* Leal B. 2002: 38).[37]

The boundary drawn here between the civil and the military domains reproduces the constitutive elements of the discourse of modernization analyzed in Chapter 4. In Lleras' formulation, the use of arms is considered foreign to politics, while controversies are conceived as the distinctive character of the civil domain: in such a discourse, social relations must not be regulated by violence within the civil domain—the "pacified space". For their part, arms are to be used not in the defense of a specific party or social group, but in the defense of the "common interests" of the "whole nation". Just as the professionalization of the military was claimed as a necessary condition for the modernization of Colombia in the late-nineteenth century, the same confinement of the military in its own professional domain was, in 1958, claimed as a necessary condition for the civilized exercise of politics. Nonetheless, the analysis developed in Chapter 4 invites us to resist the terms of mutual non-interference expressed by the "Lleras doctrine": I propose that we instead explore how each of these domains enables and constrains the other, as well as what

---

[37] In the original: "Toda la vida de ustedes ha estado dedicada a aprender a obedecer y, como consecuencia, a saber mandar, cuando les llegue su tiempo, pero a mandar personas que no deliberan sobre sus órdenes ni las discuten. Es un ejercicio radicalmente distinto del mando en la vida civil. (...) La política es el arte de la controversias, por excelencia. La milicia, el de la disciplina. (...) El manternerlas [las Fuerzas Armadas] apartadas de la deliberación pública no es un capricho de la Constitución, sino una necesidad de su función. Si entran a deliberar entran armadas. (...) Por eso las Fuerzas Armadas (...) no deben ser deliberantes en política. Porque han sido creadas por toda la nación, porque la nación entera (...) les ha dado las armas (...) con el encargo de defender sus intereses comunes, (...) y todo ello con una condición: la de que no entren con todo su peso y su fuerza a caer sobre unos ciudadanos inocentes, por cuenta de los otros. (...) Yo no quiero que las Fuerzas Armadas decidan cómo se debe gobernar a la nación, en vez de que lo decida el pueblo, pero no quiero, en manera alguna, que los políticos decidan cómo se debe manejar las Fuerzas Armadas, en su función técnica, en su disciplina, en sus reglamentos, en su personal".

savoirs are circulated across these domains. Seeing the "Lleras doctrine" through these lenses allows us to shed light on the practices of violence authorized by the relation of the civil with the military.

As shown in this Section, the demise of the military government in Colombia and the establishment of *Frente Nacional* did not exclusively result in the confinement of the military back to the barracks. Indeed, as professionalization programs in the Lancers' School intensified, the Colombian military were increasingly mobilized as an indispensable component of internal ordering practices in the second half of the twentieth century. For Leal Buitrago (2002), the autonomy of the Army during the *Frente Nacional* coexisted with the absence of a military state policy: "Once the scarce and modest existing political guidelines on the role of the military in society were not revised nor updated, the high-ranked military officers took the task of designing it in an improvised fashion"[38] (Leal B. 2002: 39). Two elements are noteworthy here: that Leal Buitrago considers that the autonomy of the military was a case of negligence on the part of the civil governments; and that there is a relation of causality between this negligence and the deepening of the military engagement with national security operations in Colombia—"national security without military state policy"[39], in his own words (Leal B. 2002: 35). Instead, I suggest that we read the regulatory silence Leal Buitrago is referring to as a consent of the civil domain regarding the mobilization of the military in internal ordering practices. As an illustration, the *Frente Nacional* nominated a high-ranked military officer for the position of Minister of War (which was only renamed Ministry of Defense in 1965), thereby allowing for the alignment of barracks, Chief of Staff, head of the Military Forces and Ministry of War.

Thus, while the "Lleras doctrine" evokes the "whole nation", "the people", "innocent people", and "controversy" as objects of the work of civil authorities, we can only make sense of these words by grasping the terms with which the use of violence was admitted during the *Frente Nacional*. In other words, if pushing the military away from (most of the) civil offices coexisted with their pervasive participation in internal order, the rationality with which violence was organized in this context

---

[38] In the original: "Al no revisarse y actualizarse las escasas y tímidas directrices políticas del papel militar en la sociedad, los altos mandos castrenses asumieron su diseño en forma improvisada".

[39] In the original: "Seguridad nacional sin política militar de Estado".

speaks to the discursive boundary between what is socially deplorable and what is socially acceptable on the road to democracy the *Frente Nacional* was claiming to perform—i.e. distinctions between innocent and guilty, the people and the anti-social, the whole nation and the foreign, the controversy and the taken for granted.

In this sense, Colombia is more an expression of the hemispheric circuit of military *savoirs* than an exception to it: my point is that the terms with which violence is organized on a given terrain cannot be reduced to the form of political regimes. As we have seen, irrespective of the institutional façade of their national governments, the military in South America understood that the *savoirs* diffused through the SoA were useful for violence to be tamed. That the hemispheric circuit contributed to a harmonized problematization of violence makes it not surprising the fact that counterinsurgency and intelligence were the themes of the most attended courses at SoA from the 1960s to the 1980s[40] (Gill 2004). Whether military concerns were concentrated on urban guerrillas or rural insurgents, "communism" came to be the amalgam connecting particular renderings of violence during that period into a general framing that made shared doctrinal and operational discussions among military professionals possible.

Here, the plasticity of counterinsurgency helps us to understand the preservation of its privileged position in the edifice of military *savoirs*. Indeed, one of the distinctive features of counterinsurgency is its emphasis on tactics, along with its population-centric approach, the centrality of intelligence deriving from the latter, and the principle of an impossible decisive victory. Throughout the decades, this characterization allowed for a constant development of tactical repertoires so as to adapt to the particularities of a specific terrain, while keeping the rationality with which the population of this terrain would be engaged intact.

Thus, the resilience of counterinsurgency speaks not only to its adherence across the democracy-dictatorship spectrum, but also to its persistence in time. Now, if one of its fundamental pillars is precisely the claim of an impossible decisive victory, the permanent pacification it suggests provides us an impossible differentiation between war and peace. If war was what the military professionals in the circuit learned, and if counterinsurgency was what they became specialized in, the constant

---

[40] See also: https://soaw.org/soa-whinsec-graduate-database. Accessed on 1st June 2021.

mobilization of counterinsurgency as a useful *savoir* to order societies in the hemisphere points to a permanent state of war against the population understood as part of the "problem of violence".

The next Section builds upon this analysis by exploring the only apparently strange coexistence between the discourse of "post-conflict" Colombia, on one hand, and the preservation of counterinsurgency as a *savoir* mobilized by the military on internal order, on the other. As we will see, the intensification of pacification under Plan Colombia during the 2000s was framed as such a successful formula for "peace" in Colombia that the country came to gradually re-position itself in the hemispheric circuit of military *savoirs*: not so much a reference as a problem anymore, but a reference for solutions to its military counterparts. This "success" also resulted in the perhaps unsurprising return of an enduring question: what to do with the military in a post-conflict Colombia? As we will see, answers articulated around this question give us an enduring rationality: peace, as coded war.

5.3 Successful Nonetheless: The Expert-Soldier and the Re-positioning of Colombia in the Global Circuit of Military Savoirs

The creation of the Lancers' School and the mobilization of the *lanceros* in counterinsurgency operations under Plan Lazo in the 1960s were among the main effects of a more systematic interaction of Colombian and U.S. military professionals. With regard to the organization of the military forces, the following decades witnessed a further specialization of the operations carried out by the *lanceros*—these agile and small units trained to fight insurgents in multiple terrains, especially the jungle. As a result, training programs dedicated to the production of efficient soldiers were gradually complexified so as to also encompass propaganda, intelligence techniques for infiltration and interrogation, as well as the training of anti-subversive armed groups—a form of illegality with tactical value for the operations.

With the implementation of Plan Colombia in 1999, these processes were taken to another level in terms of the resources mobilized, the specialization of the military forces, and the relevance of training programs to their professionalization. As we will see in this Section, the "modernization"[41] of the military forces to which Plan Colombia gave impulse was key to the Colombian "success story" and, consequently, to the repositioning of the country in the hemispheric circuit of military *savoirs*.

Importantly, decades of intense mobilization of the military in internal order operated towards increasing tensions among the military forces, on one hand, and the police, on the other, regarding the authority to solve the problem of violence in the country. Indeed, if the mid-twentieth century was marked by a problematization of violence that had communism at its center of gravity, the 1980s saw the emergence of the "problem of drugs" as a competing narrative in renderings of violence in Colombia. While the military were in charge of counterinsurgency as countercommunism, and the police were concerned with counternarcotics, their competition was focused on which problematization of violence was to be privileged within the Colombian security architecture. As the "problem of drugs" came to be interpreted as a nexus between guerrillas and drug trafficking ("narcoguerrillas"), the tensions between the military and the police were invested toward those who did more efficient work in repressing that violence.

Although exploring these tensions falls outside the scope of this book, this Section excavates the transformations of the security architecture in Colombia as the problematization of violence was re-articulated throughout the decades. In doing so, I argue that the solutions to the "problem of violence" came to be invariably translated into the expansion of this architecture and into demands for increased war power. As we will see, these remarks are directly linked to the repositioning of Colombia in

---

[41] The use of quotation marks in "modernization" here merits attention. Under Plan Colombia, the use of the term *modernization* referred specifically to the strengthening of the military forces through capacity management, weapons, equipment, and training. At the time, these were understood as leading to further military professionalization. This connection between modernization, professionalization, and military forces echoes the discourse on modernity presented in Chapter 4. However, as we have also seen in that chapter, the claim by the Colombian military to being "modern" was already at play since at least the late nineteenth century. Thus, with the inverted comas I want to underline that the use of the vocabulary of modernization under Plan Colombia must be interpreted as one more instantiation of what "the military" should be—an instantiation played out, yet again, by connecting the military to modernity. Indeed, the effects of modernity result from its constant affirmation as the regulative ideal of modernization—that is, modernity only exists as modernization.

the hemispheric circuit of military *savoirs*, for the successful case circulating in the region is both a specific expertise and a form that allows for its reproduction. In this sense, exploring the rationality with which this form and content have been undertaken in Colombia provides us a shared diagnosis of violence in the hemisphere, and at the same time it reveals a shared symptom: after all, what is consumed as a success is an easy-to-apply massive war architecture.

I want to start this discussion by recalling that the transition from the 1970s to the 1980s was not only characterized by the consolidation of drugs as a problem to be tackled by the police, but also by the incorporation of "terrorism" to the Penal Code as a juridical form criminalizing radical violence, as discussed in Sect. 2.1. By that time, César Turbay Ayala's administration (1978–1982) oscillated between the military and the police as the branch of the Colombian Armed Forces to which the repression of drug trafficking would be assigned. The Decree No. 2144 issued in 1978, for instance, concentrated in the Military Forces the power to undertake patrol and control operations aiming at "re-establishing public order". It was under this Decree that "Operation Fulminant" (*Operación Fulminante*) was held in *marijuana* crops found in the Colombian Atlantic coast in that same year, through the mobilization of the Army's 2nd Brigade with the support of the Air Force and the Navy (Lizarazo V. 2008: 45; Guanumen P. 2012: 240). In contrast, in 1982, the Ministry of Defense determined that all the drug trafficking-related actions were placed within the scope of the Colombian National Police—more specifically, of the Department of Control of Substances that Produce Physical and Psychic Addiction (COSAS, in Spanish), created in 1981.

Even before the U.S. counternarcotic agencies saw a decline in the marihuana crops as a result of their eradication campaigns, their concerns were drawn to the main networks of cocaine production that took shape during the 1980s in Colombia: the Medellín and Cali drug cartels. The impulse given by these two networks to the cocaine exports to the U.S. consolidated Colombia as the center of gravity of Ronald Reagan's supply-side approach to the "problem of drugs", as I have shown in Sect. 2.2. In this context, the DEA was raised to a privileged position in the constellation of U.S. federal agencies engaged with counternarcotic policies abroad, along with the FBI and the CIA. In 1985, the DEA had 2,234 special agents and an annual budget corresponding to US$ 362.4 million, in contrast to the 1,470 agents and US$ 75 million annual budget the DEA had at its disposal when created, in 1973 (DEA n.d.: 44).

The strengthening of the supply-side approach and the protagonism of the DEA in counternarcotic initiatives led to the intensification of the agency's participation in eradication and interdiction operations in Colombia, and to the channeling of resources from the U.S. to the Colombian National Police. An emblematic example can be found pecisely in the contrast between the design of *Operación Fulminante* (1978) and that of "Operation Quiet Village" (*Operación Tranquilandia*), held in 1984 against a major cocaine processing laboratory of the Medellín cartel. If the former had the Military Forces in charge of the operation, the latter was based on the intelligence provided by the DEA and was conducted by the National Police's COSAS. The Colombian Army had only a marginal role in *Operación Tranquilandia*, restricted to keeping the area under control once the operation was finished (Lizarazo V. 2008: 53). Actions such as this one were inscribed in a wider cooperation between the DEA and counternarcotic branches of the Colombian National Police, translated into instruction courses (for instance, on the use of human sources of information and on investigation focused on drugs) and equipment (such as vehicles used in the interception of phone calls, to mention but one case) (Lizarazo V. 2008: 52).

While the war against the cartels increasingly stimulated a close articulation between the DEA and the Colombian Police, negotiation attempts aimed at demobilizing specific guerrillas were undertaken by the Colombian Presidencies from Belisario Betancur (1982–1986) to Andrés Pastrana (1998–2002). Despite the differences among these administrations regarding the priority given to the negotiation and the results harvested (Viana 2016), all of them faced a strong resistance from the military. To a group of high-ranked military officers, the amnesties granted to demobilized groups in those talks would fuel the war, rather than contribute to peace. In an editorial published in *Revista de las Fuerzas Armadas,* General Fernando Landazábal Reyes, who had been the Ministry of Defense from 1982 to 1984, wrote:

> When on the verge of a decisive military victory over the armed groups, the political authority intervenes, once more, in order to lift the state of siege. In this way, the determination of the subversive armed groups to fight receives oxygen (...) [and they] transform the defeats they had suffered by

the military action into political victories of great resonance. (...) We hope this is the last amnesty.⁴² (Landazábal R. 1982 *Apud* Ramírez 1989: 115)

Seeing amnesties granted to guerrillas as a softened approach exposing the public order to danger, the military intensified their criticism whenever governments pursued a strategy of dialogue with those groups. Their pressure echoed in the dynamics of these negotiations, as well as in the terms with which agreements would be implemented. As an illustration, the Amnesty Law No. 35 approved in the context of the demobilization of the M-19, in 1982, was followed by an increase in the budget assigned to the Military Forces (Ramírez 2004: 114). The preparation for peace pursued through that particular law justified the resources channeled to the military as appropriate for the "civic-action programs" they were expected to perform in that context—a task that was never taken up by the military at that time (Ramírez 2004: 95). A few years later, the cease fire signed with the FARC in 1984 specified no responsibility or limit whatsoever for the military in case one of the parties breached the agreement (Ramírez 1989: 208–209).

This ambiguity allowed for the Military Forces to portray themselves as guardians of the cease fire on some occasions, and guardians of the Constitution, on others (Ramírez 1989: 209–211). Intelligence was intensified during that period aimed at surveilling whether guerrilla members were violating the ceasefire or not. Referring to the FARC as "bandits", General Miguel Vega Uribe, Ministry of Defense at that time (1984–1985),⁴³ circulated among the military branches a document whereby he recommended the intensification of intelligence operations

---

⁴² In the original: "Cuando ha estado a punto de obtener la victoria militar definitiva sobre los alzados en armas, la acción de la autoridad política interviene para levantar nuevamente el estado de sitio. En esa forma la voluntad de lucha de los grupos armados de la subversión recibe el oxígeno (...) [y ellos] transforman las derrotas sufridas por la acción militar en victorias políticas de gran resonancia. (...) Esperamos sea la última amnistía".

⁴³ The high rotativity of Ministers of Defense illustrates the tensions across the civil-military boundary that characterized this period. It is also noteworthy that the two first Ministers of Defense in the Betancur's administration (1982–1986), Landazábal Reyes and Vega Uribe, had a very similar profile: in addition to the rank "General", both were military officers with a solid background on guerrilla warfare and intelligence. Such profile reveals not only the credentials required for the highest rank to be granted in the Military Forces, but also the *savoirs* privileged for the command of the Ministry of Defense.

and a state of permanent alert to all combat units (Ramírez 1989: 209–210). Under the claim that it was impossible to distinguish those who had demobilized from those who were not committed to the ceasefire, General Vega ordered the Military Forces to "fight and repress, with no hesitation, any detected manifestation of armed groups", and added that the "FARC gangs" that disobeyed the commands given by the Military Forces had to be "eliminated" (Vega U. 1984 *Apud* Ramírez 1989: 209–210).

Here, we see with explicit contours the argument developed in Sects. 5.1 and 5.2: that the discourse of peace always carries the terms with which war is admittedly activated. At the same time, far from putting the military to a halt, this very impossibility of distinguishing those who had demobilized from those who had not—acknowledged by General Vega to his counterparts—historically provided the military with an expanded discursive authorization for their war power in the name of peace.

The radical character of the danger that came to be associated with the guerrillas and drugs in Colombia fed discourse of "crisis" and "emergency" that made the appeal to "exceptional measures" natural. The effect of such discourse has been the recurrent authorization of the displacement of the ordinary legislator by one of extraordinary character, and of the ordinary judicial system by military courts (Vanegas G. 2011: 262–263)—as expressed by the fact that five states of siege were declared in Colombia during the 1990s[44] (Vanegas G. 2011: 287). Throughout the decades, the pervasive reproduction of the vocabulary of emergency and its recurrent translation into a government through siege resulted in regulatory deposits that gradually came to be incorporated into ordinary laws. In other words, specific aspects of previous states of siege were emulated by ordinary legal forms given to the organization of violence under a "permanent state of alert".

---

[44] The total duration of those state of sieges was 647 days. To be clear, this was not a particular feature of the 1990s: during the twentieth century, Colombian governments often appealed to the state of siege as a privileged means to tackle disturbances of public order. On some of these occasions, the Constitutional Court considered the practice of governing through states of siege unconstitutional, calling attention to the massive violations of rights deriving from that practice (Vanegas G. 2011). For more information, see: Gallón G. (1979), Vanegas (2011), and Semana (1982).

A remarkable expression of such process can be found in César Gaviria's Public Order Law No. 104 (1993), approved right after a 270-day state of siege had expired (Vanegas G. 2011: 287). According to a hearing in the Congress with the government's spokesperson, the law was necessary to consolidate what the state of siege had "achieved" both in the war against the guerrillas and in the war against the drug cartels: 760 guerrilla members killed and another 1,860 detained (among whom, 20 commandants); 10,000 assaults against the Medellín cartel; and detention and killing of "the most important" second-rank leaders of that cartel (Leal B. 2002: 94–95).

Initially planned for a 2-year validity and then extended until 1997, Public Order Law No. 104 aimed at strengthening the justice system in terms of efficiency and anticorruption, as well as building a robust surveillance apparatus focused on informants' networks, phone interceptions, and auditing of national and subnational public offices (Congreso de la República de Colombia 1993). The same apparatus was invested in what were understood as two different phenomena: on one side, delinquent organizations linked to drug trafficking and terrorism (see, for instance, Articles 71, 82.1–6, 94); on the other, guerrillas, understood as "popular militias with political character" (see Article 14.d) (Congreso de la República de Colombia 1993). To the former, the penal system and the implacable use of violence against terrorism. To the latter, incentives for their demobilization and "reincorporation into society", while tacitly authorizing the Military Forces to use violence against those refusing to engage in negotiations.

In doing so, this particular law reveals that peace and war making are not only compatible, but part of the same rationality of social ordering—or, as specified in the subtitle of Public Order Law No. 104, the terms under which the "pursuit of coexistence and the effectiveness of justice" is understood as feasible. Again, in this process, the civil domain is part of the conditions that make the mobilization of war power possible. Indeed, the terms with which the use of violence would become admitted and the lethality that would result from that authorization are far from illustrating any purge of violence from the social space. Rather, they are expressions of how the civil domain is an indispensable dimension for the authorization and legitimation of more war power.

As we have seen, these demands for more war power were also shared by the military, who believed that soft measures were giving advantages to the guerrillas in the war. But the demands for more war power were also shared by the police, who claimed that they were losing the war to the drug trafficking organizations. This double push derived from the fact that they worked with problematizations of violence anchored in different phenomena. By the early-1990s, the emergence of the diagnosis of a nexus between guerrillas and drug trafficking organizations—articulated in the vocabulary of "narcoguerrillas", as discussed in Sect. 2.1—fused these two problematizations into one. In any case, the solution offered to the problem of violence in the country was unequivocally the same: the strengthening of the Colombian state through the expansion of its security architecture. In other words, it was a particular kind of state presence in "problematic terrains" that claims for "more state" or a "stronger state" implied.

Expanding this architecture often meant creating combat or investigation units with a particular specialization—as in the case of COSAS, later transformed into DIRAN, in 1987—, as well as boosting manpower in both police and military forces. As more war power is so repeatedly conflated with firepower, the expansion of this security architecture was also marked by the procurement of weapons and equipment traditionally associated with warfare.[45] At the same time, the "special character" that came to be associated with counternarcotic and counterterrorism operations offered the discursive justification for intense training programs to specialized military units—as we have seen in the case of *lanceros*—and to elite police units, as is the case of the Jungla Commands (*Comandos Jungla*), created in 1989 as a special force under the Colombian National Police's DIRAN and trained by military instructors from the U.S. and British armies[46] (El Mostrador 2018).

Throughout the years, the sedimentation of this expanded architecture had the effect of normalizing the use of violence and high levels of

---

[45] In the 2019 ExpoDefensa, a "security fair" specialized in displaying the arsenal of the Colombian Armed Forces, the Jungla Commands (*Comandos Jungla*), an elite police unit under the DIRAN, showed the repertoire of war weapons they have at their disposal for counternarcotic operations. See https://www.defensa.com/colombia/armas-comando-jungla-colombianos. Accessed on 9 June 2021.

[46] Gill (2004: 83) also remarks that Colombian police professionals attended courses on counternarcotic operations at the SoA in expressive numbers during the 1990s. More broadly, the SoA Watch database illustrates this transit of Latin American police professionals at the SoA during the second half of the twentieth century. See https://soaw.org/soa-whinsec-graduate-database. Accessed on 1st June 2021.

lethality as ordering mechanisms towards problematic groups and territories. As the decades went by, this very sedimentation operated towards a bureaucratic inertia in this security architecture: that is, the repetition of routines shaping professionalization programs and operations aligned to this war power naturalized a way of coping with and seeing the problem that gradually saw alternative views and practices fade away from the horizon of possibilities.

Despite—and because of—this robust security architecture that was gradually taking shape in Colombia, the levels of violence during the 1990s achieved unprecedented levels (Echandía 2006). As a solution to such high levels of violence, the Colombian security architecture underwent further expansion: indeed, a series of defeats suffered by the armed forces in the late-1990s were piled up as evidence of their weakness. Among these cases, the ones most recurrently mentioned were the defeats in the departments of Caquetá, Guaviare, and Vaupés—all of them in 1998.

The first one involved an ambush against the Army's Counterguerrilla Battalion No. 52, an elite force of the 3rd Mobile Brigade formed by professional soldiers trained in counterinsurgency. This attack in El Billar (Caquetá) resulted in 62 soldiers killed, and 43 made prisoners by the FARC (Villamizar 2003: 22). The alarming character associated with this event stemmed from the fact that this particular defeat involved well-trained and experienced soldiers from the Colombian Army (Rangel 1998). A few months later, both the Police and the Army were simultaneously attacked by 1,200 FARC soldiers in Miraflores (Guaviare). The offensive against the 7th Brigade's Infantry Battalion 19 "Joaquín Paris" and counternarcotic police forces resulted in 100 kidnapped, 30 killed, and 50 wounded among the armed forces personnel (El Tiempo 1998). Three months later, the military base in the capital of Vaupés, was taken by the FARC—revealing that this guerrilla had military capacity to take the capital of a department (Villamizar 2003: 25). The takeover of the Mitú municipality (*Toma de Mitú*) is repeatedly brought up as an emblematic example of mistakes to be avoided in military operations.[47]

---

[47] Ten years after the *Toma de Mitú*, many were the stories in the Colombian newspapers that recovered the event by narrating the excesses of violence used by the FARC and telling family stories of the armed forces' members that had not been liberated by the guerrilla since the takeover, in 1998. Described as "hell", "the bloodiest strike of the FARC", and a "violation of all the humanitarian law rules", *Mitú* came to represent

Here, the main concern regarded intelligence: although information that the FARC was planning the operation was ventilated three weeks before the attack took place, no action was taken to avoid or confront the attack (Villamizar 2003: 25).

Although the defeats were suffered by both the military and the police, the discourse that gained traction in the Colombian public debate was especially emphatic of a "military crisis" (El País 1998; Rangel 1998; Revista Semana 1998; Villamizar 2003). More than specific operational problems, these cases were evoked by the main Colombian newspapers and magazines as a sign that a military reform was both necessary and urgent.[48] In 1998, the Minister of Defense Rodrigo Lloreda Caicedo (1998–1999) created the Commission for the Restructuration and Modernization of the Armed Forces, formed by civil and military professionals. The Commission was in charge of assessing "what went

---

the unwillingness of the FARC to engage in peaceful talks (Martin and Jaramillo-Marín 2014). More than this: it came to be promoted as an emblematic case of the collective memory about violence in Colombia (Martin and Jaramillo-Marín 2014: 404). For us to understand the political effects of this mobilization of *Mitú*, we must take into account that the news coverage of its 10th anniversary was inscribed in a context marked by the renewal of Plan Colombia (since 2006) and by the Uribe administration's (2002–2010) indisposition towards any kind of negotiation with the FARC, in sharp contrast to his predecessor Pastrana—whose Presidency (1998–2002) ended with failed attempts to negotiate with that guerrilla. This "eventalization" (Foucault 1988) of *Mitú* offers the guerrilla's brutality as evidence for the impossibility of any negotiation, thereby authorizing the use of massive violence to tame that very brutality: in the terms of such discourse, it is because the guerrilla cheats that peace negotiations are not possible, and war is necessary.

[48] In addition to the widespread outreach of the "military crisis" narrative through high-ranked military officers and politicians, there was also a profusion of "security specialists" emerging in Colombia at that time. Among this new generation of "*violentólogos*" (La Silla Vacía 2016) was the Security & Democracy Foundation (FS&D, in Spanish), a policy center with close ties to political circles created in the context of Plan Colombia, funded with resources from the U.S. (León 2010), and led by the economist Alfredo Rangel. The establishment of FS&D cannot be dissociated from a broader context marked by the valorization of an epistemological grid with which policy diagnoses came to be disputed, as discussed in Sect. 3.1. In other words, at the same time the Foundation's emphasis on data, impact measurement and models partly derived from some of its researchers' background on Economics, the privileged position of FS&D in the debates about the military reform expresses a specific form of knowledge production about policy that came to characterize not only governmental agencies, but also the work of civil society in Colombia. The official website of FS&D (http://www.seguridadydemocracia.org/) was extinguished around 2014, when Alfredo Rangel was elected Senator through the Democratic Center Party, founded by Uribe in 2013.

wrong" and developing comprehensive reform in light of the military and police capacity.

Since, in this book, I am particularly interested in grasping how Plan Colombia affected the production of the military professional—especially that of the Army—and contributed to the repositioning of Colombia in the hemispheric circuit of military *savoirs*, I shall now focus on the propositions the Commission offered for the strengthening of the military.[49] Its diagnosis pointed to four main axes through which the "modernization" of the armed forces was to be advanced: command, equipment, mobility, and training.

When Plan Colombia was implemented, in 1999, the first significant change in the level of command had already been undertaken, when Generals Manuel José Bonett Locarno and Mario Hugo Galán were substituted by Generals Fernando Tapias and Jorge Enrique Mora in the Command of the Military Forces and the Army, respectively. Tapias and Mora were known in Colombia as *"troperos"*—that is, high-ranked officers acknowledged for their vocation for military operations, as well as for an offensive approach. An in-depth study on the military reform produced by FS&D in 2003 underlined the fact that this was the first time *troperos* achieved a position of command (Villamizar 2003: 29). The change in the profile of the Military and Army commands is related to an aspect often mentioned in "military crisis" narratives in the country: that the 1998 defeats derived from flaws in the domain of strategic intelligence, given that the forces were unable to grasp the military reorganization of the FARC. According to the study developed by FS&D,

> one can claim that the enemy was seriously underestimated. This can be partly explained by the traditional attitude [of the Military Forces] of classifying the insurgents as "bandits", "delinquents" or "thieves", ignoring

---

[49] Elsewhere, Peixoto and I have explored the hemispheric circuit of police *savoirs*, taking the Police Community of the Americas (AMERIPOL, in Spanish) as an object of investigation. In this police cooperation mechanism, Colombia came to enjoy a privileged position as regards intelligence, as well as counternarcotic and counterterrorism operations. The authority of the Colombian National Police among its hemispheric counterparts in these domains of expertise cannot be dissociated from the U.S. resources received in the context of the war on drugs since the late-1980s. See Viana and Peixoto (2019).

its military capacity and generally seeing them as despicable ordinary criminals.[50] (Villamizar 2003: 32)

In this sense, the change in the profile expressed by the choice for Generals Tapias and Mora sought to connect the whole line of command to the operational level, allowing for the knowledge produced about the enemy in the terrain to circulate in the other layers of the chain of command. Also, the new profile of the Commands of the Military Forces and of the Army was marked by an explicit acceptance of "war" as the key-word in the diagnosis of violence in Colombia, displacing the vocabulary of "maintenance and re-establishment of public order" by one of "winning the war" (Villamizar 2003: 30)—as illustrated by a motto often repeated by General Tapias: "We are at war and we are winning it"[51] (*Apud* Villamizar 2003: 30).

To achieve this goal, the "modernization" of the Military Forces under Plan Colombia involved the simplification of the structure of the General Command of the Military Forces. Four central offices (*jefaturas*) were created in 2002[52]: personnel; logistic; training and doctrine; and operations—each of these under the responsibility of a Major General (*Mayor General*), i.e. a high-ranked military officer. Interestingly, three branches were merged in this process: the Central Operations Office engulfed the offices of Operations, Intelligence and Civil-Military Relations[53] (Villamizar 2003: 60). If, as we have seen in Sect. 5.2, the BINCI formalized the fusion of intelligence and irregular warfare into the operational level, merging those three branches within the Central Operations Office crystallized that same logic within the command structure.

At the same time, this specific reorganization cannot be disassociated from the reading that part of the "military crisis" derived from the mismanagement of the "human sources" of intelligence: the population

---

[50] In the original: "En pocas palabras, se puede afirmar que se subestimó de manera grave al enemigo. Esto se explica en parte por la actitud tradicional de catalogar a los insurgentes como 'bandidos', 'facinerosos' o 'cuatreros', desconociendo su capacidad militar y en general menospreciándolos al verlos como simples criminales comunes".

[51] In the original: "Estamos en guerra y la estamos ganando".

[52] The General Command was formerly constituted by six central offices: Personnel, Intelligence, Operations, Logistic, Integral Action and Strategic Planning.

[53] By its turn, the kind of operations previously inscribed in the category of "Civil-Military Relations" were renamed "Integral Action" (*Acción Integral*) in this context.

(Villamizar 2003: 33). In this sense, the Central Operations Office was expected to coordinate the work on tactical intelligence so as to control the population before the insurgents did so—just as prescribed in classical versions of counterinsurgency doctrine since Galula (2006: 176), as discussed in Sect. 5.1.

Another tactical problem tackled by the military reform was related to the air power: the 1998 defeats of the armed forces were often mentioned as illustrations of the failure to provide aerial support to the units under attack (Villamizar 2003: 33). Here, the acquisition of airplanes and helicopters pursued a multiplication effect of the military manpower, especially through the use of some of these aircrafts for aerial assault, logistic support, transportation of troops and terrain reconnaissance. With the resources comprised in Plan Colombia, 74 helicopters were supplied by the U.S.; and additional ones were procured by the Colombian government (Vargas V. 2014: 140). Four years after Plan Colombia had been implemented, Colombia presented the third largest helicopter fleet in the hemisphere, after the U.S. and Brazil (Villamizar 2003: 50). As of 2003, the police and military forces in Colombia had 230 helicopters, among which 30 were of the assault type and most of them produced in the U.S. (Black Hawk, Bell, Huey, and Hughes)[54] (Villamizar 2003: 51).

An additional feature of Plan Colombia was the creation of specialized combat forces. Although this had been a trend from the previous decades,[55] this process was intensified with Plan Colombia. Indeed, after

---

[54] Although this enhanced airpower could have stimulated the design of joint operations, each of the branches of the Colombian Armed Forces—most notably, the Police and the Army—used some of those helicopters to reinforce their own airpower. Even the simplification of the General Command mentioned above did not result in the increase of joint operations. When addressing the case of the General Command of the Military Forces, Villamizar (2003: 65) argues that it "is more invested in administrative tasks than the actual conduction of the joint operations for which it was established. The operational control, that is, the conduction of war is in the hands of each of the Forces (Army, Marine, and Air Force) separately. And each of these forces fights, in a certain way, its own war" (Villamizar 2003: 65–66). In the original: "el Comando General (...) está más dedicado a labores administrativas que la conducción real de las operaciones conjuntas para lo cual fue establecido. El control operacional, es decir, la conducción de la guerra está en manos de cada una de las Fuerzas (Ejército, Armada y Fuerza Aérea) por separado. Y cada una de estas fuerzas pelea, en cierta forma, su propia guerra".

[55] For instance, the Colombian Army had already created the *lanceros* in the 1950s as a military unit specialized in the jungle, as we have seen in Sect. 5.2. In the context of the intensification of the war on drugs, the Urban Anti-terrorism Special Forces Group (AFEUR, in Spanish) was created in the Military Forces in 1985, with the objective

1999, the creation of specialized units in the military forces was organized according to particularities of the Colombian territory, as in the case of Mountain Battalions; to a specific skill mobilized through military operations, as illustrated by the Mobile Brigades (BRIM, in Spanish) and the Rapid Deployment Force (FUDRA, in Spanish); and according to a particular category of threat, as in the case of the Counternarcotic Brigades (BACN, in Spanish).[56]

Among those specialized forces, the BACN is an emblematic example of how the U.S. was involved in the training of these new military forces in Colombia. The creation of the first BACN in 1999 was presented by General Fernando Tapias as a necessary response to the "tough" character of the fight against drugs in some parts of the country.[57] The BACN was in charge of operations involving the fumigation of coca leaf crops; the control over chemical precursors used in the production of illicit drugs; the destruction of drug trafficking infrastructure (such as processing laboratories, camping and plane airstrips); and the arrest (and killing) of members of drug trafficking organizations. In these operations, the Brigade relied heavily on helicopters, given the difficult access to the regions where the drug trafficking activity was concentrated.

The three Counternarcotic Battalions[58] created under Plan Colombia from 1999 to 2000 were trained by the 7th Group of U.S. Special Forces in Fuerte Tolemaida. Their training program consisted of four pillars. The first one involved operations of the "ranger" kind, as well as a technical preparation focused on how to master weapons, equipment (e.g.

---

of countering and neutralizing terrorist actions in the main urban areas of Colombia. Another example is found in 1996, when the Army created the Unified Action Groups for Personal Freedom (GAULA, in Spanish) to prevent and solve cases of kidnapping and extortion.

[56] Currently, the FUDRA, the AFEUR, the GAULA, and the BACN are four of the 6 Special Forces of the Colombian Army. For more information, see https://www.ejercito.mil.co/index.php?idcategoria=279742. Accessed on 6 June 2021.

[57] Although the "baptism" of the 1st Battalion was held in August 1999, it was only with the publication of Ministerial Resolutions No. 1296 (1st September 2000) and No. 005 (8 December 2000) that the Counternarcotic Special Brigade was formally created, with a military base in Larandía (Caquetá).

[58] Currently, the Brigade comprises three maneuver units (BACN No. 1, 2 and 3), and a support one—the Counternarcotic Services and Support Battalion (BASCN, in Spanish), responsible for the provision of supplies and of logistical support to the other units of the Brigade. See https://www.ejercito.mil.co/?idcategoria=189542. Accessed on 8 June 2021.

compass, GPS, and night vision devices), and techniques such as how to build an improvised vessel. The following stage concentrated the training on tactics, including physical resistance exercises such as marching, trotting, swimming, and training in specific formations and self-defense. The third component of the training program focused on the psychological preparation of the soldiers, especially through simulations on how to deal with situations of high pressure. Finally, the program sought to familiarize the soldiers with the legal frameworks on human rights and humanitarian law, drawing particular attention to instructing soldiers on how to deal with local authorities, and how to proceed with invasion, capture and confiscation.

By combining physical preparation with the familiarization of the soldiers with terrains such as the jungle and the mountain, the BACN training program points to the persistent relevance of the "rangers" as an efficient irregular form of warfare in Colombia. Indeed, the training of this counternarcotic military force reproduces the emphasis on tactics, agility, small combat units, and psychological operations which is also at the core of the training of the *lanceros*. What is specific to Plan Colombia in this regard is the explicit incorporation of counternarcotic operations into the domain of military expertise—of which the creation of the BACN is one of its main expressions.

If irregular warfare was already a privileged military *savoir* in Colombia since the 1950s, Plan Colombia took the military organization it required to another scale. Here, the mobilization of the vocabulary of "professionalization" was understood in a considerably different way from the one analyzed in Sects. 4.2 and 4.3. More specifically, under Plan Colombia, the term "professionalization" referred to a category of soldier that was massively incorporated to the Military Forces during that period: the "professional soldier" (*soldado profesional*), i.e. soldiers who, after having concluded the mandatory military service (18–24 months), voluntarily decide to remain in the Military Forces, after receiving specific training and a salary for their work (Villamizar 2003: 61). This category of soldier is not part of the military career track and, consequently, it has no perspective of promotion, nor of salary raise: even after ten years of service, he would still remain a "professional soldier".

Such a professional category allowed for an exponential increase of military manpower within a short period of time. If, in 1998, there were

22,000 professional soldiers in Colombia,[59] in 2002, this number corresponded to 55,000 (Vargas V. 2014: 141). This growth was formally planned by the Ministry of Defense: issued in 1999, "Plan 10,000" aimed at substituting 10,000 "regular soldiers" for the same number of "professional soldiers" each year, during a three-year period (Villamizar 2003: 61). To be clear, the main condition for the rapid multiplication of combat soldiers was the fact that the preparation of "professional soldiers" involved short-term courses. Indeed, most of these soldiers were incorporated to the BRIM and to Counter-guerrilla Battalions (Villamizar 2003: 61–62) after a 14-week training program.[60] As a result, the proportion of "regular soldiers" has significantly decreased in relation to the "professional soldiers" throughout the implementation of Plan Colombia.

"Professionalizing" the Military Forces, in this sense, came to be strictly associated with an increasing incorporation of "professional soldiers" in the troops. Preparing thousands for combat required a specific infrastructure: created in December 1999, the School of Professional Soldiers (ESPRO, in Spanish),[61] based in Nilo (Cundinamarca), offered training facilities and short-term courses specialized in the physical preparation of the soldiers (with swimming, running and physical resistance exercises[62]). By its turn, the polishing of the military officers that were to become instructors of "professional soldiers" was undertaken in another branch of ESPRO at Fuerte Tolemaida.[63]

The centrality of the BACN and of the "professional soldiers" to the operations undertaken by Plan Colombia raised Fuerte Toleimada to the center of gravity of the military preparation in that context, along with

---

[59] As these numbers suggest, the use of this particular type of military professional was not inaugurated by Plan Colombia. Indeed, during César Gaviria's administration (1990–1994), the "professional soldiers" were intensively mobilized in the "integral war" against the drug cartels and the guerrillas refusing to demobilize. If, in 1990, the Colombian Army had 2,000 professional soldiers, in 1994 this number had reached 23,000 soldiers of this category (Leal B. 2002: 99).

[60] See http://www.espro.mil.co/?idcategoria=412825#. Accessed on 10 June 2021.

[61] See http://www.espro.mil.co/?idcategoria=189706. Accessed on 10 June 2021.

[62] In March 2000, the first group of instructors who attended courses in Fuerte Tolemaida for this purpose was formed by 11 commissioned officers (*oficiales*) and 15 non-commissioned officers (*suboficiales*). In addition to that, 25 s Corporals (*Cabo Segundo*) attended the Lancers' School in order to work as instruction assistants. See http://www.espro.mil.co/?idcategoria=412477#. Accessed on 10 June 2021.

[63] See http://www.espro.mil.co/?idcategoria=189706. Accessed on 10 June 2021.

ESPRO. Created as a military fortress in the 1950s, Fuerte Tolemaida received large investments under Plan Colombia for the transformation of its infrastructure into a center of excellence in military training, having its name changed to National Training Center (CENAE, in Spanish). Currently, Fuerte Tolemaida hosts nine training schools with a wide range of specializations—*lanceros*, special forces, army tactics, air assault, and military police, to mention only a few examples.[64]

As the previous pages have shown, Plan Colombia privileged three main domains of expertise of the Colombian Army: counterinsurgency, counter-terrorism, and counternarcotic. The first domain was reflected in the multiplication of specialized forces engaging with irregular warfare across a diversity of terrains and skills, as in the cases of the Mountain Battalions, the FUDRA, and the BRIM. The second is illustrated by the investment of a special force in counterterrorism that had already existed since 1985, the AFEUR, towards the intersection of guerrillas and drug trafficking—"narcoterrorism". The third was explicitly valorized with the creation of an Army Brigade especially devoted to counternarcotic operations under Plan Colombia: the BACN.

The creation of additional layers of expertise as the Colombian security architecture expanded reflects the rearticulation of the problematization of violence in Colombia discussed in Sect. 2.1. At the same time these domains express the juxtaposition of terrorism, guerrilla, and drug trafficking that came to characterize the "problem of violence" anchored in "narcoterrorism", they reveal the historical deposits of former renderings of violence, as the creation of new specialized edifices in this architecture rarely implied demolishing the ones already in existence.

In line with these domains of expertise, the transformation of the Military Forces under Plan Colombia was guided by three main concerns: (i) to deepen the specialization and to improve the mobility of forces; (ii) to expand the "professionalization" of the military through the gradual substitution of "regular soldiers" for "professional" ones; and iii) to develop an infrastructure of excellence in military training. To do so, 80% of the US$ 4.6 billion the U.S. government provided to Colombia in foreign aid from 2000 to 2006 (Isacson 2006) was invested in the acquisition of weapons, equipment, and helicopters, the improvement

---

[64] For more information on the historical transformation of Fuerte Toleimada, see https://www.cenae.mil.co/centro_nacional_entrenamiento/conozcanos/resena_historica. Accessed on 10 June 2021.

of training facilities, as well as in contracts through which U.S. military officers (especially from the U.S. Special Forces) trained the Colombian combat units.

These concrete contours allow us to understand the conditions that made the Colombian "success story" possible. The fact that such a discourse gained traction following the first six years of Plan Colombia is not a coincidence. After all, the "modernization" of the Military Forces that characterized the bulk of the work advanced under Plan Colombia was key to the translation of their manpower superiority into a tactical dominance over the guerrillas (Villamizar 2003; Rojas 2006; Rangel S. 2008). Consequently, this transformation was central for the military to claim themselves as the protagonists of the pacification of the country. Now, if Plan Colombia is an inescapable piece for us to comprehend the "success story", this means that such a discourse also relied on material conditions that allowed for the protagonism of the military.

Although the transformations that the National Police and the other Military Forces went through during the 2000s could not be addressed in detail in this book, the Colombian "success story" actually refers to the Armed Forces in general (Felbab-Brown, 2009a, b; DeShazo et al., 2009; Davis et al., 2012; Pinzón, 2015), as we have seen in Chapters 2 and 3. In this sense, it can be more accurately interpreted as the discourse emerging from an alleged successful performance of the war power undertaken by an expanded security architecture. As argued in Chapter 3, irrespective of its truthful character, the Colombian "success story" has been taken by other countries as a reference for solutions in the security domain. For Juan Carlos Pinzón, Minister of Defense from 2011 to 2015, Colombia's regeneration "back from the brink" operated a transition from "failed state" to "exporter of security" (Pinzón 2015: 8):

> Because of the sustained progress since the turn of the century, and their exceptional expertise and experience, the Colombian Armed Forces are well positioned to evolve into a regional leader in training, education, and actively participate in international peacekeeping, humanitarian assistance, and disaster relief missions around the globe. Colombia's experience successfully combating insurgent groups, illicit facilitators, transnational criminal organizations, and drug trafficking organizations, makes it uniquely capable and qualified to assist other nations that today, or one day, may face similar threats. Over the past five years Colombian armed forces have trained almost 24,000 police and military from more than 60

nations, thus, making Colombia a consistent security partner for Central America, Caribbean, and other friendly nations. (Pinzón 2015: 8)

From 2009 to 2013, the Army and the Colombian National Police trained 10,310 armed forces' professionals from Mexico; 3,026 from Panama; 2,609 from Honduras; 1,732 from Guatemala; 1,132 from Ecuador; 510 from Peru; 465 from El Salvador; and 377 from Costa Rica (Tickner 2014: 3). In the case of the Colombian Army, one of the main facilities where these training programs have been taking place is the ESPRO. The school has been hosting short-term international courses on tactical military operations against illegal organizations in the following areas: elite units; mobile units; explosive units; demolitions; and mines deactivation.[65] In this sense, ESPRO instills in its regional counterparts not only the highly-ramified specialization, but also the "professionalization" format that came to characterize the Colombian Army since Plan Colombia. Being the only school of its kind in South America, ESPRO has already received students from Brazil, Chile, China, Israel, Paraguay, Peru, United Kingdom and the U.S.[66] Also, in April 2013, the Lancers' School, one of the nine training academies found in Fuerte Tolemaida, concluded the 367th edition of its main course, which was attended by 582 students from 19 countries (among them, Brazil, Canada, Ecuador, El Salvador, France, Peru, and the U.S.),[67] in addition to the Colombian military.

More recently, the country added a global stamp to its U.S. credentials of excellence in military training. In 2017, Colombia became a North Atlantic Treaty Organization's (NATO) global partner and the main Latin American partner of this Organization, intensifying interactions with its members in regard to terrorism, maritime interdiction, demining, cyber security, and human security. In the case of demining, Colombia has been providing training through its International Demining Centre, currently acknowledged as part of the NATO Partnership Training and Education Centers.[68]

---

[65] See http://www.espro.mil.co/?idcategoria=189706 . Accessed on 10 June 2021.
[66] See http://www.espro.mil.co/?idcategoria=189706. Accessed on 10 June 2021.
[67] See http://www.cenae.mil.co/?idcategoria=344179. Accessed on 10 June 2021.
[68] See https://www.nato.int/cps/en/natohq/topics_143936.htm. Accessed on 6 June 2021.

Importantly, the Colombian expertise has been circulating as a solution to countries that allegedly face similar "security problems" as those portrayed as overcome by Colombia. Tracing analogies between the guerrillas in Colombia and organizations such as the Al Qaeda and ISIS (Kelly 2015) or, in more general terms, the so-called "transnational organized delinquency" (Ministerio de Defensa de Colombia 2012), military officers have been repeatedly claiming that the Colombian expertise on irregular warfare and infrastructure protection (Ximénez de Sandoval 2013) can be applied to countries such as Paraguay (Pelcastre 2014), Peru and Argentina (Isacson 2013). In addition, the "success story" insistently reproduced by civil and military professionals in the U.S. (Kelly 2015; The White House 2012) and in Colombia (Ximénez de Sandoval 2013) has given breath to the idea of using "professional soldiers" in peace-building operations, as well as in counternarcotic and counterterrorism operations in Western Africa, Central America, and South America.

The fact that Colombia operates as a hub for military training in the current context is only possible under the assumption that it has overcome the problems that have stigmatized the country for so many years. In this sense, the transnational circulation of the Colombian expertise relies on a distinction built between the past and the future of its Armed Forces. In this dynamic, those trained by their Colombian counterparts represent Colombia's past—and the use of violence considered to be part of this past. Not surprisingly, the promotion of the Colombian "success story" emerged simultaneously to an(other) agenda of military reform stemming from the most recent version of an all-too-familiar question: what to do with the military in a pacified Colombia (Vargas 2003; Ciro y Correa 2014; Velásquez 2015)?

One of the responses articulated to this question was the "Army of the Future" project, focused on the restructuration of the Colombian Army with the objective of, by 2030, consolidating and increasing its role in the preservation of the territorial integrity, in the protection of human security, in the training of its regional and global counterparts, and in the participation in peace operations (Ministerio de Defensa de Colombia 2016: 75). The backbone of such a transformation is the "Damascus Doctrine" (*Doctrina Damasco*), elaborated under the advice of NATO forces (Rojas G. 2017: 112; Fundación Ideas Para la Paz 2018), considered as the "most modern in the world" (Fundación Ideas Para la Paz 2018).

The vision of the "Army of the Future" emphasizes its "stabilization" mission in the "post-conflict Colombia" through joint and coordinated operations (with other military forces and the police, respectively) aimed at preserving the integrity of the national territory (Ministerio de Defensa de Colombia 2016: 50–53). Here, the Army's special forces remain a key component in the fight against hybrid threats, defined as the "diverse and dynamic combination of regular forces, irregular forces, terrorist forces and/or criminal elements" (Centro de Doctrina del Ejército de Colombia 2020: 43).

If the Army's expertise on counternarcotic and counterterrorism derived from the lessons learned from its experience in the Colombian armed conflict, the "Army of the Future" builds upon that learning process through the development of a versatile doctrine that offers flexibility to the military command (Centro de Doctrina del Ejército de Colombia 2020: 4). More specifically, this new doctrinal framework provides a "toolkit" for an "ultimate generation [military] professional", circumscribing a range of 979 "tactical tasks" that can be combined in multiple ways by "commanders in all layers and in any operational environment"[69] (Centro de Doctrina del Ejército de Colombia 2020: 4). Thus, the versatility aspired by the Damascus Doctrine is illustrated by a vision of a "multi-mission" Army (Rojas G. 2017: 100–101; Fundación Ideas Para la Paz 2018: 6), whose forces are not only adaptable to different partners, contexts, and threats, but efficiently so, once it seeks to multiply the effects of its capacity through a plastic doctrinal framework (Ministerio de Defensa de Colombia 2016: 50).

Human security is a key term in the vocabulary of the "Army of the Future", translated into the protection of natural resources and the environment, humanitarian aid, and infrastructure protection and building (González M. et al. 2017). The human component of the Damascus Doctrine also involves the strengthening of the preventive pillar against criminal and terrorist threats through a technology-fed intelligence (Ministerio de Defensa de Colombia 2016: 82; Centro de Doctrina del Ejército de Colombia 2020: 40). Before jumping to hopeful conclusions that the Army of the Future brings a novelty in this regard, we must recall that versions of a "human security approach" were never absent

---

[69] In the original: "Este gran avance multiplica exponencialmente las opciones para los comandantes de todos los escalones y en cualquier ambiente operacional".

as demands for more war power expanded the security architecture in Colombia and fueled its lethality, as we have seen in this book.

In this sense, the Army of the Future rests on a specific construction of the present, re-articulates its past, and offers, as the formula of the future, a focus on human security with a technological, multi-mission, and versatile pacification force. In circulating regionally and globally as a reference to others, the form and content of the expertise upon which the image of the Colombian military professional as the protagonist of the "success story" relies have not only credentials, but also a market.

5.4 Conclusion

If Chapter 4 focused on the civil-military boundary that constituted the discourse on the need to professionalize the military both in Colombia and in the hemisphere, Chapter 5 drew its attention to the re-articulations in the peace-war boundary, as counterinsurgency acquired a privileged position in the edifice of military *savoirs*.

The first Section begun by showing the "uncivil nature" with which the colonial populations were portrayed by French and British forces, and discussed how it authorized the use of brutal force by military engaged in "small wars". Such aspect was crucial for us to understand how civility was at the very root of the marginalization of "small warriors" as "quasi-professionals", in sharp contrast to the privileged position enjoyed by conventional soldiers in the edifice of military *savoirs*. In this context, the development of a counterinsurgency doctrine was seen as indispensable not only to an efficient social order in colonial terrains, but also to the acknowledgement of this doctrine as a military *savoir*.

With this move, my purpose was to expose the conditions under which counterinsurgency travelled from the colonial terrain to the U.S. in the mid-twentieth century, and how it was transformed into a fully professionalized *savoir* of irregular warfare. At the core of this transformation was the combination of the expertise that had been built by France in Algeria with the attempts to design a U.S. military strategy for Southeast Asia in the context of the Cold War. By the early-1960s, counterinsurgency already circulated in the hemisphere as a privileged *savoir* having the U.S. as the main reference for the professionalization of the military in Latin America.

Section 5.2 explored the effects of an intensive and durable socialization between Colombian and American military professionals, with special attention to the re-articulation of the center of gravity of professionalization programs from the Military School to the Lancers' School by the late-1950s. This process implied a transition from the classroom to the training center as the main site for the production of the military professional in Colombia, turning towards the preparation of tactically efficient bodies through short-term programs focused on the tactical level.

As we have seen, the principle of an impossible decisive victory upon which irregular warfare relies has had profound effects over the reorganization of violence in Colombia. Indeed, the emphasis on tactics and the population-centric approach deriving from that principle are the main components for us to grasp counterinsurgency's durability as a privileged military *savoir*. At the same time, they allow us to understand its elective affinities with war power as a permanently activated mechanism for social control, especially towards groups and terrains considered as part of the "problem of violence".

By exploring the conditions leading to the expansion of the security architecture built in Colombia as a response to unprecedented levels of violence during the 1990s, Sect. 5.3 sheds light on the main axes structuring the "modernization" of the Army advanced through Plan Colombia. Here, two particular aspects merit attention. The first one is related to the combination of highly specialized forces with the rapid multiplication of manpower, made possible by the massive incorporation of an easy-to-prepare category of professional soldier—i.e. those who, after the mandatory military service, joined the Army after a 14-week training program.

The second refers to the fact that this transformation of the Colombian Army is a fundamental condition for the Colombian "success story". Indeed, the U.S. resources flowing to the acquisition of weapons, helicopters, training, and to the improvement of training facilities have allowed not only for the Colombian Army to claim its protagonist role in a successful pacification, but also for Colombia to circulate as a reference to other countries in the region and the world with regard to solutions for "security problems"—especially in the domains of counterinsurgency, counterterrorism, and counternarcotic. As such, Colombia is a window for us to comprehend the organization of violence that came to be valorized in the circuit of military *savoirs*—and, consequently, for us to come to terms with the regional and global meaning of the story of the Colombian "success".

References

Books, Chapters, Articles

Arenas, J. Diario de la Resistencia de Marquetalia. Bogotá: *Ediciones Abejón Mono*, 1966.
Atehortúa C. Colombia en la Guerra de Corea. *Folios, segunda época*, n. 27, pp. 63–76, 2008.
Atehortúa C., A. L.; Vélez R., H. *Estado y Fuerzas Armadas en Colombia*. Cali: TM, 1994.
Aussaresses, P. *The Battle of the Casbah: Terrorism and Counter-Terrorism in Algeria, 1955–1957*. New York: Enigma, 2010.
Bass, T. Counterinsurgency and Torture. *American Quarterly*, v. 60, n. 2, pp. 233–240, 2008.
Brown, K. 'All they understand is force': Debating culture in Operation Iraqi Freedom. *American Anthropologist*, v. 110, n. 4, pp. 443–453, 2008.
Cardona, C. M. *Politicians, Soldiers, and Cops: Colombia's* La Violencia *in Comparative Perspective*. Dissertation presented at University of California (Berkeley), 2008.
Centro de Investigación y Educación Popular (CINEP). Del Batallón Charry Solano a la Brigada 20 una continuidad paramilitar. *Noche y Niebla* (Dossier: Deuda con la Humanidad: Paramilitarismo de Estado en Colombia 1988–2003). Bogotá, D.C.: CINEP, 2004.
Ciro G., A. R.; Correa H., M. Transformación estructural del Ejército colombiano. Construcción de escenarios futuros. *Revista Científica General José María Córdova*, v. 12, n. 13, pp. 19–88, 2014.
Davis, K. E.; Kingsbury, B.; Merry, S. E. Introduction: Global Governance by Indicators. In: Davis, K. E.; Fisher, A.; Kingsbury, B.; Merry, S. E. (eds). *Governance by Indicators:* Global Power Through Quantification and Rankings. Oxford: Oxford University Press, 2012.
Draper, M. The *Force Publique*'s Campaigns in the Congo-Arab War, 1892–1894. *Small Wars & Insurgencies*, v. 30, n. 4–5, pp.1020–1039, 2019.
Elias, N. *The Civilizing Process*. Oxford: Blackwell, 2000.
Fall, B. A Portrait of the "Centurion". In: TRINQUIER, R. (ed). *Modern Warfare*: A French View of Counterinsurgency. London and Dunmow: Pall Mall, 1985.
Few, Michael. Interview with Dr. John Arquilla: How Can French Encounters with Irregular Warfare in the 19th Century Inform COIN in our Time? *Small Wars Journal*, November 30, n.p., 2010.
Foucault, M. Practicing Criticism. In: Kritzman, L. D. (ed). *Politics, Philosophy, Culture:* interviews and other writings, 1977–1984. New York: Routledge, 1988.

Gallón G. G. *Quince años de estado de sitio en Colombia, 1958–1978*. Bogotá: Librería y Editorial América Latina, 1979.
Gallón G. G. Human Rights: A Path to Democracy and Peace in Colombia. In: Welna, C.; Gallón G. G. (eds.). *Peace, Democracy, and Human Rights in Colombia*. Notre Dame: Notre Dame University, 2007.
Galula, D. *Pacification in Algeria, 1956–1958*. Santa Monica, CA: RAND Corporation, 2006 [1963].
Galula, D. *Counterinsurgency: Theory and Practice*. New York and London: Frederick A. Praeger, 1964.
Gildea, R. *Empires of the Mind*. The Colonial Past and the Politics of the Present. Cambridge: Cambridge University Press, 2019.
Gill, L. *The School of the Americas*. Military Training and Political Violence in the Americas. Durham and London: Duke University Press, 2004.
Gómez-Suárez, A. US-Colombian Relations in the 1980s: Political Violence and the Onset of the Unión Patriótica genocide. Esparza, M.; Huttenbach, H. R.; Feierstein, D. (eds.). *State Violence and Genocide in Latin America*. The Cold War Years. New York and London: Routledge, 2010.
González M, M. A.; Pierrotty, S., M.; Rodríguez B., J. D.; Poloche Y., Y. S. *La seguridad humana en la Doctrina Damasco*: un eje de transformación hacia el Ejército del futuro. *Revista BRÚJULA*, vol. 5, n. 10, pp.8–17, 2017.
Guanumen P., M. La narcotización de las Relaciones Colombia-Estados Unidos. *Revista de Relaciones Internacionales, Estrategia y Seguridad*, v. 7, n. 2, pp. 221–244, 2012.
Guzmán B., Á.; Moreno Q., R. Autodefensas, Narcotráfico y Comportamiento Estatal en el Valle del Cauca. In: ROMERO, M. (ed.). *Parapolítica:* la ruta de la expansión paramilitar y los acuerdos políticos. Bogotá, D.C.: Corporación Nuevo Arco Iris, 2007.
Hoffman, B. Foreword to the New Edition. In: GALULA, D. *Pacification in Algeria 1956–1958*. Santa Monica (CA): RAND, 2006.
Jardini, D. R. *Thinking Through the Cold War: RAND, National Security and Domestic Policy, 1945–1975*. Meadow Lands, PA: Smashwords, 2013.
Keene, E. *Beyond the Anarchical Society*. Grotius, Colonialism and Order in International Relations. Cambridge: Cambridge University Press, 2004
Kilcullen, D. Twenty-Eight Articles: Fundamentals of Company-Level Counterinsurgency. *IO Sphere*, Summer, pp. 29–35, 2006.
Krepinevich, A. *The Army and Vietnam*. Baltimore: Johns Hopkins University, 1986.
Leal B., F. *La Seguridad Nacional a La Deriva*. Del Frente Nacional a la Posguerra Fría. Mexico, D.C.: Alfaomega, 2002.
Lizarazo V. N. S. El papel de las Fuerzas Armadas en la política antidrogas colombiana. 1985–1990. In: VARGAS VELÁSQUEZ, A. (ed.) *El papel de las*

Fuerzas Armadas en la Política Antidrogas Colombiana. 1985–2006. Bogota, D.C.: Universidad Nacional de Colombia, 2008.

Martin, J. E.; Jaramillo-Marín, J. Las conmemoraciones noticiosas en la prensa colombiana: rememorando la toma a Mitú. *Palabra Clave*, v. 17, n. 2, pp. 378–411, 2014.

Marulanda V. M. *Cuadernos de Campaña*. Bogotá: Ediciones Abejón Mono, 1973. Available at http://www.rebelion.org/docs/68099.pdf. Accessed on 10 July 2021.

McClintock, M. *Instruments of Statecraft*: U.S. Guerilla Warfare, Counterinsurgency, and Counterterrorism, 1940–1990. New York: Pantheon, 1992.

McFate, M. Anthropology and Counterinsurgency: The Strange Story of Their Curious Relationship. *Military Review*, n. 85, pp.24–38, 2005.

Neocleous, M. *War Power, Police Power*. Edinburgh: Edinburgh University, 2014.

Olave, G. El eterno retorno de Marquetalia: sobre el mito fundacional de las Farc-EP. *Revista Folios*, n. 37, pp. 149–166, 2013.

Pécaut, D. *As FARC: uma guerrilha sem fins?* São Paulo: Paz e Terra, 2010.

Pinzón, J. C. Colombia Back from the Brink: From Failed State to Exporter of Security. *PRISM*, v. 5, n. 4, pp. 2–9, 2015.

Pizarro L., E. La Profesionalización Militar en Colombia (II): El Periodo de La Violencia. *Análisis Político*, n. 2, pp. 7–29, 1987.

Porch, D. The Dangerous Myths and Dubious Promise of COIN. *Small Wars & Insurgencies*, v. 22, n. 2, pp. 239–257, 2011.

Porch, D. *Counterinsurgency*: Exposing the Myths of the New Way of War. Cambridge: Cambridge University, 2013.

Ramírez, S. *Actores en conflicto por la paz*. El proceso de paz durante el gobierno de Belisario Betancur (1982–1986). Bogotá, D,C.: Siglo XXI, 1989.

Ramírez, S. *Intervención en conflictos internos*: el caso colombiano (1994–2003). Bogotá: Universidad Nacional de Colombia, 2004.

Rangel, S. A. Colombia: perspectivas de paz y seguridad. *Revista Criminalidad*, vol. 50, n. 1, pp. 417–432, 2008.

Rid, T. Razzia: A Turning Point in Modern Strategy. *Terrorism and Political Violence*, v. 21, n. 4, pp. 617–635, 2009.

Rodríguez H. S. M. *La influencia de los Estados Unidos en el Ejército colombiano, 1951–1959*. Medellín: La Carreta, 2006.

Rojas, D. M. Estados Unidos y la guerra en Colombia. In: Sanín, F. G.; Wills, M. E.; Gómez, G. S. (coords). *Nuestra guerra sin nombre*: transformaciones del conflicto en Colombia. Bogotá, D.C.: Norma, 2006.

Rojas G., P. J. Doctrina Damasco: eje articulador de la segunda gran reforma del Ejército Nacional de Colombia. *Revista Científica General José María Córdova*, v. 15, n. 19, pp. 95–119, 2017.

Ronderos, M. T. *Guerras Recicladas*. Una historia periodística del paramilitarismo en Colombia. Bogotá, D.C.: Aguilar, 2014.

Rouquié, A. *El Estado Militar en América Latina*. Buenos Aires: Emecé, 1984.
Ruiz N., A. Discurso del Señor Ministro de Guerra, Mayor General Alberto Ruiz Novoa. *Revista de las Fuerzas Armadas*, v. IX, n. 26, pp. 237–247, 1964.
Salamone, A. Military History and the Drafting of Doctrine: FM 3-24, Relevant Case Studies or Seductive Analogies? *Small Wars Journal*, v. 20, n. 2, n.p., 2008.
Sánchez G., G.; Fals B., O.; Umaña, E. *La Violencia en Colombia*, volumes I and II. Bogotá: Carlos Valencia, 1962.
Vanegas G., P. P. La Constitución colombiana y los estados de excepción: veinte años después. *Revista Derecho del Estado*, n. 27, pp. 261–290, 2011.
Vargas V., A. The Profile of the Colombian Armed Forces: A Result of the Struggle Against Guerrillas, Drug Trafficking and Terrorism. In: Mares, D. E.; Martínez, R. (eds). *Debating Civil-Military Relations in Latin America*. Brighton: Sussex Academic Press, 2014.
Viana, M. T.; Peixoto, G. Brasil: um novo 'caso de sucesso' para a segurança pública na América Latina? *Revista Cult*, n. 244, pp.11–18, 2019.
Villamizar, A. *Fuerzas Militares para la guerra:* La agenda pendiente de la reforma militar. Bogotá, D.C.: Fundación Seguridad & Democracia, 2003.
Villatoux, M.-C.; Villatoux, P. Aux origines de la « guerre révolutionnaire » : le colonel Lacheroy parle. *Revue historique des armées*, n. 268, pp. 45–53, 2012.
Wasinski, C. Validar a Guerra: A Construção do Regime de Expertise Estratégica. *Contexto Internacional*, v. 34, n. 2, pp. 435–470, 2012.

Documents, Reports and Studies

Amnesty International. *Unmatched Power, Unmet Principles*: The Human Rights Dimensions of US Training of Foreign Military and Police Forces, 2002.
Centro de Doctrina del Ejército de Colombia (CEDOE). Conceptos Generales Básicos Doctrina Damasco VOCADOC (Vocabulario Doctrinal). Bogotá: CEDOE, 2020.
Central Intelligence Agency (CIA). Kubark Counterintelligence Interrogation. Washington, D.C.: CIA, 1963.
Congreso de la República de Colombia. Ley 104 de 1993. *Diario Oficial No. 41.158*, 31 December 1993. Available at: http://www.secretariasenado.gov.co/senado/basedoc/ley_0104_1993.html. Accessed on 10 July 2021.
DeShazo, P.; Forman, J. M.; McLean, P. *Countering Threats to Security and Stability in a Failing State*. Lessons from Colombia. Washington, D.C.: CIS, 2009.
Drug Enforcement Administration (DEA). A History of the DEA: 1980–1985. *The DEA Museum & Visitors Center*, n.d., pp. 43–57. Available at: https://www.deamuseum.org/deahistorybook/1980-1985.html. Accessed on 15 February 2021.

Echandía, C. *Dos Décadas de Escalamiento del Conflicto Armado Colombiano.* Bogotá: Universidad Externado de Colombia, 2006.

Estado Mayor General De Las Fuerzas Militares. República de Colombia. *La Guerra en La Selva.* Manual de Campaña. Bogotá, D.C.: Sección Imprenta y Publicaciones, 1944.

Felbab-Brown, V. Narco-belligerants Across the Globe: Lessons from Colombia for Afghanistan? *Security and Defence Working Paper*, n. 55. Madrid: Elcano Royal Institute, 28 October 2009a. Available at http://www.realinstitut oelcano.org/wps/wcm/connect/da0e7a80401cec18ab82eb1ecbd00d37/WP55-2009_Felbab-Brown_Narco-belligerants_Lessons_Colombia_Afghani stan.pdf?MOD=AJPERES. Accessed on 4 July 2021.

Felbab-Brown, V. The Violent Drug Market in Mexico and Lessons from Colombia. *Policy Paper* (Foreign Policy at Brookings), n. 12, March 2009b. Available at: https://www.brookings.edu/wp-content/uploads/2016/06/03_mexico_drug_market_felbabbrown.pdf. Accessed on 4 July 2021.

Fundación Ideas Para la Paz. *La Transformación del Ejército Nacional.* Una mirada comparada con los Ejércitos más modernos del mundo. Bogotá, 2018. Available at: http://ideaspaz.org/media/website/FIP_Transf ormacion_ejercito.pdf. Accessed on 10 July 2021.

Hosmer, S.; Crane, S. O. *Counterinsurgency*: A Symposium, April 16–20, 1962. Santa Monica, CA: RAND Corporation, 2006 [1963].

Human Rights Watch (HRW). *Colombia's Killer Networks.* The Military-Paramilitary Partnership and the United States. New York, November 1996. Available at https://www.hrw.org/legacy/reports/1996/killertoc.htm. Accessed on 13 February 2021.

Isacson, A. *Plan Colombia—Six Years Later: Report of a CIP Staff Visit to Putumayo and Medellín, Colombia.* Center for International Policy, International Policy Report, November 2006.

Ministerio de Defensa de Colombia. "Combatir la delincuencia trasnacional con una visión regional es la única garantía de éxito": Ministro Pinzón. Bogotá, 3 May 2012. Available at https://www.mindefensa.gov.co/irj/go/km/docs/documents/News/NoticiaGrandeMDN/503fce10-7277-2f10-e791-c714ff f98d20.xml. Accessed on 19 June 2021.

Ministerio de Defensa de Colombia. *Visión de Futuro de las Fuerzas Armadas.* Bogotá: Imprenta Nacional de Colombia, 2016. Available at: https://www.mindefensa.gov.co/irj/go/km/docs/Mindefensa/Documentos/descar gas/estrategia_planeacion/proyeccion/documentos/vision_futuro_FA.pdf. Accessed on 5 July 2021.

The US Infantry School. *Operations Against Guerrilla Forces* (31-20-1). Fort Benning (GA): The US Infantry School, 1950.

The White House. Remarks of President Obama and President Santos of Colombia in Joint Press Conference. Cartagena, Colombia, April 15, 2012. Available

at: https://www.whitehouse.gov/the-press-office/2012/04/15/remarks-president-obama-and-president-santos-colombia-joint-press-confer. Accessed on 10 July 2021.
Tickner, A. B. Colombia, the United States, and Security Cooperation by Proxy. Washington D.C.: WOLA, March 2014. Available at: http://www.wola.org/files/140318ti.pdf. Accessed on 13 February 2021.
Velásquez R., C. A. La fuerza pública que requiere el postconflicto. *Working Papers*, n. 13. Bogotá: Fundación Ideas para la Paz [FIP], May 2015. Available at: http://cdn.ideaspaz.org/media/website/document/5547dc7eef110.pdf. Accessed on 19 June 2021.
Walsh, J. M. Are we there yet? Measuring Progress in the US War on Drugs in Latin America. *WOLA Drug War Monitor*. Washington, D.C.: WOLA, Dec. 2004.

Press Articles

Bernstein, Ad. "Lt. Gen. William Yarborough Dies", *Washington Post*, 8 December 2005. Available at: http://www.washingtonpost.com/wp-dyn/content/article/2005/12/07/AR2005120702473.html. Accessed on 10 July 2021.
El Día. "Militares colombianos presos denuncian crímenes de colegas", *El Día*, 20 July 1980. Available at: http://static.iris.net.co/semana/upload/documents/Doc-1471_2007630.pdf. Accessed on 10 July 2021.
El Mostrador. "Comando Jungla: el historial de la policía colombiana que formó a Carabineros para operar en La Araucanía", *El Mostrador*, 10 July 2018. Available at: https://www.elmostrador.cl/noticias/pais/2018/07/10/comando-jungla-el-historial-de-la-policia-colombiana-que-formo-a-carabineros-para-operar-en-la-araucania/. Accessed on 10 July 2021.
El País. "El Ejército colombiano recupera una ciudad ocupada", *El País*, 05 November 1998. Available at: http://elpais.com/diario/1998/11/05/internacional/910220416_850215.html. Accessed on 10 July 2021.
El Tiempo. "Cómo cayó el fortín mayor de Miraflores", El Tiempo, 06 August 1998. Available at: http://www.eltiempo.com/archivo/documento/MAM-816674. Accessed on 10 July 2021.
Evans, M. "La verdad sobre la Triple A", *Revista Semana (Opinión)*, 30 June 2007. Available at: http://www.semana.com/opinion/articulo/la-verdad-sobre-triple/86849-3. Accessed on 10 July 2021.
Grove, J. "The Stories We Tell About Killing", *The Disorder of Things*, 6 January 2016. Available at: https://thedisorderofthings.com/2016/01/06/the-stories-we-tell-about-killing/. Accessed on 10 July 2021.
Isacson, A. "Colombia, un 'exportador de seguridad' al Continente", *La Silla Vacía*. 18 February 2013. Available at: https://archivo.lasillavacia.com/elb

logueo/adam-isacson/41518/colombia-un-exportador-de-seguridad-al-continente. Accessed on 10 July 2021.

Kelly, J. F. "Colombia's resolve merits support", *Miami Herald*, 5 March 2015. Available at: http://www.miamiherald.com/opinion/op-ed/article20047503.html. Accessed on 19 June 2021.

La Silla Vacía. "Alfredo Rangel Suárez", *La Villa Vacía* 13 July 2016. Available at: http://lasillavacia.com/quienesquien/perfilquien/alfredo-rangel-suarez. Accessed on 10 July 2021.

León, J. "El reencauche de Alfredo Rangel", *La Silla Vacía*, 20 September 2010. Available at: http://lasillavacia.com/historia/18150. Accessed on 10 July 2021.

Pelcastre, J. 2014 "Ejército colombiano entrena a soldados paraguayos para luchar contra el terrorismo y el narcotráfico". *Diálogo. Revista Militar Digital*, 26 August 2014.

Rangel, A. "El Desastre del Caquetá", *El Tiempo*, 8 March 1998. Available at: http://www.eltiempo.com/archivo/documento/MAM-745942. Accessed on 10 july 2021.

Revista Semana. "El síndrome de Jacobo", *Revista Semana*, 7 December 1998. Available at: http://www.semana.com/nacion/articulo/el-sindrome-de-jacobo/37900-3. Accessed on 10 July 2021.

Revista Semana. "¿La noche quedó atrás?", *Revista Semana*. 11 July 1982. Available at: http://www.semana.com/nacion/articulo/la-noche-quedo-atras/367-3. Accessed on 10 July 2021.

Vargas V., A. "Los militares en el Postconflicto", *El Tiempo*, 09 January 2003. Available at: http://www.eltiempo.com/archivo/documento/MAM-968820. Accessed on 5 July 2021.

Viana, M. T. "A paz é mais complexa: o referendo na Colômbia e a guerra na paz", *Rede PCECS*, 14 November 2016. Available at: https://redepcecs.com/2016/11/14/a-paz-e-mais-complexa-o-referendo-na-colombia-e-a-guerra-na-paz/. Accessed on 5 July 2021.

Ximénez de Sandoval, Pablo. "En Colombia se puede hablar de paz gracias al sacrificio del Ejército", *El País*, 30 June 2013. Available at: https://elpais.com/internacional/2013/06/30/actualidad/1372613129_443772.html. Accessed on 10 July 2021.

CHAPTER 6

Conclusion

This book takes off in Colombia and lands in the transnational circuit of military *savoirs*. Focusing on a country which is now circulating in the international community as a "success story" of an alleged transformation from an endemic violence to a prosperous "post-conflict", the book mobilizes Colombia as a point of entry to grasp transnational dynamics of production and reproduction of *savoirs* upon which the use of state violence relies.

When exploring the production of the protagonist without which the Colombian "success story" would not have been possible—the military professional—the previous chapters have exposed the impossibility of understanding this process by confining the analysis into a national container. Indeed, the Colombian military professional is produced from an alchemy of *savoirs* circulating transnationally and their corresponding frictions with the social cuts and particular political configurations of the play of forces in a given historical context. In this sense, if the active participation of the U.S. Army is key for us to understand the emergence of counterinsurgency as the privileged military *savoir* in the professionalization of its Colombian counterpart, the work of the Chilean mission in the translation of the Prussian expertise on conventional warfare into the curricula of the *Escuela Militar* left footprints in the biography of the Colombian military professional that still endure.

The concept of "transnational circuit of military *savoirs*" proposed in this book allows us to access the durable socializations among military professionals in the hemisphere, as well as the epistemological criteria underlying the valorization of specific military *savoirs* that organize and reorganize the uses of state violence in the region. A central element in this conceptual formulation is precisely the routinization of military *savoirs*, understood as a technical knowledge from which the military professional derives his authority to speak about the domain of war. Particularly, the use of *savoir* aims at expressing the combination of theoretical formulations and practical experience that characterize this military knowledge—in other words, the articulation of the classroom and training center with the experience extracted from the terrain of operations. Under these terms, "military *savoirs*" are a specific version of what Huysmans (2006) read as the specialized knowledge from which security professionals derive their authority to advance framings of security problems.

"Transnational" is, thus, used not only to characterize a circulation that extrapolates the national boundary, but also a phenomenon that is anchored in technocratic niches (Bigo 2016). As we have seen, the circulation of military professionals in the hemispheric circuit is made possible by a socialization based on similar terms, allowing for them to see themselves as part of the same community. In turn, the channels through which military *savoirs* circulate in the region—through the intense transit of military professionals, the translation of manuals, publications in specialized journals, and weapons—operate towards an increasing harmonization of the armies in the region in terms of jargon, routines and rituals.

Through these lenses, framing a specific phenomenon as a "security problem" cannot be disassociated from the technical knowledge and bureaucratic routines of security professionals (Huysmans 2006: 2–6). More specifically, the construction of the "problem of violence" that those military professionals will be called to confront is not external to a set of assumptions, doctrinal frameworks, and layers of experience that came to characterize the *savoirs* from which those very professionals derive their authority to speak about violence. In this sense, the hemispheric circuit offers not only a shared vision of what the military professional must be, but also a common understanding of the "problem of violence" that must be tackled by such professionals.

Here, the texturized discussion developed in Part One regarding the problematization of violence in Colombia provides us a glimpse of the stakes in renderings of violence with transnational adherence in the hemisphere. After all, the "success story" relies on a delinquential and apolitical understanding of the problem of violence in Colombia, around which a successful combination of an expertise on counterinsurgency, counternarcotic and counterterrorism revolved. Such a problematization, as we have seen, brushed aside concurrent renderings of violence such as the critique centered on the state as the protagonist of the problem, and not of the solution. On these grounds, the erasure of the particularities of and disputes around the problematization of violence is a key condition for shared visions of threats to be countered by military professionals. In other words, the "problem of violence" must be decontextualized so as to allow for its circulation as an object of discussions among those professionals. Not surprisingly, the "successful" Colombian formula is currently taken as a reference for countries as varied as Mexico, Brazil, Nigeria, and Afghanistan.

In addition to that, historicizing the hemispheric circuit of military *savoirs* reveals how the expertise on state violence was rearticulated throughout the decades among those professionals. The findings emerging from the discussion about the repositioning of Colombia in that transnational circuit, therefore, must not be confined in that territorial container, for they offer us forms of organizing state violence that came to be contemporarily valorized also in Latin America and, increasingly, in the world. To be sure, the analysis about the inscription of Colombia in the circuit exposed a fundamental shift in the professionalization programs from the school/classroom to the training center as the privileged site in the production of the military professional. Indeed, if the first half of the twentieth century witnessed the emergence of 4–5-year comprehensive programs concentrated in the *Escuela Militar* and expected to result in a "citizen-soldier", by the 1950s the center of gravity of the professionalization slid to short-term courses (12–14 weeks) held in the *Escuela de Lanceros*, the main site for the specialization of the military on irregular warfare. As we have seen, Plan Colombia took the production of what I called the "expert-soldier" to another level by the early 1990s, by deepening the specialization of the Army branches and expanding its manpower by relying on even shorter professionalization courses. This particular form of organizing state violence is part of what makes Colombia a reference in the security domain in the contemporary context: an easy-to-replicate and easy-to-deploy specialization program.

Importantly, there is a specific content that came to be valorized in the transnational circuit: counterinsurgency. The new guise provided by the U.S. Army to this old military *savoir* was actually distilled from colonial ordering practices undertaken by French and British military officers and, since the 1960s, counterinsurgency was constantly recycled so as to remain fit for the times. Its durability as a privileged *savoir* in the transnational military edifice is specifically connected to its emphasis on tactics, allowing for the repeated rearticulation of its tactical repertoires, while preserving the doctrinal pillars upon which it relies.

This book sheds light on the endurance of counterinsurgency especially because of the affinities its population-centric approach presents with police work. Read along with the principle of an impossible decisive victory that lies in its doctrinal basis, the book proposes to think counterinsurgency as a rationality with which ordering practices in general are undertaken, finding among military circles only a contour specific to this professional domain. As I argued in the previous chapter, the durability of counterinsurgency as a privileged military *savoir* in Colombia gradually resulted in the normalization of the mobilization of the population in tactical operations—with and without their awareness and consent. It also resulted in the naturalization of counterinsurgency as a modality of war regulating social relations, either through the deployment of the military forces in public security operations, or through the training of elite units of the police by military instructors. In this process, counterinsurgency was accommodated as a privileged ordering *savoir* on the grounds of the resilience with which its war power provides politically useful effects in society. The fact that the Colombian "success story" allowed for the repositioning of Colombia in the transnational circuit reveals the regional and global adherence not only of the form and content with which state violence came to be organized in that country, but also of shared conceptions of the "problem of violence" to be tackled by the mobilization of the "Colombian expertise".

The confusion between war and peace brought to light through the discussion about counterinsurgency exposes yet another blurred boundary: that between the civil and the military domains, particularly in reference to the mobilization of civilians in military operations and the juxtaposition of functional scopes that we came to historically associate with the police, on one side, and the military, on the other. This divide was approached in this book through an additional angle: the systematic breach of the civil-military boundary as a condition for its enactment.

More specifically, I have shown how the Chilean military mission often negotiated with the civil domain the Congressional approval of regulations for the military career, as well as the margins within which the mission could undertake its professionalization programs with autonomy while in Colombia. Finally, I have argued how the expansion of the security architecture in Colombia since the 1980s was far from a process that happened in spite of the civil domain: it relied on the approval of laws and decrees that either piled up states of siege, or incorporated aspects from the institutional fabric emerging from such contexts as part of the regular security architecture. As the transnational circuit reminds us, this must not be taken as a Colombian idiosyncrasy, but as general lines through which the breach of the civil-military divide operates as a condition for the mobilization of the Colombian "solutions" in other countries.

Now, if the book reveals the mirage of three fundamental boundaries that came to organize our imaginaries of how state violence must be organized (internal–external; civil-military; and peace-war), this does not imply arguing that they are nothing, i.e. that they do not have concrete effects in the world. Indeed, the analysis explores how the internal–external divide authorizes both the historical emergence of "Colombian problems" and "Colombian solutions" as discursive articulations confined in national containers. Also, it shows how the civil-military boundary authorizes the monotonous repetition of professionalization programs as new formulae aimed at addressing the problems in the use of violence by military and police professionals, as evidenced in the discourse on the need to humanize the Colombian public force in the "post-conflict". Lastly, the boundary between peace and war authorizes the "success story" of a war that has been won and, consequently, the periodization inaugurating the Colombian "post-conflict".

Under these terms, the book offers a transnational perspective to investigate the phenomenon of the reorganization of violence. As we have seen, the book focuses on the rearticulation of the mechanisms through which the *savoirs* organizing the use of state violence are transmitted within a transnational circuit of military professionals, instead of reproducing the logic of presence/absence of violence that often characterizes approaches towards this topic. In doing so, it provides analytical elements for us to resist both the methodological nationalism and the institutionalist perspective when addressing the phenomenon of the organization of violence, for they do not allow us to grasp how the military *savoirs* circulate across buildings and countries, how it traverses society, and with what effects. In this sense, the book offers the transnational circuit every time we formulate questions centered on the *Colombian* military, or any other national qualification we want to use. As such, it challenges the framing with which so often studies in Social Sciences—especially those of "violentology" and on military professionalization—formulate the systematic mobilization of the Colombian military in internal ordering practices as an anomaly of that country, for instance. After all, what is understood as a confusion in the spatial (outside) and functional (war) domains that pertain to the military is actually produced through the durable socialization between U.S. and Colombian military professionals—which, in turn, needs to be inscribed in a wider circuit of *savoirs*.

This book also speaks to conflict studies, particularly those devoted to post-conflict, both in terms of the assumptions underlying the post-conflict discourse, and the investment of such studies towards the search for the political group, the economic factor, the foreign "spoiler" or the addiction that better explains the "Colombian tragedy". In contrast, this book insists on the importance of digging into the terms under which we came to identify Colombia as a "problematic country". As we have seen, the concept of "problematization" sheds light on those processes, by pointing to the political stakes in the historical articulation of the "problem of violence" as one of delinquency, while locating the encounter of such discourse with the one constituting the war on drugs and a worldwide increasing delinquentialization of the phenomenon of war. Furthermore, the book exposes how the problematization of violence in Colombia, as an expression of problematizations of violence circulating regionally and globally, vested discursive continuities with new guises throughout the decades.

If Colombia has been circulating as a successful formula of conflict transformation to be replicated in other parts of the world, this book does more than putting in evidence the limits of the "post-conflict" discourse. It convokes us to interrogate how state violence faded from the discursive landscape of the "success story", as well as to acknowledge the continuous circulation of modalities of war amid the "post-conflict", either those exported to other countries as part of the "Colombian success", or those rearticulated into humanized versions of the Army or the Colombian National Police.

Challenging the terms upon which the "post-conflict" in Colombia is anchored is also key for us to understand a fundamental professional politics running through the Colombian "success story". Here, this book also offers a particular political-conceptual take, by posing questions to the politics of a professional field that pursues the global circulation of models and best practices as easy-to-adapt and easy-to-apply formulae fit for problematic contexts. To these model solutions, the making of the "Colombian problem" is a reminder of the historical sedimentations underlying claims about the present—a past that lives on despite attempts to bury it through claims to novelty of either problems or solutions. And to the repeatedly disappointed promises of peace, the circulation of military *savoirs* constituting the reorganization of violence is a reminder of the conditions under which the line between peace and war is sustained. These askew responses offer neither clear problems nor easy solutions. Instead, they reveal the double bind in which claims to success and peace often give rise to, and, with this, the stakes involved for those of us desiring to turn it down.

REFERENCES

BOOKS, CHAPTERS, ARTICLES

Bigo, D. Sociology of Transnational Guilds. *International Political Sociology*, v. 10, n. 4, pp. 398–416, 2016.

Huysmans, J. *The Politics of Insecurity: Fear, Migration and Asylum in the EU*. London: Routledge, 2006.

Bibliography

Books, Chapters, Articles

Afeikhena, J. Lessons from Colombia for Curtailing the Boko Haram Insurgency in Nigeria. *Prism*, v. 5, n. 2, pp. 94–105, 2015.

Almario, J. Colombia: The Genesis of the World's First Narco-Democracy. *Executive Intelligence Review*, v. 19, n. 30, pp. 41–42, 1992. Available at: https://www.yumpu.com/en/document/read/3893406/view-full-issue-executive-intelligence-review. Accessed on 05 July 2021.

Archila, M. Luchas laborales y violencia contra el sindicalismo en Colombia, 2002–2010. ¿Otro daño "colateral" de la Seguridad Democrática? *Controversia*, n. 198, pp. 161–218, June 2012.

Arenas, J. Diario de la Resistencia de Marquetalia. Bogotá: *Ediciones Abejón Mono*, 1966.

Atehortúa C. Colombia en la Guerra de Corea. *Folios, segunda época*, n. 27, pp. 63–76, 2008.

Atehortúa C., A. L. *Construcción del Ejército Nacional en Colombia, 1907–1930. Reforma Militar y Misiones Extranjeras*. Medellín: La Carreta, 2009.

Atehortúa C., A. L. El golpe de Rojas y el poder de los militares. *Folios*, n. 31, pp. 33–48, Primer Semestre 2010.

Atehortúa C., A. L.; Vélez R., H. *Estado y Fuerzas Armadas en Colombia*. Cali: TM, 1994.

Atkins, G. P.; Thompson, L. V. German Military Influence in Argentina, 1921–1940. *Journal of Latin American Studies*, v. 4, n. 2, pp. 257–274, November 1972.

Aussaresses, P. *The Battle of the Casbah: Terrorism and Counter-Terrorism in Algeria, 1955–1957*. New York: Enigma, 2010.
Bartelson, J. Double Binds: Sovereignty and the Just War Tradition. In: Kalmo, H.; Skinner, Q. (eds.). *Sovereignty in Fragments – The Past, Present and Future of a Contested Concept*. Cambridge: Cambridge University Press, 2010.
Bass, T. Counterinsurgency and Torture. *American Quarterly*, v. 60, n. 2, pp. 233–240, 2008.
Bedregal, G. *Los Militares en Bolivia. Ensayo de interpretación sociológica*. LaPaz, p. 23, 1971.
Bergquist, C. *Coffee and Conflict in Colombia, 1886–1910*. Durham (NC): Duke University Press, 1989.
Bewley-Taylor, D. R. *International Drug Control: Consensus Fractured*. Cambridge: Cambridge University Press, 2012.
Bonditti, P. Violence, 'Terrorism', Otherness. Reshaping Enmity in Times of Terror. In: Campbell R. (ed). *Violence and Civilization: Studies of Social Violence in History and Prehistory*. Oxford: Oxbow, 2014.
Bonilla, A. Vulnerabilidad internacional y fragilidad doméstica: la crisis andina en perspectiva regional. *Nueva Sociedad*, n. 173, pp. 50–64, June 2001.
Botero Jaramillo, N. El problema de los excluidos. Las leyes contra la vagancia en Colombia durante las décadas de 1820 a 1840. *Anuario Colombiano de Historia Social y de la Cultura*, v. 39, n. 2, pp. 41–68, Jul–Dic. 2012.
Brown, K. 'All They Understand Is Force': Debating Culture in Operation Iraqi Freedom. *American Anthropologist*, v. 110, n. 4, pp. 443–453, 2008.
Bushnell, D. *The Making of Modern Colombia: A Nation in Spite Itself*. Berkeley (CA): University of California Press, 1993.
Campbell, D. *Writing Security: United States Foreign Policy and the Politics of Identity*. Minneapolis: University of Minnesota Press, 1992.
Cardona, C. M. *Politicians, Soldiers, and Cops: Colombia's La Violencia in Comparative Perspective*. Dissertation presented at University of California (Berkeley), 2008.
Carvajal C., C. La Policía Nacional en el posconflicto. *Revista Criminalidad*, v. 47, n. 1, pp. 38–48, 2004. Available at: https://www.policia.gov.co/sites/default/files/RevistaCriminalidadco.pdf. Accessed on 04 July 2021.
Casallas R. J. A. *Cooperación Técnico Militar del Ejército Colombiano al Ejército de Honduras*. Universidad Militar Nueva Granada, Programa de Relaciones Internacionales y Estudios Políticos, Bogotá, November 2015. Available at: http://repository.unimilitar.edu.co/bitstream/10654/7842/1/CasallasRu%C3%ADzJaimeAlberto2016.pdf. Accessed on 05 July 2021.
Castaño C., A. *La Policía. Su origen y su destino*. Biblioteca Escuela de Policía "General Santander", Vol. VIII. Bogotá: Cahur, 1947.
Castro, C. *O Espírito Militar: um antropólogo na caserna*. Rio de Janeiro: Zahar, 2004.

Castro, C. The Army as a Modernizing Actor in Brazil, 1870–1930. In: Silva, P. (ed.). *The Soldier and the State in South America: Essays in Civil-Military Relations.* New York: Palgrave Macmillan, 2001.

Centro de Investigación y Educación Popular (CINEP). Del Batallón Charry Solano a la Brigada 20 una continuidad paramilitar. *Noche y Niebla* (Dossier: Deuda con la Humanidad: Paramilitarismo de Estado en Colombia 1988–2003). Bogotá, D.C.: CINEP, 2004.

Chapman, P. *Bananas: How the United Fruit Company Shaped the World.* Edinburgh: Canongate, 2007.

Chernick, M. *Acuerdo posible: solución negociada al conflicto armado colombiano.* Bogotá, D.C.: Aurora, 2008.

Chernick, M. Economic Resources and Internal Armed Conflicts: Lessons from the Colombian Case. In: Arnson, C. J.; Zartman, I. W. (eds.). *Rethinking the Economics of War: The Intersection of Need, Creed, and Greed.* Washington, D.C.: Woodrow Wilson Center Press, 2005.

Ciro G., A. R.; Correa H., M. Transformación estructural del Ejército colombiano. Construcción de escenarios futuros. *Revista Científica General José María Córdova,* v. 12, n. 13, pp. 19–88, 2014.

Craig, R. B. Domestic Implications of Illicit Colombian Drug Production and Trafficking. *Journal of International Studies and World Affairs,* v. 25, n. 3, pp. 325–350, 1983.

Crandall R. Explicit Narcotization: US Policy Toward Colombia During Samper Administration. *Latin American Politics and Society,* v. 43, n. 3, pp. 95–120, 2001.

Crandall, R. *Driven by Drugs: US Policy Toward Colombia.* Londres: Lynne Rienner, 2002.

Davis, D.; Kilcullen, D.; Mills, G.; Spencer, D. (orgs.). *A Great Perhaps? Colombia: Conflict and Convergence.* London: Hurst, 2016.

Davis, K. E.; Kingsbury, B.; Merry, S. E. Introduction: Global Governance by Indicators. In: Davis, K. E.; Fisher, A.; Kingsbury, B.; Merry, S. E. (eds.). *Governance by Indicators: Global Power Through Quantification and Rankings.* Oxford: Oxford University Press, 2012.

Draper, M. The *Force Publique*'s Campaigns in the Congo-Arab War, 1892–1894. *Small Wars & Insurgencies,* vol. 30, n. 4–5, pp. 1020–1039, 2019.

Echandía, C. *Dos Décadas de Escalamiento del Conflicto Armado Colombiano.* Bogotá: Universidad Externado de Colombia, 2006.

Elias, N. *The Civilizing Process.* Oxford: Blackwell, 2000.

Enloe, C. *Nimo's War, Emma's War. Making Feminist Sense of the Iraq War.* Berkeley: University of California Press, 2010.

Fall, B. A Portrait of the "Centurion". In: TRINQUIER, R. (ed.). *Modern Warfare: A French View of Counterinsurgency.* London and Dunmow: Pall Mall, 1985.

Feldmann, A. E. Measuring the Colombian "Success" Story. *Revista de Ciencia Política,* v. 32, n. 3, pp. 739–752, 2012.

Fellowship of Reconciliation (FOR); Coordinación Colombia-Europa-Estados Unidos (CCEEU). *"Falsos positivos" en Colombia y el papel de asistencia militar de Estados Unidos, 2000–2010.* Bogotá, D.C.: FOR and CCEEU, 2014.

Fernández, M.; Esteves, P. Silencing Colonialism: Foucault and the Modern International. In: Bonditti, P.; Bigo, D.; Gros, F. (eds.). *Foucault and the International. Silences and Legacies for the Study of World Politics.* New York: Palgrave Macmillan, 2017.

Few, Michael. Interview with Dr. John Arquilla: How Can French Encounters with Irregular Warfare in the 19th Century Inform COIN in our Time? *Small Wars Journal,* Nov. 30, n.p., 2010.

Fonnegra, G. *Las Bananeras. Un testimonio vivo.* Bogotá: Círculo de Lectores, 1986.

Foucault, M. *Discipline and Punish.* New York: Second Vintage, 1995.

Foucault, M. Nietzsche, Genealogy, History. In: Rabinow, P. (ed.). *The Foucault Reader.* New York: Pantheon Books, 2010 [1984].

Foucault, M. Polemics, Politics, and Problematizations: An Interview with Michel Foucault. In: Rabinow, P. (ed). *The Foucault Reader.* New York: Pantheon Books, 2010 [1984].

Foucault, M. Politics and the Study of Discourse. In: Burchell, G.; Gordon, C.; Miller, P. *The Foucault Effect: Studies in Governmentality.* Chicago: University of Chicago Press, 1991.

Foucault, M. Practicing Criticism. In: Kritzman, L. D. (ed). *Politics, Philosophy, Culture*: interviews and other writings, 1977–1984. New York: Routledge, 1988.

Foucault, M. *Security, Territory, Population.* New York: Palgrave Macmillan, 2007.

Foucault, M. The Order of Discourse. In: Young, R. (ed.). *Untying the Text: A Post-Structuralist Reader.* Boston, London and Henley: Routledge, 1981 [1971].

Franco R., V. L. *Orden contrainsurgente y dominación.* Medellín: Siglo del Hombre, 2009.

Gallón G. G. Human Rights: A Path to Democracy and Peace in Colombia. In: Welna, C.; Gallón G. G. (eds.). *Peace, Democracy, and Human Rights in Colombia.* Notre Dame: Notre Dame University, 2007.

Gallón G. G. *Quince años de estado de sitio en Colombia, 1958–1978.* Bogotá: Librería y Editorial América Latina, 1979.

Galula, D. *Counterinsurgency: Theory and Practice.* New York and London: Frederick A. Praeger, 1964.

Galula, D. *Pacification in Algeria, 1956–1958.* Santa Monica, CA: RAND Corporation, 2006 [1963].
García-Peña, R. P. Un país problema en un mundo intervencionista. In: Leal B., F. (ed.). *En la encrucijada: Colombia en el siglo XXI.* Bogotá, D.C.: Norma, 2006.
Gildea, R. *Empires of the Mind: The Colonial Past and the Politics of the Present.* Cambridge: Cambridge University Press, 2019.
Gill, L. *The School of the Americas: Military Training and Political Violence in the Americas.* Durham and London: Duke University Press, 2004.
Gómez-Suárez, A. US-Colombian Relations in the 1980s: Political Violence and the Onset of the Unión Patriótica Genocide. In: Esparza, M.; Huttenbach, H. R.; Feierstein, D. (eds.). *State Violence and Genocide in Latin America. The Cold War Years.* New York and London: Routledge, 2010.
González M, M. A.; Pierrotty, S., M.; Rodríguez B., J. D.; Poloche Y., Y. S. *La seguridad humana en la Doctrina Damasco*: un eje de transformación hacia el Ejército del futuro. *Revista BRÚJULA*, v. 5, n. 10, pp. 8–17, 2017.
González R., J. D.; Masullo J., J.; Sánchez M., C.; Restrepo T., J. A. Registrar, cuantificar y debatir. ¿Cómo se ha medido la violencia contra trabajadores sindicalizados en Colombia? *Controversia,* n. 198, pp. 57–110, June 2012.
González, F. E.; Bolívar, I. J.; Vázquez, T. *Violencia Política en Colombia.* De la nación fragmentada a la construcción del Estado. Bogotá, D.C.: CINEP, 2003.
Guanumen P., M. La narcotización de las Relaciones Colombia-Estados Unidos. *Revista de Relaciones Internacionales, Estrategia y Seguridad,* v. 7, n. 2, pp. 221–244, 2012.
Guzmán B., Á.; Moreno Q., R. Autodefensas, Narcotráfico y Comportamiento Estatal en el Valle del Cauca. In: ROMERO, M. (ed.). *Parapolítica: la ruta de la expansión paramilitar y los acuerdos políticos.* Bogotá, D.C.: Corporación Nuevo Arco Iris, 2007.
Hilgers, T.; Macdonald, L. (eds.). *Violence in Latin America and the Caribbean: Subnational Structures, Institutions, and Clientelistic Networks.* Cambridge: Cambridge University Press, 2017.
Hoffman, B. Foreword to the New Edition. In: Galula, D. (ed.). *Pacification in Algeria 1956–1958.* Santa Monica (CA): RAND, 2006.
Huysmans, J. *The Politics of Insecurity: Fear, Migration and Asylum in the EU.* London: Routledge, 2006.
Inayatullah, N.; Blaney, D. L: *International Relations and the Problem of Difference.* New York: Routledge, 2004.
Isacson, A. Failing Grades: Evaluating the Results of Plan Colombia. *Yale Journal of International Affairs,* pp. 138–154, Summer/Fall 2005.
Jaramillo M., J. Expertos y comisiones de studio sobre la violencia en Colombia. *Estudios Políticos,* n. 39, pp. 231–258, 2011.

Jardini, D. R. *Thinking Through the Cold War: RAND, National Security and Domestic Policy, 1945–1975*. Meadow Lands, PA: Smashwords, 2013.

Kapoor, I. Acting in a Tight Spot: Homi Bhabha's Postcolonial Politics. *New Political Science*, v. 25, n. 4, pp. 561–577, 2003.

Keene, E. *Beyond the Anarchical Society. Grotius, Colonialism and Order in International Relations*. Cambridge: Cambridge University Press, 2004

Kilcullen, D. Twenty-Eight Articles: Fundamentals of Company-Level Counterinsurgency. *IO Sphere*, Summer, pp. 29–35, 2006.

Krepinevich, A. *The Army and Vietnam*. Baltimore: Johns Hopkins University, 1986.

Leal B., F. *Estudios sobre el estado y la política en Colombia* (Tomo II). La contribución de Francisco Leal Buitrago. Bogotá: Universidad de los Andes, 2016.

Leal B., F. *La Seguridad Nacional a La Deriva. Del Frente Nacional a la Posguerra Fría*. Mexico, D.C.: Alfaomega, 2002.

Lizarazo V., N. S. El papel de las Fuerzas Armadas en la política antidrogas colombiana. 1985–1990. In: Vargas Velásquez, A. (ed.) *El papel de las Fuerzas Armadas en la Política Antidrogas Colombiana. 1985–2006*. Bogota, D.C.: Universidad Nacional de Colombia, 2008.

López R., A. *Remedios nocivos: las orígenes de la política colombiana contra las drogas*. Bogotá, D.C.: Penguin Random House Group Editorial, 2016.

Loveman, B. *For la Patria: Politics and the Armed Forces in Latin America*. Wilmington (DE): Scholarly Resources Books, 1999.

Lynch, J. As origens da independência da América Espanhola. In: Bethell, L. (org.). *História da América Latina: da Independência a 1870*, vol. III. São Paulo: EDUSP, 2004.

MacCoun, R. J.; Reuter, P. *Drug War Heresies: Learning from Other Vices, Times, and Places*. Cambridge: Cambridge University Press, 2004.

Mainwaring, S.; Bejarano, A. M.; Pizarro L., E. An Overview. In: Mainwaring, S.; Bejarano, A. M.; Pizarro L., E. (eds.). *The Crisis of Democratic Representation in the Andes*. Stanford: Stanford University, 2006.

Malaguti, V. *Introdução Crítica à Criminologia Brasileira*. Rio de Janeiro: Revan, 2011.

Martin, J. E.; Jaramillo-Marín, J. Las conmemoraciones noticiosas en la prensa colombiana: rememorando la toma a Mitú. *Palabra Clave*, v. 17, n. 2, pp. 378–411, 2014.

Marulanda V., M. *Cuadernos de Campaña*. Bogotá: Ediciones Abejón Mono, 1973. Available at: http://www.rebelion.org/docs/68099.pdf. Accessed on 10 July 2021.

McClintock, M. *Instruments of Statecraft: U.S. Guerilla Warfare, Counterinsurgency, and Counterterrorism, 1940–1990*. New York: Pantheon, 1992.

McFate, M. Anthropology and Counterinsurgency: The Strange Story of Their Curious Relationship. *Military Review*, n. 85, pp. 24–38, 2005.

Mills, G. The Door Through Which Much Follows? Security and Colombia's Economic Transformation. In: Davis, D.; Kilcullen, D.; Mills, G.; Spencer, D. (orgs.). *A Great Perhaps? Colombia: Conflict and Convergence*. London: Hurst, 2016.

Montenegro R., L. E.; Durán E., P. A. Lucha contra el narcotráfico: transferencia de una experiencia. *Revista Criminalidad*, v. 50, n. 2, pp. 57–70, 2008. Available at: https://www.policia.gov.co/sites/default/files/RevistaCriminalidadco.pdf. Accessed on 05 July 2021.

Morelli, F. Entre el antiguo y el nuevo régimen. La historia política hispanoamericana del siglo XIX. *Historia Crítica*, n. 33, Enero-Junio, pp. 122–155, 2007.

Muller, J. Z. *The Tyranny of Metrics*. Princeton e Oxford: Princeton University Press, 2018.

Neocleous, M. *War Power, Police Power*. Edinburgh: Edinburgh University Press, 2014.

Nunn, F. M. Foreign Influences on the South American Military: Professionalization and Politicization. In: Silva, P. (ed.). *The Soldier and the State in South America: Essays in Civil-Military Relations*. New York: Palgrave Macmillan, 2001.

Olave, G. El eterno retorno de Marquetalia: sobre el mito fundacional de las Farc-EP. *Revista Folios*, n. 37, pp. 149–166, 2013.

Orozco A., I. *Combatientes, rebeldes y terroristas. Guerra y Derecho en Colombia*. Bogotá, D.C.: Temis, 1992.

Orozco A., I. La democracia y el tratamiento del enemigo interior. *Análisis Político*, n. 6, n.p., 1989.

Orozco A., I. Los diálogos con el narcotráfico: historia de la transformación fallida de un delincuente común en un delincuente político. *Análisis Político*, n. 11, n.p., 1990.

Pabón A., N. El papel de las Fuerzas Armadas en la política antidrogas colombiana, 1998–2006. In: Vargas V., A. (ed). *El papel de las Fuerzas Armadas en la Política Antidrogas Colombiana, 1985–2006*. Bogotá, D.C.: Universidad Nacional de Colombia, 2008.

Palacios, M. *Coffee in Colombia, 1850–1970. An Economic, Social, and Political History*. Cambridge: Cambridge University Press, 1980.

Pamplona, M. A. Nação e modernidade nos escritos de Sarmiento e Nabuco. *Letterature d'America*. Anno XVII-XVIII, n. 75–76, pp. 25–65, 1997/1998.

Pécaut, D. *As FARC: uma guerrilha sem fins?* São Paulo: Paz e Terra, 2010.

Pécaut, D. *Crónica de cuatro décadas de política colombiana*. Bogotá, D.C.: Norma, 2006.

Pécaut, D. La contribución del IEPRI a los estudios sobre la violencia en Colombia. *Análisis Político*, n. 34, pp. 64–79, 1998.

Peñaranda, R. The War on Paper: A Balance Sheet on Works Published in the 1990s. In: Bergquist, C.; Peñaranda, R.; Sánchez G., G. (eds). *Violence in Colombia. 1990–2000: Waging War and Negotiating Peace.* Wilmington (DW): Scholarly Resources, 2003.

Pereira F., A. Violencia en el mundo sindical. Un análisis cualitativo sobre una práctica persistente en Colombia, 1986–2011. *Controversia*, n. 198, pp. 13–56, June 2012.

Pinzón, J. C. Colombia Back from the Brink: From Failed State to Exporter of Security. *PRISM*, v. 5, n. 4, pp. 2–9, 2015.

Pizarro L., E. La Profesionalización Militar en Colombia (1907–1944). *Análisis Político*, n. 1, pp. 20–39, 1987.

Pizarro L., E. La Profesionalización Militar en Colombia (II): El Periodo de La Violencia. *Análisis Político*, n. 2, pp. 7–29, 1987.

Pizarro L., E. La profesionalización militar en Colombia (III): los regímenes militares (1953–1958). *Análisis Político*, n. 3, pp. 6–30, 1988.

Porch, D. *Counterinsurgency: Exposing the Myths of the New Way of War.* Cambridge: Cambridge University, 2013.

Porch, D. The Dangerous Myths and Dubious Promise of COIN. *Small Wars & Insurgencies*, v. 22, n. 2, pp. 239–257, 2011.

Ramírez, S. *Actores en conflicto por la paz. El proceso de paz durante el gobierno de Belisario Betancur (1982–1986).* Bogotá, D.C.: Siglo XXI, 1989.

Ramírez, S. *Intervención en conflictos internos: el caso colombiano (1994–2003).* Bogotá: Universidad Nacional de Colombia, 2004.

Rangel, A. (org.). *Sostenibilidad de la Seguridad Democrática.* Bogotá: Fundación Seguridad & Democracia, 2005.

Rangel, S. A. Colombia: perspectivas de paz y seguridad. *Revista Criminalidad*, vol. 50, n. 1, pp. 417–432, 2008.

Rasmussen, D. W.; Benson, B. Rationalizing Drug Policy Under Federalism. *Florida State University Law Review*, v. 30, n. 679, pp. 679–734, 2003.

Rey E., M. F. La educación militar en Colombia entre 1886 y 1907. *Historia Crítica*, n. 35, pp. 150–175, Enero-Junio 2008.

Rid, T. Razzia: A Turning Point in Modern Strategy. *Terrorism and Political Violence*, v. 21, n. 4, pp. 617–635, 2009.

Rodrigues, T. Tráfico, Guerra, Proibição. In: Labate, B. C.; Goulart, S. L.; Fiore, M.; MacRae, E.; Carneiro, H. (orgs.). Salvador: UFBA, 2008.

Rodríguez H. S. M. *La influencia de los Estados Unidos en el Ejército colombiano, 1951–1959.* Medellín: La Carreta, 2006.

Rojas G., P. J. Doctrina Damasco: eje articulador de la segunda gran reforma del Ejército Nacional de Colombia. *Revista Científica General José María Córdova*, v. 15, n. 19, pp. 95–119, 2017.

Rojas, D. M. Estados Unidos y la guerra en Colombia. In: Sanín, F. G.; Wills, M. E.; Gómez, G. S. (cords.). *Nuestra guerra sin nombre: transformaciones del conflicto en Colombia*. Bogotá, D.C.: Norma, 2006.

Rojas, D. M. Plan Colombia II: ¿más de lo mismo? *Colombia Internacional*, n. 65, pp. 14–37, 2007.

Ronderos, M. T. *Guerras Recicladas. Una historia periodística del paramilitarismo en Colombia*. Bogotá, D.C.: Aguilar, 2014.

Rouquié, A. *El Estado Militar en América Latina*. Buenos Aires: Emecé, 1984.

Ruiz N., A. Discurso del Señor Ministro de Guerra, Mayor General Alberto Ruiz Novoa. *Revista de las Fuerzas Armadas*, v. IX, n. 26, pp. 237–247, 1964.

Ruiz V. J. C.; Illera C. O.; Manrique Z. V. *La tenue línea de la tranquilidad. Estudio comparado sobre seguridad ciudadana y policía*. Bogotá, D.C.: Universidad del Rosario, 2006.

Safford, F. Política, Ideologia e Sociedade na América Espanhola do Pós-Independência. In: Bethtell, L. (org.). *História da América Latinai: Da Independência a 1870*, vol. III. São Paulo: EDUSP, 2004.

Safford, F.; Palacios, M. *Colombia – Fragmented Land, Divided Society*. Oxford: Oxford University Press, 2002.

Salamone, A. Military History and the Drafting of Doctrine: FM 3–24, Relevant Case Studies or Seductive Analogies? *Small Wars Journal*, v. 20, n. 2, n.p., 2008.

Sánchez G., G. (org). *Colombia: violencia y democracia*. Bogotá, D.C.: Universidad Nacional de Colombia, 1988.

Sánchez G. G.; Fals B. O.; Umaña, E. *La Violencia en Colombia*, vols. I and II. Bogotá: Carlos Valencia, 1962.

Sarmiento, D. F. *Facundo – o civilización y barbarie*. Buenos Aires: Biblioteca del Congreso de la Nación, 2018.

Scalercio, M. A. *As armas e as consciências*. Tese de Doutorado, Instituto de Relações Internacionais, Pontifícia Universidade Católica do Rio de Janeiro. Rio de Janeiro, 2015.

Thoumi, F. E. Illegal Drugs in Colombia: From Illegal Economic Boom to Social Crisis. *The Annals of the American Academy of Political and Social Science*, n. 582, pp. 102–116, 2002.

Thoumi, F. E. The Numbers Game: Let's All Guess the Size of the Illegal Drug Industry! *Journal of Drug Issues*; pp. 185–200, Winter 2005.

Tickner, A. B. Intervención por invitación: claves para la política exterior colombiana y sus debilidades principales. *Colombia Internacional*, n. 65, pp. 90–111, 2007.

Tickner, A. B. Morales C., M. Narrating Success: Colombian Security Expertise and Foreign Policy. In: Bagley, B. M.; Rosen, J. D. (eds). *Colombia's Political Economy at the Outset of the 21st Century: From Uribe to Santos and Beyond*. Washington, D.C.: Lexington, 2014.

Trace, M.; Roberts, M.; Klein, A. Assessing Drug Policy Principles and Practice. *Drugscope Report* n. 2, London: Beckley Foundation Drug Policy Programme, 2004.

Uprimny Y., R.; Chaparro H., S.; Oliveira, L. F. C. *Delito de drogas y sobredosis carcelaria en Colombia*. Documentos Dejusticia n. 37, Bogotá, D.C.: Dejusticia, 2017.

Urrego A., M. Á. El movimiento sindical, el período de la violencia y la formación de la nueva izquierda colombiana, 1959-1971. *Diálogo de Saberes*, n. 38, pp. 135-145, 2013.

Valladares, L. P. *A invenção da favela: Do mito de origem a favela.com*. Rio de Janeiro: Editora FGV, 2005.

Vanegas G., P. P. La Constitución colombiana y los estados de excepción: veinte años después. *Revista Derecho del Estado*, n. 27, pp. 261-290, 2011.

Vargas V., A. *Las fuerzas armadas en el conflicto colombiano: antecedentes y perspectivas*. Medellín: La Carreta, 2012.

Vargas V., A. The Profile of the Colombian Armed Forces: A Result of the Struggle against Guerrillas, Drug Trafficking and Terrorism. In: Mares, D. E.; Martínez, R. (eds). *Debating Civil-Military Relations in Latin America*. Brighton: Sussex Academic Press, 2014.

Vargas, E. V. Fármacos e outros objetos sócio-técnicos: notas para uma genealogia das drogas. In: Labate, B. C.; Goulart, S. L.; Fiore, M.; MacRae, E.; Carneiro, H. (orgs). Salvador: UFBA, 2008.

Viana, M. T.; Peixoto, G. Brasil: um novo 'caso de sucesso' para a segurança pública na América Latina?, *Revista Cult*, n. 244, pp. 11-18, 2019.

Villa, R. D.; Viana, M. T. Internacionalização pelo envolvimento de atores externos no conflito colombiano: atuação da OEA na desmobilização de grupos paramilitares na Colômbia. *Dados - Revista de Ciências Sociais*, v. 55, n. 2, pp. 403-445, 2012.

Villamizar, A. *Fuerzas Militares para la guerra: La agenda pendiente de la reforma militar*. Bogotá, D.C.: Fundación Seguridad & Democracia, 2003.

Villatoux, M.-C.; Villatoux, P. Aux origines de la «guerre révolutionnaire»: le colonel Lacheroy parle. *Revue historique des armées*, n. 268, pp. 45-53, 2012

Walker, R. B. J. Europe Is Not Where It Is Supposed to Be. In: Kelstrup, M.; Williams, M. C. (eds.). *International Relations and the Politics of European Integration: Power, Security and Community*. London and New York: Routledge, 2000.

Wasinski, C. Validar a Guerra: A Construção do Regime de Expertise Estratégica. *Contexto Internacional*, v. 34, n. 2, pp. 435-470, 2012.

Weber, M. Politics as a Vocation. In: Owen, D.; Strong, T. B. (eds.). *The Vocation Lectures*. Cambridge: Hackett, 2004.

Documents, Reports and Studies

Amnesty International. *Unmatched Power, Unmet Principles: The Human Rights Dimensions of US Training of Foreign Military and Police Forces*, 2002.
Cárdenas, M.; Casas-Zamora, K. *The "Colombianization" of Mexico*. Washington, D.C.: Brookings Institution, 21 September 2010. Available at: https://www.brookings.edu/opinions/the-colombianization-of-mexico/. Accessed on 05 July 2021.
Castro Blanco, E. El Derecho como positivación fáctica de exclusión a los vagos en Colombia. In: *Diálogo de Saberes*, No. 34 (Ene-Jun. 2011), pp. 163–196.
Central Intelligence Agency (CIA). Human Resource Exploitation Training Manual (DRV HUM 4082). Fairfax: CIA, 1983. Available at: http://nsarchive.gwu.edu/NSAEBB/NSAEBB122/CIA%20Human%20Res%20Exploit%20A1-G11.pdf. Accessed on 15 February 2021.
Central Intelligence Agency (CIA). Kubark Counterintelligence Interrogation. Washington, D.C.: CIA, 1963.
Centro de Doctrina del Ejército de Colombia (CEDOE). Conceptos Generales Básicos Doctrina Damasco VOCADOC (Vocabulario Doctrinal). Bogotá: CEDOE, 2020.
Colectivo de Abogados 'José Alvear Restrepo'. *Libertad sindical y derechos humanos en Colombia*. Bogotá, D.C.: Colectivo de Abogados, 13 June 2005. Available at: https://www.colectivodeabogados.org/libertad-sindical-y-derechos-humanos-en-colombia/. Accessed on 14 February 2021.
Congreso de la República de Colombia. Ley 104 de 1993. *Diario Oficial No. 41.158*, 31 December 1993. Available at: http://www.secretariasenado.gov.co/senado/basedoc/ley_0104_1993.html. Accessed on 10 July 2021.
Coordinación Colombia-Europa-Estados Unidos (CCEEU). *Informe Alterno sobre la Situación de las Desapariciones Forzadas en Colombia Presentado ante el Comité Contra la Desaparición Forzada de Naciones Unidas*. Bogotá, D.C.: CCEEU, September 2016. Available at: http://coeuropa.org.co/wp-content/uploads/2016/10/Informe-Desaparici%C3%B3n-forzada-arreglado-10-oct-ilovepdf-compressed.pdf. Accessed on 14 February 2021.
Coordinación Colombia-Europa-Estados Unidos (CCEEU). *Informe Alternativo al Septimo Informe Presentado por el Estado de Colombia al Comité de Derechos Humanos de las Naciones Unidas*. Bogotá, D.C.: CCEEU, October 2016. Available at: http://coeuropa.org.co/wp-content/uploads/2017/01/Informe-alternativo-al-SEPTIMO-INFORME-11-enero-2017.pdf. Accessed on 14 February 2021.
Coordinación Colombia-Europa-Estados Unidos. *Informe Alternativo presentado por las organizaciones de la Sociedad Civil al 7mo Informe presentado por el Estado Colombiano ante el Comité de DDHH de las Naciones Unidas*. Bogotá: Coordinación Colombia-Europa-Estados Unidos, 2017. Available at: http://coeuropa.org.co/wp-content/uploads/2017/01/Informe-alt

ernativo-al-SEPTIMO-INFORME-11-enero-2017.pdf. Accessed on 04 July 2021.

DeShazo, P.; Forman, J. M.; McLean, P. *Countering Threats to Security and Stability in a Failing State. Lessons from Colombia*. Washington, D.C.: CIS, 2009.

DeShazo, P.; Primiani, T.; McLean, P. *Back from the Brink. Evaluating Progress in Colombia, 1999–2007*. Washington, D.C.: CIS, 2007.

Drug Enforcement Administration (DEA). A History of the DEA: 1975–1980. *The DEA Museum & Visitors Center*, n.d., pp. 24–42. Available at: https://www.deamuseum.org/deahistorybook/1975-1980.html. Accessed on 15 February 2021.

Drug Enforcement Administration (DEA). A History of the DEA: 1980–1985. *The DEA Museum & Visitors Center*, n.d., pp. 43–57. Available at: https://www.deamuseum.org/deahistorybook/1980-1985.html. Accessed on 15 February 2021.

Ejército de Chile. La llegada al país de los restos del General de División don Emilio Körner. *Memorial del Ejército de Chile*. Santiago (Chile), Talleres del Instituto Geográfico Militar, Año XIX, Ago. 1924, pp. 115–118.

Estado Mayor General De Las Fuerzas Militares. República de Colombia. *La Guerra en La Selva. Manual de Campaña*. Bogotá, D.C.: Sección Imprenta y Publicaciones, 1944.

Felbab-Brown, V. Narco-belligerants Across the Globe: Lessons from Colombia for Afghanistan? *Security and Defence Working Paper*, n. 55. Madrid: Elcano Royal Institute, 28 October 2009. Available at: http://www.realinstitut oelcano.org/wps/wcm/connect/da0e7a80401cec18ab82eb1ecbd00d37/WP55-2009_Felbab-Brown_Narco-belligerants_Lessons_Colombia_Afghani stan.pdf?MOD=AJPERES. Accessed on 04 July 2021.

Felbab-Brown, V. The Violent Drug Market in Mexico and Lessons from Colombia. *Policy Paper* (Foreign Policy at Brookings), n. 12, March 2009. Available at: https://www.brookings.edu/wp-content/uploads/2016/06/03_mexico_drug_market_felbabbrown.pdf. Accessed on 04 July 2021.

Felbab-Brown, V. Lessons from Colombia for Mexico? Caveat Emptor. *Brookings*, 24 February 2012. Available at: https://www.brookings.edu/articles/lessons-from-colombia-for-mexico-caveat-emptor/. Accessed on 14 February 2021.

Fellowship of Reconciliation (FOR). *Military Assistance and Human Rights*: Colombia, U.S. Accountability, and Global Implications. Bogotá, D.C.: FOR, July 2010. Available at: https://peacepresence.org/2010/09/22/report-mil itary-colombia-us/. Accessed on 15 February 2021.

Fundación Ideas Para la Paz. *La Transformación del Ejército Nacional*. Una mirada comparada con los Ejércitos más modernos del mundo. Bogotá, 2018. Available at: http://ideaspaz.org/media/website/FIP_Transf ormacion_ejercito.pdf. Accessed on 10 July 2021.

Hosmer, S.; Crane, S. O. *Counterinsurgency: A Symposium*, April 16–20, 1962. Santa Monica, CA: RAND Corporation, 2006 [1963].
Human Rights Watch (HRW). *Colombia's Killer Networks: The Military-Paramilitary Partnership and the United States*. New York, November 1996. Available at: https://www.hrw.org/legacy/reports/1996/killertoc.htm. Accessed on 13 February 2021.
International Crisis Group (ICG). Colombia: President Uribe's Democratic Security Policy. *Latin America & Caribbean Report* n. 6, 13 November 2003. Available at: https://d2071andvip0wj.cloudfront.net/06-colombia-president-uribe-s-democratic-security-policy.pdf. Accessed on 14 February 2021.
International Crisis Group (ICG). War and Drugs in Colombia. *Latin America & Caribbean Report* n. 11, 27 January 2005. Available at: https://www.crisisgroup.org/latin-america-caribbean/andes/colombia/war-and-drugs-colombia. Accessed on 13 February 2021.
Isacson, A. *Colombia: Don't Call it a Model*. Washington, D.C.: WOLA, 14 July 2010. Available at: https://www.wola.org/sites/default/files/Drug%20Policy/notmodel.pdf. Accessed on 19 June 2021.
Isacson, A. *Plan Colombia – Six Years Later: Report of a CIP Staff Visit to Putumayo and Medellín, Colombia*. Center for International Policy, International Policy Report, November 2006.
Ministerio de Defensa de Colombia. "Combatir la delincuencia trasnacional con una visión regional es la única garantía de éxito": Ministro Pinzón. Bogotá, 03 May 2012. Available at: https://www.mindefensa.gov.co/irj/go/km/docs/documents/News/NoticiaGrandeMDN/503fce10-7277-2f10-e791-c714fff98d20.xml. Accessed on 19 June 2021.
Ministerio de Defensa de Colombia. *Visión de Futuro de las Fuerzas Armadas*. Bogotá: Imprenta Nacional de Colombia, 2016. Available at: https://www.mindefensa.gov.co/irj/go/km/docs/Mindefensa/Documentos/descargas/estrategia_planeacion/proyeccion/documentos/vision_futuro_FA.pdf. Accessed on 05 July 2021.
Ministerio de Hacienda y Crédito Público. Generación de empleo 2010–2013: Superando las metas. *Reportes de Hacienda*, v. 6, año 2. Bogotá: Dirección General de Política Macroeconómica, Ministerio de Hacienda y Crédito Público, 12 December 2013. Available at: https://docplayer.es/8632435-Generacion-de-empleo-2010-2013-superando-las-metas.html. Accessed on 19 June 2021.
Palau, L. *Colombia en 1907 – bajo la administración del Sr. General Rafael Reyes*. Bogota: Imprenta Nacional, 1907.
Policía Nacional de Colombia. *Manual de Operaciones Especiales*. Bogotá, D.C.: Policía Nacional de Colombia, November 2009. Available at: http://web.archive.org/web/20120603010154/http://www.policia.edu.co/policia/doc

umentos/doctrina/manuales_de_consulta/108218_Manual%20Operaciones. pdf. Accessed on 13 February 2021.

Policía Nacional de Colombia. *Revista Criminalidad*, v. 23. Bogotá, D.C.: Policía Nacional de Colombia, Departamento de Información, Criminalidad y Estadística, 1980. Available at: https://www.policia.gov.co/revista/volume n-23. Accessed on 13 February 2021.

Policía Nacional de Colombia. *Revista Criminalidad*, v. 30. Bogotá, D.C.: Policía Nacional de Colombia, Dirección Central de Policía Judicial, 1987. Available at: https://www.policia.gov.co/revista/volumen-30. Accessed on 13 February 2021.

Policía Nacional de Colombia. *Revista Criminalidad*, v. 48. Bogotá, D.C.: Policía Nacional de Colombia, Dirección Central de Policía Judicial, 2005. Available at: https://www.policia.gov.co/sites/default/files/RevistaCriminalidad2005.pdf. Accessed on 15 February 2021.

Presidencia de la República de Colombia. Declaración del Presidente Juan Manuel Santos en el lanzamiento de la Cátedra para la Paz. 25 May 2015. Available at: http://wp.presidencia.gov.co/Noticias/2015/Mayo/Paginas/20150525_07-Declaracion-del-Presidente-Juan-Manuel-Santos-en-el-lanzamiento-de-la-Catedra-para-la-Paz.aspx. Accessed on 19 June 2021.

Presidencia de la República de Colombia. Palabras del Presidente Juan Manuel Santos en su posesión para el período presidencial 2014–2018. Bogotá, 07 August 2014. Available at: http://wsp.presidencia.gov.co/Prensa/2014/Agosto/Paginas/20140807_03-Palabras-del-Presidente-Santos-en-su-posesion-para-el-periodo-presidencial-2014-2018.aspx. Accessed on 19 June 2021.

Presidencia de la República de Colombia. Palabras del Presidente Juan Manuel Santos en la presentación de la segunda edición del libro '100 Colombianos'. Bogotá, 31 January 2014. Available at: http://wsp.presidencia.gov.co/Prensa/2014/Enero/Paginas/20140131_03-Palabras-del-Presidente-Juan-Manuel-Santos-en-la-presentacion-de-la-segunda-edicion-del-libro-100Colombianos.aspx. Accessed on 19 June 2021.

Project Counselling Service, Comisión Intereclesial de Justicia y Paz, Corporación Colectivo de Abogados José Alvear Restrepo y Fundación Comité de Solidariedad com Presos Políticos. *El desmantelamiento del Paramilitarismo: Aprendizajes y Recomendaciones desde las Víctimas*. Bogotá, D.C.: Project Counselling Service, November 2014. Available at: https://issuu.com/cajar/docs/201411_desmantelamiento_-_final. Accessed on 15 February 2021.

Reyes, R. Exposición de Rafael Reyes. Presidente de la República de Colombia a sus compatriotas. In: *Gaceta de Santander*, No. 3764 (January 23, 1906).

Sanclemente, M. (Ministro de Guerra). Informe de los Ministros del Despacho efectivo dirigidos a la Asamblea Nacional Constituyente y Legislativa en 1907. In: *Diario Oficial*, No. 12.913 (April 3, 1907).

Sweeney, J. P. Colombia's Narco-Democracy Threatens Hemispheric Security. *The Heritage Foundation Backgrounder*, n. 1028, 21 March 1995. Available at: http://thf_media.s3.amazonaws.com/1995/pdf/bg1028.pdf. Accessed on 05 July 2021.

The US Infantry School. *Operations Against Guerrilla Forces* (31-20-1). Fort Benning (GA): The US Infantry School, 1950.

The White House. National Security Decision Directive n. 221. "Narcotics and National Security", Washington, D.C., 08 April 1986. Available at: http://www.fas.org/irp/offdocs/nsdd/23-2766a.gif. Accessed on 13 February 2021.

The White House. Remarks of President Obama and President Santos of Colombia in Joint Press Conference. Cartagena, Colombia, April 15, 2012. Available at: https://www.whitehouse.gov/the-press-office/2012/04/15/remarks-president-obama-and-president-santos-colombia-joint-press-confer. Accessed on 10 July 2021.

Tickner, A. B. *Colombia, the United States, and Security Cooperation by Proxy*. Washington, D.C.: WOLA, March 2014. Available at: http://www.wola.org/files/140318ti.pdf. Accessed on 13 February 2021.

U.S. *Congress*. An Act to Provide for the Establishment of Strategic Planning and Performance Measurement in the Federal Government, and for Other Purposes. Washington, D.C.: U.S. Congress, 05 January 1993. Available at: http://govinfo.library.unt.edu/npr/library/misc/s20.html. Accessed on 15 February 2021.

U.S. Department of State. Press Briefing on Board Plane. Secretary Colin L. Powell (03 December 2002). Available at: https://2001-2009.state.gov/secretary/former/powell/remarks/2002/15668.htm. Accessed on 13 February 2021.

U.S. Government Accountability Office (GAO). Drug Control. Agencies Need to Plan for Likely Declines in Drug Interdiction Assets, and Develop Better Performance Measures for Transit Zone Operations (GAO-06–200). November 2005. Available at: http://www.gao.gov/new.items/d06200.pdf. Accessed on 15 February 2021.

U.S. Government Accountability Office (U.S. GAO). The Drug War: Colombia Is Undertaking Antidrug Programs, but Impact Is Uncertain (GAO/NSIAD-93–158). August 1993. Available at: http://archive.gao.gov/d49t13/150027.pdf. Accessed on 13 February 2021.

U.S. House of Representatives. Proceedings and Debates of the 108th Congress Second Session. *Congressional Record*, v. 150, Pt. 17. Washington, D.C.: Government Printing Office, 10 October 2004. Available at: https://www.govinfo.gov/content/pkg/CRECB-2004-pt17/pdf/CRECB-2004-pt17-Pg23242.pdf. Accessed on 13 February 2021.

UNCTAD. *World Investment Report Overview 2014*. Investing in the SDGs: An Action Plan. Geneva: UNCTAD, 2014. Available at: http://unctad.org/en/PublicationsLibrary/wir2014_overview_en.pdf. Accessed on 19 June 2021.

United Nations High Commissioner for Refugees (UNHCR). Report of the United Nations High Commissioner for Human Rights on the situation of human rights in Colombia (A/HRC/19/21/Add.3). New York: Human Rights Council, 31 January 2012. Available at: http://www.hchr.org.co/documentoseinformes/informes/altocomisionado/report2011.pdf. Accessed on 15 February 2021.

Veillette, C. Andean Counterdrug Initiative (ACI) and Related Funding Programs: FY2007 Assistance. *CRS Report for Congress*, RL33370, 18 April 2006. Available at: https://www.everycrsreport.com/files/20060418_RL33370_f5d0ccd0c6e5a696c183495b4a1d0d39c4071857.pdf. Accessed on 13 February 2021.

Veillette, C. Colombia: Issues for Congress. *CRS Report for Congress*, RL32250, 4 January 2006. Available at: https://www.everycrsreport.com/files/20060104_RL32250_2df02f67ff23fe997c54a61253eedc6467c89ccc.pdf. Accessed on 13 February 2021.

Velásquez R., C. A. La fuerza pública que requiere el postconflicto. *Working Papers*, n. 13. Bogotá: Fundación Ideas para la Paz [FIP], May 2015. Available at: http://cdn.ideaspaz.org/media/website/document/5547dc7eef110.pdf. Accessed on 19 June 2021.

Walsh, J. M. Are we there yet? Measuring Progress in the US War on Drugs in Latin America. *WOLA Drug War Monitor*. Washington, D.C.: WOLA, Dec. 2004.

Press Articles

Albright, M. "Colombia's Struggles, and How Can We Help", *New York Times*, 10 August 1999. Available at: http://www.ciponline.org/colombia/00081002.htm. Accessed on 05 July 2021.

Bernstein, Ad. "Lt. Gen. William Yarborough Dies", *Washington Post*, 08 December 2005. Available at: http://www.washingtonpost.com/wp-dyn/content/article/2005/12/07/AR2005120702473.html. Accessed on 10 July 2021.

Diálogo. "Ejército colombiano entrena a soldados paraguayos para luchar contra el terrorismo y el narcotráfico", *Diálogo*, 26 August 2014. Available at: https://dialogo-americas.com/es/articles/colombian-army-trains-paraguayan-soldiers-to-fight-terrorism-drug-trafficking/. Accessed on 19 June 2021.

El Día. "Militares colombianos presos denuncian crímenes de colegas", *El Día*, 20 July 1980. Available at: http://static.iris.net.co/semana/upload/documents/Doc-1471_2007630.pdf. Accessed on 10 July 2021.

El Espectador. "Críticas a Santos por asegurar que 'el posconflicto ya comenzó en Colombia'", *El Espectador*, 16 June 2015. Available at: https://www.elespectador.com/politica/criticas-a-santos-por-asegurar-que-el-posconflicto-ya-comenzo-en-colombia-article-566564/. Accessed on 19 June 2021.

El Mostrador. "Comando Jungla: el historial de la policía colombiana que formó a Carabineros para operar en La Araucanía", *El Mostrador*, 10 July 2018. Available at: https://www.elmostrador.cl/noticias/pais/2018/07/10/comando-jungla-el-historial-de-la-policia-colombiana-que-formo-a-carabineros-para-operar-en-la-araucania/. Accessed on 10 July 2021.

El País. "El Ejército colombiano recupera una ciudad ocupada", *El País*, 05 November 1998. Available at: http://elpais.com/diario/1998/11/05/internacional/910220416_850215.html. Accessed on 10 July 2021.

El Tiempo. "Cómo cayó el fortín mayor de Miraflores", El Tiempo, 06 August 1998. Available at: http://www.eltiempo.com/archivo/documento/MAM-816674. Accessed on 10 July 2021.

El Tiempo. "Ejército rechaza informe de Human Rights Watch", *El Tiempo*, 26 November 1996. Available at: http://www.eltiempo.com/archivo/documento/MAM-601138. Accessed on 15 February 2021.

El Tiempo. "Fuerte réplica de Uribe a ONG", *El Tiempo*, 09 September 2003. Available at: http://www.eltiempo.com/archivo/documento/MAM-1006587. Accessed on 15 February 2021.

El Tiempo. "Fuerza Antiterrorista en Bogotá", *El Tiempo*, 15 January 1991. Available at: http://www.eltiempo.com/archivo/documento/MAM-10076. Accessed on 13 February 2021.

El Tiempo. "Grave lo de Arauca", *El Tiempo*, 08 September 2004. Available at: http://www.eltiempo.com/archivo/documento/MAM-1532348. Accessed on 15 February 2021.

El Tiempo. "Noventa minutos de búsqueda final", *El Tiempo*, 04 December 1993. Available at: http://www.eltiempo.com/archivo/documento/MAM-270373. Accessed on 13 February 2021.

Evans, M. "La verdad sobre la Triple A", *Revista Semana (Opinión)*, 30 June 2007. Available at: http://www.semana.com/opinion/articulo/la-verdad-sobre-triple/86849-3. Accessed on 10 July 2021.

Grove, J. "The Stories We Tell About Killing", *The Disorder of Things*, 06 January 2016. Available at: https://thedisorderofthings.com/2016/01/06/the-stories-we-tell-about-killing/. Accessed on 10 July 2021.

Gutkin, S. "DEA Agent attacks Colombia as 'narco-democracy'", *Washington Post*, 1st October 1994. Available at: https://www.washingtonpost.com/archive/politics/1994/10/01/dea-agent-attacks-colombia-as-narco-dem ocracy/410189e6-0878-48b9-925a-127ce47148f1/. Accessed on 20 June 2021.

Isacson, A. "Colombia, un 'exportador de seguridad' al Continente", *La Silla Vacía*. 18 February 2013. Available at: https://archivo.lasillavacia.com/elblogueo/adam-isacson/41518/colombia-un-exportador-de-seguridad-al-continente. Accessed on 10 July 2021.

Kelly, J. F. "Colombia's Resolve Merits Support", *Miami Herald*, 05 March 2015. Available at: http://www.miamiherald.com/opinion/op-ed/article20047503.html. Accessed on 19 June 2021.

La Silla Vacía. "Alfredo Rangel Suárez", *La Villa Vacía* 13 July 2016. Available at: http://lasillavacia.com/quienesquien/perfilquien/alfredo-rangel-suarez. Accessed on 10 July 2021.

León, J. "El reencauche de Alfredo Rangel", *La Silla Vacía*, 20 September 2010. Available at: http://lasillavacia.com/historia/18150. Accessed on 10 July 2021.

Manrique Z., V. "¿Cómo debe responder la Policía a un posconflicto?", *Revista Semana*, 23 May 2013. Available at: http://www.semana.com/opinion/articulo/despues-la-habana-como-debe-responder-policia-posconflicto/344167-3. Accessed on 05 July 2021.

Pelcastre, J. 2014 "Ejército colombiano entrena a soldados paraguayos para luchar contra el terrorismo y el narcotráfico". *Diálogo. Revista Militar Digital*, 26 August 2014.

Presidencia de la República de Colombia. "Estamos creando un país distinto con oportunidades para todos los colombianos: Presidente Santos". *Presidencia de la República de Colombia*, 31 January 2014. Available at: http://wsp.presidencia.gov.co/Prensa/2014/Enero/Paginas/20140131_02-Estamos-creando-un-pais-distinto-con-oportunidades-para-todos-los-colombianos-Presidente-Santos.aspx. Accessed on 19 June 2021.

Rangel, A. "El Desastre del Caquetá", *El Tiempo*, 8 March 1998. Available at: http://www.eltiempo.com/archivo/documento/MAM-745942. Accessed on 10 July 2021.

Revista Semana. "¿La noche quedó atrás?", *Revista Semana*, 11 July 1982. Available at: http://www.semana.com/nacion/articulo/la-noche-quedo-atras/367-3. Accessed on 10 July 2021.

Revista Semana. "El síndrome de Jacobo", *Revista Semana*, 7 December 1998. Available at: http://www.semana.com/nacion/articulo/el-sindrome-de-jacobo/37900-3. Accessed on 10 July 2021.

Revista Semana. "Los violentólogos". *Revista Semana*, 15 September 2007. Available at: http://www.semana.com/nacion/articulo/los-violentologos/88236-3. Accessed on 13 February 2021.

Ruiz B., J. "Nuestras Fuerzas Armadas en el postconflicto", *Revista Semana*, 02 March 2014. Available at: http://www.semana.com/opinion/articulo/fue

rzas-armadas-en-el-postconflicto-opinion-del-general-r-jaime-ruiz/385666-3. Accessed on 05 July 2021.

Vargas V., A. "Los militares en el Postconflicto", *El Tiempo*, 09 January 2003. Available at: http://www.eltiempo.com/archivo/documento/MAM-968820. Accessed on 05 July 2021.

Viana, M. T. "A paz é mais complexa: o referendo na Colômbia e a guerra na paz", *Rede PCECS*, 14 November 2016. Available at: https://redepcecs.com/2016/11/14/a-paz-e-mais-complexa-o-referendo-na-colombia-e-a-guerra-na-paz/. Accessed on 05 July 2021.

Viana, M. T. "Colombia's New Presidency: Peace as Business (As Usual)", *e-IR*, 31 July 2018. Available at: https://www.e-ir.info/2018/07/31/new-presidency-in-colombia-peace-as-business-as-usual/. Accessed on 15 February 2021.

Ximénez de Sandoval, Pablo. "En Colombia se puede hablar de paz gracias al sacrificio del Ejército", *El País*, 30 June 2013. Available at: https://elpais.com/internacional/2013/06/30/actualidad/1372613129_443772.html. Accessed on 10 July 2021.

INDEX

A
ACI. *See* Andean Counterdrug Initiative (ACI)
Administrative Department of Intelligence Services (SIC), 75
Administrative Department of Security (DAS), 75
AFEUR. *See* Urban Anti-terrorism Special Forces Group (AFEUR)
Afghanistan, 1, 239
Air Force, 3, 10, 181, 191, 209, 219
Algeria, 132, 169–174, 178, 181–184, 199, 228
AMERIPOL. *See* Police Community of the Americas (AMERIPOL)
Andean Counterdrug Initiative (ACI), 48
Anti-extortion and Anti-Kidnapping Special Corps (COPES), 41
Antinarcotic Division (DIRAN), 48, 65, 214
anti-subversive armed groups, 200, 201, 207

architecture, 1, 9, 14, 41, 62, 66, 68, 75, 83, 167, 208, 209, 214, 215, 223, 224, 228, 229, 241
Arenas, Jacobo, 195
Argentina, 23, 117–123, 128, 131, 133, 137, 145, 226
arms industry, 138, 139
Army of the Future, 226–228
Atehortúa Cruz, Adolfo León, 94, 188
Aussaresses, Paul (General), 183, 184, 199

B
BACN. *See* Counternarcotic Brigades (BACN)
banditry. *See bandolerismo*
bandits, 35, 211, 217
bandolerismo, 34, 35, 189, 193
bandoleros, 35, 195, 196
Benidorm Agreement, 189
Betancur, Belisario, 210, 211

© The Editor(s) (if applicable) and The Author(s), under exclusive license to Springer Nature Switzerland AG 2022
M. T. Viana, *Post-conflict Colombia and the Global Circulation of Military Expertise*, Critical Security Studies in the Global South, https://doi.org/10.1007/978-3-030-96103-9

Bigo, Didier, 238
BINCI. *See* Intelligence and Counterintelligence Battalion (BINCI)
Bolivia, 49, 124, 131–133, 203
boundary, 5, 11–13, 35, 82, 93, 95, 96, 100, 107, 111, 129, 158, 165, 204, 206, 211, 228, 238, 240, 241
bourgeoisie, 104–108
Brazil, 3, 20, 49, 121, 131–133, 145, 219, 225, 239
BRIM. *See* Mobile Brigades (BRIM)
brutality, 118, 119, 121, 166, 168, 171, 182, 184, 186, 216
brutal, 154, 169, 228
Bugeaud, Thomas-Robert (General), 169–174, 184, 185
bureaucracy, 109, 112–115, 120, 129
bureaucrat, 112, 120
bureaucratization, 109–111, 113, 127
bureaux arabes, 171, 173

C
Callwell, Charles (Major General Sir), 167
campesino, 35, 78, 79, 193–195, 200
Canada, 3, 225
carabinieri, 136
carceral system, 59, 72–75
caudillismo, 99, 117–119, 121, 123, 124
caudillo, 99, 100, 117–120, 122, 124, 128, 156
CCEEU. *See* Coordination Colombia-Europe-United States (CCEEU)
cease fire, 211
CENAE. *See* National Training Center (CENAE)
Central America, 1, 69, 124, 225, 226
Central Intelligence Agency (CIA), 46
Central Workers' Union (CUT), 77
Charry Solano, Ricardo (Lieutenant Coronel), 201
Chile, 20, 120, 125, 127, 131, 133–138, 145, 146, 148, 225
Chilean Army, 125, 133–136, 140, 147–150, 153, 156, 157, 187
Chilean (military) mission, 12, 100, 141, 142, 146, 149–158, 160, 184, 188, 193, 237, 241
China, 225
CIA. *See* Central Intelligence Agency (CIA)
CINEP. *See* Research and Popular Education Center (CINEP)
Citizen security, 21, 22, 96
citizen-soldier, 12, 13, 142, 148, 149, 153, 166, 239
civic action, 177, 178
civil, 8, 11–13, 22, 34, 35, 61, 71, 92–96, 99, 100, 102, 113–115, 118–120, 123–128, 141, 143, 144, 146, 149, 152, 153, 159, 160, 179, 180, 182, 183, 187, 194, 199, 203–205, 211, 213, 216, 226, 228, 240, 241
authority, 99, 100, 114, 118–120, 123, 126, 128, 141, 144, 146
domain, 93, 94, 123, 129, 152, 153, 204, 205, 213, 240, 241
elite, 12, 95, 119, 124–127, 189, 203
-military, 11–13, 93–96, 100, 115, 123, 125–127, 160, 182, 228, 240, 241
-military action, 187, 194
civilization, 12, 95, 99, 101, 107, 114, 117–123, 149, 150, 154–156, 159, 160, 167, 177, 178
civilité, 104, 107, 119, 126

civility, 122, 154, 155, 166, 167, 228
Civilization and Barbarism, 117
civilizing process, 102, 104–108, 116, 118, 167
The civilizing process, 11, 99, 102, 159
uncivilized, 99, 167
cocaine, 29, 39, 47, 65, 66, 68, 69, 209, 210
Colombia Battalion No. 1, 188, 191, 192
Colombian National Police, 1, 3, 5, 10, 21, 22, 34, 36, 39, 48, 62, 66, 67, 75, 101, 209, 210, 214, 217, 225, 242
colonial, 13, 116, 132, 155, 165, 168, 169, 171–174, 178, 182, 184, 186, 228, 240
Comandos Jungla. *See* Jungla Commands (*Comandos Jungla*)
communism, 35, 136, 184, 189–191, 193, 200, 206, 208
communist, 175, 189, 192, 199
conscription, 12, 131, 134, 140, 149, 150
Conservative Party, 189
Coordination Colombia-Europe-United States (CCEEU), 74, 79, 80, 84
COPES. *See* Anti-extortion and Anti-Kidnapping Special Corps (COPES)
COSAS. *See* Department of Control of Substances that Produce Physical and Psychic Addiction (COSAS)
counterinsurgency, 13, 14, 47, 48, 95, 165, 166, 172–174, 176–188, 190, 197, 199, 201, 202, 206–208, 215, 219, 223, 228, 229, 237, 239, 240

counternarcotic, 1, 8, 9, 21, 22, 24, 44–49, 57–60, 62, 63, 65–71, 73–75, 85, 208–210, 214, 215, 217, 221, 223, 226, 227, 229, 239
Counternarcotic Brigades (BACN), 220–223
counterterrorism, 21, 22, 50, 214, 217, 223, 226, 227, 229, 239
court, 104, 105, 107, 110, 124, 212
courtization of warriors, 105, 106, 108, 110, 115
court society, 102, 105, 106, 108
criollo, 117, 126
crisis, 145, 190, 212
culture, 92, 118, 147, 172
curriculum, 113, 130, 132–134, 142, 148, 153, 172, 187, 199
CUT. *See* Central Workers' Union (CUT)

D

Damascus Doctrine (*Doctrina Damasco*), 226, 227
DANE. *See* National Administrative Department of Statistics (DANE)
DAS. *See* Administrative Department of Security (DAS)
DEA. *See* Drug Enforcement Administration (DEA)
decisive victory, 169, 177, 184, 206, 229, 240
delinquency, 8, 23, 32, 36, 74, 75, 82, 226, 242
delinquentialization, 242
transnational organized, 23, 226
democracy, 32, 50, 91–94, 189, 190, 203, 206
narco-, 2, 6
Department of Control of Substances that Produce Physical and Psychic Addiction (COSAS), 209, 214

DIJIN. *See* Judicial Police and Intelligence Central Division (DIJIN)
DIRAN. *See* Antinarcotic Division (DIRAN)
disciplinarization, 129, 143, 149, 150
discourse, 1, 3–5, 11, 12, 29, 35, 43, 46, 58, 59, 63, 73, 74, 78, 83, 95, 99–102, 104, 106, 107, 110, 113–116, 119, 120, 123–127, 129, 137, 139–144, 146, 152, 158–160, 167, 178, 190, 204, 207, 208, 212, 216, 224, 228, 241, 242
  discursive, 1, 11, 12, 58, 59, 73, 74, 100, 101, 106, 107, 116, 123, 159, 191, 212, 241, 242
  discursive field, 9, 24, 57–59, 63, 71–73, 83–86
  of modernization, 11, 95, 99–102, 106, 107, 110, 113–116, 123, 125–127, 129, 137, 139–143, 159, 160, 178, 204
  order of, 59, 72
Doctrina Damasco. See Damascus Doctrine (*Doctrina Damasco*)
doctrine, 13, 96, 113, 129, 138, 148, 165, 173, 174, 176, 177, 179, 181, 184, 185, 187, 190, 195, 198, 199, 202, 203, 218, 219, 227, 228
Drug Enforcement Administration (DEA), 21, 45–47, 65, 69, 209, 210
drugs, 1, 8, 28, 36–40, 42–45, 48, 51, 59, 63–71, 80, 84, 209, 210, 212, 220
  drug cartels, 21, 36, 40, 41, 48, 65, 92, 209, 213, 222
  drug trafficking, 2, 3, 8, 9, 20, 24, 37, 40–43, 45, 47–52, 59, 64–67, 69, 81, 208, 209, 213, 214, 220, 223, 224
  war on, 8, 10, 42, 43, 51, 60, 65, 67, 217, 219, 242

E

Ecuador, 3, 49, 127, 133, 146, 225
education, 19, 20, 108, 112, 122, 123, 126, 146, 148, 150, 151, 224
efficiency, 9, 39, 63, 67, 70, 130–132, 169, 172, 198, 213
Ejército del Futuro. See Army of the Future (*Ejército del Futuro*)
Elias, Norbert, 11, 99, 102–116, 123, 159, 178
ELN. *See* National Liberation Army (ELN)
El Salvador, 3, 133, 225
emergency, 212
enemy, 110, 145, 165, 167, 170–172, 174, 178, 179, 184, 190, 196, 197, 201, 217, 218
enmity, 177, 179
  internal, 124
Escuela de Lanceros. See Lancers' School (*Escuela de Lanceros*)
Escuela del Estado Mayor. See General Staff College (*Escuela del Estado Mayor*)
Escuela de Soldados Profesionales. *See* School of Professional Soldiers (ESPRO)
Escuela Militar. See Military School (*Escuela Militar*)
Escuela Militar de Cadetes. See Military School of Cadets (*Escuela Militar de Cadetes*)
Escuela Superior de Guerra. See Superior War College (*Escuela Superior de Guerra*)

ESPRO. *See* School of Professional Soldiers (ESPRO)
Europe, 12, 13, 60, 81, 94, 95, 100–103, 106–108, 110, 113, 115, 116, 118, 120, 122–124, 127–129, 137, 139, 140, 159, 166, 173, 187
expertise, 1, 3, 4, 10, 13, 22, 23, 93, 96, 128, 130, 132, 166, 169, 181, 186, 192, 200, 203, 209, 221, 223, 224, 226–228, 237, 239, 240
expert-soldier, 13, 96, 239
externalization, 44–46, 57
extrajudicial killings, 9, 24, 27, 28, 77–80, 86

F

failed state, 6, 224
 failing state, 20, 27
FARC. *See* Revolutionary Armed Forces of Colombia (FARC)
FBI. *See* Federal Bureau of Investigation (FBI)
Federal Bureau of Investigation (FBI), 21
FIP. *See* Ideas for Peace Foundation (FIP)
Fiscal Year (FY), 71
forced disappearances, 9, 24, 27, 79, 86
Fort Benning, 195
Fort Bragg, 183, 184, 199
Fort Leavenworth, 184
Foucault, Michel, 7, 23, 30, 45, 58–60, 63, 72–75, 81, 82, 96, 103, 106, 216
France, 3, 32, 95, 112, 131, 133, 134, 140, 159, 169, 184, 186, 225, 228
 French army, 132, 169, 171, 175, 180

French court society, 102
French (military) mission, 125, 130–132, 139, 140
French model, 132
French officers, 132, 133
Franco-Prussian War, 131, 132, 134
Frente Nacional, 203, 205, 206
FS&D. *See* Security & Democracy Foundation (FS&D)
FUDRA. *See* Rapid Deployment Force (FUDRA)
Fuerte Tolemaida. *See* Tolemaida Fortress
FY. *See* Fiscal Year (FY)

G

Gaitán, Jorge Eliécer, 92, 94
Galula, David, 173–184, 219
gangs, 212
GAO. *See* U.S. General Accounting Office (GAO)
gaucho, 121, 122
GAULA. *See* Unified Action Groups for Personal Freedom (GAULA)
Gaviria Trujillo, César, 213, 222
General Staff College (*Escuela del Estado Mayor*), 155
Germany, 32, 133, 150
GOES. *See* Special Operations Group (GOES)
Great Britain. *See* U.K.
guerra sucia, 40, 92
guerrilla, 2, 8, 23, 28, 32, 34, 35, 38–43, 46–51, 59, 60, 77, 80–82, 133, 169, 170, 185, 189–193, 195, 196, 198, 200, 206, 208, 210–216, 222–224, 226
 narcoguerrilla, 8, 10, 24, 42, 43, 46–49, 59, 60, 77, 83, 85, 208, 214

H

hearts and minds, 168, 169, 172
helicopters, 47, 219, 220, 223, 229
Honduras, 3, 203, 225
HRW. *See* Human Rights Watch (HRW)
human rights, 3, 9, 21, 24, 27–29, 32, 59, 74, 77, 79–84, 86, 201, 202, 221
  activists, 59, 79, 83
  organizations, 9, 24, 83
  violations, 3, 9, 24, 79–84, 86, 201, 202
Human Rights Watch (HRW), 28, 74, 77, 79, 80, 83, 199, 200
human security, 96, 225–228
Huysmans, Jef, 62, 238

I

IACHR. *See* Inter-American Commission on Human Rights (IACHR)
IDB. *See* Inter-American Development Bank (IDB)
Ideas for Peace Foundation (FIP), 20, 226, 227
IEPRI. *See* Institute of Studies on Politics and International Relations (IEPRI)
independent republic, 194, 195, 201
India, 171, 181
Indochina, 132, 173, 175, 183
Institute of Studies on Politics and International Relations (IEPRI), 33, 34
instruction, 135, 148, 152, 154, 156, 186, 188, 189, 195, 197, 201, 210, 222
intelligence, 9, 21, 22, 28, 46, 48, 52, 59, 63, 74–80, 83, 85, 170–173, 183, 187, 197, 199–201, 206, 207, 210, 211, 216–219, 227

apparatus, 9, 59, 63, 74, 76–79, 85, 171, 173
  report, 78, 80
  service, 28, 76
  unit, 76
Intelligence and Counterintelligence Battalion (BINCI), 201, 202
Inter-American Commission on Human Rights (IACHR), 79
Inter-American Development Bank (IDB), 22
internal-external boundary, 241
IRA. *See* Irish Republican Army (IRA)
Iraq, 31, 165, 179, 185
Irish Republican Army (IRA), 183
irregular warfare, 13, 170, 179, 185, 187, 192, 195, 196, 201, 202, 218, 221, 223, 226, 228, 229, 239
ISIS. *See* Islamic State in Iraq and Syria (ISIS)
Islamic State in Iraq and Syria (ISIS), 23
Israel, 225

J

Judicial Police and Intelligence Central Division (DIJIN), 21, 33, 34, 36, 75
Jungla Commands (*Comandos Jungla*), 214
jus ad bellum, 167
jus in bello, 167
justice, 20, 28, 92, 118, 213

K

Kilcullen, David, 177, 179, 180
Korean War. *See* War in Korea
Körner, Emil (Captain), 131, 134, 135, 150

L

Lacheroy, Charles (Colonel), 174, 175, 178, 182
Lancers' School (*Escuela de Lanceros*), 3, 13, 166, 188, 195–199, 202, 205, 207, 222, 225, 229, 239
Landazábal Reyes, Fernando (General), 210, 211
Leal Buitrago, Francisco, 205
Liberal Party, 142, 189, 190
literacy, 126, 137, 146, 148–150
Lleras Camargo, Alberto, 189
Lleras doctrine, 203–205
Lyautey, Hubert (General), 132

M

Malaya, 181, 183, 200
manual, 12, 76, 77, 137, 138, 140, 186, 190, 191, 196, 197, 238
Marín, Pedro Antonio. *See* Marulanda Vélez, Manuel
Marulanda Vélez, Manuel, 195
massacres, 2, 29, 81, 168, 200
metric, 8, 24, 29, 57, 62–64, 66, 67, 69, 71, 72
Mexico, 1–3, 20, 22, 69, 124, 127, 225, 239
military apparatus, 59, 139
military campaign, 126, 130, 133, 149, 150, 193, 198
military career, 12, 128, 129, 134, 135, 137, 139, 140, 150, 151, 155–157, 221, 241
military crisis, 216–218
military mission, 12, 125, 129, 131–133, 138, 154, 155, 172, 176, 196, 197
military officers, 31, 32, 49, 84, 92, 93, 124, 128, 131, 133, 137, 138, 140–142, 149–151, 166, 168, 174, 179, 181, 183, 185, 188, 191–193, 195, 198–200, 202, 205, 210, 211, 216, 218, 222, 224, 226
military operations, 2, 8, 66, 75, 77, 79, 80, 94, 137, 141, 193, 215, 217, 220, 225, 240
military professional, 5, 6, 10–14, 94, 95, 100, 101, 123, 125, 128–131, 133, 137–141, 152, 153, 159, 160, 165, 178, 187–189, 191, 197, 198, 202, 206, 207, 216, 217, 222, 226, 228, 229, 237–239, 241, 242
military reform, 113, 216, 217, 219, 226
military school, 5, 12, 95, 96, 113, 115, 129–134, 137–140, 147, 149, 170, 180, 183–186, 188
Military School (*Escuela Militar*), 13, 134, 135, 141, 142, 146, 148, 150–153, 155, 156, 166, 188, 201, 229, 237, 239
Military School of Cadets (*Escuela Militar de Cadetes*), 149
Mobile Brigades (BRIM), 215, 220, 223
modern, 95, 100–104, 106, 108–115, 118, 129, 133, 147, 152–154, 158, 167, 169, 178, 183, 188, 208
discourse of modernization. *See* discourse
modernity, 12, 100, 116, 123, 159
modernization, 4, 100–102, 106, 116–118, 122, 123, 128, 137, 141–143, 159, 168, 204, 208, 217, 218, 224, 229
montonera, 118
Morantes Jaime, Luis Alberto. *See* Arenas, Jacobo
Mountain Battalions, 220, 223
Movement of State Crime Victims (MOVICE), 79

MOVICE. *See* Movement of State Crime Victims (MOVICE)

N
Naranjo Trujillo, Oscar (General), 21
National Administrative Department of Statistics (DANE), 33
National Liberation Army (ELN), 77
National Security Decision Directive (NSDD), 43, 44, 46
National Training Center (CENAE), 223
native, 171, 177, 197
NATO. *See* North Atlantic Treaty Organization (NATO)
Neocleous, Mark, 107, 177, 178
New Granada, 125–127
New Public Management, 60, 61
NGO. *See* non-governmental organization (NGO)
Nigeria, 1, 23, 239
non-governmental organization (NGO), 22, 77, 80
North Atlantic Treaty Organization (NATO), 225
NSDD. *See* National Security Decision Directive (NSDD)

O
Office of National Drug Control Policy (ONDCP), 71
ONDCP. *See* Office of National Drug Control Policy (ONDCP)
Operación Fulminante. *See* Operation Fulminant
Operación Marquetalia. *See* Operation Marquetalia
Operación Tranquilandia. *See* Operation Quiet Village
Operation Condor, 203
Operation Fulminant, 209, 210
Operation Marquetalia, 194, 195
Operation Quiet Village, 210

P
pacification, 4, 5, 7, 12, 91, 95, 99, 101, 104, 106, 108–110, 125, 127, 137, 140, 141, 143, 144, 159, 176–178, 180, 182, 193, 198, 203, 206, 207, 224, 228, 229
pacified social space, 12, 96, 101–110, 113–115, 117, 119, 120, 159, 178
Panama, 3, 49, 143, 203, 225
Paraguay, 23, 225, 226
paramilitary, 2, 28, 34, 47, 75, 79–83, 178, 199, 200
partidas, 169
Pastrana, Andrés, 19, 27, 210, 216
peace, 4, 5, 7, 19, 20, 29, 82, 96, 101, 102, 107, 113, 135, 136, 143–145, 177, 178, 191, 195, 206, 207, 210–213, 216, 226, 240, 241, 243
Peace Agreement, 2, 7, 20, 21
process, 2, 20, 27
-war, 11, 13, 95, 96, 165, 228, 241
peasant. *See campesino*
Pécaut, Daniel, 33, 35, 49, 189, 190, 195
Penal Code, 8, 34, 36–39, 42, 51, 129, 209
Peru, 3, 22, 23, 49, 102, 124, 127, 131–133, 137, 138, 203, 225, 226
Philippines, 181, 186, 200
Pinzón, Juan Carlos, 1, 3, 4, 10, 23, 29, 224, 225
Pizarro Leongómez, Eduardo, 94, 142
Plan 10,000, 222

Plan Colombia, 4, 14, 27, 28, 47, 57, 60, 63, 64, 66, 67, 78, 80, 82–85, 96, 166, 198, 207, 208, 216–225, 229, 239
Plan Lazo, 193–195, 198, 199, 207
police, 1, 3–5, 8, 9, 13, 14, 22, 23, 33, 35–37, 41, 45–48, 52, 59–63, 65, 74–79, 82, 96, 101, 107, 131, 136, 177, 178, 183, 186, 208, 209, 214–217, 219, 223, 224, 227, 240, 241
   apparatus, 78, 85
   operations, 2, 9, 46, 74, 75
Police Community of the Americas (AMERIPOL), 217
Politics as a Vocation, 11, 99, 102
population, 13, 33, 46, 60, 74, 92, 132, 145, 151, 155, 158, 165, 171, 172, 174–177, 179, 180, 197, 206, 207, 218, 219, 228, 229, 240
   -centric approach, 13, 175–177, 206, 229, 240
post-conflict, 2, 4, 5, 7, 20–22, 166, 207, 237, 241, 242
problematization, 6–10, 23, 30, 34, 41–43, 45, 46, 51, 57–59, 62, 63, 72, 76, 77, 82–86, 94, 123, 125, 179, 189, 190, 202, 203, 206, 208, 214, 223, 238, 239, 242
professional, 12, 22, 91, 93, 100, 101, 105, 108, 113–115, 117, 126, 128, 129, 136, 148, 157, 168, 169, 192, 204, 215, 221–223, 227, 229, 240, 242, 243
   military, 5, 6, 10–14, 94, 95, 100, 101, 113, 115, 123, 125, 128–131, 133, 137–141, 144, 146, 149, 152, 153, 159, 160, 165, 172, 178, 186–189, 191, 193, 197, 198, 202, 206–208, 216, 217, 222, 226, 228, 229, 237–239, 241, 242
   police, 95, 178
professionalization, 12–14, 93–96, 99, 101, 102, 110, 113–115, 123, 125, 127–129, 131–141, 143, 144, 146, 147, 149, 150, 153, 155, 159, 160, 165–168, 173, 186–188, 191, 193, 198, 204, 207, 221, 223, 225, 228, 229, 237, 239, 242
professionalization programs, 5, 10–13, 95, 100, 116, 123, 133, 141, 146, 149, 153, 154, 156, 158, 159, 166, 187, 188, 193, 197, 198, 202, 205, 215, 239, 241
professional soldier (*soldado profesional*), 221
progress, 3, 27, 65, 69, 70, 95, 113, 116–119, 122, 144, 177, 224
Prussia, 95, 132, 133, 139, 140, 153, 159, 172, 186, 187
psychological operations, 168, 174, 175, 192, 199, 221
public health, 38, 68, 70
public order, 8, 36, 38–40, 42, 76, 93, 193, 211, 212, 218
   disturbance of, 51

Q
quadrillage, 175
Quiroga, Juan Facundo, 117, 121

R
race, 122, 123
RAND Corporation, 180, 181
ranger, 195, 220, 221
   Ranger Course, 195
   Rangers School, 195

Rapid Deployment Force (FUDRA), 220
rationalization, 102, 109, 112, 122, 145
ratonnades, 175
razzias, 171, 172, 174
Reagan, Ronald, 43, 209
regroupement, 174, 175, 185
regulative ideal, 12, 96, 100, 102, 109, 116, 123, 159, 208
Research and Popular Education Center (CINEP), 79, 201, 202
Revolutionary Armed Forces of Colombia (FARC), 2, 7, 20, 21, 47, 48, 195, 211, 215, 216
revolutionary war, 174–176, 178, 182, 184, 185
Reyes, Rafael, 125, 141–146, 152
Rojas Pinilla, Gustavo (General), 93, 192
Rosas, Juan Manuel, 120–122
Rouquié, Alain, 93, 94, 116, 120, 124, 125, 127–131, 133, 136, 137, 140, 149–151, 155, 167, 187
royal mechanism, 104
Ruiz Novoa, Alberto (General), 192–195
Russia, 134, 172

S

Santos, Juan Manuel, 19–21
Sarmiento, Domingo Faustino, 12, 99, 100, 116–123, 159
School of Professional Soldiers (ESPRO), 222, 223, 225
School of the Americas (SoA), 187, 206
Security & Democracy Foundation (FS&D), 216, 217
self-defense groups, 174, 200

SIC. *See* Administrative Department of Intelligence Services (SIC)
SoA. *See* School of the Americas (SoA)
social movements, 7, 33, 39, 76–79
sociogenesis, 102, 103
soldado profesional. *See* professional soldier (*soldado profesional*)
South America, 2, 49, 91, 100, 124, 142, 146, 202, 203, 206, 225, 226
Spain, 32, 118, 120, 122, 128, 134, 168, 169
Special Operations Group (GOES), 41
state of siege, 210, 212, 213
strikes, 38, 42, 82, 136, 140, 143
success story, 2–5, 7–10, 14, 20, 22–24, 27–29, 57–59, 62, 72, 74, 78, 82, 84–86, 91, 96, 166, 208, 224, 226, 228, 229, 237, 239–242
Suchet, Louis-Gabriel (General), 168, 169
Superior War College (*Escuela Superior de Guerra*), 155, 201
Switzerland, 133

T

tactics, 13, 96, 129, 133, 134, 138, 153, 154, 169–174, 179, 184, 197, 199–201, 206, 221, 223, 229, 240
terrorism, 1, 2, 8, 14, 35, 38–43, 49–51, 76, 77, 84, 209, 213, 223, 225
  narcoterrorist, 24, 48, 50, 59
  war on, 8, 50
Thousand Days' War, 32, 92, 125, 133, 141, 143, 144
Tickner, Arlene, 3, 20, 28, 44, 92, 225
Tirofijo. *See* Marulanda Vélez, Manuel

Tolemaida Fortress, 3, 4, 220, 222, 223, 225
torture, 27, 76, 175, 183, 184, 186, 194, 195
training, 3–5, 10, 13, 14, 47, 76, 95, 96, 112, 113, 115, 131, 145, 148, 166, 186, 188, 191–193, 196–200, 207, 208, 214, 217, 218, 220–226, 229, 238–240
   facility, 198
   program, 186, 188, 199, 207, 214, 220–222, 225, 229
transnational, 3, 6, 11–13, 94, 95, 97, 138, 165, 166, 224, 226, 237–242
Trinquier, Roger (Lieutenant Colonel), 183, 184
Turbay Ayala, César, 35, 40, 209

U

U.K.
   British military officers, 76, 240
UNHCHR. *See* United Nations High Commissioner for Human Rights (UNHCHR)
Unified Action Groups for Personal Freedom (GAULA), 220
unionists, 9, 24, 59, 74, 77–80, 85, 86
   labor unions, 77, 78, 86
United Nations High Commissioner for Human Rights (UNHCHR), 79, 83
Urban Anti-terrorism Special Forces Group (AFEUR), 219, 220
Uribe Vélez, Álvaro, 49
Uruguay, 121, 124
U.S. Army Special Warfare School, 183, 186, 199
U.S. General Accounting Office (GAO), 47, 66
U.S. Special Forces, 220, 224

V

Valencia Tovar, Álvaro (General), 188
Vargas Velásquez, Alejo, 4, 5, 47, 48, 80
Venezuela, 49, 91, 124, 133, 138, 140
Vietnam, 180, 184, 200
violence, 2, 4–12, 14, 19, 23, 24, 28, 31–36, 40–43, 48, 51, 57, 59, 63, 64, 71, 72, 75–77, 79, 82–86, 91–97, 99–104, 106–111, 113–120, 123–128, 136, 139, 142, 143, 159, 167, 168, 170, 177–179, 189, 190, 193–195, 201–206, 208, 209, 212–216, 218, 223, 226, 229, 237–243
   legitimate, 108, 109, 190
   monopolization of, 99, 101, 103, 104, 107–111, 113, 114, 117, 123, 125, 127, 142, 143
   political, 32, 34, 35, 108, 109, 113, 114, 193
Violencia, La, 31, 92, 94, 189, 190, 195, 203
violentología. *See* violentology
violentólogos. *See* violentology, violentologist
violentology, 31, 34, 92, 242
violentologists, 41

W

Walker, R.B.J., 124
war, 1, 4, 5, 7, 13, 14, 28, 31, 34, 35, 38, 40, 49, 66, 91–94, 96, 100–104, 106, 107, 110, 111, 113–120, 124–128, 131, 133, 135, 136, 139, 143, 144, 149, 155, 159, 166–172, 174–178, 183–185, 188, 190–192, 196, 206–208, 210, 212–216, 218,

219, 222, 224, 228, 229, 238, 240–243
 conventional, 167, 169–171, 188, 192
 independence, 12, 116, 117, 120, 124, 125, 127, 139, 143, 159
 making, 94, 96, 101, 106, 213
 modality of, 166, 240
 small warriors, 167, 186, 228
 small wars, 166–173, 228
 warlike actions, 113, 114, 119, 127
warfare
 conventional, 166, 167, 169, 172, 186, 192, 237
 irregular, 13, 170, 179, 185, 187, 192, 195, 196, 201, 202, 218, 221, 223, 226, 228, 229, 239
 modern, 168, 170, 172, 188
War in Korea, 13, 188–192, 195
War of the Pacific, 128, 133, 134
war power, 177, 178, 212, 213, 240

Washington Office on Latin America (WOLA), 69
weapons, 4, 12, 47, 65, 138–140, 192, 214, 220, 223, 229, 238
Weber, Max, 11, 99, 102, 109–116, 123, 159
WEF. *See* World Economic Forum (WEF)
Western Africa, 226
WOLA. *See* Washington Office on Latin America (WOLA)
World Economic Forum (WEF), 21

Y
Yarborough, William P. (General), 199, 200

Z
zapadores, 144–146

GPSR Compliance

The European Union's (EU) General Product Safety Regulation (GPSR) is a set of rules that requires consumer products to be safe and our obligations to ensure this.

If you have any concerns about our products, you can contact us on

ProductSafety@springernature.com

In case Publisher is established outside the EU, the EU authorized representative is:

Springer Nature Customer Service Center GmbH
Europaplatz 3
69115 Heidelberg, Germany

www.ingramcontent.com/pod-product-compliance
Lightning Source LLC
LaVergne TN
LVHW011006250326
834688LV00004B/97